THEY HAD NO CHOICE
RACING PIGEONS AT WAR

THEY HAD NO CHOICE
RACING PIGEONS AT WAR

Garry McCafferty

TEMPUS

First published 2002

PUBLISHED IN THE UNITED KINGDOM BY:

Tempus Publishing Ltd
The Mill, Brimscombe Port
Stroud, Gloucestershire GL5 2QG

PUBLISHED IN THE UNITED STATES OF AMERICA BY:

Tempus Publishing Inc.
2A Cumberland Street
Charleston, SC 29401

Tempus books are available in France and Germany
from the following addresses:

Tempus Publishing Group   Tempus Publishing Group
21 Avenue de la République   Hockheimer Strasse 59
37300 Joué-lès-Tours   D-99094 Erfurt
FRANCE   GERMANY

British Library Cataloguing in Publication Data.
A catalogue record for this book is available from the British Library.

ISBN 0 7524 2403 3

Typesetting and origination by Tempus Publishing.
PRINTED AND BOUND IN GREAT BRITAIN.

CONTENTS

ACKNOWLEDGEMENTS

I hope that this book will give you an insight into the major part that pigeons and members of the National Pigeon Service contributed to the war effort. We must also remember the breeders and the people at home who were so involved.

I would like to take this opportunity to add my own personal thanks to all those caught up in the conflicts, who fought so that my family and I can live in a free society. These days, I look at my pigeons in a totally different light; their ancestors gave their all, even though they had no choice.

I would like to thank the following, without whose help this book would not have been possible: The Osman Family – Lt Col A.H. Osman, Major W.H. Osman and Colin Osman. The Racing Pigeon Publishing Company, *British Homing World* and *Pigeon Sport*. Thanks also to Mr C.M. Standerwick, Mr Dennis Sanders, Mr Tom Silk, Mr Martin Hough, Mr Dave Brown, Mrs Southern, Miss Pat Southern, Dennis Bottomley, Jeff Metcalfe, Danny Buckland, Jack Curtis (The Big Fella), C.G. Lowe and the War Office. the Royal Signals Corps, Brian Newsome, Mr Owen Vaggers, the late Mr Eddie Gilbert, Mr Derek Partridge, Sean Aherne for the front cover painting, Mr Dennis Woolf, Mr Harry Aldridge, Mr Tony Kehoe, John Platt, Mr J. Inch, Mr John Tucker, Mr H.C. Woodman, Mr Ralph White, Mr Eric Smallman, Mr Geo Barrett, Mr Fred Wiltshire, Mrs Sandra Williams and not forgetting Kirsty Heselwood, for typing the manuscript.

FOREWORD

The idea behind this book is quite simple, and is twofold. Firstly, it aims to present the facts about the heroic flights made by these sixteen ounces of feathers and bones that undoubtedly helped this country to win two world wars. Secondly, it means to put on record the individual stories of our brave troops, and those at home who were so very much involved in the National Pigeon Service and other units.

The format of the book is somewhat unconventional, as there are no traditional chapters as such; instead there is a continuous stream of stories of personal experiences and memories of those dark and distant days. Many of the contributors are sadly no longer with us and that in itself is the main reason that this work must be published, so that we will have a permanent record to commemorate these much-missed members of our great sport.

During my research, I have to admit that at times it brought great emotion, as I discovered the incredible bravery and valour that both the pigeons and their minders showed. Although I was born seven years after the Second World War, I felt that I was there and part of it, such were the experiences told to me by ex-members of the forces and their families.

I feel humble to have been asked to put this book together, and proud that I have in some way done my bit to remember how it was. It is important to remember the incredible situations that these people and pigeons went through so that we can enjoy the freedom we have today. Of course, there are bound to be stories of the war years that will come to light in future years – perhaps one day another book will be written to accommodate them.

PROLOGUE

The old man sat alone staring at the flickering remnants of the fire and pulled the blanket tighter around his shoulders, as there was no more coal. He would make a warm drink and go to bed – it was warmer there. As he stood, it was still possible to glimpse the strong, muscular man he had once been, but age catches up with us all. The man was in his eightieth year and was now alone, but he wouldn't give up his home, a place where he and Alice had spent so many happy times. It was eight years since she had died, and he missed her.

In the kitchen, waiting for the milk to warm, he looked out of the window to the loft at the bottom of the garden. The memories of the years of racing he had enjoyed and the successes he had achieved came flooding back. His mind also drifted back to those dark, terrible days of the war and the great comradeship of his mates in the Army. He smiled as he remembered the times in the Pigeon Service, when he was in charge of the mobile lofts in the Far East. Despite the war raging around them, looking after the birds brought some kind of sanity. Those brave men, those heroic pigeons, they were never really given the praise they so richly deserved. The man's smile was replaced with tears, as he recalled the friends who lost their lives in front of him, and the pigeons they loved that failed to return.

After the war, he had returned to civilian life and the world of pigeon racing. He wished that he had kept in touch, but time passes so quickly and promises fade.

Once the man had gone to bed, he picked up the *Pigeon Weekly* as usual and began to read. As he turned the pages, he was transfixed by an article about the forthcoming Remembrance Sunday walk past at the Cenotaph. He couldn't believe what he was reading: 'For the first time ever, pigeon men can attend in their own right and not just as soldiers or members of the forces,' said the newspaper, 'The Royal British Legion has now acknowledged what pigeons and pigeon personnel did in the war effort.' There was a telephone number to book a seat on a coach. He decided he would go and pay tribute to the fallen – tomorrow he would find his medals.

The day dawned in London, when he stood shoulder to shoulder with fellow pigeon men and women. He looked resplendent and proud as the Steward announced: 'Pigeon Section next'. It was a wonderful feeling as they walked towards the monument. The applause of the crowd was deafening. Passing the Cenotaph, he saluted and was relieved of his poppy cross, emblazoned with a pigeon. There were tears, many tears, but at last he could say goodbye properly. God bless the lads and God bless the pigeons. God willing, he would return next year.

1

THE EARLY DAYS

References to pigeons are found throughout the ages. It is said that they were even kept in ancient China. Alexander the Great was know to have used them, and pigeons brought back the first news of victory at Waterloo.

Pigeons have been used in countless wars throughout history. It is recorded that pigeons relayed the news of Caesar's conquest of Gaul. In the thirteenth century, Genghis Khan organised a pigeon relay service across Asia and most of Europe.

Messages were sent into Paris during the siege of 1870 to 1871. Letters were sent from London, photographically copied in a much-reduced form on thin films of collodion and sent into the capital by carrier pigeon. The film was then relayed onto a screen by magic lanterns, which were very popular at the time. The pigeon service was carried out under extremely unpleasant conditions during the winter months of 1870 to 1871, but during that time thousands of messages were carried over the Prussian lines and delivered safely to Paris. On 3 February 1871, one lone pigeon arrived in the French capital carrying 40,000 messages using this early example of micro-film.

In a lecture on the subject, Colonel Osman reported that lecturer Captain G.G. Aston of the Royal Marine Artillery gave the following table of figures of the pigeons used during the siege of Paris and those that made it home with a message:

September and October 1870. Liberated 105, arrived home 22.
November 1870. Liberated 83, arrived home 17.
December 1870. Liberated 49, arrived home 12.
January 1871. Liberated 33, arrived home 3.
February 1871. Liberated 22, arrived home 3.

The percentage of safe arrival was very small, largely due to the fact that this was an emergency service which had been adapted to suit the circumstances. In later conflicts, the arrival rate became much higher as birds were trained and handled by experts.

The British army used a limited number of pigeons during the Boer war, when it became necessary to communicate with the besieged garrison at Ladysmith. Pigeons were used to carry despatches and plans out of Ladysmith and the service proved so successful that a number of small pigeon lofts were established by the Army.

During the early part of the First World War, the use of pigeons was controlled by the Intelligence Corps, but in the spring of 1915 pigeons were successfully used to bring back situation reports during the enemy attack on Ypres. As a result of these operations, the First Corps Pigeon Service was organised in the Second Corps during the month of May. From this date, the growth of the forward carrier Pigeon Service was rapid. The carrier pigeon had already been recognised as a trustworthy and speedy means of conveying messages over distances that were far greater than the newly-introduced trench wireless set was capable of reaching. Not only were the pigeons quick, but they seemed to be untroubled by gunfire whilst in flight and were less susceptible to gas effects than human beings.

Pigeon messages went straight from battalion headquarters, or from pigeon posts in the trenches, to Division or Corps headquarters. As the majority of messages were intended for the Brigade to which the battalion belonged, some delay was inevitable but it was reduced to a minimum by locating the lofts near to the signals office of the formation which the bird served. Pigeon messages were treated as priority and were given preference over all 'less important telephone traffic'.

Records show that the message from the trenches could be relied upon to reach the brigade headquarters in ten to twenty minutes, according to the distance that the pigeon had to fly. The men in the trenches appreciated the use of pigeons because, prior to their introduction, quite a number of soldiers had been killed while acting as messengers. It was difficult at first to ensure that the soldiers did not overfeed the birds and make pets of the carrier pigeons, a problem which was gradually overcome.

As the service increased and more men were trained as 'pigeoneers', (this was prior to the introduction of the trade of loftsman), a great degree of efficiency was attained. Having trained handlers ensured that the pigeons were properly handled and fed, and protected against the rats infesting the trenches. The new organisation gave a pigeon station at each Brigade sector of the front and at each station was a basket containing four pigeons, under the charge of a specially trained soldier.

In June 1915, the Carrier Pigeon service was reorganised. An establishment of ten pigeon stations with each army was authorised and a similar number for the cavalry Corps. In order to cater for this new requirement, the enlistment of 60 pigeon 'Specialists' was authorised and the service was transferred to the R.E. Signals Service. The plane for the First Army Pigeon Service for December 1915 shows that fifteen pigeon stations had been established, with eight reserve 'baskets' giving a total of 202 birds.

As the war progressed, it became necessary to increase the service even further. The lessons learned during the Somme Offensive showed that there was a need for a 'mobile loft', which could be moved from location to location as the need arose. The proposal for the mobile service called for six motor and sixty horse-drawn lofts, with the motorised loft holding fifty and the horse drawn loft seventy-five birds, so that the new mobile service would give an additional 4,800 pigeons to the Signal Service. The mobile loft proved to be a success, as by 1917 it was reported that the service was extremely efficient, with several hundred messages being passed by the pigeon service during every battle. The established figure was again increased during July 1917, when the horse-drawn lofts were increased to 120 and six other mobile lofts, and the use of pigeons had been extended so that they were also used by artillery officers on forward observation duties and by tank crews.

The Pigeon Service at this time had, according to the history of the Royal Engineer Signal service, far outstripped the forward wireless service in its practical utility. It was invaluable in the later action of the war and in particular during a retreat. It was found that the mobile lofts were not as 'mobile' as had been hoped. Horses were difficult to find at short notice and with the roads completely congested during one retreat, forty horse-drawn and motor mobile lofts were lost to the enemy. Most of these had been destroyed by fire and the birds dispersed, so that no mobile loft was captured complete with birds.

The Carrier Pigeon service continued throughout the war and at the conclusion of the conflict there were 22,000 pigeons in the service, with 150 mobile lofts and 400 pigeoneers.

Following the formation of the Royal Corps of Signals in 1920, the newly-formed Corps took over the responsibility for the Pigeon Service. During the years inbetween the two wars, lofts were established and loftsman became a trade within the Corps. In the early stages of the war, there was no co-ordination between the Navy and the Army. Each command took such steps in organising as were expedient, and no doubt for a time there was an element of overlap.

Hardly had the naval Pigeon Service been established when Lt-Col. A. H. Osman OBE received an urgent message from the War Office to meet Col. Maud. The two men had a discussion about pigeons and the need for a Home Defence Pigeon Service for the whole of the Eastern Coast of England. Col. Osman was seen as the best person to set up the project. He decided the answer to the request was to form a volunteer service, and not actually requisitioning lofts. By this means, fanciers capable of conditioning their birds and keeping them fit could be called on in an emergency and would be at the disposal of the command. If necessary, should the enemy effect a landing, these owners could at once be put in uniform. Col. Maud thought the scheme an excellent one and begged Osman to undertake the work of its immediate organisation, with the rank of Captain.

Outside of the Higher Command, few of the public were aware of the fear that was entertained of a serious invasion and the steps taken to meet such an emergency. It was pointed out to Col. Maud that the Colonel's paper, 'The Racing Pigeon', might be the means of obtaining volunteers and birds for the service. The only conditions in which he would undertake the work were if he were given an honorary rank, without pay. It was on these terms that Colonel Osman was appointed to organise and command the first Carrier Pigeon Service in the British Army.

While in the midst of selecting sites for Home Defence depots and arranging details, a call came from France to enlist sixty men for active service in the Carrier Pigeon Service. It was impossible to deal with this matter as well as proceed with the organisation at hand. These sixty men were therefore enlisted at Leeds by the N.H.U., but at a later date, when the Home Defence Service was established and in working order, all other men and Carrier Pigeon Service requirements for the Army were dealt with by the Carrier Pigeon Service Headquarters, Horse Guards, under the command of Col. Osman.

At the outbreak of war, the British Army had not paid any serious consideration to the use of pigeons, evidently relying upon the field telegraph signals and wireless. The enemy, however were much more adequately prepared for war than the Allied forces, as during the earliest days of the war, they brought into use a well-organised Pigeon service, with mobile lofts fully equipped with pigeons.

In the defence of Verdun, pigeons proved their great value and were eventually the only means of communication for this front when all other means had failed. Some of the messages sent during February and April 1916 were of a thrilling nature. The following are translations of the actual messages carried from Verdun by pigeons:

28 February. 14.40. 2 Pigeons. Colonel 166 at (place) Verdun. *A strong enemy attack has outflanked Champion and is now directed on the Tresnes Montgirmont Eparges. (Telephonic) cut by a strong bombardment. We are resisting. 334.*
29 February. 8.40. *During the day yesterday and night the bombardment of the position continues. No infantry attack in Section one, a deserter gave himself up last night at Bois Carre. According to him the Germans have withdrawn troops to take them to the right bank.*
6 March. 17.45. *Enemy attack continues at Bethincourt at 19.45 barrage obtained lately has not been able to impede progress. About a battalion has been able to concentrate in the woods between Bethincourt and Rafficourt. Artillery has fired on these woods. All communications broken with 1 brigade, (Corbeaux Woods) Bethincourt always held by a battalion of the 22ON. All dispositions taken for holding on Morthomme. Very violent bombardment of our lines, send relief to Souville urgently.*
15 April, 6.26 a.m. *The German counter attack has been repulsed by the companies occupying the Hautville trench and he has entrenched a line in front of this own line at the front. Artillery barrage is necessary on A.U.C. 9x. The first battalion of the 36th is in position a little N. of the Driant Trench. Serious losses, at least fifty per cent of the effectives. Reinforcements urgent.*

These and other despatches were carried through shell fire and barrage whilst the defence of Verdun held out. It is said the defence of Verdun won the war; if so, pigeons, by their courage, helped to win it.

Major Alec Waley, who was appointed O.C. Carrier Pigeon Service on the French front, gave some interesting details in an article in the *Morning Post*, about the use of pigeons in the battle of the Somme and the important messages carried by them in this great battle. The following extracts are from the article:

> It was 25 September that the Guards Division were to attack Les Boeufs and Goudecourt. The pigeon lofts which served the division were two mobile lofts sited at Minden Post, a few hundred yards behind Carnoy and thus about ten miles as the pigeon flies from Les Boeufs. From early in the morning the pigeon despatch riders had been carrying the birds up in large stock baskets to the different battalion headquarters and to the Guards advanced division R.C. at Bernafay Wood.

Recording the advance:

It was a typical September day and good for flying, but the artillery preparation was deafening and tested the birds to the limit. Messages began to come in from 2.00 p m. and the regularity with which the birds homed, and thus the advance could be followed, was quite remarkable.

The messages given below are well worth studying. The lofts would contain a few officers and men awaiting the birds. The birds would be seen arriving from afar, over the howitzer batteries before a few circling flights around the lofts, lower and lower, then a flutter onto the lofts and into the trapping box.

The message carrier would be taken off the pigeon's leg at once, its little flimsy message form extracted and the text phoned through instantly to Corps and Division H.Q.s, before the birds were fed.

In every message, 'R.D.' stands for the hour that which the Division received the message, with some going through in remarkable time.

From: Give to Gain, 25 September 1916.
Messages now received from all Companies in brown line. Just about to advance to Blue at proper hour. Artillery fire a bit short. Shovels wanted. Have seen Colonel Campbell and shall proceed myself to village, resistance feeble.

Place: Green Line, 2.55 p.m. Sender's signature; R. McCalont, Lt-Col. R.D.
3.20 p.m. from Gallant to Gain, 25 September 1916.
Have only one officer left, could Newton and Transport Officer be sent up tonight. Am now advancing through the village of Les Boeufs supported by the 2nd Battalion Coldstreams. Sender's signature: C.M., time 2.45 p.m. R.D. 3.10 p.m. from D85 to Z8.
25 September 1916.
Message from Welsh guards reports enemy are turning their left flank, which is not in touch with the 21ˢᵗ Division, a battalion urgently wanted to fill the gap.

Place 3, 3.37 p.m. sender's signature: R.S. Lambert, Capt. R.D. 3.59 p.m. from O.C., L.F. Coy, 2nd battalion Scots guards to Great. *The 2nd Battalion Scots Guards have reached and consolidated their objective. 1st Brigade, on our right, have pushed through Les Boeufs and are digging themselves in about 50 yards E. side of the village. The 21st Division appears to be held up on the left flank of the 4th Grenadiers, who are on the left of this battalion and are very badly in the air. For this reason, the left half Battalion 1st Grenadiers were unable to push on to the third objective and have not dug themselves in 100 yards behind the second objective. Am trying to establish defensive flank on the left Grenadiers of the 4th. All the Officers of the 4th Grenadiers appear to be casualties.*

Place; N.33D.73, 3.50 p.m. Sender's signature: V.A. Cochrane Baillie, Lt. R.D 4.25 p.m. From D.85 to Z 8, 25 September 1916. *Message received from the front line D.87, 3.15 p.m., reports D.83 on third objective. D.87, D.85 on sunken road. N34A and D. troops appear to be echeloned towards the left. Message from left company D.85, 2.15 p.m. Reported being at N.33 D.22 with their left not in touch with the 21st Division, who are held up on the first German line. A bombing fight is now in progress on the left of D.89, about N.32, D.74 situation at that point dangerous.* Sender's signature: R.S. Lambert, Capt., 5.15 p.m.

On this day on the Somme front, over 400 operation messages came back from tanks and the attacking forces: not a bad record for the pigeons and a good mark to the stout lads who had to take them up with them over barbed wire, trenches and shell craters into the unknown.

In the battle of the Somme, the French alone used 5,000 pigeons and only two per cent of the birds released with messages failed to return, despite shell fire and adverse weather conditions on many occasions. Also, the loss of that percentage of the pigeons did not necessarily mean the failure to deliver any important messages carried, as these were always sent in duplicate on important occasions.

From the tanks, pigeons proved of great service to communicate with the base; in fact, they were often the only means of communication. Sometimes, when they were liberated from the tanks the birds seemed stupified, no doubt due to the fumes of the oil. Colonel Osman strongly recommended the use of small closed baskets for use in the tanks, similar to our show baskets.

At this time, there was a lot of instruction for the Tank Corps at Wool, and every Officer and man who was to serve in the Tank Corps had to thoroughly master the handling of pigeons. At the conclusion of the war there were 22,000 pigeons, 150 mobile lofts and at least 400 C.P.S. Pigeoneers in the C.P.S. Good reports came from GHQ Salonika, where Sergeant F. Shaw was sent out to establish the service. The Egyptian service was established by Sergeant H.C. Knott. In fact, there was not a single unit of the C.P.S. Army Pigeon Service that proved a failure.

On the morning of 8 October 1914, Commander Denuit, the head of the Belgium Pigeon Service, took a flaming torch to the Great Columbier in Antwerp and with tears streaming down his face, burnt alive 2,500 of the finest pigeons in the world rather than left them fall to the hands of the Germans. You can only imagine what this sacrifice cost him, especially if you are a pigeon fancier yourself. The brave commander was only just in time, as the Germans captured Antwerp at noon.

DEDICATION:

IN MEMORY OF
PIONEER R. BLUNDELL
ROYAL ENGINEERS

Who died aged twenty-seven years on Friday, 1 November 1918.
Pioneer Blundell, Carrier Pigeon Service, son of Mr & Mrs J. Blundell of Crossens, Southport, husband of Margaret Blundell, of 149 Heysham Road, Southport. Remembered with Honour. Étaples military cemetery, Pas de Calais, France. In the perpetual care of the Commonwealth War Graves Commission.

2
THE SPECIAL SECTION

In the Second World War, with the fall of Holland, Belgium and France, the possibility of dropping pigeons with an invitation of co-operation to the people of these overrun areas became practicable once more. At that time there were large numbers of pigeons in the United Kingdom, which during peace time had raced the south road from points on the Continent. It was not known if these birds, when liberated singly under such exceptional conditions, could be counted on to face the channel crossing, but experiments were met with success. In this war, a more direct method of supply could be used, however; aircraft were continually crossing the European Coast on various missions, and could drop pigeons into selected areas.

During the last month of 1940 and the early part of 1941, the supply of pigeons used with Special Section was drawn by local arrangement from a few specially selected lofts or groups of lofts, situated in South Eastern and Southern England, the greatest care being taken to ensure that the least possible information was available to the loft owners regarding the work being undertaken.

It soon became apparent that even by restocking these lofts with the young birds, the opportunities of the Service could not be fully developed. By 1942, a system based on groups of fanciers working under Pigeon Supply Officers was adopted. With the new system, it was possible to work out a plan whereby the individual fancier was not called upon to jeopardise the bird strength of his loft to a point where the quality of his birds would be affected, but could be maintained in a position to furnish birds for service as long as such calls should be made on him. The National Pigeon Service assisted in this work, which grew to a point where some 1,300 civilian lofts throughout Eastern, South Eastern and Southern England were training and supplying birds regularly, reinforced in the final operational phases with the birds drawn from Midland lofts.

The pigeon fanciers of the British Isles, co-ordinated through the National Pigeon Service, have supplied birds to the Army, Air Force, Home Guard, Police and other services. For the use of such birds, these fanciers have received a small rent in the form of payment for service flights, but in the instance of Special Section, such a rent was not really applicable because the majority of the birds employed could not be expected to return. Therefore, it can be said, greatly to the credit of the fanciers working with Special Section, that beyond the fact that once a bird was nominated for this service it was fed at public expense, a fancier received no compensation in the event of loss, other than the knowledge that through the voluntary sacrifice of some of his birds and his own work in training them, he was forwarding the Allied cause.

It must be remembered that, without knowledge of the results obtained, these men and women who trained and supplied pigeons for these operations did so to the detriment of their sport. Through winter and summer alike, they added yet one more

NATIONAL PIGEON SERVICE

Conditions of Membership

(*a*) Membership is restricted to those who train and breed homing pigeons and who maintain a loft of at least 20 pigeons of quality approved by the Committee of the National Pigeon Service. Prospective membership will be subject to the approval of the Committee, who will examine all applications before membership forms and badges are issued.

(*b*) Members are required to give an undertaking that they will volunteer their services and/or their birds to H.M. Government as required if and when necessary.

(*c*) The fact of being a member of the N.P.S. which is a voluntary body, does not exempt a member from any obligations in connection with National Service which may be enforced by H.M. Government from time to time. On the other hand, membership of the N.P.S. does not preclude a member from joining or being a member of any other National Service organisation.

(*d*) All approved members will receive a badge of membership, together with a certificate of membership.

(*e*) All members will be required to adhere to the instructions of the Committee of the N.P.S. which will act under the direction of the Secretary of State for Air.

(*f*) Members may resign from the N.P.S. at any time after one month's notice to the Committee and at the same time will return their badge and certificate of membership.

Any member who, in the opinion of the Committee of the N.P.S. is deemed unsuitable for any reason, may be called upon to resign.

(*g*) Pigeons and lofts belonging to members may be inspected by the Committee of the N.P.S. or any representative deputed by them at any time.

(*h*) Those members selected for co-operation with R.A.F. Stations are not expected to be members of any other National Service organisation, in order that they can devote their maximum time to their pigeon duties.

NPS membership conditions.

Tom Silk's NPS membership card.

task to the long hours of war work, Home Guard and fire-watching which already crowded their lives. On the other hand, the people of occupied territories risked life and liberty to do their part with slim hope of its achievement. These facts emphasise the co-operation and good faith of those who played the main part in this sterling work.

Some groups stand out as pigeoneers in this work, and carried on through to the final phases of the war with a splendid record of perfor-mance. The Ipswich group under 'Herbie Keys', The Folkestone Fanciers with 'Johnny Banks', as pigeon supply officer, Weston-super-Mare organised by Mr Parratt and Shepherd's Bush under Gaston Noterman are those with the longest terms of service to their credit. Among the big individual lofts which contributed such a lot in the opening phases which should be mentioned are those of Mr A. Chester Beatty, Mr Fuller Isaacson, Mr Hardcastle and Mr Fowler of Chard, who were perhaps the first in this field.

In the early days, comparatively small numbers of birds were used, but the system of dispatch and the equipment employed was materially the same throughout the term of operations. Then, as later, birds sent on service were collected from loft owners the day prior to despatch and taken to an airfield. There they were fitted with message containers and packed in the round single bird cartons with parachutes attached, together with bags of food to last ten days, instructions, questionnaires and so on. Finally, when briefing was completed and it was known which planes were to be used, the containers were packed on board to be taken overseas.

With luck, on the second morning after the birds had been taken from their lofts, they were found by some Belgian or Frenchman lying in a field. Records do not show how many birds ever reached their destination or how many of those that fell on occupied soil were picked up by the Germans, their agents or those lacking the will to fight who handed them to their overlords, claiming the largest rewards that were offered. That the Germans were stung to intense effort in their attempts to stop the ever-growing traffic, which brought the Allies news of enemy strength and movement, is evidenced by the lengths to which they went in an attempt to stop it. An illustration of this occurred when, during the German defeat in Belgium, a headquarters was overrun, with its adjoining loft buildings and storage rooms. In these were found great numbers of containers, with accompanying equipment stored there, in the lofts were many birds wrung with British 1940/1941 rings. There is no doubt that, disguised as Allied pigeons, these birds were used with Special Section equipment and dropped in certain areas in an attempt to trap those who were working with the Service behind the German lines.

Messages covering the widest range of fact have been received through this service, and it should be a source of satisfaction to the people of southern England to know, for example, that long before the V1 appeared to plague them, birds of their own training had brought information of the German plan. It is almost beyond belief, but in the old-type message container, a bird brought back a message of 5,000 words and fifteen sketch maps, giving a wealth of detail.

The development and organisation of Special Section arranged through the medium of the civilian fancy is of considerable interest, from a small beginning, when up to 100 birds were used. The numbers increased to a point where some 1,500 birds were used. During the latter years, a few old-time channel birds were still to be found in fanciers' lofts and, due to the war, the majority of clubs in Southern England were racing on the north road.

Because service requirements were directly opposed to the majority of civilian interests, a meeting was called of the Pigeon Supply Officers representing Special Section groups, the National Pigeon Service committee members concerned being invited to attend. At the meeting, the service requirements were defined with regards to what training would be necessary to qualify pigeons, and it was pointed out that such training would not only cut across the racing interests of group members, but that the great increase in training and supply of birds would have to be accomplished with no further increase in the number of signals personnel who could be devoted to this work. At the meeting, general policies were adopted by a majority vote. To express common equity, a principle was established: namely, that as far as possible service demands for operational birds would be based proportionally on the total number of nominated birds in each group, this system being reflected in turn within the groups themselves. Since most groups were built on existing civil club organisations, when birds were nominated for service by the members of a group, necessitating the provision of a certain number of fit, trained pigeons for an operation, each member of that group was to ensure that he had enough birds ready so that his loft provided its just proportion of the birds required from the group as a whole.

It was pointed out that failure on the part of the club member to do this resulted in other club members having to make up this deficiency. It was the responsibility of the Pigeon Supply Officers, in fairness to the other members of the group, to see that each member fulfilled his obligation.

DEFENCE REGULATIONS, 1939.

REGULATION 9.

Number....... 65

PERMIT TO KEEP RACING OR HOMING PIGEONS.

To All whom it may concern.

By Virtue of the Powers vested in me under the provisions of Regulation 9 of the Defence Regulations, 1939, I hereby grant permission to the Person named below *19.6.41.* in possession of Racing or Homing Pigeons, not exceeding *40.* in number, to be kept (*in open loft*) at...... *12 Rowan Place New Brunswick*

NAME OF HOLDER.

Surname ...... *Silk*

Christian Names...... *Thomas.*

Registered Postal Address ...... *12 Rowan Place.*

New Brunswick.

...... *J. Hardy*
Signature of ~~Chief Constable~~ (or Superintendent).

...... *Haworth York n.R.* Police Station.

...... *T. Silk.*
Signature of Holder.

Date...... *6th April 1940*

The holder of this Permit is not authorised thereby to liberate any racing or homing pigeon away from its own loft. In order to carry any racing or homing pigeon, it is necessary to obtain the prescribed official label (a) from the Secretary of the National Pigeon Service, 22, Clarence Street, Gloucester, if the birds are for transit only, and not for liberation (green label); (b) in other cases, from the police (yellow label).

The holder should carefully note the provisions of the Regulation, which is printed on the other side.

THIS PERMIT MAY BE REVOKED AT ANY TIME.

[7545] 29175/845 2,200 bks. 9/39 4006 G & S 704   [P.T.O.

Tom Silk's permit to keep pigeons.

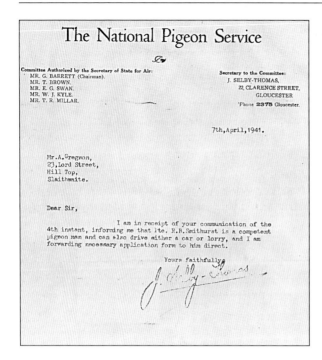

A letter from the NPS.

A plan of training was decided on, which covered points from the east coast down and around to the south west. Groups by individual arrangements were to introduce their birds into this programme either in a clockwise or anti-clockwise direction. In the majority of instances, consignments of birds for training which had to pass through London or which originated in the London area, were collected on certain nights of the week by section personnel, being convoyed to the liberation points on the following morning. The groups situated in the extreme south west who could not participate in the general plan, trained largely in an easterly or south easterly direction, by local arrangement.

It was decided that Pigeon Supply Officers would keep training records of all nominated birds, so that on the receipt of a service demand some ten days prior to the date on which the birds were required, they were in a position to know, from their records, which of their groups' birds had successfully completed sufficient training to ensure a good chance of them homing from operations.

It must be of considerable satisfaction to pigeon-fanciers generally to know how this plan for an equal distribution of the burden of service requirements met with almost universal acceptance and that the co-operation received from the fancy was such that during all the subsequent operational periods, on no occasion did the work planned have to be curtailed due to failure in the supply of trained pigeons fit for service.

Subsequent meetings were held, at which various problems were discussed and solved; plans were also made for the coming months to meet the conditions anticipated. Great credit is due to the Pigeon Supply Officers and National Pigeon Service Committee members for their interest and work, particularly when it is remembered that the Pigeon Supply Officers undertook these responsibilities and the work involved without remuneration.

Some idea can be formed of the size and proportions of this undertaking when it is realised that as service pigeons were sent overseas throughout the year, so the training and conditioning of birds also had to be continued, with attendant losses. Fifty thousand birds is a fair estimate of the number of pigeons nominated for service by fanciers and placed in training during the period, covering all Special Section operations from which were drawn the 17,000, plus birds sent overseas.

At the close of the service, most groups had sufficient trained old birds and enough young birds in training to carry through the commitment to supply an average of 1,000 to 2,000 service birds per month, should this be required of them.

Records established that twice the number of returns could be expected where yearlings and old birds are used, compared with young birds under the same conditions. Plans, therefore, were aimed at ensuring that there would be between twelve and fifteen thousand trained birds in Special Section lofts at the end of any year and that, in addition, approximately 20,000 young birds would be trained from Special Section lofts each year to provide the service birds needed in the subsequent year, a few being required in the current year during that period when the moult curtailed the use of old birds, although fanciers were asked to do all they could to stagger this condition in their pigeons.

However, the objective outlined above was only realised in the summer of 1944, when some 28,000 nominated birds were in training. In the latter part of the year, the enemy was driven from France, Belgium and southern Holland and a point was reached when the continuation of the service was no longer practicable on the scale previously in force.

The problems that developed from this undertaking can be judged by the fact that the collection of some 300 crates of birds in an evening, between 7p.m. and midnight, was by no means unusual. This meant that between three and four hundred pigeons had to be watered and housed for the night and shipped to catch early trains to their liberation points the following morning, with the possibility during bad weather of a holdover which might double the number of birds to be handled the subsequent day. The patience and good spirit shown by the fanciers cannot be over-emphasised. This will be appreciated when it is realised that, throughout the year, these fanciers voluntarily sacrificed two evenings a week and in good and bad weather alike, despite blackout, brought their birds to collecting stations by bicycle, pushcart and bus, with all the inconvenience such circumstances imply in time of war.

While the individual training programmes of groups varied in detail, in principle, liberations were made from points all around the coast, so that the birds reaching the English shore at any point from the continent would find themselves on a familiar line of flight. Training involved both mass and single liberations to ensure, as far as possible, both the quality and condition of birds used. Liberations at sea were also arranged on the largest scale practicable during the spring and summer. Fanciers will be interested to note that during the winter months, despite the uncertainty of the weather, velocities of over 1,700 yards per minute were occasionally obtained in training pigeons from the coast.

The majority of pigeons sent on service homed from points in Northern France, Belgium and southern Holland, but there were birds which brought messages from as far afield as the Bordeaux area on the west, the upper Rhone Valley on the south, and northern Denmark to the east, a distance of just under 500 miles.

As might be expected, it was during the late spring and summer months that the percentage of returns was greatest, resulting no doubt from a combination of factors.

During this period, not only did the birds have better flying weather and more hours of daylight in which to home to their lofts, but with the very early hours of daylight they were less likely to be overlooked by those collaborating, who in turn would be less subject to discovery at that time of day.

On occasion, birds from Special Section lofts were diverted for purposes other than their normal role; they were taken on combined operations and other important missions where contact with this country was necessary. When, in the winter of 1943, it became apparent that during the following spring or early summer, pigeons might be required for service with the opening of the second front, certain groups at points along the south coast were first rested and then, in co-operation with the United States Army Signals, training was organised. When the time came for these groups to be transferred to the command they were to serve, the plan proved itself and the birds were ready when D-Day came, several hundred being used by the American Army at Portsmouth and Plymouth, where the lofts were.

The following table of returns will prove of interest to Special Section fanciers, for it shows what they have accomplished during four years of continuous service; and how by furnishing pigeons in continuously large numbers they have not only neutralised the intense German countermeasures built up in anticipation of a Western front, but have increased the flow of information reaching these shores at a most critical period of the war.

Records for the four years during which this service has operated show that 16,554 birds were dropped in enemy-held territory, of which 1,842 or eleven per cent returned to the United Kingdom.

TABLE OF RETURNS
Beginning of Service to September 1941. Despatched 616, returned 139.
October 1941 to March 1942. Despatched 74, returned 14.
April 1942 to September 1942. Despatched 1,342, returned 267.
October 1942 to March 1943. Despatched 1,664, returned 113.
April 1943 to September 1943. Despatched 3,793, returned 528.
October 1943 to March 1944. Despatched 2,819, returned 161.
April 1944 to September 1944. Despatched 6,246, returned 620.

It should be understood that throughout all operations, in order to maintain the maximum security and to deny enemies as much knowledge as possible about the scope of the operations and the degree of success obtained, this service was split in terms of responsibility.

All of the records maintained by the branch of the Service responsible for this type of work, and the Special Section personnel, as a signals unit working with those fanciers whose express duty was the supply of properly trained birds, have been subject to the same restriction of information.

It is important, therefore, that fanciers who find discrepancies in this list of returns understand the reason why. For instance, where planes were forced back through weather conditions or enemy action, landing at some British Airport, the pigeons they carried were liberated and the fanciers to whose lofts these pigeons homed forwarded the message carriers in the belief that their birds had returned from abroad; no record is available of such birds. Then again, the fact that some pigeons returned without a message container did not necessarily signify that the flight had been without value, because such methods were sometimes used as a pre-arranged signal and thus conveyed intelligence to the department concerned.

While the Special Section Service was in operation, the fanciers working with it could have no knowledge of the collective value which individual efforts made possible. Winter months were discouraging, returns being comparatively poor and training difficult. It was then that interest in the Section's work began to flag, recognising this trend. In the autumn of 1943, Mr J. Humphreys of Tottenham, as chairman, started the organisation of a show for service pigeons to stimulate interest and a committee composed of Special Section Pigeon Supply Officers served, with Mr H. Smith as secretary and Mr G. Noterman as treasurer.

The show, in aid of the Merchant Navy Seamen's Fund, was arranged for 12 December, at the Scottish Drill Hall in London. An auction of gift birds was planned in conjunction with it. Good support was given by the fancy, with some 600 entries. His Majesty the King, along with many of the leading fanciers in the United Kingdom, donated birds to be auctioned in support of the charity and, after all the expenses had been paid, a cheque for £485 was passed to the credit of the Merchant Navy Seaman's Fund.

In September 1944, with the progress being made on the Allied fronts, it was apparent that Special Section could only be of service to the country for a few months longer. The committee, which had acted in 1943, thought that another pigeon show, to be held in December, might be welcomed by the fancy. The show was planned to be something of a closing ceremony, emblematic of the bond which common service with Special Section had fostered among loft owners.

The committee, with an increased membership, decided that as a closing gesture, on this occasion the proceeds were to benefit the Royal Signals War Memorial Fund and asked that Maj.-Gen. L.G. Phillips, CB, CBE, MC, director of signals, be invited to attend the opening ceremony. The officers appointed by the committee on this occasion being the chairman, Mr H. Keys with Mr R. Wallis as secretary and Mr J. Banks as treasurer.

The date of 2 December was the date selected for the show of Service Pigeons (Army Division), as it was to be called. When, in October, the closing down of the service removed the necessity for strict security enforcement, the Director of Signals chose this as the occasion when public recognition might be given to the splendid work to which so many of the fancy had contributed so much. However, competition was limited to those loft owners who had supplied birds for Special Section operations, and the entries restricted to a single pigeon from each loft, except in the two classes open to all birds that had completed operational flights.

The show was splendidly supported, with 1,017 entries. Over 100 gift birds from outstanding lofts were accepted for auction, these included one from the King, and six pigeons with remarkable Army service records presented by the National Pigeon Service.

On the day of the show, attendance exceeded expectations. Thousands must have visited this exhibition and the drill hall was packed when the director of signals gave the following address: 'There are many of you present today who have been working with the Special Section, Army Pigeon Service, a unit of the Royal Signals and I am very glad in my capacity as director of signals, to be given this opportunity to thank you all for your magnificent work in connection with this service.

'In the past, the work of the Special Section has for obvious reasons been kept surrounded in mystery, but today I am in a position, partially at any rate, to lift the veil and help you appreciate more fully the valuable contribution you have made to the service.

'In the war of 1914 to 1918, by means of balloons and other devices, a limited number of pigeons based on Army lofts in France were dropped behind enemy lines for use by agents and well disposed civilians in getting information back to British Army headquarters. In 1940, after France had been occupied by the Germans, this fact was recalled and steps were taken, with the help of the then recently formed National Pigeon Service, to start a pigeon service with a similar object in view.

'To ensure success, three main essentials had to be met: a constant supply of pigeons that could reasonably be expected to home from across the Channel from distances up to 300 miles; a means of delivering these birds in good condition to the possible users in areas from which information was required; and the presence of persons well disposed to us and possessing great courage in the selected areas, to make use of the pigeons once delivered. The first of these essentials, the supply of pigeons, was solved by the good will of the National Pigeon Service Committee and the unfailing zeal of the many civilian loft owners with whom the Special Section had co-operated. In the first instance, the pigeons used were birds previously trained by their owners for cross-channel racing, but supplies of this nature were limited. It therefore became necessary to augment this source if the ever-growing demands of this service were to be met. This was achieved by taking on lofts whose birds had not previously been trained for cross channel work and by filling up and even increasing the size of many lofts, through drafts of young birds supplied from the lofts of other members of the National Pigeon Service.

'The number of birds at the disposal of Special Section has continually increased until, during the last few months, it has reached the vicinity of 30,000, including young birds under training, found from some 1,200 individual lofts which, in turn, have been organised into fifty groups each under a Pigeon Supply Officer.

'In addition to the actual owners of lofts that have co-operated with the Special Section, I would like to thank these P.S.O.s for their work in conjunction with the running of these groups, the members of the National Pigeon Service Committee for their very great help they have given in the organising of new groups and provision of young birds, and the owners of the lofts from which these young birds were obtained. In doing so, I would stress the point that both for the supply of birds used for operational flights and young birds; no payment in money was made. The respective loft owners reward was limited to free corn for a proportion of the birds in their lofts, and the sense of work well done.

'You have lately read in the papers how, through the services of the RAF, arms and supplies were dropped to members of the Maquis. In the same manner, pigeons packed in special containers have during the last four years been continually dropped over areas from which information was required. Naturally, information was normally required from areas where the presence of German troops was suspected and consequently not only did a number of birds dropped get into the hands of the Germans, but also any person retaining a bird ran a considerable risk. We know that the Germans offered large sums of money for any pigeons handed over to them, organised special search parties to find pigeons that they suspected of having been dropped, and death was the penalty for being found in the possession of one. Under these circumstances you can readily understand that in the natural course of events only a proportion, I might say a small one, of birds were ever released to fly home to this country. This, I think, should make clear the necessity for the large number of birds that have been required.

'During the four years that this service has been in existence, well over 1,000 birds have returned with messages, of which a proportion have strayed to lofts other than their own. That this would happen had been appreciated and by the use of a special green-coloured carrier and the co-operation of the police, arrangements were made by which messages found on stray birds were rapidly collected and forwarded to Wing House. The finding of some of these messages was almost miraculous.

'In one case, a policeman watching a pigeon flying over saw a carrier fall from its leg and on finding it discovered it was one of the magic green ones and dealt with it in the proper manner. In another case, a small boy found a dead pigeon in a ditch with two such carriers on its legs, they were found in Falcon's nest on the south cost of England.

'One stray landed on a trawler off the south cost of Ireland and, having rested, was last seen joining, as the trawler owner reported, a west bound vessel. Even this pigeon turned up eventually, complete with message, at its own loft in Weston-super-Mare.

'I should like to thank the police and the many pigeon fanciers not directly connected with the Special Section, who, by their help in forwarding messages found on strays, did much towards the success of this work.

'Many of you have probably wondered when taking the green message carrier off your pigeons' leg, what sort of messages were inside. Time does not permit for me to give you the details of all of them, but I propose to give you extracts from a few which I thank will show you have vitally important they were.

'Latterly, many of them have given the exact positions of flying-bomb sites which were in due course passed to the right authority, a matter that should be of considerable interest to people living in London and the southern counties.

'Others gave positions of Headquarters and information regarding troop movements and the like. In one case, one message gave such detailed information as regards a Headquarters, including times when most officers were present, that a subsequent raid by our bombing planes had excellent results.

'In certain cases messages were of a more flippant nature, one gave details about how the writer had put a German, wishing to get out of the war, on a road where he knew the Maquis were, thereby making certain that the German's wish was granted.

'Again, another message included a short note from a grounded airman telling his wife that he was safe and well. This pigeon it is felt, certainly delivered the goods.

'During the time that the Special Section work has been in operation, pigeons have been dropped over France, Belgium and even in Holland and Denmark. The percentage of returns from different areas has varied considerably and it was evident to a certain extent that people trapped in any new areas had to be educated by the continuous dropping of pigeons before they were prepared to make use of these birds to get information to this country. This, I think, was only natural as they always had to be on their guard against traps laid by the Gestapo.

'The longest flight from which a pigeon returned was some 400 miles, the average distance being in the vicinity of 200 miles.

'I have now ladies and gentleman, given you some insight into the work in which you have participated and it only remains for me to say how much your co-operation has helped the war effort and once again to thank you all very much.'

The chairman, in thanking the director of signals for his recognition and appreciation of the service given by the fancy to the country, stressed the importance of continuing the friendships within the fancy, which has been the happy result of working together.

The director of signals then presented three medals, bearing the Royal Signals emblem, as a memento for remarkable service. A medal was presented to Mr H. Keys of Ipswich, as the Pigeon Supply Officer of the group with the greatest number of recorded service returns. The second medal was presented to Mr Bryant, on behalf of his son, whose pigeon, NURP.38.BPC6 had homed three times from the Continent on the later occasion in November, the performance in this instance being the deciding factor.

Mr J.H. Catchpole, of Ipswich, owner of NUHW.37.CEN335, was awarded the third medal. In July 1942, his bird homed from a distance of 480 miles from northern Denmark, which was judged the most outstanding single performance made on Special Section Service.

Immediately following the address and presentation of medals, the auction of gift birds which had started in the afternoon resumed, and interest reached a climax when the N.P.S. Service birds were offered.

As a result of the work and support of the Special Section loft owners, the show for service pigeons (Army Division), raised the splendid sum of £1,212 10 shillings and 7d net for the benefit of the Royal Signals War Memorial Fund.

Although the Special Section was not formally closed down until January 1945, the speech given by the director of signals on 2 December 1944 in fact marked the true termination of the effort which Special Section fanciers had so long sustained. In closing this section of the book, it might be well to echo the sentiment expressed by Mr Keys; namely, the hope that this voluntary work, so steadfastly undertaken to help the country in a time of need, would continue to be the cause of wider friendship and better understanding within the fancy itself.

3

THE SHOW FOR SERVICE
PIGEONS (ARMY DIVISION)

The show for service pigeons (army division), was held on 2 December 1944, at The Drill Hall, 59 Buckingham Gate, Victoria, London. This was in aid of the Royal Corps of Signals War Memorial Fund (a post-war club for all ranks of signalmen).

The show consisted of twenty classes, of which classes one and two were cocks of any age which had flown in Special Sections operations, and hens of any age which had done the same. It was clearly stated that 'all birds, having returned from operations overseas, are eligible for exhibit, and ring numbers of such birds will be verified against special service records. The date of operation flights will be shown with entries.'

'The civilian loft having the bird with the greatest number of recorded service returns will be judged the winner if there is a tie on performance. The [prize will go to the]fancier whose bird is judged to have given the most outstanding single performance on service'.

Conditions of entry were as follows: 'All Special Section lofts, past and present in good standing may enter only one service pigeon in any one of the classes 3 to 16 inclusive. And in cases where such a loft does not nominate an entry, the P.S.O. is empowered to allocate the vacancy thus created to another loft within the group, with the proviso that no loft enters more than two birds. In the event of two entries being made by one loft, these must be entered in different classes.'

Lofts operated with Special Section in the Midlands were told: 'Loft owners in the Birmingham, Wolverhampton and Worcester Federation areas who wish to compete, must have at least one bird accepted and basketed for Special Section service and their entries for classes 3 to 16 inclusive must be selected from those birds in their loft which club records substantiate.'

PROGRAMME SHOW FOR SERVICE PIGEONS
(ARMY DIVISION)

THE DRILL HALL, 59 BUCKINGHAM GATE,
VICTORIA, LONDON, S.W.1
2 DECEMBER 1944
in aid of
ROYAL CORPS OF SIGNALS WAR MEMORIAL FUND
(POST WAR CLUB FOR ALL RANKS SIGNALS)

PRESIDENT – H.E. KEYS ESQ., IPSWICH
HON. SECRETARY – R.J. WALLIS ESQ., PLAISTOW
HON. TREASURER – J. BANKS ESQ., FOLKESTONE

COMMITTEE

H.A. BRIDGE ESQ., THUNDERSLEY
A.F. PAYS ESQ., MITCHAM
H.J. HUMPREY ESQ., TOTTENHAM
F.E. SAMES ESQ., OLD FORD
H. JONES ESQ., PORTSMOUTH
F. SEAMAN ESQ., WOKING
V.E. LOVE ESQ., ENFIELD
H. SMITH ESQ., CATFORD
G. NOTERMAN ESQ., SHEPHERDS BUSH
J. WRIGHT ESQ., WALTHAMSTOW

JUDGES

W. ANDREWS ESQ., FARNBOROUGH
R. HAYCOCK ESQ., WREXHAM
W.G. BUCKINGHAM ESQ., LONDON
E.H. LULHAM ESQ., CHINGFORD
E. COLCLOUGH ESQ., FLIXTON
S.A. MOON ESQ., HAYWARDS HEATH
W.E.H. DICKENS ESQ., ELLESMERE
GILES SHARROCKS ESQ, HASKAYNE
T. DAVIDSON ESQ., LONDON
J. SLADE ESQ., ENFIELD
J. GAZE ESQ., LOWESTOFT

H.F. SMITH ESQ., NEWPORT
A.R. HANCOCK ESQ., WEST MALLING
A. WARD ESQ., OXTED
F.J. HARMER ESQ., LOWESTOFT
ARTHUR WRIGHT ESQ., MANCHESTER

AUCTIONEERS

J. BANKS ESQ., FOLKESTONE
L. GILBERT ESQ., FOREST HILL

12 NOON – DOORS OPEN TO THE PUBLIC.   2.30 P.M. – SALE OF GIFT BIRDS.

4.00 p.m. Maj.-Gen. L.G. Phillips CB, CBE, MC, director of signals, plans to be present to thank Special Section loft owners for their work.

Presentation of mementoes will be awarded to the Pigeon Supply Officer whose group has received the greatest number of service bird returns on Special Section work.

Copies of this programme, priced 1/6, post free. Apply to Hon. Secretary,
c/o 18 Sackville Street, London W.1.
Single bird containers of cardboard are available at 2 shillings at The Auctioneers Table.
Original pedigrees and transfer forms can be obtained at the time of purchase.

The committee wishes to publicly express their thanks for the generous contributions, which have been received in support of the show from the following:
H. A. Bridge Esq., Thundersley. Gold medal for best opposite sex classes 1 and 2.
A £5 special classes A & B, (Special Section personnel only).
Brinkler, Osbourne and Young of London, all pens and trestles supplied free of charge.
S. Fuller Isaacson of Muswell Hill. Supply and printing of admission tickets.
Major S.H. Heap of The Royal Signals. £2 best cock in show.
R. Jolly Esq., of Wigan. £2 donation to the fund.
T. Morgan Esq., Airdrie. Gold medal, best bird in classes 1 and 2.
A. Pays Esq., Mitcham. £2 best hen in show.
Major Pearson £5 five shilling for classes 1 & 2.
Racing Pigeon, London. £2 two shillings to fund Lt-Col. G.R. Starr MC. Bottle champagne, bottle of Vermouth to be auctioned.
W. Wasden Esq., Sheffield. Ten shilling donation to fund.
Thames Estuary Group. £10 donation to fund.
W.H. Hardcastle Esq. £5 donation to fund.
'Yorkie' The Beehive, Mitcham. 30 shillings donation to fund.

The committee takes this opportunity of thanking the Judges, Auctioneers, Stewards and all those whose voluntary help has been such a contribution to the organisation of this event.

CLASSES

Class 1. Cocks (any age). Flown Special Section operations (unlimited entry).
Class 2. Hens (any age). Flown Special Section operations (unlimited entry).
Service Birds (any ring). Trained for Special Section operations.
Class 3. Old cocks, blue or chequers, (B.DK.B.BLK.VEL), (hard colour).
Class 4. Old hens, same as Class 3.
Class 5. Old cocks. Red, red chequer or mealy, (hard colour).
Class 6. Old hens, same as Class 5.
Class 7. Old cocks. Pied or white w/flighted, (any colour).
Class 8. Old hens. Pied or white flighted, (any colour).
Class 9. Cocks any age. Fancy colour, (other than colours in Classes 3 to 8 inclusive).
Class 10. Hens any age. Fancy colour, (other than colours in Classes 3 to 8 inclusive).
Class 11. Young cocks. 1944 rung blue or chequers. (B.DK.B.BLK.VEL). Hard colour.
Class 12. Young hens. 1944 rung blue or chequers. (B.DK.B.BLK.VEL). Hard colour.
Class 13. Young cocks. 1944 rung. Red, red chequers or mealy, (hard colour).
Class 14. Young hens. 1944 rung. Red, red chequers or mealy, (hard colour).
Class 15. Young cocks. 1944 rung. Pied or white flight, (any colour).
Class 16. Young hens. 1944 rung. Pied or white flight, (any colour).

Special Class A. Any age cock.
Special Class B. Any age hen.

Entries from Special Personnel only.
These birds do not quality for competition in any other Classes; awards for these Classes are being donated by H.A. Bridge Esq.

Classes 1 and 2: it should be clearly understood that all birds having returned from operations overseas are eligible for exhibit and ring records of such birds' numbers will be verified against Special Section records. Date of operational flight will be shown with entries.

Special Prizes. £2 best cock in show. £2 best hen in show.
Medal. Best bird in Classes 1 and 2.
$2\frac{1}{2}$ Guineas for best cock in Class 1.
$2\frac{1}{2}$ Guineas for best hen in Class 2.
Prize Money. £2 10 shillings per class. Distribution. First prize: 25 shillings,

Second: 15 shillings, Third: 10 shillings, Fourth: commended award card only.
Entry fee 2 36 (??) per bird all Classes.
Birds to be penned in the London area at 18 Sackville Street, before midnight on Thursday 30 November 1944.
Provincial area birds to the same address by midnight Friday, 1 December 1944 and having flown a distance in excess of 100 miles on the south road during the 1944 season.

After the show there was a sale of very famous pigeons by an arrangement with the National Pigeon Service Committee. 'The birds mentioned below, with outstanding records of performances in conjunction with military operations, may only be purchased by loft owners who are members of the National Pigeon Service. They will be sold with the proviso that none of them will be publicly exhibited without previous permission of the National Pigeon Service Committee.'

Lot 92. 'MARQUIS'. 'This blue chequer cock, bred in 1942, has been sent four times on varying operations and due to his reliability was only used on the most important missions. First, in April 1943, he was sent on service returning 4 days later, and again in the same year returning from Amiens with 'the goods'. In February 1944, in thick weather, he was sent with Combined Operations, returning to his London loft on the same day in good time. Again in the D-Day operation, he was sent to France and returned with an important operational message for the fourth time.' He was sold for £15 10 shillings, then resold for £22 pounds, making £37 10 shillings in total.

Lot 93. 'THE DUKE OF NORMANDY'. 'After six days in the basket, this grand cock bred in 1941, was landed with special invasion paratroopers deep behind the German beach defences and was liberated at 6.00 a.m. on D-Day. Despite the barrage and gunfire, he faced the northerly Channel gales and heavy rain, to drop with an operational message at his loft in London within 24 hours. It may well be that this bird was the first to reach an English loft from the soil of France. It is established without question that he was the first bird to return from British troops on D-Day operations.' He was sold for £17.

Lot 94. 'LE DAUPHIN'. 'This splendid red cock, bred in 1942, has survived hard operational work without a single mistake for three years, and was chosen for long distance work with paratroopers sent deep into France. Recognising the almost impossible task to be achieved, only the most reliable and finest birds were sent. This pigeon was the only bird to survive this mission, arriving back within 24 hours.' He was sold for £35.

Lot 95. 'WILLIAM OF ORANGE'. 'Bred in 1942, this handsome mealy cock during training flew 68 miles in 59 minutes and was specially selected for service with the airbourne troops landing at Arnhem. He was liberated with an operational message at 10.30 a.m. on 19 September 1944 and arrived at its London loft in 4 hours and 25 minutes, after covering 260 miles singled up, flying 135 miles across open seas.' It is doubted that the velocity of 1,740 Y.P.M. over such a distance has ever been equalled. He was sold for £135.

Lot 96. 'BEACHCOMBER'. 'This famous pigeon, bred in 1941, was the first bird to arrive at operational headquarters with messages dispatched from the beach while the Dieppe raid was in progress. He was one of a pair released during a period of radio silence; his companion was killed by enemy gunfire. In addition to this performance, he has been employed and returned for Special Section work. Included in his training were single up flights from Berwick, Penzance and Belfast to his home loft at Reigate.' He was sold for £31.

Lot 97. 'BAY OF TUNIS'. 'A blinding rainstorm in North Africa did not prevent this 1942 bred blue chequer pied cock from bringing a first report of the fall of Tunis to the first Army Signals headquarters British North African Expeditionary Force. Settled to a new location within three days, this bird solved the problem of communications in bad weather over impassable roads for a stretch of thirty-two miles, thus establishing the flexibility of pigeons used in modern warfare.' He was sold for £26.

On 21 October 1944, a letter was sent to R.J. Wallis, the Show secretary, from Lt-Gen. H.C.B. Wemyss from the War Office. It read:

> Dear Mr Wallis. Thank you for your letter of 13 October 1944 to the secretary, Royal Signals Corps Committee, who passed it on to me. On behalf of all ranks of the Royal Corps of Signals, I gratefully accept your offer to donate the proceeds of your pigeon show and sale of gift birds to the Royal Signals Memorial Fund. The Army Pigeon Service, due to its activities, seldom comes into the limelight, but the excellence of this essential means of communication has been demonstrated on many occasions during the present war and the last one. If my military duties will permit, I will do my best to visit the show myself; meanwhile I wish it every success.
>
> Yours faithfully,
> H.C.B. Wemyss.

4

PIGEONS IN THE RAF

Air Vice Marshal Coryton, Commanding Officer of the RAF's 5 group in 1940, disapproved of a new idea that he suspected was dreamed up by some boffin or a newly-commissioned young Officer bringing his ideas into the service. His group had been chosen as the guinea pig for the idea of carrying pigeons in aircraft which could be released to fly home with a message, indicating where the aircraft had come down.

Scathingly, after the first experiments, he wrote that there had been no record of a life having been saved due to pigeons being carried in Bombers, nor was he satisfied that the morale of his crews would be anyway improved by their presence.

But he spoke too soon, or had not read the full facts. At this time of Coastal Command Aircraft, all aircraft, since their operations were mainly over the sea, used pigeons and intended to continue to do so. Group Captain V.E. Noon, though lower in rank, on 5 July 1940, wrote critically in reply that it was his opinion that if having a Pigeon Service meant that one life could be saved, then the establishment of such a service – with one Corporal and two Aircraftmen on each station, which Coryton had said was a waste of manpower – was justified. There was much discussion at all rank levels and the pigeon fanciers of Britain saw themselves being called up to continue a job they loved instead of having to abandon their birds for the duration.

In the file AIR14/1582, parts one and two at the Public Records Office, there is much evidence to prove that it was good idea:

> Halifax T of 51 Squadron, operating from Snaith, was reported missing 11/12
> July 1943. A hen, pigeon number NPS.41.NS7102 owned by Mr Stephenson
> of Moorends, Thorne, returned to its loft on 16 June, having flown probably
> 500 miles, enabling the position of the Halifax to be located.

In a further report after detailed investigations and questioning, it is stated that aircrew liked their pigeons and did not regard then as an extra chore but a last chance of being found if force-landed. They had confidence in them and had more faith in their flesh and blood than in the dinghy transmitter that was regarded as cumbersome, unreliable and unlikely to be used if the crew were injured.

Considerable research had been done at Farnborough as to the advantages of pigeons, since the trails of the transmitter were still in their early stages and not likely to be established in all aircraft for some time. A report from the Chief Signals Officer of 5 Group in 1941 confirms the statements of crews who valued having a last link available for assistance if the W/T was unserviceable.

One wonders, therefore, about the origin of Coryton's prejudice. Especially since it was not a new idea, but had begun before the war by obtaining the voluntary services of civilian pigeon owners, who were formed into an association called the National Pigeon Service (NPS). This was based at Clarence Street, Gloucester, with local addresses established in July and August 1940 to cover the whole country. The High Wycombe West End Homing Society, for example, offered their services from their HQ at the Rose and Crown in Desborough Road.

It was not as easy as first imagined, however, to recruit sufficient civilians to fill the requirements. Therefore, it was decided to provide lofts manned by the RAF on the larger stations, and 5 Group in Bomber command were chosen to demonstrate the feasibility and value of the idea. One of the firms who were contracted to build these lofts was Tarran Ltd, Clough Road, Hull, of which there are many detailed plans in the files. It is interesting to note that all this was considered a man's job and WAAF members were not to be considered suitable, although no reason was given. Had there been no female fanciers?

So when 5 Group started their 'Gardening' operations on 8 November 1940, that is mine-laying in the North Sea and off the East Anglia coast, they carried pigeons in specially-constructed cages, supplied with food and drink. On several occasions after that, the birds were released and flew home to base safely, and missing aircraft were located or accounted for. But still the CO of the group was sceptical and said no rescue had as yet had been effected which could be attributed to the Pigeon Service. Hindsight shows us that it was too early to come to such a conclusion.

Pigeon 40YHS129 was picked up by 11 Maintenance Unit at Chilmark on 23 July 1940, another was caught at Bramcote with ring markings NURP.40KX250 on 22 July. A third reached North Coates, Fitties, on 17 July – NONU395FC1995. One came in from the Atlantic to Steval carrying blue ring C938.NURP.37LL350 and wing mark 35054.

Private owners were warned in August 1940, when the threat of invasion was very close, that all pigeons in the areas likely to fall into enemy hands must be immediately destroyed. It is not explained why. The exceptions were those used by the Army and the Air Force. The local NPS representative were to supervise the destruction.

The Pigeon Service Instruction School, for the training of the birds and the men detailed to look after them, was established at Felixstowe. It was not long before reports of the need for such trained birds became apparent. A Baltimore with engine failure ditched in the Mediterranean 100 miles from its base and one bird was drowned. An air search failed to find the aircraft but the crew were later picked up by launch as a result of the second bird's safe return to its loft. NO1263MEPS143, with a message attached to its leg, saved their lives.

An aircraft from Coningsby in September 1942 was located after the finding of a pigeon NPS.42.25794, that was established as having flown 250 miles.

Another famous release resulted in a message. As a result, ten lives were saved from the catalina from Sullom Voe which had ditched north west of the Shetlands at Rouas in October 1943. There were heavy seas and the aircraft could not take off. In addition, visibility was less than 100 yards; in spite of these conditions, the pigeon got through. This bird was 'White Vision', whose full story is told later in the book.

At OTUs (Operational Training Units), crews were given one hour's extra training in order to learn how to deal with pigeons, and included in the files are their detailed training sheets crowded with instructions. These sheets were issued to everyone dealing with the birds, both on the ground and in the air.

Special care was needed when launching them. They had always to be sent off into the wind in the same direction as the aircraft was flying. The airmen who looked after them were called 'pioneers', but there were still protests that so many were being employed and that this was a waste of manpower.

That was something with which Wing Commander Cliff DSO would no doubt have disagreed. He was rescued when his Beaufort came down in the sea due to engine failure. He, with three crewmembers, were saved by the presence of pigeon IWS.40NEHU, alerting the high-speed launch from Leuchars which rescued them in February 1942. Although the bird was wet and covered in oil, it had managed to fly between 120 and 140 miles to find help.

The birds' normal flying altitude was considerably lower than that of most aircraft and great care had to be taken in the launching, always in a downward direction if possible, or the bird could be injured or disorientated. They suffer from a lack of oxygen at 20,000 feet, with some losing consciousness in the aircraft, but they soon recover if brought lower and they can then still find their way home from sea level. There were careful instructions as to the manner of release from different types of aircraft. Such as, from a Beaufort, the bird had to go down the port side door or side gun window, but if from the gunner's entrance hatch, it had to be thrown upwards facing ahead and as far away from the cabin as possible to enable it to get over the tail.

There was, however, no satisfactory release from a Mosquito and no fighter aircraft seems to have carried them, presumably because of lack of room in the cockpit.

When an aircraft ditched into the sea and the birds were wet, instructions said, they must not be dried by hand but must be given time to dry themselves in the air. 'Allow it to take its time, it will know when it is fit to go.'

Each station allocated a pigeon loft had on average 200 birds in each one. A total of 49 stations are listed in all. Simple arithmetic tells us that the two pigeons to each bomber on the 1,000 bomber raids was not too difficult to achieve. RAF Elvington had 209 and Methwold 335.

A report from RAF Wattisham describes how the message panels were mounted on webbing, with a padded backing fastened around the birds' legs with a press-stud. Indelible pencil was used for the message and the three white panels, each measuring a half by seven eights, were to be moistened before use. The padding was grooved in order to accommodate the metal identification ring and the tablets attached to the inside of a watertight container with a lid. If those needing rescue were in a dinghy, the message was to begin with the letter D, followed by the time of ditching, the time of the pigeon's release and the location. If launched while the aircraft was flying, the D was replaced by an A, and if crashed on land, an L.

Special colours were used for these containers. An RAF SOS message was of blue Bakelite with a white patch on the side, the Army used red, while black indicated the police. Yellow was the colour for authorised commercial usage, but any other colour was of unknown source and had to be approached with caution.

By 1944, the service was in process of being withdrawn as the wireless transmitter was by then was more reliable and satisfactory. Some birds had been collected by officials from private lofts and were now returned to their owners, many of whose names appear in the records. A sign of the times was that when one station wanted to organise a pigeon competition, permission was refused because it was considered too expensive and the use of transport unnecessary.

Occasionally there had been confusion which gave rise to the suspicion that there had been insufficient training for remand birds. For instance, when L4047 of 44 Squadron force-landed at Tackley near Upper Heyford, the pigeons were removed from the aircraft. The duty pilot, not realising their importance, thought they had been confined long enough and released them in error. In due course this set in motion the search and rescue procedure when it was not required.

These three reports offer many useful and interesting insights into the little-known employment of nature's wings for the help of mankind. And it is not for nothing that some pigeons were awarded high decorations for their courage and endurance.

5

OUR FEATHERED AIRFORCE

A Report from 1939

The RAF is to recruit 250,000 racing pigeons for use as messengers. In times of emergency, radio can easily be jammed, but trained birds 'get through' nine times out of ten.

Britain's most democratic sport is to play a big part in National Defence. Owners throughout the country are offering the Air Ministry their valuable racing pigeons for use in peace or war. Realising the usefulness of these birds as message carriers in emergency, the Ministry is co-operating with the committee preparing a special fanciers' register.

A chain of lofts will be organised to work with the RAF stations, and trained pigeons will be taken in reconnaissance aircraft.

Those whose pigeons are expected to serve will receive an annual grant. At this time, the sport of pigeon racing has become very big and with the season just starting, 400,000 fanciers, drawn from every grade of society, are getting busy. Strongholds of the sport are the industrial areas of Lancashire and Yorkshire, where millions of pounds are invested, the bulk of it by the working man, and thousands of pounds are distributed by clubs every year as prize money.

But surely, you would say, the homing pigeon has outlived its usefulness in peace or war. Communications, if ever there is another war, would be far too speedy and effective to leave any niche for the humble pigeon. Maybe, but with the development of radio transmission has come the radio 'barrage' to jam messages, and there is always the risk of breakdown or of a situation where the use of one's radio might mean betrayal to the enemy.

In such situations, the pigeon might spell the difference between life and death. They saved many lives in the last war and could do it again if necessary.

The endurance of these birds is staggering. One was released from a ship in the middle of the Atlantic and two and a half days later arrived at his loft in New York, one thousand miles away.

Another bird, following the same instinct which has baffled all scientific investigators, found its way safely home over 1,500 miles of land and sea.

During the war, when as many as 1,000 birds were used in one engagement, these tiny winged messengers ignored creeping gas clouds and shattering barrages; they flew above them apparently unaffected by the heaviest gunfire. Nine out of ten reached home.

The British Forces in the First World War used 100,000 pigeons in France, Salonika, Egypt and Mesopotamia. Organisers of the new National Service intended to recruit 250,000 for peacetime operations with the Royal Air Force.

Pigeons saved many lives and solved many problems of communication. Baskets of them were, for instance, often dropped by night, well behind the enemy lines, to be retrieved and used later by some intrepid British agent.

At sea, the birds proved invaluable. A flying boat came down with engine trouble twenty-two miles off the Scottish coast. One of the two pigeons on board was drowned when water flooded into the cockpit and when the basket was hauled out onto the wing, they saw that the other, probably their sole remaining hope of rescue, would, without speedy attention, be dead within minutes.

While the pilot scribbled a message, his companion wrapped the stricken bird in a woollen muffler and snuggled it inside his tunic. Gradually, the warmth had an effect and at last the bird rose, circled unsteadily and then headed west.

Less then half an hour later, the exhausted bird arrived at its RAF loft, having flown the twenty-two miles in twenty-two minutes. This is not a record, as a pigeon has been known to fly more than a mile in half a minute, but it is nevertheless a remarkable feat. The airmen were taken off the sinking plane just in time.

Often the messages that the little birds carried were vivid chapters in the dramas of life and death. For example, early one morning, this message was brought to a loft in Flanders Seaport: 'Short shot down ten miles NNE Newport, one enemy down, my tanks shot. French TBD on way, send fighters'. A minute later another message: 'Short landed OK, I shot one down but he did not crash, my tank's no good, can't climb, send fighters quick'. Eighteen minutes later came this message: 'I am shot down, hit in tank radiator, Roger's dead, send boat, Paine'. Soon another pigeon arrived: 'Machine turning to port, have jettisoned everything but am on wing tip, sea calm, nothing in sight. Machine has seemingly steadied, think it will float for a time'. A break then, 'My love to my mother, tell her I am not worrying. If machine sinks will swim to buoy close by me'.

This was the last message. Graham Paine reached home after his plane had been taken in tow by a patrol vessel. They found the wing tip of the other machine still sticking out of the sea, but it was empty.

Once, a British submarine, which had captured a German trawler and its crew, broke down in enemy territorial waters. A carrier pigeon was sent out, and a British escort vessel went out to take them both out of the danger zone.

So, once more, hail to the National Pigeon Service, ready if needed, and credit to the British working man who made it possible.

24 June 1939.

It is a curious fact that, while each step in the telegraph system and radio from 1900 onwards seemed as if it must reduce the value of the racing pigeon in war, the reverse has proved to be the case. Pigeons were used more extensively in the Second World War than in any other. We owe the means of developing such a service entirely to the British racing pigeon fancier and the intelligent thoroughbred which evolved through generations of long-distance racing.

In 1939 it was decided to organise a voluntary National Pigeon Service made up of civilian pigeon fancier volunteers, co-ordinated by a National Pigeon Service Committee under the Air Ministry to provide a pigeon service for the services.

When the war came, however, it was found that an all-civilian organisation was unsatisfactory and the RAF Pigeon Service was formed by recruiting pigeon fanciers and appointed experts as technical officers. This RAF section demanded an unusually high degree of long-range reliability in difficult conditions.

Not only were many aircrews' lives saved as a result of pigeon communication, but naval small craft, Civil Defence, the Intelligence Service and SHAEF made use of the RAF services with success. The service extended from Iceland to Singapore and from the Bahamas to India, employing about 500 'pigeoneers' and some 50,000 pigeons.

The maximum number of RAF Pigeon Officers covering the activity at any time was three, which left nearly everything to the skill and initiative of the selected NCO Pigeoneers. Some idea of the esteem in which this service was held by the ever-critical civilian expert, may be gathered from the fact that the RAF-bred pigeons 'Ruhr Express' and 'Per Ardua' raised £420 and £360 respectively when sold by auction, making a new world record price for racing pigeons. Just after this, a civilian racer changed hands for £500.

In December 1939, it was decided to form an Army Pigeon Service to consist of eight lofts and a headquarters section. In May 1940, an officer was transferred from the Air Ministry Pigeon Section to take charge of the Army Pigeon Service, and for a time men were recruited and trade tested by the RAF until the new organisation got on its feet. From this small beginning, the very extensive Army Pigeon Service developed, covering almost all the theatres of war.

The overrunning of the Low Countries and France in 1940 had a marked effect on the employment of pigeons. Firstly, the threat of invasion led to the organisation of Emergency Pigeon Services by the Army, Police and Civil Defence; and secondly, the situation brought enemy-occupied territory, in which the civilian population was friendly, within effective pigeon range of this country.

Use of home-based pigeons for communication with agents in enemy-occupied Europe began in a small way. In October 1940, the Air Ministry selected a famous civilian loft, and equipped an agent with two pigeons for a task which presented considerable difficulty, since the pigeon would have to be maintained undercover in France, by a man without previous experience of pigeons, for a week or more while he obtained the relevant information.

The agent was very carefully instructed in pigeon management and the rest was very successful. The two pigeons arrived almost together, from a point almost 300 miles distance, in six hours and forty minutes, after eleven days' detention. October is, in fact, probably the worst month to fly a pigeon any distance owing to the state of the moult and other circumstances.

The civilian owner, the late R.W. Beard of Kenley, received a letter of congratulations and thanks from the secretary of state for the airforce, which he fully deserved for the skill with which he had prepared the two pigeons for the task.

Following this success, the use of pigeons by the intelligence service gradually increased, with varying success.

The Dutch Section, in particular, using RAF Felixstowe with increasing confidence, obtaining an average return of seventy per cent, despite the hazards. Their best loads were thirty-eight microfilms on one pigeon, and an eight-page message with diagrams and 2,000 words on another. In pre-aeroplane and pre-radar days, one of the chief difficulties was delivering the pigeons to the agent, or even to a given area.

If a pigeon was smuggled through, as it had to be in the old days, the long detention in cramped confinement was a severe handicap for the subsequent flight. Nowadays, however, we possess the means to direct an aircraft accurately, at night if necessary, to a pinpointed location. And it is this factor, more than any other, which resulted in the use of pigeons by the Allies more extensively in the Second World War than in any other previous war. It was also this factor, in conjunction with the presence in Southern England of large numbers of civilian lofts – most of whose pigeons had experience of racing from France in peacetime – which led to the most extensive intelligence operation of the war. It was most important to obtain information on the mood of the civilian population in enemy-occupied territories, which were not effectively covered by our agents. This operation was organised by the Special Section of the Army Pigeon Service, in liaison with the intelligence section concerned.

The method, in brief, was to convey a large number of suitably-trained pigeons to the desired area by air at night, to drop them singly in small cartons with parachutes. The cartons contained full directions to the finder and usually a questionnaire as to the information desired.

It was, of course, a matter of chance as to who the finder would be and, indeed, whether they would be found at all. There was also the hazard of the drop itself, when it was inevitable that the losses would be heavy; in fact, no service loft could sustain them and remain operational. However a large number of civilian owners were organised into groups in the south and south east counties, and subsequently in the Midlands, and these in turn supplied the pigeons, stood the loss and received reinforcements from other National Pigeon Service breeders.

Upwards of 27,000 pigeons were maintained and prepared for the task and over 17,000 were dropped. Of these, fewer than 1,900 returned, but the information they conveyed was of inestimable value.

When this service was started in 1941, there was a good supply of experienced peacetime cross-Channel racers and the percentage returns were over twenty-two per cent. As time went on, these racers disappeared and were replaced by younger birds, often hastily trained for the job. The returns dropped considerably. The average over the whole operation from 1941 to VE Day was about 10 per cent.

Now a few words on the boomerang system of training, (that is, training birds to fly out from home to an out station and return again), carrying messages both ways if necessary. This technique was developed simultaneously by the Army Experimental Section and the RAF Pigeon Research Section, and was used successfully through the Arakan campaign. In one case, a reliable Boomerang service of thirty miles was established in fifteen days. Boomerang, although only developed by the British Services during the last war, was, according to captured documents, a standard system in the German Pigeon Service in 1925. The degree of control and adaptation to special tasks, which is possible in the employment of pigeons, goes far beyond Boomerang, as had been demonstrated by the Research Station.

R.C.A.F. Pigeon Manual 1943

1. TRAINING
In order to ensure the successful operation of this branch of the service, care should be exercised in choosing the personnel.
(a) In addition to those qualifications necessary for enlistment as an AC2 Standard, pigeoneers should be fully qualified to:
(I) Care for and feed pigeons properly.
(II) Train and condition birds for racing.
(III) Breed them successfully
(IV) Instruct others in (I), (II) and (III) above.
Knowledge: They should have a thorough knowledge of the capabilities, limitations and habits of homing pigeons.
Personal Traits: A pigeoneer who is boisterous and of a turbulent nature tends to frighten and upset the pigeons, thereby reducing their effectiveness.
The successful pigeoneer should possess:
(I) Dependability – Regular and prompt in carrying out all his duties.
(II) Kindness – In order to gain the confidence of the pigeons.
(III) Patience – Considerable time and repeated effort are necessary to properly train the birds.
(IV) Neatness – To provide a sanitary and attractive loft for the pigeons and keep a legible set of records.
(V) Thoroughness – Close attention to all details.
(VI) Firmness – To enforce discipline in the handling of the pigeons.
(VII) Power of accurate observation – Able to observe details readily and accurately in order to note and learn characteristics of individual pigeons in the loft.

2. PIGEON TRAINING

All pigeons, except those specifically reserved for breeding purposes, undergo training continuously from the time they are hatched until the ages of 7 to 10 years. Pigeons can be trained for both day and night flying, but for the time being the RCAF will concentrate on day flying and the data contained herein on night flying is purely informative.

(a) The training of a pigeon begins in the nest compartment.

(I) The first step in training the youngster is to teach it to understand that the can rattle means food. This training is continued during its stay in the breeding loft and during the early stages of the second step.

(II) Youngsters should be taken out of the nest boxes when they are from three to four weeks old and placed in the young bird loft. They should be placed in an open-ended basket on the floor and fed and watered there. It is quite probable that this basket will constitute their home for the first seven to ten days they are in the young bird loft. This procedure removes all fear of baskets from their mind and they will always regard a training basket as their second home.

(b) The second step is the training of the youngster to trap. It is essential that pigeons trap immediately upon return from any flight, in order that messages carried by them can be delivered with the least possible delay to the officer in charge of the operations room.

When new birds are received which do not know how to trap, place a settling cage over the lighting board or dormer and proceed with the new birds as with the youngsters above.

Begin the first trapping exercises in the morning after the loft has been cleaned, the next about 2.00 p.m. and the third about one hour before sunset. At the beginning of the third day, teach the pigeons to fly from the hand to the lighting board and require them to trap as before. First, hold the pigeons only a few feet away from the lighting board; as they become stronger on the wing, gradually increase this distance until the point of launching is at the maximum distance from which the loft is visible, not to exceed one mile.

Continue these trapping exercises three times daily for the first week. At the end of this period, all the pigeons should have been trained to trap readily. In case there are one or more obstinate or unruly pigeons that do not trap quickly, place them in a nest compartment for a period of two feedings, allow them water but no food and permit them to observe the other pigeons as the latter are being fed, then repeat the trapping exercises. This method will usually correct their tardiness.

Adjust the former or trap to permit entry into, but not exit from, the loft.

Always station a pigeoneer at the loft to be on the lookout for return of pigeons after a liberation and have him give a few grains of food to each returning pigeon as a reward. Note – Where RCAF lofts have dormer traps situated in the roof of the pigeon loft, there is no need for lighting boards.

(c) Upon completion of training in (b) (II) above, pigeons should be ready to receive intermediate training.

The birds should first receive a sufficient number of exercise flights, normally two each day until they can fly easily for periods of from 40 to 60 minutes. If the birds are moulting, these training flights should not begin until the heaviest part of the moult is completed.

Birds should never be released through the trap or dormer for exercise flights. Always release birds through the window and see that they return through the dormer or trap.

Once training is started, it should be concentrated. Birds are given four or five training flights a week starting at about three miles, with gradually increasing distances until at the end of one month they have flown 100 miles successfully. In each of the training flights, the first release at a new distance if possible should be in a group and thereafter by means of single tosses.

Pigeons that have received this training are in proper physical condition and can now fly distances of from 150 to 200 miles.

After the pigeons are a year old, they are mated for the first time. During this period they are to be trained as in (c) (I) above and after working up to 100 mile flights they are ready for long distances up to 300 miles. Yearlings should not normally be flown over 300 miles. They are kept in condition with forty to sixty mile flights twice a week.

The training of old birds is exactly the same as for yearlings, except that after the old birds have made on hundred mile flights they are ready for distances of five to six hundred miles. They are kept in condition in the same manner as are yearlings.

While pigeons are moulting, the amount of work is to be reduced. When a new shipment of homing pigeons is received at a loft, it is necessary to confine the pigeons in the loft to acquaint them with their new surroundings. In addition, they should be allowed to spend their time in the aviary or settling cage where they can observe and familiarise themselves with the surrounding country. During confinement, spend a great deal of time taming the Pew birds. Allow them their own section of the lot and permit individual birds to select their own perches. See that they are not disturbed and talk to them constantly in order that they may soon feel at home. In general, youngsters strong enough to fly should be confined for about three days. Old birds may require confinement of up to six days to settle.

At the expiration of this time, the traps of the loft should be opened and the pigeons allowed to go out on their own initiative. The best time for this first liberation is late in the afternoon, before the pigeons have had their last feed of the day. Dark or overcast days are ideal. After twenty to thirty minutes of liberation, the pigeons are called by the can rattle and given their evening food. On this liberation, do not drive the pigeons out of the loft. If they are driven they will fly wildly and, without knowledge of the country, may lose themselves and fail to return. The normal young pigeon, on being permitted to go through the window for the first time of its own free will, will perch on the lighting board or roof of the loft and probably make a few short flights in the air, returning to the roof of the loft after each one, venturing farther and farther away in each succeeding flight.

On the second day of liberation, the window is to be opened at about noon and the pigeons are allowed to go out of their own free will, to remain outside for perhaps thirty minutes; then they are called in by the can rattle and given a very slight amount of food. Give them another flight of thirty minutes, terminating just before the evening feeding time.

On the third day, open the window before the pigeons are fed in the morning and allow them to go out of their own free will and fly around the loft for perhaps thirty minutes; after which call them in by the can rattle and give them the regular amount of food. In the afternoon, about 4 or 5 o'clock, depending upon weather conditions, allow them another flight.

Never feed a pigeon anywhere except inside the loft. Never allow a pigeon to alight upon the ground, a tree or a building; only on the lighting board or roof of the loft. After pigeons have been thoroughly settled and trained to a loft, do not allow them to remain an indefinite time on the roof of the loft; always call them in by the can rattle and give them a few grains of food.

Never send a pigeon in poor condition out for a flight; in the case of healthy pigeons, when taken out always liberate them and allow a flight home, reducing the distance if necessary. Never carry back a pigeon that is able to fly to the loft.

After the first moult, the young pigeons may be expected to show their first desire to mate. If it is not desired to let them mate at this time, the cock and hen pigeons should be separated and placed in separate compartments or lofts. The nest boxes should be closed.

When pigeons are mated, they are continued in training, even after eggs are laid. If the eggs are to be destroyed, both cook and hen may be taken out on the same practice flight. If the eggs are to be hatched and the squeakers developed, only one of the mates is sent out on any one flight, the other remaining with the nest. Incidentally, the homing tendency of the pigeon is heightened during the breeding season by his domestic desires, and his reliability is increased thereby.

3. (a) General – the training of pigeons for night flying is a relatively recent development and must still be considered somewhat experimental. However, the training methods presented have proved quite successful and should be followed. It is anticipated that changes in method may occur in the future.

The night loft – this should be situated as far as possible from wires, trees or other eminencies which might injure the birds in flight.

Shutters – since night-flying pigeons are trained and fed at night, they must be given an opportunity to rest during the day. Doors and windows of a night loft are equipped with shutters that exclude light, without cutting off circulation of air.

Lights – when birds are working at night, the interior of the loft is brightly illuminated. A light is placed above the trap in such a position that it shines faintly on the lighting board. No lights should be placed on the outside of the night loft.

Lighting board – the lighting board is larger than that normally used for day birds. It should have a length of at least five feet and extend out from the loft by at least three feet. Aluminium paint should be used on the lighting board to make it faintly luminous; the board should be repainted frequently. This would not apply where lofts have a dormer type of trap.

Stocking the night loft – continued breeding of night-flying pigeons has not demonstrated that the ability to home at night is transmitted to the youngsters. In fact night birds, because of their changed mode of living, are seldom in fit condition for breeding and will usually produce youngsters that are below the desired physical standard. For these reasons it is best to stock a night loft with youngsters from proved day fliers.

Preliminary training – youngsters should be placed in the night loft when 28 days old. Breaking them to the loft and trap should be done in the daytime. During the first two weeks the schedule given for day birds is to be followed.

Exercise – during the third week, the single-toss day flights are to be continued as for day birds. In addition, the youngsters should be exercised late in the afternoon so that they learn to trap to the loft at dusk. They should be fed at this time by artificial light. Night birds should never be released for exercise after dark. To drive birds from a lighted loft out into the darkness is certain to result in injuries and losses. The youngsters continue their exercising progressively later, being released late in the daylight but so that their flying arrival is made in the dusk and darkness of light. After the fifth week they should be ready for night training.

Preliminary night training – Even after years of experience, pigeons never lose their fear of flying at night. This fact is most important in the training of youngsters. The pigeoneer must bear in mind that the bird he tosses into the dark is always very frightened. If youngsters are given their first night training tosses in the evening, after dark, they are confused and frightened and are likely to fly blindly into wires and trees, or settle to the ground and await daylight. Youngsters that settle to the ground on the first few night flights will do so on subsequent flights and seldom develop into reliable night fliers. Morning tosses in the darkness just before dawn have proved by far the most successful in the training of night fliers.

Youngsters tossed in the morning before dawn are as confused and frightened as if tossed in the evening; however, before they can stray very far from the loft area, or attempt to settle to the ground, it becomes light; and they can easily find their way to the loft. Continued tosses in the morning before daylight will impress upon the bird that, even though he is confused or lost, all he need do is remain in the air until there is sufficient light for him to find his way home. Having thus overcome his initial fear, his natural instinct and intelligence will come to his aid and he will attempt to find his way home through the darkness. After a number of successful flights to the loft in the darkness before dawn, the pigeon will have gained enough confidence to be safely tossed in the evening, or at any time during the night.

Direction training – Night-flying pigeons are very directional and cannot be successfully flown from all directions. A bird flying well from the south will usually not be reliable if released from the north. A few pigeons will fly equally well from all directions, but these must be considered exceptions. For this reason, night birds should be trained only for the direction from which they will be used. To attempt to deviate from this course by more than 45 degrees is certain to reduce greatly the effectiveness of the pigeon. If it is expected that night birds will be required for flights from two directions, for example from the south and from the west, two teams of pigeons should be trained, one for each direction.

Altitude training – night birds that fly close to the ground upon release cannot be considered reliable messengers, even though they do return to the loft in good time. Such birds are almost certain to fly eventually into wires or trees and injure themselves. Therefore, a well-trained night bird should immediately ascend to a high altitude upon release and make his flight to the loft at such altitude. The following method has been very successful in teaching young night birds to ascend at once upon release and to remain high in the air. A field of high corn, cane or reeds in the vicinity of the loft is selected. On a clear, moonlit night the youngsters are gently tossed one at a time into the tops of this vegetation. The pigeons will not be flying fast enough to injure them- selves. However, they become so frightened in attempting to fly clear that upon freeing themselves they rise straight into the air to a high altitude. Two or three such tosses are generally sufficient to teach youngsters to climb rapidly to a great height immediately upon release. The training is not necessary in the case of youngsters which are exercised with old night birds and who learn to follow the latter to high altitudes. Birds for this training must have successfully completed the training indicated in (f) above.

Releasing – night birds should always be forcibly tossed into the air when released at night. Night birds should never be group tosses, or released from a basket. An open spot as far as possible from wires, trees and buildings should be selected for the release of night birds. These points should be stressed in the training of handling and using personnel.

Advanced training: continuous training flights are necessary to keep night fliers in condition for use. Each bird should be given at least two training flights a week. 'Tight' birds should be trained for flights up to thirty miles, with the average flight being made at distances of from fifteen to twenty miles. Night birds should be trained to carry message holders during training flights.

Care and daily routine – to give night birds sufficient rest, the shutters on the loft doors and windows should be kept closed in the morning and the pigeoneers should not enter the loft or disturb the birds in any way. At about 11.00 a.m. the shutters should be opened and the birds allowed to go into the aviary while the loft is being cleaned. After the loft is cleaned, the birds should be lightly fed and then provided with a bath if the weather is favourable; the shutters are then closed. If pigeons are not being sent out for training or signal communication flights, they should be exercised in the evening. The evening meal should be at about 9.00 p.m., at which time the birds should be given all the feed they can clean up.

Flight Records – the keeping of the Pigeon Flight Record is of extreme importance in preparing night birds for communication flights. In addition to the usual notes posted in the flight record, the failure of a bird to home at night and the weather conditions during a flight should be listed. Accurately-kept records will readily show that certain birds home poorly from some directions but do better from others. Such birds should then be trained only over the course on which they make the best returns. By noting the weather, the records will show that some birds fly well in rain and fog, while the speed of others is greatly reduced. This information enables the pigeoneer to supply units with reliable birds for varying conditions.

6

THE NATIONAL PIGEON SERVICE

RECORDED BY TOM SILK

At the outbreak of the Second World War, the British Government decided that the pigeons recruited from civilian lofts would be needed for the Army, Navy and the Air Force. Restrictions were immediately imposed on all fanciers, corn was rationed, and fanciers who decided that they would not join the National Pigeon Service received no corn ration.

Pigeon fanciers supplied many thousands of pigeons for all the armed services; many, sadly were lost on active service. Many pigeons were awarded The Dicken Medal – the pigeon VC for outstanding service.

Tom Silk kept a record of all the times his birds went on service and the messages brought back with the pigeons. York and District fanciers first supplied pigeons to the Army in 1940, and in 1943 they were transferred to the Royal Air Force and supplied pigeons for every bomber. Tom recorded where the bombers went, and the number of planes lost. This information was taken from the daily papers and the wireless. He does not claim that his contribution was any different to any other loft except that he kept a detailed record in his notebook. He felt that the younger generation would be surprised at the amount of planes that we lost and how many bombs were dropped over enemy territory.

Tom was fortunate that the manager of the firm that he worked for was a captain during the First World War and willingly allowed him to despatch one of his staff to the Signals Department at Fulford Barracks with any message a bird brought home. Tom's wife had to maintain a constant watch for the pigeons arriving home while on service. All lofts worked on a roster system, two days on service and two days free. The birds would be left in baskets before the handlers went to work, and would be picked up by men from the forces.

Major Hutton was in charge of the Army pigeons and Wing Commander Lee Raynot controlled the Pigeon Service.

York fanciers first went on service with the Army in July 1940, with their birds going within a 100 mile range. They served Doncaster, Spurn Head, Pennistone and Nottingham; even with snow on the ground, many still carried messages.

January 1943 saw the birds transferred to the Royal Air Force supplying pigeons for Bomber Command at Linton-on-Ouse, approximately five miles north of York. Again the birds were collected early in the morning and were on service for two nights then returned or liberated at Linton-on-Ouse, depending on weather conditions.

Two pigeons were carried in every bomber in a metal container. Attached to each bird's leg was a plastic band, and the aircrew carried a plastic tube and a message pad.

Planes returning back to base were often damaged and were forced to ditch in the sea. The crew would give the latitude and longitude on the pad supplied and attach it to the pigeon's leg, then release the bird. Sadly, many of the pigeons and crew sank before this could be done.

Tom Silk's team usually consisted of six to ten birds. The following is a complete record of Tom's own birds in service:

1 January 1943. Bad weather, snowing, no raids reported.

2 January. Lovely weather but very cold, no raids reported.

7 January. Bitter cold and snowing, no raids reported.

8 January. Still cold and snowing, no raids reported.

10 January. Moonlight but foggy, big raid on Berlin, 22 bombers missing.

Tom had two birds in planes brought down over Berlin and lost.

18 January. Thick fog, mines laid in enemy waters.

25 January. Fine but no raids reported.

26 January. Fine but dark night, raids on Lorient and Bordeaux, two bombers missing.

31 January. Fine but cold night, no raids reported.

1 February. Rain and foggy, no raids reported.

6 February. Fine frost night, mines laid in enemy waters and western Germany, three bombers lost.

7 February. Fine night, very heavy raid on Lorient, seven bombers missing.

14 February. Full moon, heavy raids on Lorient, over 1,000 tonnes of bombs dropped, eight bombers missing.

18 February. Full moon, heavy raid on Wilhelmshaven, four bombers missing.

24 February. Lovely night but dark, raids on Wilhelmshaven and Western Germany. No planes reported missing, our bombers returned after 11.00 p.m.

25 February. Lovely night, bombers setting off at 7.00 p.m. Raid on Nuremburg and Western Germany, nine bombers missing.

2 March. Dark cloudy night, bombers raided western Germany, three bombers missing.

3 March. Dark night, heavy raid in Hamburg and Western Germany, ten bombers missing.

8 March. New moon, cold and frost, heavy raid on Nuremburg and Western Germany, seven bombers missing.

9 March. Lovely night but very cold, heavy raid on Munich and western Germany, mines laid in enemy waters, eleven bombers missing.

14 March. Moonlight but foggy, no raids reported.

15 March. Lovely night, no raids reported.

20 March. Moonlight, no raids reported.

21 March. Full moon, heavy white frost, no raids reported.

26 March. Lovely still night, bombers going off at 8.00 p.m. Duisberg heavily raided and also western Germany, planes returning at midnight, four bombers missing.

27 March. Lovely night, bombers going over at 7.50 pm, returning after 3.00 a.m. Berlin heavily raided, 900 tonnes of bombs dropped, nine bombers missing.

1 April. Nice fine night, no raids reported.

2 April. Fine starry night. St Nazier and Lorient bombed and mines laid, two bombers lost.

7 April. Gale blowing and very cold, no raids reported.

8 April. Fine but cloudy, heavy raids on targets in Ruhr. Mines laid, twenty-one bombers lost.

13 April. Lovely night, half moon. Spezia in Italy and North West Germany, three bombers lost.

14 April. Lovely night, very heavy force of planes leaving from 9.15 p.m. Stuttgart very heavily raided, twenty-three bombers missing.

19 April. Full moon, no raids reported.

20 April. Full moon, lovely night, very heavy raid on Stettin and Rostock, mines laid in enemy waters. Thirty-one bombers missing.

25 April. Dark night, strong gale, no raids reported.

26 April. Dark night, strong wind blowing, very heavy raid on Duisberg for forty-five minutes. 1,400 tonnes of bombs dropped, (thirty tonnes every minute), seventeen bombers missing.

1 May. Fine night, mines lost in enemy waters, all planes returned.

2 May. Fine night, no raids reported.

7 May. Cold and raining, no raids reported.

8 May. Raining and a gale blowing, no raids reported.

13 May. Lovely night, half moon, very heavy raid on Berlin, Bochum, Czechoslovakia and the Ruhr. 3,000 tonnes of bombs dropped, thirty-four bombers missing. Lost one pigeon on service.

19 May. Full moon, no raids reported.

20 May. No raids reported.

25 May. Fine night, bombers going over from 11.30 p.m., very heavy raid on Dusseldorf, 2,000 tonnes of bombs dropped, (ten tonnes every minute, twenty-seven bombers missing).

26 May. Thundery evening, no raids reported.

31 May. Overcast and raining, no raids reported.

1 June. Thunderstorms and heavy rain, no raids reported.

6 June. Dull night, no raids reported.

7 June. Dull warm night, no raids reported.

Tom had two birds liberated, (destination unknown), during the night as an experiment; both homed next morning.

12 June. Lovely night, half moon, bombers going over in force from 11.00 p.m. to midnight. Bochum heavily raided, twenty-four bombers missing.

13 June. Lovely night, clear, mines laid in enemy waters and also targets in Germany, one bomber missing.

This concluded operations for two months as there was a change of squadron. The Royal Canadian Air Force then took over at Linton-on-Ouse.

19 August. Fine warm night, no raids reported.
20 August. Fine night, rain early morning, intruder patrols.
25 August. Fine night after a thundery day, mine laying and intruder patrols, one bomber missing.
26 August. Dark night, heavy rain, no raids reported.
31 August. Fine but dark night. Ten birds on service, very heavy raid on Berlin, forty-seven bombers missing. Lost one pigeon brought down over Berlin.
1 September. Fine night, no raids reported.
6 September. Fine night, ten birds on service. Munich heavily raided, sixteen bombers missing.

This was the last time the birds went on service. The pigeons were replaced when dinghy bleepers were installed in the inflatables, with built-in canopies. During the many nights that Tom's birds were on service, a total of 333 planes were lost.

Yorkshire was the main base for England's bombers, with eight airfields within ten miles of Linton, meaning that day and night, the aircraft were always flying. The York supply officer was Harold Wood, and serving at Linton were Sgt Hughie Ambler and Cpl John Tucker, ('Pepys' of the *British Homing World*), both from Southend-on-Sea. Tom became great friends with the two men and at weekends they would stay at his house. As you would imagine, pigeons were discussed until the early hours of the morning, with many top fanciers visiting too.

Tom quotes one incident which he thought funny but very sad. He had a bareless mealy hen that naturally was very white. The aircrews called her 'the white one'. Some of the crews who had her on board during a raid and returned safely looked on the bird as a lucky charm. Some regarded her as a dove of peace and did not want her with them. This, you can be assured, was all in serious vein. It was life and death every time for these gallant men and the hen was on duty thirty-one times, and so may have had sixty-two operations.

'Observer' of the *British Homing World*, Sgt Les Davidson, was of course with the Pigeon Service and would visit Tom to see the birds. On one occasion, Tom had in the nest a couple of strange-coloured squeakers, bred from a pair of show pigeons which the late C.R. Snow had sent to him to look after. One glance at them and Leslie said they were 'silvers' – as readers know, his knowledge on colours was legion.

7

THE ROYAL AIR FORCE 1939-1944

BOMBER COMMAND, LINTON-ON-OUSE,

YORKSHIRE, ENGLAND

GROUP FOUR AND GROUP SIX

Few bomber bases in Britain had a more distinguished record during the Second World War than RAF Linton-on-Ouse, near York. Twin-engined Whitleys from the base were in action on the first night, when they dropped propaganda leaflets over Germany.

It was not long, however, before leaflets were replaced by bombs. As Britain's air power increased, so crews from Linton ranged far and wide. Targets included Berlin, Hamburg and the vast industrial complex of the Ruhr.

The Whitleys were eventually replaced by four-engined Halifax aircraft, and in 1942 Linton was involved in the war's first 1,000 bomber raid on Cologne.

The following year, the Canadians took over the airfield and were in constant action until Germany surrendered, flying Lancasters as well as Halifaxes. They formed part of the all-Canadian No. 6 Group, which expanded until it had fifteen bomber squadrons, most of which were based in the Vale of York.

Night after night, local villagers watched the planes set off to attack targets in Germany and occupied Europe. Daytime was equally busy, with air exercises and test flights taking place after ground crews, often working in the open in atrocious weather, had completed their work.

Inevitably, many aircraft crashed and many men died. Some were returning from operations in badly-damaged aircraft; others were on training flights. Sometimes the weather was to blame. One squadron from Linton lost three out of fourteen Halifaxes which had taken off in icy conditions in March 1945 to attack Chemnitz.

One bomber crashed on York, killing six of the seven crew and five civilians and injuring eighteen more. The fuselage fell in Nunthorpe Grove and one of the engines landed on Nunthorpe Grammar School. The seventh member of the crew, pilot officer John Low – the wireless operator/air gunner – had a miraculous escape. He bailed out far too low for his parachute to deploy fully, but when the plane exploded on hitting the ground, the blast blew him higher into the air and he escaped with serious injuries. The happy sequel was that he married the girl who nursed him back to health in hospital.

Long before the Canadians arrived, Linton was on the receiving end of a raid. Three

German planes attacked the base in May 1941. The station commander, Group Capt. F.M.H. Garroway, who had only taken up his appointment the previous day, was among thirteen personnel killed. Thirteen more were injured.

Colin Young, of Kippax, Leeds, then an airframe fitter, remembers the attack. 'A stick of bombs fell across the parade ground and there were several other casualties when the NAAFI was hit', he said. Mr Young, now a volunteer helper at the Yorkshire Air Museum at Elvington, also recalled the horrendous losses. 'One of my ground crew pals volunteered for flying duties and, after training as a Flight Engineer, returned to Linton. He went down on his first operation. They used to reckon that if you survived your first four operations, you had a better chance of survival. But I remember a navigator who, before setting out on his thirtieth op., the last of his tour, packed his bags ready to get a train home the following morning. He didn't return from the raid.' Among personalities stationed at Linton was Leonard Cheshire, the legendary bomber pilot and holder of the Victoria Cross. He was there as a pilot officer in 1940 and later returned as Commanding Officer of 76 Squadron, flying Halifaxes. He pleaded for design changes to be made to the tail section of the Halifax because pilots were experiencing a lack of control and there had been many crashes. After proving his point by putting the four-engined bomber deliberately into a spin (and only just recovering in time), he persuaded the designers to alter the shape of the fin.

Many of the aircrew lived at nearby Beningbrough Hall, the home of the Countess of Chesterfield, and at Aldwark Manor. The crews at Beningbrough made good use of the ferrymen who took them across the River Ouse to enjoy a few beers at the Alice Hawthorn pub in Nun Monkton. These ferrymen certainly had an eye to business. They would charge twopence to cross the river – but anything up to half-a-crown for the return journey after 9.00 p.m.

'The alternative was an eleven-mile walk, via Aldwark Bridge', said Bill Steel, a retired RAF Sergeant. Bill was curator of the Memorial Room at Linton, dedicated to all ranks who served at the base during the war, until his death in January 1992.

Photographs and information reached him from far and wide. One letter from a former engine fitter, who was at Linton in 1940 and 1941, paints a dramatic picture of those far-off days. 'It was a grim time for us all', he wrote.

On one occasion before a raid, the bomber he had served taxied towards the take-off point and then stopped. 'I went out to see what the trouble was. I found the pilot slumped over the controls sobbing and crying. The crew just looked vacant. They had had enough. A relief crew took over.'

When the Canadians came, they gave their squadrons not only numbers but exotic names such as Goose and Thunderbird. The crews took part in all the major raids on Germany, hammered French targets in preparation for the Allied invasion and attacked flying bomb sites.

For the statistically-minded, more than 9,500 operation sorties were flown from Linton during the war and 321 bombers were lost.

After the war, Linton became a fighter base. Since 1957 it has been the home of the RAF's No. 1 Flying Training School, providing basic instruction for tomorrow's pilots.

8

76 AND 78 SQUADRONS

During the four months mentioned, May to August 1941, there were two Royal Air Force Squadrons, 76 and 78, under the command of Leonard Cheshire and W/C Warner stationed there.

The Squadron's aircraft were four-engined Halifax heavy-duty bombers, able to carry as heavy a load of bombs as any aircraft in RAF service at that period of time, with a flying range that encompassed Berlin. Quite a keen rivalry developed between 76 and 78.

John Tucker was Corporal in charge of pigeons at Linton, September 1942 to March 1944, for eighteen months, with two L.A.C. s. It was their duty to ensure that all aircraft leaving the 'drome' had on board two pigeons in metal containers, with push-on lids to make the containers water-tight in the event of ditching. John's immediate superior was Sgt W.L.B. Davidson, stationed at 4 Group Headquarters, Heslington House, York. Today we know Leslie as the *British Homing World* scribe, 'Observer'.

Until such time as the station loft could be stocked and the inmates trained, pigeons for RAF requirements were supplied to the station by the York and District National Pigeon Service under the direction of Mr Wood. He had a grand team of fanciers to call on: Tom Silk, J. Watson, H. Tate, J. Harrison, C. Robshaw, J. Sidewell, A. Sleightholme, H. Thompson, Kirby and Kettlewell, amongst others. These fanciers sent pigeons to Linton which were as good as any in the land, many with records to their name. Pigeons were flown any distance up to five hundred miles, and many were lost on service.

Kirby and Kettlewell, when asked if they would allow one of their birds to be released from an aircraft flying at 3,000 feet in complete darkness to demonstrate a pigeon's capability, sent a good one. Its performance is recorded by a few lines in *Pigeons in World War Two*; bearing in mind the conditions, with release of the pigeon over the mouth of the Wash, it is an injustice to say so little about it.

John Tucker recalls an item of humour. 'Our Leslie, on one of his loft inspections, had arranged an interview with W/C Cheshire. On his way to keep the appointment, he omitted to salute a passing officer. He was called to order and gave his explanation that, at Group Headquarters, with so much gold braid about, this was acceptable procedure. When ushered into W/C Cheshire's office, you can imagine how the Sergeant felt to find he was before the man he had not saluted. The upshot of the interview was that all future aircrews joining the Squadron from that date had to attend that station loft for instruction on handling pigeons, which was very beneficial to aircrew and mind-relieving to John.'

In 1943, when squadron bombing became RAF policy, the squadron's efforts were intensified and a greater number of aircraft went on missions. From May to August, they reached a peak with the 'Thousand Aircrafts Raid'. Squadrons 76 and 78 met their quota, earning the honour of most sorties flown and the heaviest tonnage of bombs dropped; however, the price paid was grievous. The squadrons were decimated, as would be shown if correct figures were ever issued for this period of time. John is sure they would exceed those quoted by Tom Silk from the numbers issued then. On each of these aircrafts were two pigeons. Two events set John Tucker thinking. Firstly, after training a new crew, he asked if there were any questions. He was asked how far they could see. In John's answer, he mentioned the third eyelid, and one crewman turned and asked his companion, 'Is he kidding, sir?' 'No, he is not,' was the reply. 'Tell them of the bastard wing, wing flights and tail correlation, Corporal, then they will all know something about flying.'

That man was also a fancier and, on parting, his remarks were 'See you again, Corp., when I get time, it would be pleasant to swap a few reminiscences.' But he never saw any of them again.

Secondly, a wireless operator/air gunner came to the office and said: 'Corp., am I daft or do pigeons talk to each other?' 'Well, they have a language of a kind', John replied. 'He will coo her up when he's interested and has an habit of ooh-ing and aah-ing when nesting. Also, when danger is about, a pigeon will grunt an alarm signal to the flock. What makes you ask?' The gunner replied: 'Well, Corp., its like this – your two tins of pigeons go on a shelf above my radio set. When we get above 3,000 feet I put on my oxygen mask, at 26,000 feet those damn pigeons have their heads stuck out of the cardboard lining to their tin as large as life, looking at what's going on, not attempting to escape or even being frightened. Not even when all hell breaks out when Gerry opens up the ACK-ACK.'

The young man came again a time or two and liked to sit in peace and share a cup of tea, but then he, too, was gone. In August 1943, the two squadrons were stood down to regroup, and many crews went to Pathfinder squadrons, including W/C Cheshire. It was not known what became of W/C Warner. Other personnel went to retrain on Lancasters, which were faster and with a higher flight ceiling than the Halifax, giving added safety.

Later came the first all-Canadian squadron of the Royal Canadian Air Force. Previously, Canadian personnel had flown as RAF crewmen. John did not doubt that the valour and bravery of the Canadians would have been equal to that of 76 and 78. But they were not at Linton in August 1944 when 76 and 78 left the base.

It came under 6 Group Command. The Sergeant in charge of pigeons was H.V. Ambler, a friend and club member of John's at Southend-on-Sea. With no operational flying at Linton for a brief period of time, in his off-duty periods John and Sergeant Ambler would visit many of the Yorks and District fanciers, always finding a welcome and lofts of excellent pigeons.

Tom Silk was not a Yorkshire man, but a Londoner. His daughter Jean, a nurse, emigrated to Australia, then Mary and Tom went out there to be near her. Tom's son still lives in Yorkshire and is a dedicated fancier and proud to own an N.H.U. Gold Medal (Meritorious Performance). Tom has now turned ninety-four and still going well.

As secretary of Essex Central Federation he was excellent, until one came to the audit – he always had more cash in the bank than he should have, due to purchases made from cash in his pocket, with the account logged but never taken out of the funds. John recalls an entry in his diary from 1943. 'Keeps but a small family of pigeons that have flown well from the long-distance events. The birds have quite a lot of Gurney blood in their breeding. His birds always came to the Station in immaculate condition.'

Mary and Tom and others in the York area sent their best pigeons to Linton and, as you will see from Tom's diary, many were lost on service along with many aircrew. Some aircrew escaped by parachuting from stricken aircraft to spend years as prisoners of war. Linton never had a pigeon come back to its NPS Base.

John says, 'The credit and honour for those four months in 1943, in respect of Linton-on-Ouse RAF Station, belong to 76 and 78. One cannot live amongst men as those without being affected. This month we will honour their memory.'

9

COLUMBINE VOYAGERS OF VALOUR

BY JOHN 'PEPYS' TUCKER

Columbia species – Diovan, Dove, Pigeon. It is of the pigeon voyagers of World War Two that I write, for they also served their country's needs from around 1940 to 1945. Many perished at home and abroad, yet brought glory to their kind. I write not of the street pigeon, that urchin of town street, square or park, but about the thoroughbreds, similar in appearance to Stan Guppy's Continental Queen, whose voyage of approximately 500 miles on one day, covering 945 YPM, constituted a record – she was the first pigeon to accomplish this in the south west regions of Great Britain.

A few months later, in 1940, the war with Germany saw the 'Queen' and thousands of her kind become members of the National Pigeon Service, a voluntary organisation comprised of the National Homing Unit, H.M. Government and some 27,000 pigeon keepers, (fanciers as we know them).

Fanciers were given the opportunity to become RAF or Army pigeon keepers, subject to a proficiency test. I took mine, passed, and was put on reserve. A few weeks later I was called up and fitted out at RAF Station Uxbridge to become one of the number two school of pigeon keepers at Calshot Seaplane Base in July 1940.

After a few weeks at Calshot, Cpl W. Douglas of Stanley Street, Tyne Dock, was in charge and amongst the illustrious pupils assembled were J.W. Perkins, W. Downs, A. Newell, W. Gillingham, J. Ambler, E. Gault, E. Game, R. Norman, W. Yates, G. Williamson, Eric Smith, C.J. Cranstoun, E. Hudson and Nicols, all well-known first-class pigeon racing fanciers.

Initially, the Royal Air Force requirement was for all coastal command aircraft patrolling the coastal waters and sea-lanes of the United Kingdom to have two pigeons in a two-section wicker basket. Later, the basket was substituted by a tin with a clip-on lid and a screw top air safety valve to prevent the pigeon getting wet if the plane ditched. SOS forms and colour-coded message carriers were either attached to the leg of the pigeon by carrier ring or strapped to the lid of the tin by plastic ribbon. A member of the crew had to fill in details of the ditching position including the latitude and longitude, if known, and release the pigeon once the crew were safely in the rubber dinghy.

As for the NPS, during the next five years their members, men and women, were to maintain, keep trained and supply to Military and Civilian groups, their pigeons. Some 27,000 were maintained, of which 17,000 were used for various missions.

Some 46,500 birds were furnished to the American forces, resident at that period of time in the United Kingdom. Many of these were part of the invasion force and saw service on the continent to the war's end. To my knowledge, quite some number were returned to America when victory came. To meet the requirements of Great Britain's Air Force and Army Pigeon Sections, 200,000 young birds were bred, at no cost, to stock service lofts, static and mobile, many of these seeing service overseas in Africa, the Middle East, Italy and elsewhere.

Sgt John Errat, B.E.M., received that honour for his devotion to duty as an army pigeoneer from 1941 onwards.

The men and women of these isles with race-trained lofts of pigeons gave grand service to the National Pigeon Service from 1940 until the RAF and Army lofts could be established. There were the pigeons for any of the Military and Civilian service requirements, that is police, fire and Home Guard but, principally, for the Army.

They were bearers of every type of message from the front line – for the RAF who sent 'save our souls' from ditched or crashed aircraft, for the Special operations executive [personnel] who used pigeons for reconnaissance raining units, and for agents infiltrating enemy territory. {They were also] 'seeded', packed in cardboard containers, attached to a parachute and dropped from an aircraft over quite an area of Europe. These had a request message enclosed in their containers; some came back, no message, just released by kind-hearted finders, some were taken by the enemy with false information, others carried details of great importance that helped towards the Allies eventual victory.

Shortly after our school was posted, I found myself at RAF station North Coates on the edge of the North Sea, with Cpl Graham Atkinson and two Scots lads as company. Stationed at North Coates were 22 Squadron, Beaufort Torpedo/Bombers, RAF Coastal Command and 812 Squadron, Swordfish survivors of the aircraft carrier 'Courageous'. The Beauforts were to attack shipping and ports with torpedoes or bombs, and the Swordfish at that period of the war was mine-laying in coastal waters to keep German battleships bottled up. Our aircraft losses were severe and many grand pigeons supplied by Grimsby and the surrounding area were lost, yet those fanciers sent their equal to replace them. A few of the names that come to mind are: Sandy Smith, J. Askew, Tunnard & Car, Ford & Ford, E. Braithwaite, G. Dobbs, P. Bemrose, and Miller. Alas, of the names quoted only two are alive to my knowledge.

Of the wives of Syd Ford and George Dobbs, Mabel Ford is now well into her eighties and partially blind. She is still articulate and a joy to talk to. She and her workmates at Watmaugh's Biscuit Factory sent hundreds of pounds to the Racing Pigeon Red Cross Fund. In those days she was an expert dancer.

Hilda Dobbs, wife of George, then of Side Lane, South Road, always had a slice of cake and a cuppa when one collected pigeons from her. Both looked after and kept their husbands' pigeons racing and there was never a question mark against the fitness of birds sent for service. 'Mabs' raced on her own when Syd was ill.

Shortly promoted to Corporal, I was posted to 16 Group, Chatham, Kent. The loft was on Chatham Downs, close to the hospital. Four weeks later, I was posted on to Detling. The Sergeant in charge at Chatham decreed that the grass around the loft would be cut, smart, neat and tidy, but from the air [it was] a bull's eye, a good marker for the hospital. With W/T masts adjacent, it was felt that the hospital could be mistaken for a Military Installation and bombed, so the loft was moved into Chatham Barracks, leaving a certain Sergeant with a red face. At Detling, I took charge of an RAF loft of pigeons from a Cpl Lomas, son of a well-known Croydon fancier. Training facilities were very limited, due to strict service rationing at that time; yet Cpl Lomas, with the co-operation of the Commanding Officer of a Spitfire Wing, then stationed at Detling, had found the answer to releasing pigeons from a Spitfire without damage to the pigeon. This technique was used on Mosquitos, two aircraft that were seldom issued with pigeons, when he ascertained that pigeons were capable of night flight. Experiments were made by releasing pigeons at night from high-speed launches in the Dover area. Quite good results were obtained, but with the station loft sited under trees, the pigeons crash-landed into the trees, resulting in broken wing flights. As floodlighting was taboo, the experiment had to be aborted, as wing flights need time to grow.

After a change of personnel, I had Corporal Harry Clayton and Leading Aircraftman, Alf Clench, and we had a good crew. Flight Lieutenant Hill, then Signals Officer, arranged that District Registered Letter Service take a basket of Voyagers to other RAF Stations and letter delivery points. We made liberations from an Anson Aircraft, training Wireless Operators/Air Gunners covering the area of Portsmouth, West Sussex, Felixstowe and Suffolk – our pigeons qualified to become part of a communication system covering the British Isles, in the event of enemy action putting the telephone system out of service. I boast, but out of four lofts, Detling came up trumps for both time and reliability on a trial run.

Following a spell at RAF Linton-on-Ouse, Yorkshire, my next posting was again to RAF Detling and to my surprise, my Sergeant in charge of 4 Group Bomber Command plus Leading Aircraftsman, was Alf Clench. Group Sergeant W.L.B. Davidson was at RAF Hurn with Sergeant Tom McLean and a certain Corporal, Jack Adams, (King Jack). Tom McLean was Group Sergeant of the Hurn area, near Bournemouth. The Hurn Pigeon Section was the most successful loft for returns; unfortunately Tom today is registered semi-blind, but still cheerful in himself when I phoned him for information and memories. Both Leslie and Jack have gone.

Being with Sergeant Davidson and Alf Clench was like a homecoming into the loft, with Alf and Learned Corporal H. Clayton, who had carried on with the loft inmates when I was posted. A few new recruits [were there] but many old favourites, including a barren hen I knew the breeder of and which won two half-crown bets I had with Leslie.

We were not surprised to be ordered to liaise with the War Office on its pigeon requirements. 11 April 1945 came and a consignment of pigeons were seeded over the Ruhr Pocket, some 300 miles from base; among that consignment were Detling pigeons. My transport during this time was a six-cylinder Standard box van.

On 13 April, filling up the M.T. section, a voice from the office shouted, 'Get back to the loft, Corp., they have got one and it's urgent.' I put my foot down and was soon back at the loft.

An excited Leslie and Alf informed me that 29018 had brought a capsule containing surrender terms from a General von Model. Our Sergeant who, from his schooling, had a knowledge of German, had passed the capsules information on to Wing House Piccadilly by phone, as they wanted the message and capsule pronto.

The van's engine was built to go and I was off. At the bottom of Strood Hill I had to stop for six sailors who surrounded the van and wanted a lift to London. I agreed but told them I was in a hurry; anyway, up the hill we went and never have six men had a faster trip to town. When there were dropped off, one asked if the war was over and I replied, 'Yes, read the papers', and with a laugh I was on my way. Wing House had a commendation from the person who accepted the capsule and its contents. To this day I cannot remember his name. Me, I was right chuffed. The RAF had come up with a winner, fastest time, longest distance, RAF-born and bred. So it was away to Detling, just in case, me and a weekend pass. One or two other birds came back, but no messages, just liberations.

In September 1945, I was in the company of Leslie Davidson, Sergeant Ron Shepherd and other RAF and Army personnel in the grounds of The Royal Hospital, Chelsea, where a flower show was open to the public. A packed audience of many nationalities watched Ron Shepherd's seekers being put out of circling aircraft to seek their loft, [which were] panniers placed in an open space, surrounded by people, stalls and noise. It was a wonderful performance for, as Sergeant Shepherd said, he had never had an audience this size before.

We also saw 'Ruhr Express', 29018, auctioned and purchased by R. and D. Bishop for £425 when a Croydon publican stopped bidding. We three wondered if the 'Express' would have been an exhibit had the man continued bidding.

(From the memories of John Tucker).

10

A GHOST STORY

Harry Aldridge couldn't for the life of him think why he had waited all these years, forty-eight to be precise, to tell the story. It all started in December 1943, when Harry's misfortune, or so he thought at the time, was to be one of the hundred or so Royal Artillery personnel manning the six 4.5 foot anti-aircraft guns in Cornwall, with the forbidding Atlantic Ocean to the west and situated on the northern perimeter of Cornwall's number one military airfield. Harry's off-duty periods were either spent encased in blankets in his tents or huddled around the totally inadequate stove in the Nissen hut that they called the rest room. Harry was in charge of the aircraft spotters, doing round the clock duty in the lookout above the underground command post, and he was also the batteries' aircraft recognition specialist. It was inevitable that sooner or later he would become friendly with some of the RAF personnel. They were 'kindred spirits in the maelstrom of life, the flotsam and jetsam on the waves of time.'

In one of his frequent visits to the airfield and the RAF pigeon section, Harry got to know Sergeant George Salter of the pigeon unit. George hailed from Maidstone, a fancier of some repute before joining the RAF. Harry also made the acquaintance of young Sergeant Jimmy Armitage. Jimmy came from Southport, and was the son and grandson of dedicated fanciers. He was a rear gunner in Halifax Bomber *C for Charlie*.

The Coastal Command Liberators and Halifax bombers flew round-the-clock sorties off occupied France's western seaboard in search of German U-boats, which were creating such havoc with the Atlantic convoys that were Britain's lifeline to the Americans.

Harry's first impression of the RAF pigeon unit was the seemingly endless supply of pint mugs of delicious tea, strong and sweet, in spite of wartime restrictions. There must have been a hundred or so birds in the lofts; however, there was one pigeon he found it impossible to take his eyes off, a white grizzle cock. It was a truly magnificent specimen with beautiful feather quality, which extended down his legs, almost to the tip of his toes.

Looking into the imponderable depths of his eyes, Harry remarked to Sergeant Salter, 'I bet this one's pedigree is a bit special.' 'It is, Harry,' Salter replied, 'San Sebastian, Mirandi, Bordeaux and Liborne are race points that abound his ancestry.'

The bird was known as the 'Ghost', not only because of his colour, but also by his lightning trapping. It came as no surprise to learn that this pigeon was earmarked for Special Services. His many training flights were from the French coast, usually liberated from aircraft. It was rather a coincidence that, of all the lofts in the British Isles supplying birds to the service, the 'Ghost' should have come from a loft at St Just, just thirty miles south of where they were. He had come as a twenty-eight-day-old squeaker some two and a half years previously.

Harry and the rest of the personnel had arrived in this location after quite a long spell in the thick of the action on the south coast, on the bombing run up to London. As a result, they were quite pleased that the only time that they were in action was to engage the occasional lone German reconnaissance aircraft, probably trying to get a few photographs of the airfield. A few salvoes of heavy anti-aircraft shells usually had the enemy looking for a less hostile patch of sky. Everyone was looking forward to a quiet Christmas, as past experience showed that the RAF and the Luftwaffe honoured an unwritten truce over Christmas and Boxing Day.

As it was approximately 6.00 p.m. on Christmas Eve, Harry was a bit surprised to hear a four-engine aircraft warming up at the far end of the runway, adjacent to the look out post. About ten minutes later, Harry peered into the darkness and could just manage to make out the speeding form of Halifax *C for Charlie* as it became airborne opposite to where he was standing. He recalled feeling sorry for his pal, Sergeant Jimmy Armitage in the rear gun turret, having been dropped into what would probably be the last offensive mission before Christmas.

The first flurry of snow swept across the airfield, Harry readjusted his balaclava and helmet and just as he recoiled from the icy blast coming in from the north, the message to 'stand to' came up from the command post. Harry sounded the general alarm, jumped down the steps to the command post and glanced over the plotting table. There was the target, the small illuminated dot moving across the map on course for their area. Harry was back in the lookout post just as six guns let go their first salvoes, but the enemy pilot eventually had no stomach for this kind of reception and quickly turned south and out of range. As the guns stopped firing, he just about made out the faint drone of the engines as he flew away to the south west. Harry had an uneasy feeling that this aircraft was a night fighter. By his reckoning, it was now on the same course as *C for Charlie* and about thirty miles astern of her.

At eight o'clock that evening, he came off duty for a four-hour break and drifted across to the RAF Naafi canteen for a pint, where he ran into Sergeant George Salter. Harry told him of his uneasy feeling about *C for Charlie*. 'That's funny, Harry,' he said, 'I had a queer feeling about this flight; I don't know what made me do it, but I sent your favourite, 'Ghost', on this trip – I hope all goes well.'

After taking off, *C for Charlie* flew south, the nine-man crew carrying out all the usual tests and checks on instruments, engine temperatures, oil pressures and fuel lines. In fact, the control panels on a Halifax comprise over eighty various dials, levers, switches etc, and, as they left the coast behind, the gunners fired a few short bursts to check the machine guns.

The pilot levelled off at 1,000 feet as cloud cover was down to 1,200 feet. The Rolls Royce Merlin engines rumbling sweetly, the darkness of the outside world broken only by the stabbing flames of the exhaust pipes. About an hour after leaving the Cornish coast, the pilot altered course on the second leg in search of enemy shipping. It seemed as if the patrol was going to be fruitless as the crew had not seen any sign of the enemy. However, the boredom of this evening's operation hardly had chance to make itself felt when the unexpected happened. The Messerschmitt 110 nightfighter dived out of the clouds to starboard, raking the outer engine with shell-fire. A long black plume of smoke poured from the engine nacelle as the engine stopped. The inner starboard engine was overheating, the cooling system having been damaged, so the pilot had no choice but to cut the engine.

Jimmy Armitage and the upper gunner had not been caught completely unawares, as they both managed to get in a quick burst of gunfire. As the Messerschmitt turned away, the last they saw of it was the plane heading in the direction of the French Coast with an engine on fire.

However, the crew of *C for Charlie* had their own problems, as the Halifax was losing height. The loss of two engines made it almost impossible to maintain altitude and the plane was now only 600 feet above the cold, angry sea. The pilot decided that a forced landing was on the cards, so the navigator checked their position and found it to be approximately seventy miles south west of Land's End.

The crew took up positions near to the escape hatches as the pilot made his approach to ditching. Jimmy Armitage grabbed the pigeon container just before the plane hit the water. The starboard wing hit the sea first and as it dug in the water, the fuselage at the route of the wing burst open, allowing the sea to pour in. However, this did provide an escape route and they all managed to scramble out onto the partly-submerged wings, where they got the inflatable dinghy afloat. Lady Luck had been kind to them all, as they had all escaped with minor sprains, cuts and bruises.

It wasn't until the comparative safety of the dinghy that the effects of their injuries were being felt. Sergeant Jimmy Armitage decided it was time to examine the pigeons with the aid of the torch provided in the survival kit. He surprised to find 'Ghost', as he was not used for routine flights. He was worried about the condition of the birds, as they had obviously been totally submerged into the sea at the point of impact – apart from being wet through, they had, it seemed, taken in quite a lot of sea water. He decided that he would put the birds up singly at daybreak – it was going to be a long wait. Apart from the cold, seasickness was a problem for many members of the crew.

When dawn eventually came, visibility had deteriorated somewhat and was only about a mile, and even less in the snow squalls. It was with some misgivings that Jimmy tossed out the first bird, keeping the 'Ghost' back until he saw how the first pigeon cleared. What followed gave little hope, as the first bird made no attempt to gain height; for a moment, he looked like he was going to join the crew in the dinghy, before he flew aimlessly out to sea.

After some twenty minutes, Jimmy took the 'Ghost' from the container. The bird had dried out, but the immersion in salt water had had a bad effect on these pigeons. He tossed the 'Ghost' into the air but, unlike the first bird, he got up, circled a couple of times, and made off to the north east. 'That looks better,' said Jimmy to the rest of the crew. 'If he keeps going, he'll make it to the coast at Land's End'.

The failure of *C for Charlie* to return to base was of great concern. Aircraft and shipping were being alerted for a sea search, but the weather was deteriorating rapidly. Sergeant George Salter and other loftsmen watched and waited for an arrival of bird and message, inwardly despairing in view of the conditions, the sky getting darker by the minute. Then, suddenly, out of the murk, a bird dived into the loft, but before entering, glanced through the doweled front. There stood the 'Ghost' on the front of his nestbox. Just as George entered the compartment, the telephone rang in the small office adjoining. One of the loftsmen went to answer it as the Sergeant went to get the message, if any, from the 'Ghost'. However, the bird had completely disappeared. George searched everywhere, but there was no 'Ghost' to be found. The chap who answered the telephone called to George with a message from headquarters. The Sergeant read the message and said 'It appears that the 'Ghost' was picked up off the floor of the loft in St Just where he was bred. He died in the hands of the old chap who reared him.' 'He was faithful to the last', said George quietly to the group of loftmen gathered around him. 'The message he delivered had the crew's position, all are alive, and with a bit of luck, they should be picked up in the next hour or so.' The other bird was never seen again. Sure enough, the crew were picked up by a motor Torpedo boat at 10.45 a.m. on Christmas morning. Their injuries were not too serious and after a spell in sick bay, all departed for a fortnight's leave.

Shortly after this episode, Harry's regiment moved across country to the south east near Burnham-on-Crouch, into what was known as the gun belt, to engage the Flying Bombs on their way down to London. They then had improved radar and shells with a magnetic fuse. During the next few months, the battery of six 4.5-metre guns shot down dozens of them over the coast and marshlands. With the other batteries further down the coast, together with the RAF Tempest, Mustang and Mosquito fighter aircraft, very few flying bombs were reaching London. The Buzz Bomb (Doodlebug) was finished.

After a spell in Egypt and the Sudan, which included a crocodile shooting expedition near the Senar Dam, the war at last came to an end and Harry went home to get demobbed. He kept in touch with his friends in the RAF and it was eighteen months later that he travelled from his home in the Midlands to the wedding in Maidstone of ex-Sergeant Jimmy Armitage and Julie, the daughter of Sergeant George Salter, ex-RAF Pigeon Unit officer.

Harry stayed with George and his wife for a few days after the wedding and, as was to be expected, it didn't take them long to get round to the pigeons. As Harry looked into the front of the loft, there stood a white Grizzle cock, just as when he had first seen and admired its sire. It had the same feathered legs and beautiful eyes. 'What do you think of him?' George asked as he put him onto Harry's hands. 'This is a perfect pigeon,' he replied. 'This was the last youngster we managed to breed from "Ghost",' said George. The following spring, Harry was delighted to take possession of a squeaker from Maidstone, a Grizzle that was earmarked for the stock loft. Fanciers have asked Harry for the last forty years where the feathered legs come from. Until now, he had always thought that it was too long a story to tell.

11

THE MIDDLE EASTERN PIGEON SERVICE

1942-45

January 1942 saw the birth of the Middle East Pigeon Service with its headquarters at Digla, near Cairo, Egypt. It included a school where pigeoneers wanting to join the organisations were tested on their ability as fanciers before being enlisted into the service. Here, also, was the breeding centre, which received considerable assistance from the South African Pigeon Service, who sent a number of drafts of pigeons from that country. Later on, birds also began arriving from the UK.

The Commanding Officer of the M.E.P.S. was Lt-Col. J.A. Hollingsworth, a perfect gentleman. Anyone who served under him always received the upmost civility and courtesy. Sergeant-in-command of the school was Alf Peberty from Leicester. Anyone who was at Digla will always remember Alf's familiar voice crying out 'on parade'. Another great fancier at HQ was Sergeant W.H. Smith of Braidwood, Lanarkshire, the 1938 S.N.F.C. Nantes winner. Also at Digla in those days was Sergeant Tom McDaid of Liverpool, whose knowledge of pigeons was remarkable. Sadly, the other three fanciers have passed on, but will always be remembered by the lads of the M.E.P.S.

Major Fred Hartford from London was responsible for the organisation of pigeon lofts throughout Syria, while Captain Walters was stationed at Jerusalem and in charge of lofts in that area. The Pigeon Service operated in an area which stretched from the Turkish border to the Lebanon, a distance of over 200 miles, and the lofts were attached to the 9th Army stationed in Palestine. Sergeant T. Crotch from Norwich was at Agir with Signalman Matthews and Leading Aircraftsman Smith, while Corporal Jack Porter from Stalmine near Blackpool was in charge of the loft at Sarafand.

In June 1942, two mobile lofts, numbers 108 and 88, left Digla for the western desert. Sergeant Jack Errett from Tottenham, Signalman W. Button from Ipswich and Signalman Cheadle from Eccles accompanied loft number 108. Corporal J. Crossland of Halifax, Signalman Eades of Doncaster and Signalman Mallett from Northwich were in charge of loft 88.

At this time, the German and Italian Armies had pushed the British and Commonwealth troops right back into Egypt, to a place that would soon gain world renown – El Alamein. It was here that General Auchinleck halted the Axis advance. Loft number 108 was at Burg El Arab and loft 88 at Inkingi. Birds from all forward areas were trained to home to the HQ in the rear.

The third mobile loft to arrive in the battle area was accompanied by Corporal Knox

The National Pigeon Service mobile lofts.

from London, Signalman Scholes of Barnsley and Leading Aircraftman Ashdown from Kent. These two men visited units of the 13th Corps and 30th Corps, where they instructed personnel in the handling and use of pigeons.

Pigeons were very soon in use with the 9th Australian Division, the 51st Highland Division, the 1st and 2nd New Zealand Divisions and the 4th Division.

Sergeant J. Errett was made in charge of the section with W. Button promoted to Corporal and in charge of 108 loft. Loft number 88 was doing good work with the Royal Air Force and birds used with the reconnaissance patrols.

On 22 October 1942, all the birds were sent out from 108 loft, and for two days the loft was empty. The birds began to arrive early on 25 October and after a feed and a drink were sent out again. This continued for the next six days and over 100 messages were carried over this period, a result of the necessity of maintaining wireless silence.

With the breakthrough by the 8th Army on 3 November, 108 loft moved forward to Mersa Matruh, with one loft moving up to Tobruk. The birds were resettled and put into service with the Australian Air Force at Gambut – anyone who saw service there would remember it for its violent dust storms.

The next move involving lofts 88 and 108 was to Benghazi. Corporal Crossland was still in charge of loft 88, assisted by Signalman Elkins and Leading Aircraftman Lomasc. Now in charge of 108 was Corporal J. Wales, helped by two Irish pigeoneers, Corporal Button and his pigeoneers having moved forward with the advancing 8th Army.

Such was the demand for pigeons that a further four mobile lofts were sent to Benghazi for the use of the Air Force's Bomber Group and the 9th United States Army Air Force with their Liberator Bombers. This airfield was at Birka, two miles west of

Benghazi. Personnel accompanying these lofts included Sergeants J. Ambler of Keighley and D. Kendall of Huddersfield. Pigeoneers A. Birch, A. Hosmer, G. Silson of London, M. Bone, T. Blackburn of Middlesborough, C. Brett from Kent, J. Leishman of Banknock, J. Smart of Blantyre and D. Day of Nailsworth. Also attached was Private Jim Tellis, an American from Baltimore.

It was from Birka that the 9th U.S.A.A.F. made the great raid on the oil fields of Ploesti in Romania, and also from here that they conducted many bombing raids on Italy.

Corporal J. Jackson from County Durham was in charge of the loft at Missarata, which supplied birds in that area. On 23 January 1943, the victorious 8th Army entered Tripoli, the last remaining capital of Mussolini's former empire. With the fall of Tripoli, the work of the M.E.P.S. in the western desert was complete and the army term pigeons had punched their way from Alamein to Tripoli, a distance of some 1,400 miles.

Two pigeons received the Dicken Medal for outstanding services. 'George' (blue chequer cock M.E.P.S. 42/1263) from the loft of D-Day, was a well-known National flyer who saved the lives of four airmen who came down in the Mediterranean. Sergeant Ramsey, one of the four, related how this valiant pigeon saved their lives.

'We had to ditch our aircraft off the coast of Benghazi, we were on our way back from an operation and we carried two pigeons in metal containers. On impact, they broke up and sank at once. The bird in the fore position was hurled through the nose of the aircraft, the observer going the same way. Luckily for us, he spotted the container sinking, the lid having burst open, releasing the bird from the container. He held it in one hand and swam to the dinghy, but the other bird went down with the aircraft. The survivor was in a sorry state and after drying it as best we could, we

NPS members in the desert.

Members of the NPS. Note the sardine boxes used to make pigeon lofts.

rested it for a few hours. We then thought that it might get away with its message, but, although it did its best, it just went straight into the water again. This happened several times until it did eventually get airborne. We did not think for one minute that it would reach base. The situation was not good – this was our only chance of rescue. However, it was not many hours before the good old Navy came and picked us up, suffering from cuts and exposure. Without doubt, we owe our lives to that pigeon'.

All four airmen, Flight Lieutenant N. Crompton of New Zealand, Flight Sergeant Howell of Newfoundland, Sgt Deverall of Bristol and Sgt Ramsay survived the war.

The only other pigeon to receive The Dicken Medal was blue hen NPS43/WD593, 'Princess'. At six months old, this pigeon delivered an important message from Crete to Alexandria, a distance of over 500 miles, mainly over water. She was parachuted into Crete with a number of British agents, who were to observe enemy troop movements and also establish contact with local guerrilla forces.

The agents landed with two canisters containing pigeons and a powerful wireless transmitter. The shock of landing damaged one of the valves of the transmitter, rendering it useless. As a result, 'Princess' was released to carry a request for a replacement part to be dropped by parachute. This message was successfully delivered. Unfortunately, she died within a fortnight and the award of the Dicken Medal was made posthumously. This was classed as one of the finest achievements ever recorded by a service pigeon. This particular bird was trained by Corporal Parsons from the service loft at Alexandria.

The next theatre of operations for the pigeons of M.E.P.S. was Sicily and Italy, where two sections – 9HQ and 21HQ – were operational. Commanding 9HQ was Major Wonter Smith, who before the war flew pigeons with the Idle H.S. in Yorkshire. Others in the section included Sgt Parry, Sgt Crossland, (who took over from Sgt Parry), Sgt Alex King of Wilshaw, Corporal Semple, Wilton, Corporal Smith and Signalmen Cartwright, Gill, Sweet, Dalton, Clough, Cartlidge and Hebden. The latter were joined at a later date by Signalmen Greer, Byrne, Jenkinson, Warman, Jeans, Trueman, Woodhouse, Forster, Francis, Thorpe and Edwards. This section was completely mobile and comprised of six lofts. It was latterly commanded by Major Hartford.

The other section, 21HQ was under Major W.B. Dikson and comprised of Corporals Mallinson, Moore, Grace, Picks, Chambers, Steward, Parker. Signalmen Ebden, Smith, Faber, Box, Stafford, Nesbit, Walker, Osbourne, Dormer, Coates, Simms, Elkin, Robinson, Ivey, Hollis, Anderson, Knight, Husskison, Booth, Mulligan and Hubbleday.

Eight thousand messages were carried by 9HQ in Italy, in operations with the 8th Army and the famous 13th Corps. Notable performances by M.E.P.S. included that of mealy cock 42.16368 'Italia', which flew Spitza in ten hours and fifty minutes after being dropped south of Rome by intelligence people. This bird carried a message which resulted in the rescue of 100 high-ranking officials held prisoner behind German lines.

Another great performance was put up by Dark Chequer hen M.E.P.S. 42.2442. This bird was trained on the mobile system and was sent under the charge of Signalmen Smith and Francis to the island of Avar off the Greek Dalmatian coast. This bird settled into its new loft in five days and was sent out with forward patrols in that area. The most important information it carried was the news that the German Army was planning to invade the island. This warning enabled the British and Allied troops to be withdrawn safely. A testimonial was received by Major Wonter Smith in charge of 9HQ.

In addition to these outstanding feats, many messages were carried from Albania to Brindisi during raids by Major Grey and No. 2 Commando.

MR WOODMAN'S STORY

During the D-Day landings, 6 June, pigeons and fanciers alike played an important part. It is only fitting to recall H.C. Woodman's account of the Plymouth Pigeon group's involvement in that operation.

By the end of 1943, Major Heap and L.T. Spencer had visited Cecil Street several times. Between them, plans were formulated to turn the group over from Special Section – to teach American pigeoneers our way of handling pigeons and to memorise the location of the forty-three lofts of the group, spread over an area of about fourteen square miles.

On 28 December, Mr Woodman received a letter from L.T. Spencer from his head-quarters at Tidworth near Aldershot, informing him that pigeoneers, staff, and Sgt Herbst with privates Mozer, Dzingle and Kadlowboski would all be arriving that afternoon for a prolonged stay at his headquarters and would he please have 200 racers ready for a most important exercise on the evening of 30 December?

The next night, at opposite ends of the city, two Plymouth fanciers – Charles Bygraves and Fred Thorn, transport officers for the group – climbed into their trucks and discreetly called at the lofts of the group members. They collected the birds and brought them to the secret bird room at Cecil Street.

Around the walls of these rooms were forty twenty-bird panniers, arranged in tiers. They placed the birds in these baskets, which were capable of holding 700 pigeons for days at a time, and returned the empty baskets. That evening, the pigeoneers examined the birds in four-bird American Army pigeon containers; then, the boxing-up completed, they had supper and went to bed.

Sgt Herbst and Mr Woodman were up at six a.m. the following morning and while enjoying an early cup of tea, they heard a faint knock on the door. Mr Woodman opened the door to welcome Ernest Cookson, a Transport Driver of the USA 29th Division – he was to hear that knock on the door many times before D-Day. While Ernest was enjoying a cup of tea, Herbst and Mr Woodman loaded the seventy containers, each with four pigeons, into the truck and with a 'cheerio' Ernest, now back in his cab, slipped into gear and departed as silently as he had come.

The pigeons sent to the first exercise were away for seven days and on the seventh day the phone rang to say that Fred Thorn had one of his pigeons back with the goods, which in this case turned out to be a vital coded message from the combat exercise area. It was later discovered that Fred's pigeon had flown many miles after being cooped up for a week. During that day, several more birds returned with coded messages. So ended their first American Operation with the 29th Division US Army.

The American brass hats, realising the potential in the use of racing pigeons, pressed them harder to hasten the organising of the D-Day communication lines for their invasion army.

By the Plymouth Group's contacts with the 29th Division, they now knew the other part of the 280th US Pigeon Company. The 208th had a section operation under a Sgt Don Harding and were based at Bere Alston and Tavistock. Don Harding's section now became responsible for the training of the group's pigeons.

The pigeons were collected by Fred Thorn and Charlie Bygraves and taken to the NPS Headquarters. They were again picked up next morning by Ernest Cookson, who took them away to Bere Alston and Tavistock, where they were taken to training points stretching from Falmouth in the west to Sidmouth in the east. Liberations were very frequent, the idea being to train each pigeon like an athlete, giving them plenty of workouts. On some days they were taken out on a landing craft and there, in panniers upon the deck of a tank carrier, would hear the shattering roar of guns of all types, as the ships fired everything they had at the mock defenders. Very often the birds were liberated during the salvoes and flew madly home.

During January, February and March, Lt Tom Spencer, QC of 280th Company, came to stay with the platoon at Cecil Street. After dinner, he and Mr Woodman worked on the plans of the D-Day operations. The Plymouth Group had forty-three good lofts to play with, and all of these lofts were situated between Modbury, fourteen miles to the west of Plymouth, to Pensilva near Liskeard, in rugged country of moorland. It was on large sheets of paper that they had to mark the fancier's house, his loft, his telephone, or nearest phone if he did not have one, his ability to billet a pigeoneer and the nearest police station. When all the lofts had been mapped, they were divided into different sections. The original plans that were eventually presented to Lt Spencer, who in turn presented them to Supreme Headquarters Allied Expeditionary Force, were sketched out on big sheets of greaseproof paper laid out on Mr Woodman's floor. It took weeks and weeks to plan this huge operation.

May 1944 came, and during the early part of this month they had their final tryout with the 280th Pigeon Company. Although the group did not know at the time, this was a great mock invasion exercise, with 324 pigeons liberated under realistic war conditions with live ammunition being used. Fifteen pigeons failed to return to their lofts, the remainder carrying scores of messages which kept the pigeoneers rushing from the lofts in their jeeps to messages or radio centres with vital attack messages.

Three weeks before D-Day, Lt Spencer, for security reasons, took all the pigeons into the security of a big army camp at Plymouth.

Seven days before the actual D-Day operation, Mr Woodman thought there was just another practice, an invasion exercise. On 28 and 29 May, 520 pigeons were picked up from the war-battered city of Plymouth. During the following days, the group's fanciers were becoming restless at the prolonged absence of the birds.

On the day of the invasion, 5 June, Mr Woodman slept late, until his wife woke him to tell him the invasion was on. He was out of bed in a jiffy, standing there in his pyjamas. He looked out of the window as a jeep came out of the lane opposite the house, coming away from the loft of Taw, Doidge and Woodman, and so came D-Day, with 28 fully-armed American pigeoneers patrolling the 48 lofts. By 6.00 p.m., three Plymouth pigeons had flown the 160 miles from the beachhead, but none carried the message required.

An airborne division had been flown to Normandy on 6 June and strapped to the stomachs of eighty of the toughest US Paratroopers, in little round containers, were eighty of the Plymouth group's best pigeons. The flights' records at the back of this book give the details of this. No wireless contacts were to be made. The Division's mission was one of chaos and destruction, with reinforcements asked for via the pigeons, but as the day wore on no message arrived.

During the evening, American pigeon officers visited Cecil Street and asked if there was a chance of a pigeon coming through from this division. By now the weather was deteriorating fast, the wind was gale force and from the north-west, and they were told there was just a chance. The jeeps were speeded up to make their visits every ten minutes instead of the usual twenty minutes in the morning. The drama was being played to its climax. 8.00 p.m. passed, then 9.00 p.m., and it would be dark at 10 p.m. Just after nine, it happened. William George was keeping a lonely vigil at his loft when he saw the pigeon come, pitch on the board and fly round to the trap entrance. 'Clang' went the bolt wires and 'Paddy', Bill George's red chequer cock dropped into the loft. A shrill ring was heard from the alarm bell, but it was not needed. Bill caught 'Paddy' and removed the red message container. Down the lane hurried the jeep, and from it dropped the three pigeoneers, for about the twentieth time that day. They climbed up the ladder to the loft, and stared at the message container in Bill's hand and then they smacked Bill on the back with delight. Each of the three gave Bill a pound note and then they dashed off to the message centre.

The honour of the 280th Signals Pigeon Company was saved. Next morning, another airborne division was flown in to rescue the soldiers. The message was very dramatic. It appeared that the division dropped in a district where a German Army Corps was on manoeuvres. As they came floating down, they met a warm reception and it was made known later that some Plymouth racing pigeons – which homed on D-Day, covered in human blood and without messages – were freed from containers by bullets ripping through the drums attached to the paratroopers.

By the time D-Day had come to a close, the patrolling jeeps had used over a 1,000 gallons of petrol in their patrols.

Day after day after the invasion, birds were coming home, many as we know used by the French resistance movement and thus still helping the Allied cause. Yet again this proves the commitment and bravery of fanciers in the war effort; without the help of the likes of Mr Woodman and his group the outcome of the war could have been so different.

In 1940, a fancier called Fred Cox was drafted to work at the army pigeon loft at Horse Guards parade. Being a sculptor by trade, Fred gained first prize for his work called 'Pigeon in Flight' in the National Portrait Gallery. Fred was, at that time, a very successful fancier, racing into London with his brother. The Cox brothers were really renowned for their racing exploits and it was therefore inevitable that one of them would be of more use in the pigeon loft management at the rear of 10 Downing Street. In fact, he had many distinguished visitors such as Messrs Eden, Halifax and Churchill, who popped in to see him and the birds.

The first loft there was a First World War mobile; this was later changed to a seventy-foot long modern loft. This particular loft was for use with the Signals and Pigeon Service. These birds were used by the RAF, and also on manoeuvres and in unison with various French Resistance Movements. The birds were dropped by parachute from various aerodromes into Northern France. A lot of good fortune was required here, as they sometimes fell into enemy hands. If everything worked to plan they would have to home from points such as Ghent, Nantes, Lyons and even as far as Barcelona. This they did but, with such risks involved, quite a few also went missing. Once these birds were dropped into various locations, they were taken care of and their containers disposed of.

During this time, one such resistance movement in Holland was at Kinrool. Mrs Marie Louise Cartwright, in one of her letters, stated that an English bomber crashed near their village. Their unit was the first at the scene. Marie recalls this incident in good detail. One of the crew, a Sgt Williams, was killed and was buried in the village. The captain was taken prisoner, but the resistance movement managed to get the rest of the crew away before the Germans arrived. The aircrew were returned to British shores through various Resistance networks. Marie stated that they knew they got back alright because of a message on their radio saying 'The birds are back in the cage'. Within this aircraft were two pigeons in their containers. One was drowned in a ditch, but the other was released with a message and of course, they knew that it had arrived back in England safely.

Marie worked as an interpreter, operating between the Dutch and Belgium border, and she gave a graphic description of how five members of her group were caught by the Germans in possession of pigeon containers. They were to pay a terrible price because they were shot in a field at the rear of her home.

Her village of Kinrool had a good record of getting British aircrews back to England and was known to the Germans as the 'English village'. Marie stated that they were very proud of that but the price they paid was horrific, as over thirty of the group had been shot. She said that before these incidents, the only time that she had had any experience with pigeons was when they were killed for the table. Sadly, this brave woman passed away in December 1989.

We move on to the story of 'Felix', whose proper name was Philip Schneidau. He was half French and half British, but opted for British nationality when he was twenty-one years old. He was thirty-seven and had been an international hockey player for France, before he was dropped by parachute from a Whitley. He had to arrange his return himself. He was to be picked up by a Westland Lysander, learn about pigeons, then change his appearance for, as an international sportsman his face was well known.

He was instructed in the use of pigeons by Squadron Leader W.D. Lea Rayner who had been in the Army Pigeon Service in the First World War and was a Captain in Ireland. Lea Rayner was to become a Wing Commander and was in charge of the RAF Pigeon Service in the United Kingdom. He told Felix that the two pigeons he was taking with him should be placed in a pair of socks with the toes cut out and put in a rucksack. It was at this time that wireless transmitters for the agents were not in full use so the pigeons were the only way of communicating with the UK.

Felix was eventually dropped from the Whitley bomber near to Montigny on the evening of 9 October 1940. When he arrived in France, he boarded out the pigeons with an old friend who kept pigeons of his own. More then a week later, the Lysander failed to turn up so he attached identical messages to the two birds' legs and released them at 8.00 a.m. on a Sunday morning. They arrived at the civilian loft at East Grinstead at 4.30 p.m. and, as arranged, the owner telephoned for a dispatch rider who signed for the messages and set off for the Air Ministry in London on his cycle. The Duty Clerk at the Air Ministry signed for these messages at 6.30 p.m., but it was another thirteen hours before there was anyone on duty who had the authority to set the pick up into action.

Hundreds of fanciers passed through the pigeon service units during the war and before being accepted, they underwent selection tests to test their suitability. It was soon found that the best men, with few exceptions, came from certain parts of the country where competition in racing was at its keenest. There were of course some very amusing incidents during the selection process. Fanciers were required to apply for these positions and were called up for an interview in due course.

Understandably, commanders of platoons etc were reluctant to let their best men go, but a Major A. Neilson Hutton, who conducted interviews with a lot of the men, stated that he sometimes turned men down for being unsuitable for such reasons as not knowing the incubation period, or how many flights pigeons had. Surprisingly, they were men who kept pigeons before being called up. It was evident from the very start that only the best applicants, with sound knowledge of their subject would be successful. When one looks at the calibre of men in the Pigeon Service and what was required of them, it was clear that this was a wise formula. Some of them stayed in Britain, many within RAF locations, but others, as we know, went with mobile lofts to within reasonable distance of the front lines.

R.A.F. Pigeon Form No. 1628.

PIGEON MESSAGE FORM.

To :—

From :—

Series No.   Date

Time of origin :

Sender's Signature : | Time received
                              | at loft :

Should this bird fail to return to its own loft, the finder is requested to telephone or otherwise deliver the message it carries to the nearest R.A.F. Unit, or Post Office. It may save life if this is done promptly.

R.A.F. Form 1326

S.O.S.

Colour Code   Aircraft No.   Date

Time

*Position

*If this is blank, see outside carrier and transmit.

Preserve Container and forward with Message

If this message is found, please transmit to Air Ministry Signals immediately.   (See overleaf.)

TO FINDER :—
If at sea, transmit by W/T for retransmission to Air Ministry via your G.P.O. W/T Station on S.O.S. wave.

If in United Kingdom telephone to nearest Police or R.A.F. Station for retransmission. Alternatively, telephone (forward charge)
HOLBORN 3434, Ex. 1254 (between 0900 and 1900 hours only)
or ABBEY 3411 and ask for Signals Officer (between 1900 and 0900 hours only).

Give FULL particulars in message, e.g.: "S.O.S. Colour—yellow in orange ; Aircraft No. M. 6199 ; 23/5/40 ; 1345 hours ; Position : 55°—14'N. 2°—21'E. In rubber dinghy."

It may be that the time, position and further detail is not filled in ; the message, giving colour code, aircraft number and date, is not less important on that account.

Do not delay ! Do not lose the Container !
(*12403—10988) Wt. 17180—702 150M 6/43 T.S. 700

The pigeon form. The message was put in a plastic container with a screw top, and attached to the bird's leg using a plastic band.

THE LATE EDDIE GILBERT

Eddie Gilbert served in the Army Pigeon Service in both the UK and the Middle East for five and a half years. Even before the outbreak of war, fanciers in Kings Lynn had their birds on service with the RAF based at Bricham Newton, where they were sent twice a week. At that time, Eddie was secretary of the South Road Club and he volunteered for the Pigeon Service in May 1940. Once accepted, he went to Aldershot, where he met up with other volunteer pigeon personnel. After a short spell with the mobile loft at Billingham, Eddie moved on to the headquarters at York, where he helped the contrac-

Eddie Gilbert's loft, Hadera, Palestine, 1942-43. Eddie lived with the birds.

tors to erect a forty-foot loft in Fishergate Gardens. On completion, he was put in charge of it and actually lived in it. In 1942, Eddie was posted to the Middle East, where he was to oversee the service loft there.

This loft housed all the South African pigeons which had to be broken into it. Eventually the birds settled and were trained for service in the desert. In fact, Eddie had the first two pigeons to fly from the desert headquarters back to Maadi. One bird was carrying the first message to be received from the base during the campaign. A week or so later, Eddie was posted to a new loft in Palestine, as there was no pigeon service in place at that time. On arrival he had to report to the CSO 9th Army, who proved to be good friends to the British pigeon lads.

When the battle in the desert was over, some of the lofts were pulled down, with several of the lads finishing up at the signals base. As time went by the crew were recalled to the Pigeon Service, where they were to train the 'Nomad' birds. Once again it was back to Palestine to re-open the Gaza lofts, with only twelve birds. Even after only one night in the loft, they were let out, with everyone returning to the basket and fed only on peas to break them. After just two weeks training, these pigeons were running a service of ninety miles from Haifa; all this took place in 1944.

This was not the end of Eddie's involvement, as he was then asked to report to the 9th Army Headquarters Signals to take pigeons into Turkey. However, Turkey did not enter the war, so it was decided to send the birds to the Syrian Hills and the Arab Legion, where a small loft was started up. Eddie was to continue moving about with the birds and did service in Gaza again and in Syria. Thus, he saw a lot of the Middle East with the Pigeon Section.

The Service was closed in October 1945 and Eddie and his pals were demobbed and home for Christmas.

TROON MAN'S MIDDLE EAST EXPLOITS

In an issue of the well-known periodical *Racing Pigeon,* in an article on the war-time Middle East Pigeon Service, a Troon man, Mr John Whyte of 21 Walker Avenue, is shown

Middle East loft. John Whyte is second from left in the back row.

At Desert HQ, 1943.

in one of the numerous photographs used to illustrate a fascinating story of the work of the little-publicised branch of the Royal Corps of Signals.

The Number 9 Headquarters Section working in Italy (then in the North African theatre of war), was responsible for over 8,000 operational messages being carried by pigeons, in addition to working from the forward areas with Assaulting Units. The pigeons were carried by aircraft on air operations and on a number of occasions when planes came down in the sea, the SOS messages sent by releasing the pigeons were responsible for the subsequent rescue of the crews.

The photograph in the periodical shows Mr Whyte and other signals personnel standing beside a row of mobile pigeon lofts at the Pigeon Service Training Centre, which had been set up near Cairo in January 1942. In 1941, Mr Whyte was posted to the Signals in the Middle East. He was soon experiencing, like everyone else in the 8th Army, the change of fortunes of war, which characterised the desert campaign in the early days of the Tobruk and Benghazi periods. It was in July 1942 that John was transferred to the Pigeon Service and after a spell of initial training he was posted for operational duties with the Long Range Desert Group. This was an interesting and mobile phase in his Army Service, but something no less intriguing, although less mobile, was to follow.

In 1943, he was assigned to a job that can be best described as Special Service duties and for the next two years, indeed until the end of the war, he led a rather eventful life. John's area of operations covered both land and sea, on and around the many islands of the Greek Archipelago in the Aegean Sea.

Many of the islands were occupied by the Germans, but not completely, and it was the seldom mentioned 'little war' that concerned John. His job entailed long periods in which he had no direct contact with Allied troops and during one spell lasting fully nine months he scarcely saw a Britishman – his companions were Greeks and there were occasional glimpses of Germans on some of the other islands.

It was, therefore, with great pleasure and appropriate celebration that he later met two Troon men on different islands. They were Mr Peter Strachan of 5 West Porland Street, serving in the RASC Boat Service and Mr Fred Meldrum of 11 Bank Street, a member of the RAF and at that time serving on an Air Sea Rescue Launch.

While John's duties were principally concerned with the Pigeon Service, he had many exciting experiences in other operations, and war, as innumerable war memoirs show, can be a queer business at times.

He has many recollections of life as it is lived in the twentieth century in those islands, which have histories going back many centuries. John got to know Chios and Samos very well – two islands which had a highly refined form of civilisation hundreds of years before the beginning of the Christian era. John found that people living there were not lacking in the abiding human qualities of courage and of self sacrifice. They were friendly, helpful and generous and more than ready to do a favour.

John's exciting memories include the role played by the little ships and the men who sailed them with quiet courage under the very nose of the enemy.

The army had, a reputation, not without foundation, for a certain unorthodoxy in finding the right man for the right job – many a good butcher, for instance, found himself carving a career in the Medical Corps. Where the Pigeon Service was concerned, however, every effort was made to obtain men with practical experience in the training and handling of birds. John Whyte was an obvious choice, for he had been a fancier since his boyhood days. It is doubtful if he ever imagined when he adopted the hobby while still at school that his boyish inclination to have pigeons of his own would eventually add a chapter to his life which, if fully told, would read stranger than fiction.

Before the war, John was a painter and decorator with a local firm. He flew his pigeons under the name of Whyte and Lapsley (Lapsley being his stepbrother's name). All were one family, with John being the eldest of five brothers and two sisters, although sadly the two sisters died very young. The partnership flew in Troon Homing Club and flew very well. In 1935, in the Scottish National Flying Club Nantes race, they took 36th Section and 77th Open, winning the grand total of five pounds six shillings with a velocity of 703 YPM, over 591 miles, with 1,724 birds competing. On 26 May 1937, they entered the Irish Hospital Dublin Pigeon Derby Sweepstakes –30,000 birds competed, and they finished tenth in the Kyle federation, though the Open position is not known. Then along came the war and there was no more pigeon racing for a while.

After the war, once John was demobbed, his son Ralph always encouraged him to start up again but he kept putting if off, although he did visit a few lofts on Sundays after going to the football on Saturdays. Eventually Ralph won and persuaded his father to set up again, starting with some tumblers from Ralph's brother-in-law. After about a month, John felt the old feeling coming back and racing pigeons was once again part of his life. Ralph would travel over on Saturdays to watch the birds coming back from the races and, as in previous years, he won his fair share.

He won the club's Channel Cup six times in nine years, but then due to lack of

Training pigeons in the Middle East.

members the Troon Club finished in 1972. John had had enough and gave up again. It was at this time that Ralph was flying his own pigeons in Mossblown, so it was now John's turn to visit him. John Whyte had always said that his biggest thrill was when Ralph won the National race from Nantes in 1977. What a night they had at the presentation awards. Sadly, John passed away in 1982, but nobody will ever forget the man from Troon.

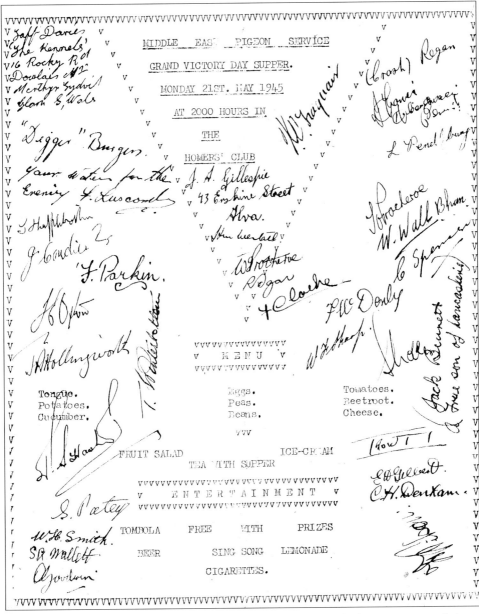

Middle East Pigeon Service Victory Day supper menu, with the signatures of those members who attended.

Feeling the cold in the desert.

Left: *Len Parry of Essex, 1943.* Right: *Tom Rix at the HQ loft, Maadi, 1942.*

Pigeon Service HQ, Maadi, 1943.

The lads from the Pigeon Service, Cairo, 1943.

A local fancier on a Turkish island.

Releasing the birds in 1942.

12

WAR OF LITTLE WINGS
THE FOUR BRAVE MEN OF HANVEC

The road from the village of Hanvec, Finistère, wound across the common of Loperic and Jean le Minn was riding his cycle on this early, cold and misty late spring morning, on the way to the farm where he worked. As he pedalled along, his spirits rose with the sun that was slowly dispersing the mist and Jean began to sing an old Breton folk song, his eyes continuously searching the landscape. Suddenly, away from the road, he saw two white mushroom-like mounds. Dismounting, he walked across the springy turf to the white patches.

They were two small linen parachutes and attached to the strings of each parachute was a small round cardboard container. Jean knew what he was looking at, as he had heard that the RAF dropped the famous secret service pigeons in containers such as these. Quickly he cut away the containers. Nearby was a large mossy stone, so, pulling it aside, he put the now badly folded parachutes into the shallow cavity. Pressing the stone back on top of them, Jean covered the base with dead bracken. Then, thrusting his hand into the containers, he transferred each pigeon, a red chequer hen and a blue pied cock, into his coat pockets. Two sealed envelopes, two small bags of seed, two cardboard containers and two small boxes containing four green leg message carriers were also in there. Jean ripped up the containers into small pieces, which he scattered in the grass as he walked back to his cycle. It would have taken a clever soldier to have noticed that the RAF had dropped two English racing pigeons in that vicinity during the night.

With his heart beating fast, Jean carried on his way to the farm where he hid his find in the barn. With the birds safe, Jean furtively opened one of the envelopes and read the heading of the questionnaire. His eyes opened wide with amazement, as they were indeed English spy pigeons which he had found. The message said:

> You have had the good luck to find this pigeon, take advantage to serve your country. This is a unique opportunity which may not occur again, make the most of it. Help us to drive the enemy out of your country, to give you back your liberty and property. Send us information about the enemy, what he does, what he thinks. Read our questionnaire carefully and follow our instructions exactly. We shall be able to reward you when victory is won. We shall not forget your efforts. You can collect important information, this pigeon can bring it to us, we can make use of it.'
> INSTRUCTIONS: As soon as you get home, give the pigeon food and water; leave him enough room to move about in comfort until it is

released. Look after it for several days if necessary, it has a very important part to play.

When you have studied the questions, collect your information and write it carefully. Destroy all these papers and the pencil, put the message in the tubes and push it as far as it will go into the cylinder. When you fix the tubes to the pigeon's leg, make sure the end of the tube is uppermost. Do not use your own name, use an invented name, a number or a motto, for it will enable us to find you later to reward you for your deed of fidelity. When you have fixed the time for dispatch, fix the tubes to the pigeon's legs very carefully. Release the bird at dawn in fine weather. If this is impossible, put the pigeon on a roof, a window sill, a wall or tree. Do not release the pigeon in the afternoon, evening or the early hours of the night if you can avoid it. Do not release the pigeon in wet or foggy weather. Give the bird a tablespoon of the grain supplied and a drink; give it another drink half an hour before liberating it, but do not give it anything to eat at this time.

Jean turned the questionnaire and read the other side:

Very important: do not forget to mention the date and the name of your locality in your message, and do not talk about it.

After reading the questionnaire through, Jean made up his mind what to do about the pigeons. He had decided that this was a job for George Blaiso, the contractor at Hanvec and his very good friend. After finishing work, he pedalled hurriedly across the common, the pigeons now secreted in his cyclebag, the documents and containers in his pockets. At last he reached Monsieur Blaiso's sitting room, where they were shortly joined by the village schoolmaster.

Four copies of the message were then written, telling the English Intelligence that a certain château was being used as a German army headquarters and a supply depot. The four copies were inserted into the leg carriers; two were handed to Jean and two given to another man.

In Jean's bedroom, early next morning in the dark hour before dawn, two people stood near the window. Jean went to open the lower portion of the window, but his wife pulled him back as the sound of a German patrol could be heard approaching. When the sound began to fade away, the window was gently opened and the blue pied cock rested on the window sill. The crouching pigeon rose on its legs, as the pale pink and turquoise blues of morning lit up its once darkened resting place. It turned around fussily and passed its beak through its long flight feathers, preening itself. A moment later it was gone, soon to be joined by the red hen; as silently as they arrived, they flew away.

The next night, Blaiso, listening to the BBC, heard the French announcer say, '584, 584, the corn is ripe for reaping'. A few nights later, the château was destroyed by the RAF from St Eval.

The Special Section of the Wing House owed a lot of their success to the French Resistance movement and it is only fit and proper to mention north west France and two of England's greatest friends.

H.C. Woodman, who wrote these articles, said that it brings back vivid memories of a French Resistance worker and hero, one Celestin Floch who lived at 20 Quay De Leon, Morlaix, and his colleague, Captain Ernest Siberil, a small boatbuilder of the fishing village of Carontec, not far from Morlaix. These two French heroes were the last link of a resistance lifeline that returned shot-down RAF personnel from the Brest area back to England. The work was done by vessels of all kinds, usually stolen from coastal villages and towns in the area. They audaciously stole the harbourmaster's launch at Brest and sent it across to England with airmen, loyal French soldiers and others.

In the early days of the Occupation, a great friend of Siberil's was an elderly French fisherman who made many trips to the Channel Islands and then, with refugees, to England. After some months of this work, the old man was suspected by the Gestapo and tried, but on account of his great age he was sentenced to only one year in prison. After six months he became very ill and was released to go home, with the promise that he would return as soon as he was better. On arrival back home, he soon contacted Siberil, who had arranged for him to sail to England. The departure was fixed for the Tuesday night in a high-speed German patrol boat that Siberil was repairing and making seaworthy, but even under the circumstances, Captain Siberil affirmed that the vessel could not be made ready in time.

Then came another complication – a German sea mine was washed ashore and into the path of a small rowing boat, in which the old man was to be transferred to a small fishing vessel. To make matters worse, the Germans had mounted a guard over the mine, so how would they be able to get the old man out? Captain Siberil sent to the local 'estaminet' for a certain lady, a member of the Resistance, who came down to the beach and enticed the sentry to take her to a remote place on the beach to make love, whilst Siberil put the old man on the boat for England.

Celestin Floch of Morlaix, was a great fancier and had a fine loft of racers at home. To fool the Germans, he mixed them up with tumblers, fantails and other pigeons. The German soldiers who inspected the civilian lofts in the Brest area never questioned the validity of the loft; most of them were ignorant of the many breeds of fancy pigeons.

One day, a German soldier who was an experienced fancier came to Morlaix. He visited the loft, immediately spotted the racers and gave a warning to Floch. As soon as the German left, the pigeons were transferred to a farm some miles away. Later, through the comradeship of the sport, Celestin and the German soldier became friendly, but the friendship didn't last too long as the German was transferred to the Russian front. Back came the racers to Morlaix and operations commenced again.

In June 1943, Captain Silberil came under suspicion by the Gestapo and word reached Floch through the pigeons that Siberil and his family were to be arrested. Floch's job in the movement was as the dispenser of false indentity papers.

He knew that he had to get to Celestin. He jumped on his bicycle and rode the six miles to Carontec in the dark. The trip had to be made over rocky coastal paths. Unfortunately, because of the terrain, Celestin fell from his bicycle and broke his ankle.

Although in great pain, he continued his journey to deliver the news and to issue false papers to the Captain and his family, who then went underground for four months. Madame Siberil and her son lay hidden in an underground cellar, never once coming into daylight. During this time, the Captain's young son contracted tuberculosis.

In November 1943, the Captain, harassed and sought after by the Gestapo, sailed for the haven to which he had sent so many fettered spirits, England.

Altogether, these wonderful members of the Maquis sent twenty small boats and their valuable cargoes to England. Mr Woodman had the honour of entertaining Celestin Floch and Captain Siberil after the war, when they stayed with him for two weeks.

Celestin became very well known to the members of the Plymouth Group. Captain Silberil, as the leader of the modern piracy that paid off, is now known as Captain Ernest Siberil, Legion of Honour, and Croix-De-Guerre.

After the war, Celestin became president of the Morlaix Flying Club and bred from pigeons from Mr Woodman's father-in-law, Peter Taw, who sold Captain Siberil two cocks and two hens from Dennis White's Champion Suffolk Punch strain – their progeny won eleven firsts and one second in their first year of racing.

Mr Woodman looked up the group records and found that pigeon HW43N.2360 returned from Morlaix on 8 September 1943; for some reason he never did get round to asking Celestin if he sent the bird back, but you can be sure that the grand pigeon fancier of Morlaix had something to do with it.

13

FRANK HOUGH OF MACCLESFIELD

Frank was another of our gallant lads who served so bravely in locations so very far away from home. Frank was seconded from his unit to the scheme as he had kept pigeons and raced at home. His first posting was with the Pigeon Service in Burma and India, and this was the letter he took with him:

Subject – Army Pigeon Service, No.SC/4554, 23 Div Sigs 30/1/43. To: 3/3 G.R.
Ref. 23 Div Letter No. G.523/19 of 29 Jan herewith by hand of the pigeoneer
No. 2367622 Sigmn Hough. F., who is accompanied by No. A9174 Sigmn Fateh Mohd, (Punjabi Musalman), the Indian pigeoneer.
They have with them: (a) rations for 14 days, (b) rations for pigeons for about a month, (c) 8 pigeons, (d) training baskets etc.
You are requested to arrange for their accommodation and future rations of personnel and pigeons.
The 15 cwt truck will take them as far as Sanshak and will be returned on 1 Feb to Rear HQ, 23 Div Sigs at Thoubal.
You are requested to give them every assistance in the construction of the loft as early as possible, so that the training of the birds may not be delayed.
Signed Lt-Col. 23 Div Sigs.

And this was the letter sent ahead of them:

From: G523/19, 23 Ind Div, 29 Jan 1943. To: 3/3 G.R.
Army Pigeon Service – Div Sigs are sending you eight carrier pigeons with one BOR Pigeoneer and one IOR Pigeoneer. The pigeons are for use between your patrols and advanced HQ at Chammu. To house them, a small loft will have to be built.
The pigeons are untrained and it will be some little time before they are ready for operational purposes. The BOR is experienced in the working of the birds and he has a copy of *The Homing Pigeon,* which is a guide to their handling. For the success of the scheme, it is important that you take a keen interest in the welfare and training of the birds and see that the pigeoneers are given every facility. If the scheme is a success your own communication problems should be simplified considerably.
Message holders have been demanded by wire and will be sent to you immediately on receipt.
The IOR Pigeoneer is a P.M.

Will you please render progress report every 10 days. Something quite brief is all that is required.

Signed Lt-Col. G.S.

Frank was to stay at this posting for less than six months and he left the pigeons with the Indian pigeoneer as he was recalled to his unit due to the Japanese expansion on the continent.

This was the copy handed over to Signalman Fatehkhan A9174 on 1 May 1943:

2 pigeons, red chequer cock 41T32 and blue hen 41.130.

42 bird baskets, 42 wire netted boxes and locks, 2 food troughs, 2 water troughs, 2 army books (P.S. message) 418, 8 performance cards, 12 message containers, 1 (*Roman Urdu*) book (*The Homing Pigeon*).

You will notice only one pair of pigeons was left. Frank told his son Martin that they had trouble with hawks initially when setting up the lofts in the jungle. It was so bad that Frank had to use his rifle to clear them from the surrounding area.

One story he told was about the first training toss, when they sent the pigeons to the next village in the valley, via the Naga tribesmen. When the pigeons failed to return, Frank asked the Gurkas who were attached to his unit to investigate. They returned saying that the Naga tribesman thought that the pigeons presented in baskets were presents and had eaten them. That was one avenue of training that was not used again.

Two other letters sent at the time from Captain J Roberts OC No. 3 Company read:

SUMMARY OF SERVICES. MESSAGES SENT, MESSAGES RECEIVED.

Please keep records giving the above information and ensure that they are forwarded to me on the first of each month. Some hens will be sent forward to you at the first opportunity, but actual breeding must not be done at working lofts, any eggs laid should be destroyed.

17 March.

Ref. Your reports, re: pigeons. Several returns required to be submitted each month and the following information must be forwarded:

Birds lost on service (Ring numbers must be given).

Birds lost from training or from the loft (Ring numbers must be given).

Birds died or destroyed (Ring numbers must be given).

When the birds have been trained and issued to units the following additional information must be forwarded on the first of each month:

Date, Unit using pigeon services, number of birds sent and received, flying distances, ring numbers, time taken, weather conditions.

This is how the Pigeon Service worked in the jungle.

Frank Hough, 1943.

14

A LETTER

To The Secretary
National Pigeon Service
22 Clarence Street
Gloucester

No. 2310/30/Signals 2
General Staff Branch
Signals Directorate
New Delhi
G.H.Q.A.P.O.
22 October 1945

Dear Sir,

In 1942 and 1943, the Indian Pigeon Service, which is part of the Indian Signal Corps, received considerable reinforcements of pigeons from the United Kingdom. These proved invaluable in the establishment of services in India and Burma and in May 1944, the Chief Signal Officer of the Fourteenth Army reported that pigeon lofts had proved themselves in operations.

The Service was considerably extended and young pigeons, bred from the original UK stock, withstood successfully the difficult climatic conditions in this theatre. Many were dropped by parachute behind the enemy lines and some returned with important information. Mobile lofts were used in Burma and the 'Boomerang' system was especially successful in the Arakan Campaign. Lofts were prepared for Malaya but the cessation of hostilities made their use unnecessary.

In India pigeons have been valuable in maintaining communications on the North West Frontier between small columns and their bases.

There is no doubt that the success achieved by the Army Pigeon Service in this theatre was the direct result of the excellent quality of the pigeons donated by the members of the National Pigeon Service. The assistance was greatly appreciated and I shall be obliged if you will kindly convey our grateful thanks to those fanciers who contributed pigeons for shipment to India.

Yours sincerely
(Signed) H.D. Beadon Brigadier
A/Signal Officer in Chief

15

INDIAN PIGEON SERVICE
(INDIAN SIGNALS)
JULY 1946

As we know, the Pigeon Service operated in many countries during the war years. We have heard that, among others, mobile lofts and Army Pigeon Services were based in Palestine, Africa, Egypt, Burma and Crete. One other location where the Pigeon Service

Members of the Indian Pigeon Service, Headquarters Indian Signals. From left to right, back row: Hari Singh, Seshaya, Ganga Dharan, Charan Singh, Kashiya, S. Venkatia. Fourth row: W/C Mana Khan, C/I/T. Mohd Aslam, Nk. Ramzan Ahmed Shah, Nusrat Hussain, Sgmn Fazal Karim, Karim Bux, Said Mohd, Mohd Sultan. Third row: Sgmn Zaman Shah, Hafiz Ullah, Nk. Wali Mohd, Sgmn Sardar Mohd, L/Nk. Mohd Bashir, Nk. Mohd Feroz, Sgmn Mohd Tazim, Nk. Allah Ditta, L/Nk. Imanat Ali, L/Nk. Ghulam Mahbob. Second row: L/Nk. Abdul Aziz, Haq Niwaz, Mohd Sadiq, Nk. Mohd Aslam, Dvr. J. Mackenzie, Sgmn B.K. Plummer, Sgmn L.C. Ridley, Nk. Johangir Khan, Sgmn Fateh Din, Sgmn Abdul Majid, Sgmn Abdul Jalil. Front row: Hav. Sher Mohd, Cpl R. Flaxman, CSM R.C. Talbott, Capt. W. Mathieson (I. Sigs), Major W.H. Law, (R. Sigs), Sub Mohd Akram, Sgt D. Bottomley, L/Cpl J. Coates, Hav./C. Din Mohd.

The British ranks of the Indian Pigeon Service, Indian Signals. From left to right, back row: Sgmn L.C. Ridley, L/Cpl J. Coates, Sgmn B.K. Plummer, Dvr. J. Mackenzie. Front row: Sgt D. Bottomley, Capt. W. Mathieson (I. Sigs), Major W.H. Law, (R. Sigs), CSM R.C. Talbott, Cpl R. Flaxman, 'Floss' the dog.

was invaluable was in India, where birds were deployed at Bangalore, Calcutta, Karachi, Rawalpindi and New Delhi. At the latter there were 400 pigeons based within twenty-four lofts, which demonstrates just what a massive operation it was to supply messages to the lofts at the various headquarters.

One of the members of the Indian Pigeon Service was Sergeant Dennis Bottomley. Dennis, like the rest of the NPS, did a sterling job under very difficult conditions. Today, Dennis is enjoying his retirement in Howarth, Yorkshire, from where he has sent these two wonderful photographs of those dark days of the war campaign in India.

16

THEY ALSO SERVED

Sunday 17 September 1944 dawned bright and clear, in this, the 263rd week of the Second World War. However, the relative peace of a wartime Sunday in the South East of England was shattered, as the first elements of the greatest airborne force in history took off.

Their principal objective was a bridge over the Lower Rhine, at a place few had heard of before, but which had become forever synonymous with courage – Arnhem. In addition to the 35,000 strong Allied Airborne Army, complete with artillery, vehicles and equipment, were eighty-two pigeons, one of whom is the subject of this story – mealy cock NPS.42.NS.15125.

Since the Allied invasion on D-Day, 6 June, weeks of bitter fighting now found the British 2nd Army poised on the Belgian Dutch border. Field Marshal Montgomery's plan was to lay a 'carpet' of airborne troops through Holland to enable the tanks and heavy artillery of his 2nd Army to strike quickly into the industrial heart of Germany, the Ruhr and bring the war to an end.

Along the route to be taken were three bridges. For the plan to succeed, these bridges had to be taken and held intact to enable the army to cross. First in line was the bridge at Grave over the Maas; next and largest was the bridge over the Waal at Nijmegen. The third and most vital bridge, key to the success of the whole operation, was the bridge over the Lower Rhine at Arnhem.

The 101st US Airborne Division, under the command of Major General Maxwell Taylor, was to be responsible for holding the smaller bridges over the canals between Eindhoven and Grave, as well as dealing with any enemy opposition along their stretch of the corridor. The 82nd US Airborne, led by Brigadier James Gavin, were to land on the stretch between Grave and Nijmegen and capture a ridge known as the Groesbeek Heights and take and hold the Nijmegen bridge. Commanded by Major General Urquhart, paratroops of the 1st British Airborne were to land sixty-four miles behind enemy lines and eight miles from their objective and hold the Arnhem Bridge until the 2nd Army reached them. Allied Commanders estimated that the Army would be there in two days.

The first news of the unopposed landing by British troops was flown to London by pigeons released by Corps, Commanders. As night fell, elements of 1st Airborne Division held the north end of the Arnhem Bridge. The bridge at Grave had been captured intact and the bridge at Nijmegen was still in enemy hands.

As for the progress of the 2nd Army: led by the Irish Guards, part of the Guards Armoured Division had encountered heavy resistance and had only been able to cover seven miles. The operation was already dangerously behind schedule. It had been believed that enemy forces in the Arnhem area were weak. However, British paratroopers soon found themselves facing hardened SS troops who were in Arnhem for rest and refit. On Monday 18 September, Lt-Col. Frost, with 500 men, were surrounded at the bridge. German Forces now occupied most of the town, therefore preventing any attempt at reinforcement. Troops detailed to hold the dropping zones in readiness for the second lift were also under heavy mortar and machine gun attack. Despite heavy resistance, the 4th Parachute Regiment came in, but was pinned down almost immediately. All day the British force at the bridge held. Although they were lightly armed, they stopped the German Army from crossing and successfully beat off repeated infantry attacks from the town.

The weather in Holland on Tuesday 19 September was clear. At 10.30 a.m. that morning, a mealy cock – NPS.42.NS.15125 – was liberated to fly to London. He covered the 283 miles, of which 135 miles were over open sea, in 284 minutes. The time taken would please most of us even now, but there were also difficulties. His condition, feather-wise, would have not been very good as this was late in September and the moult must have been well advanced. To fly alone over unfamiliar territory after being in confinement for three days, and being put up in the midst of a very noisy battle, says much for the constitution of the pigeon and the standard of care he must have received. In addition to these difficulties, he had further problems to face at the home end. The North Sea and most of southern England were fog-bound to the extent that the third lift, made up of Polish Forces under the command of Major General Stainislaw Sosabowski, was abandoned. The message carried gave information about the desperate situation at Arnhem Bridge and contained an urgent plea for re-supply. Due to the pigeon's efforts, an attempt at re-supply was made by Allied aircraft, which took off from an airfield in the Midlands unaffected by fog. Unfortunately, by the time this drop went in, the battle lines had altered and most of the supplies fell into enemy hands.

On Wednesday 20 September, the gallant force, still holding the northern end of Arnhem Bridge despite attacks by tanks and heavy artillery, were in a desperate situation. They were short of food and ammunition, with the original force of 500 now cut to approximately 150 men still capable of fighting. The houses in which they stood were being reduced to rubble as they came under heavy tank, mortar and artillery attack. The cellars were packed with wounded men. Time after time, these gallant few fought off enemy attacks. As houses became untenable, the troops dug themselves into the gardens and carried on. Eventually the situation became so grave that the wounded were in danger and the decision was made to withdraw. Only a handful of men were able to fight out, leaving the wounded in the care of the medics.

The position was soon overrun by German troops, who evacuated the wounded. An attack by British ground forces and American Airborne troops had taken Nijmegen Bridge, but they were still a long way from the troops besieged at Arnhem. Things did not improve, and it was found to be impossible to fly in the Polish brigade, but some supplies did reach the Division.

British troops had now been forced into a small area near Oosterbeek and were under heavy mortar and artillery fire. The weather continued to be bad, but in spite of this it was possible to fly in the majority of the Polish Parachute Brigade on

21 September. Nothing could be done on the next day, but the balance was dropped on 23 September. Despite the steep banks and heavy enemy fire, a brave attempt by Polish forces to support British troops went ahead and 200 men crossed the Rhine. But, despite further attempts to reinforce the troops on the night of 24 September, these were unsuccessful. South of the river, the enemy had twice cut the advance of the 2nd Army and although progress was steady, it was too slow.

The situation at Arnhem was by this time desperate and on 25 September it was decided to withdraw the bridgehead. That night, during a heavy rainstorm, 2,163 men of the British Airborne were ferried across the Rhine under heavy fire, leaving behind 1,200 dead and 6,642 missing, wounded or captured. In the nine days of Operation Market Garden, combined losses – airborne and ground forces in killed, wounded or missing – amounted to more than 17,000.

The bird NPS.42.NS.15125 became known as William of Orange and was awarded the Dicken Medal for his epic flight. After the war, he was brought back from the Army Pigeon Service by his breeder, Sir William Proctor Smith, and he died in 1960. In telling this story, the author makes no apology for the description of the whole operation as an example of courage and fortitude by all those involved. It has no equal.

Arnhem War Cemetery is situated not far from the last stronghold of the men who fought there. This sombre monument is the scene of a ceremony carried out every year on the weekend nearest to 17 September. Following a simple service, flowers are placed on every one of the graves of the British and Polish men who lie there.

HE DIDN'T DIE ALONE

One of the most moving stories I uncovered in my research for this book came from Eric Smallman of Kent. Eric is now in his nineties and not in the best of health and he wanted the world to know the story of his best friend in the Forces, Tom Millar.

Eric and Tom were called up together and served with the infantry in France. There was a terrible battle during which the British troops came under very heavy bombardment, which left many brave lads dead. Eric had been wounded as he tried to seek cover in No Man's Land. Tom, also badly injured, managed to make it into a trench, where he realised that his injuries were critical. In the meantime, Eric had been picked up by stretcher-bearers and taken to a field hospital.

It was some days later that Eric had recovered enough to inquire about his friend. Sadly, he was to discover that his great friend had died in the trench surrounded by dozens of his dead comrades. Some time later, Eric was fortunate to find the medic who found Tom, who told him that he had passed his personal possessions on to his company captain. He added that, when he removed Tom's dog tag from around his neck, a dead pigeon was also found inside his tunic.

Eric wasn't surprised that Tom would be near a pigeon, as before the war he was a well-known pigeon fancier, but how a pigeon came to be with Tom in the trench baffled him for many years.

After being demobbed, Eric went back to his old job as a baker but he never forgot his pal and, as a tribute to him, he subscribed to *Pigeon Weekly*, although he didn't have the first idea about pigeon racing. For many years he took this journal as, in some way, it kept the memory of Tom alive.

It was not until the early 1970s that he received a parcel that filled in the missing pieces of Tom's final hours. The package was sent by Tom's son, Brian, who had discovered various papers and pigeon-related papers that were kept by his late father, while he was going through some old stuff in the attic. On reading through, he found references to Eric and how his father had regarded him as a great friend. Brian thought it only right that these personal items should be sent to Eric in Tom's memory.

So after some investigating Brian found Eric's address and sent them on. It goes without saying that it was a very emotional time for Eric as he laid the contents upon the table and recalled those terrible days of the war. One of the items was a rather grubby and badly-worn little red diary that had the original black stubby pencil lodged in its spine. Carefully and tearfully, Eric read the contents that were to recall this fateful day when Tom was to die for his country.

As time went on and the years passed, Eric would often read Tom's words and he never really gave much thought as what to do with his personal effects. That was until he picked up the *Pigeon Weekly* last year and by chance read of the forthcoming book that I was writing on the war years. It wasn't long until I was to receive a call from Eric, who thought it would be a great tribute to his friend if the story were included in the book. A few days later I was to receive the diary, which I have to say was heartbreaking to read. I have set out below the last entry written by Tom before he died:

> Things don't look too good, I've been badly hurt, my left leg has been blown away from the knee, I don't think I will last much longer as I am losing too much blood. I'm in the South trench but everyone is dead, there is no movement, only the smoke and the smell. Please tell Mary and the children that I love them with all my heart, I hope they don't feel bad of me. I can't write much more, I am weak. I know I will soon be with my Maker, I am not afraid. I thought I was on my own but a red pigeon has just fallen from the sky and is just a few inches from me. He must be on service too. We make a good pair, I have one leg left, and he is missing a wing. I will keep him warm, we will go on together, goodnight, God bless, Tom.

GEO BARRETT, OBE

In 1947, Geo Barrett, OBE, reminisced about the National Pigeon Service. In September 1938, a resolution was passed by the International Pigeon Board for presentation to the under-Secretary of State, War Office, to the effect that, in the event of hostilities, the members of the unions affiliated to the Internal Pigeon Board would be pleased to place their birds and, when possible, their own services, at the disposal of the War Office.

The resolution of the International Pigeon Board was passed to the Director of Signals, Air Ministry and a conference was called by the deputy Director of Signals, Air Ministry in February 1939. When the original NPS committee was formed, it consisted of Mr T. Brown, then president of the International Pigeon Board, Major W.H. Osman and Geo Barrett, OBE – at that time, president of the National Homing Union. Mr J. Selby Thomas was appointed secretary to the newly-formed committee.

The committee was empowered, if circumstances demanded, to co-opt additional members to the committee. Eventually the committee consisted of seven members: Messrs T. Brown, E.G. Swan, T.R. Millar, R. Ingham, W.E. Hickmott, W.J. Kyle, and Geo Barrett as chairman. Each member of the committee was allocated to one of the respective military areas and was responsible for the Pigeon Service Activities in that command.

Originally, membership of the NPS was open to all true fanciers who maintained a loft of at least twenty trained pigeons of a standard approved by the committee. All members enrolled in the service were issued with a badge and certificate of membership. In 1940, it was necessary to agree to a policy to restrict recruitment to the Service to allow for sufficient members who would be in a position to supply the anticipated number of trained birds and produce the required number of young pigeons. This step was also necessary in view of the impending shortage of pigeon foods.

One of the first duties of the committee was the formation of a number of groups of NPS members who would be in a position to supply pigeons in the first instance, for use by Coastal Command. The actual supplying of pigeons for operational purposes was first begun in the RAF in November 1939. In May 1940, the War Office inaugurated the Army Pigeon Service and at a later stage groups were formed for the supplying of pigeons to the Home Guard, Police and Civil Defence Services.

Possibly the most important service was the supplying of birds for intelligence work overseas. Special Section groups of NPS members were formed and the members of these groups loaned their birds, knowing that possibly only a small percentage would ever return to their lofts. In spite of this, they sent their best birds and many an old favourite returned with important information from France, Holland, Belgium, Denmark and Norway. The people in these countries often risked severe punishment and even their lives in handling these pigeons, in order that they could get back to Britain carrying their vital messages.

Some 200,000 young birds were reared for use by the Services by the members of the NPS and the breeders' only compensation for the production of these young birds was a free grant of one CWT of pigeon food for every eight youngsters which they supplied to the Services. A fine lot of birds to the value of half a million sterling was sent and it is to the great credit of the breeders that only a very small percentage of the birds supplied had to be rejected.

It is pleasing to know, in spite of a demand by the Army authorities, that after strenuous efforts by the National Pigeon Service Committee, racing was allowed to proceed throughout the war period.

At the end of 1940, the situation in regard to pigeon food caused grave concern and conferences were called between the Ministry of Food, Air Ministry, War Office Representatives and the NPS Committee and it was eventually decided that the rationing of pigeon food and the control of selling prices would be necessary. The actual rationing of pigeon food came into force in 1941 in accordance with the Foodstuffs National Priority Mixture Order 1941. It was found to be necessary, owing to the shortage of the necessary grains, to confine the issue of ration cards to those fanciers who had been enrolled to membership of the NPS and who were either supplying trained birds or producing young birds for use by the various services. This, of course, came as a great blow to fanciers outside the NPS, but at the time of the original formation of the service, members did not come in the numbers which had been anticipated. Therefore, having missed the opportunity to enrol, large numbers of fanciers were deprived of the benefit of being able to obtain rationed pigeon food.

Unfortunately, the pigeon food situation became much worse as the war progressed and it became even worse after the cessation of hostilities. Geo Barrett was convinced that fanciers had quite a good deal when compared with others such as the fancy pigeons, cage birds and poultry.

It is very difficult to compress into this article full details of all that should be said about members of the NPS who came forward and so ably assisted the committee. Geoff hoped that no one would be slighted because he was not able to mention the names of all those who did such splendid work. But I must place on record the very helpful way in which he and fellow members of the committee were given birds worth many thousands of pounds for service, without any seeking or receiving of compensation when birds were lost.

Many thousands of miles were travelled by the members of the NPS Committee in their visits to lofts in their respective areas, and in attending meetings for the formation of NPS Groups.

The organisation of office work, which included thousands of forms, the issue of many thousands of food coupons and arrangements for meetings with the service departments, was carried out in a manner that was a great credit to the secretary. Mr J. Selby Thomas proved that in him we had an able organiser. The thanks of the committee are due to the National Homing Union for the loan of his services during the whole of the war period. I would also like to mention the very efficient staff who worked under Mr Selby Thomas.

In spite of criticism, not always just, or in the best taste, I think the committee and the members generally are satisfied that they did a good job and have nothing to regret – they were able to assist the country at a time when things were very black indeed.

17

LIFE IN THE ARMY PIGEON SERVICE

On transfer to the Royal Signals, Fred Wiltshire's light infantry training record stood him in good stead on a great many occasions. First of all there were tests to pass at the Holding Unit at Aldershot, both written and practical, before they were passed out. On getting through the tests, which took a month to complete, Fred and the others had postings to all parts of the country. Fred's first posting was Hitchen, where he met Sid Small, the NCO in charge of the loft, and he spent a happy few weeks looking after the birds and travelling to the various lofts in the command round the east coast, delivering their supply of corn. Being the holding unit for the command, they had drafts of young pigeons, to eventually be dispatched to the fixed lofts as required in the command.

At last, a message came through to report to Holt. This was one of the lofts Fred had delivered corn to. There he was introduced to Corporal Sid Edwards and he soon recognised some of the youngsters sent out from Hitchen a few weeks earlier. After settling in and getting to know what was expected, his kit finished up in the office attached to the loft, where he slept to get the birds out for their early morning exercise and also late at night. There was also the daily cleaning and scrubbing out to be done, plus preparing the birds for service. The birds had to be ready at all times; there was constant training to be done if the pigeons were not wanted for service.

From Holt it was to Yarmouth, to take over the loft while their Corporal went on leave. Here, everyone was under constant alert as 'Jerry' paid a visit night after night and the 'ACK' guns continually blazed. Eventually Fred returned to his old loft at Holt, and then there was a further posting to Colchester to take over the lofts there.

This loft had not been painted for some time, or whitewashed, and after words with the officer responsible for stores they had enough paint and whitewash to last until the end of the war.

When a draft of youngsters were sent as replacements, Fred rang the CO, complaining that ninety per cent were ridden with canker and asking who was responsible. A few weeks later he was back in Aldershot on draft for overseas for his trouble. The feeling of the men on draft was, if you complained there was only one place for you – out of the country.

The First World War mobile lofts were still there, but they soon had new ones plus half-a-dozen called 'mousetraps'. These were easily erected and housed thirty birds. They were invaluable as they could be set up very quickly on any terrain. The other lofts were built like present-day caravans and had to be towed. The personnel's time was spent getting the birds used to them, particularly with the 'mousetraps' – although it could be said that it took the men longer to get used to these new lofts than the pigeons. Major Neilson Hutton was in charge and many an unfortunate man felt his wrath for overfeeding whilst trying to break birds out. Whilst there, one NCO failed to salute a brigadier, the punishment being that the section was given two hours' square-bashing every day, with Fred having to take them. This lasted for a fortnight, as one morning RSM Brittian, the senior RMS of the British Army, was drilling a squad of OCTU cadets. As he was marching them in their direction, Fred saw him out of the corner of his eye and encouraged the men to really give their best. RSM Brittian halted his squad and in no uncertain terms told his men that he wanted them to drill as well as Fred's men. This resulted in a word of congratulation to the OC from the RSM.

The next morning, assembling the squad ready for their two-hour stint, Fred was told to take them on a route march as a reward for their work the previous day, with instructions to march them to Ash. In Ash there was a café that made the finest cup of tea for miles around. After a quick word to fall out, the lads were soon inside and arrived back in time for lunch. From then on there was no more drill.

Time was then taken up with lectures on every subject they were likely to encounter. There was also training on the two-way system and they eventually established a regular service. Then there were a few schemes as part of the training on how to behave when the real thing happened and then there was embarkation leave. One or two men were recalled to make up the advance party to take the birds and equipment overseas. In the party were Sid Shorter, Roy Mundy and Curly Johnson, who became loft manager to Fuller Isaacson after the war. Fred was in charge of this party of men.

Five days in Liverpool followed, while the ship was undergoing a refit. The trip overseas proved to be very eventful as the next boat to them in the convoy was torpedoed. On reaching the Bay of Biscay, they faced the roughest seas for fifteen years according to one of the sailors. Things didn't improve, as Fred was to have his first set-to with authority. The birds in baskets were hanging over the side of the ship, with orders that no one was to pass a certain point. Fred asked to see the ship's adjutant to get permission to rescue the birds that looked like they were going to a watery grave. With difficulty this was obtained and after a little trouble the baskets were retrieved without loss, and the birds were securely battened down. The destination was eventually reached in the dark, with the lads spending all night unloading the equipment and getting it ashore without incident.

On their first trip to Algiers, where they had landed, Sid Shorter and Fred found a merchant seaman in a bad way with a knife wound under his nose. They escorted him back to the port only to find that his ship had sailed. They left him with the port authorities, knowing that he would be well taken care of. Thanks to Sid, they eventually found their way back to billets, but it took some working out.

The following days consisted of looking after the birds, while the nights were free as it was dark at 7 p.m. A month later, the rest of the lads arrived. It was all action then, lining the loft up and letting out the birds for the first time.

Losses were particularly heavy for the first day or two. This was understandable under the circumstances to everyone except Major Hutton. He called Fred to his office and instructed him to take complete charge of the lofts, with the following words: 'I'll have your guts for garters if you lose any more birds.' It is uncertain whether it was luck or good judgement on everyone's part, but they never lost another pigeon while at that location.

Orders came to move on and they soon found themselves travelling through the Atlas Mountains – and suffered a slight setback when one of the lofts had slid over the mountain. Fortunately, it was one of the two-wheeled affairs, and the pin it stood on when stationary had slipped down and dug into the ground, thus holding the loft. When it was eventually hauled up, they found a white-faced Roy Mundy inside, so this was a serious matter at the time as personnel were not supposed to travel in the lofts but it certainly caused a few laughs later on.

The soldiers' job was to get behind German lines and establish communication in the event of a wireless silence. It was no fun watching the convoys going through and being dive-bombed, machine gunned and facing heavy artillery fire. All this time, Fred and his boys were moving from location to location, sometimes ten miles, sometimes forty miles. The lofts were well split up by now, but they all had the same job to do.

The birds did a wonderful job, mainly due to the patience of the men in charge. After one battle, Captain Smith and Fred went to inspect their next move. The carnage that greeted them was terrible – just seventy-nine men out of a whole battalion were left. Fred picked up a rifle there and kept it with him for the rest of his time in North Africa. Meanwhile, the troops were emphatically told never to go outside the white lines beyond where the mine detectors had gone, as the Germans had laid mines everywhere.

The lads obeyed the instructions, but in one instance the unit they were attached to had half a dozen men scattered to the winds through disobeying the orders. When Fred and the soldiers arrived at Medges el Bab, they were confronted by mountains of wheat, but the fear of being mined was enough to keep them away. They turned their attention to erecting the 'mousetraps' on the roof of a high building; this did not deter the birds, and, in fact, they performed with distinction. It was here that the message came, delivered by pigeon, of the fall at Tunis. On receipt of the message, it was delivered to a dispatch rider, who had instructions to take it to headquarters, where it was relayed to England by wireless. Through this operation the news of the fall of Tunis was known by the English before the majority of people in North Africa. The pigeon was later named 'The Bey of Tunis'.

It was here, at Medges el Bab, that Fred was performing the duties of guard commander. As he left the guardroom to inspect the guards, he was greeted by German soldiers in their dozens, who had been asleep all along the road, having given themselves up, knowing that the end was near. Fred carried on past them to see the sentry, who was talking to a German sergeant who spoke good English. He said that most of the men had just come from Russia and were thankful that the war was over. It was a very relieved guard commander that returned to the guardroom that day.

With hostilities over, the troops moved on to Tunis to await news of their next move. It was at this time that Fred went into a field general hospital outside the town to give Fred Adamson his 'mousetrap'. He would erect it on a ship moored between North Africa and Sicily. The birds now had to work in conjunction with the troops in Italy. Fred had instructions to let out the 'Bay' first, in order to get the rest settled, and they all did a first-class job. Their location aboard the ship did not upset the birds at all, as they had become used to moving around so much during the trip from Algiers to Tunis. The 'Bay of Tunis' was a super pigeon and the credit for the whole job was entirely his. During the troops' travels, they captured an Italian mobile loft and Harold Barnett, who was an engineer in civilian life, soon had it in working order – the engine had to be repaired before it was usable. It was to prove an added asset, particularly as there was soon to be a replacement set of birds sent by the Americans. All the lofts were called in, with the personnel split into three shifts of four hours each.

After a time, they travelled back to Algiers, half the section going by road, the others by train. They were not like the English trains, being just a flat bed on wheels, but the section arrived safely and were anxious to get back with the pigeons.

Final orders came through and they embarked on an American Liberty ship, destination unknown. They eventually finished up on the Clyde in the middle of winter, and finally reached Yorkshire and home, for a spot of well-earned leave.

18

MIDDLE EAST PIGEON SERVICE MEMORIES

BY J. INCH OF PORTSMOUTH

Mr Inch was one of those men who went right through Italy with 9 HQ and 21 HQ. Firstly, he went with Sgt Peberdy down to Brindisi and later travelled with Sgt Ted Crossland under the command of Major Harford. Mr Inch also had the experience of going across the Adriatic to the islands of Vis and Lagosta, just opposite Split on the mainland of Yugoslavia.

At a time when the Germans occupied all of Yugoslavia and Greece, Mr Inch and his company were attached to Special Service and a commando group. It was not much of a job then, as they could not train the birds from the mainland during the day as Jerry had the run of the coast down to Albania. To 'out' in an MTB during daylight would mean certain death from the German patrol planes, but they did get a few birds across as the Commandos made contact with the Yugoslav partisans at night. The birds were liberated during the day to get back to the island of Vis. The losses were terrific due to the birds not having enough training and, above all, these islands were full of hawks, which terrified the bird.

Mr Inch remembers the first attempt to settle the birds after just three days on the island. It was an hour before dusk and, along with G. Francis, he let the pigeons out and kept them circling the loft, before dropping them and playing around with them with the corn tin. All seemed well, when all of a sudden the birds started circling higher and higher and two huge hawks appeared. That was the last they saw of this team of birds.

Mr Inch had enlisted in 1942, and the first four months consisted of hard infantry training with the Hampshires. He had then asked for a posting to the Royal Corps of Signals, (Army Pigeon Section), and was sent to Aldershot for five weeks of Army pigeon schooling.

Along with his two mates, G. Francis and Fred Adamson of Brentform and Bacup, he was posted to Scotland. Then there was a period of leave, but before he knew it they were recalled and on their way to North Africa with the 1st Army. These three soldiers were sent in advance of any other pigeon personnel.

After six weeks in Algiers, they were eventually picked up by Major Hutton's section. From Algiers they went through North Africa and finished up at Tunis.

Most of the birds were supplied by the American Pigeon Service, but pigeons were hardly used in this part of North Africa.

After the capture of Tunis and the end of the African campaign, most of the pigeon personnel were sent back to England, but Mr Inch and a few others were sent to Italy to join up with Sgt Alf Peberdy, a real pigeon man. After a short stay at Brindisi, the breeding centre for all the mobile lofts in Italy, they had the pleasure of meeting some grand fanciers – Bobby Jenkinson of Huddersfield, Ernie Smith of London and Bob Wilton of Street, amongst others.

From Brindisi, many birds were trained at sea to fly back from Albania. Often, the pigeons were taken out several miles by motorboat for release.

As time went by, Mr Francis and Mr Inch were sent with a basket of pigeons to establish a loft on the island of Vis. This, they recorded, was one of their greatest experiences. After a few weeks on Vis they were relieved and sent back to Brindisi.

The next posting was to join some of the lofts operating a few miles from Monte Casino. From here, all the lofts were continually on the move, never staying static for long.

The Germans made their longest stand at Rimini and here three lofts were kept going. From here, hundreds of messages were carried by the pigeons. Mr Inch was in the company of Corporal Wilson, Sergeant Alex King, Corporal Ernie Smith and others. On the first night, they pulled into Catolica, a mile from Rimini. The group was going to set up camp in a field but changed plans at the last minute. Luck was certainly with them, as during the night Jerry sent over a few planes and dropped bombs in the very field they had left.

The lads were to stay here for eight weeks, up to their necks in mud. Eventually, they were moved into the mountains overlooking Bologna, but the enemy was on its last run. From then on it was a holiday, with these brave lads going on to Venice and Austria to finish their Army service.

While at Klagenfurt, Mr Inch met Reub Barnett of Dulwich. Reub was one of those disappointed fanciers who was unlucky and could not get posted to the Pigeon Service. He had to be content as a 'DON R', but he had nevertheless fixed up a loft in the German barracks at Klagenfurt.

19

THE NAVAL PIGEON SERVICE

When the War Committee was formed, I expressed an opinion that it might be called upon to discuss the use of pigeons as messengers in the near future. Hostilities had not been in progress many months before this view materialised and the Admiralty decided that pigeons might render useful services.

One of the earliest steps taken by the enemy was to lay mines in the North Sea to endanger our merchant shipping, as well as naval work. It became necessary to organise a service of trawlers for minesweeping, for which service our fishing fleet of trawlers bravely responded. Many of these trawlers, when they put to sea, had no means of reporting progress or communicating with their base.

I felt I could not accept the position of lieutenant in the RNVR offered to organise this service, but Mr Romer, having at that time just retired from professional work and having relatives in the Navy, was offered and accepted the post, with my son as assistant.

My son had previously, on several occasions, offered himself for active service, but on account of defective eyesight and varicocele, he had been rejected. He was therefore glad of some opportunity of service in the war.

The owners of the lofts to be employed were chosen from those living as near the coast as possible. The service was placed under the direction of Col. Dixon, a most efficient officer and organiser, with Lieut. Romer as expert pigeon officer.

Having obtained a list of suitable lofts, letters were semt to the owners asking for their co-operation and the use of their birds – in not one case did they meet with refusal. Although the service was started in October 1914, when the birds were badly in moult, I at once put every bird in my loft in training, as my home loft was only thirty miles from the coast.

I had sixty birds at that time. Over thirty had flown 400 to 500 miles as my loft had just got to the top of its form in 1914. Although these birds were trained day after day throughout the winter of 1914, and from then on throughout the war, my losses were comparatively small. The distance birds had to fly for the Naval Pigeon Service was from seventy to 150 miles. By giving them constant liberty in all weathers, they covered these distances, both in winter and summer, with regularity. As an example, on three successive weeks I had one pigeon return from the middle of the North Sea bringing dispatches and she was one of those subsequently awarded a certificate of merit for her work in this service. Some of these messages were of a thrilling nature, but the receivers were not allowed to divulge their contents.

In some cases, they were in code and, of course, it was then impossible to decipher them. I remember one of the dispatches my birds carried from the North Sea described an attack made upon the minesweeping fleet by a zeppelin, the first time that a zeppelin had ever left Germany to attack us. The skipper of the trawler described what had taken place and reported that the minesweepers remained uninjured and were able to continue their work after the zeppelin had tried to destroy them. Evidently, at this stage, the zeppelin crew's aim was not very accurate over the sea.

When it is remembered the rough passage these birds had, sometimes sparsely fed, and that they were often handled by brawny sailormen who had been given but a few lessons in fastening messages on the birds before use, it is surprising how consistently and well they homed.

This is a credit to their breeding and to the owners who, like myself, did not hesitate to offer their very best for the service. On one occasion, I lost three of my most valuable birds and never heard of them again. I felt sure that, if given their liberty, at any distance or in any weather, these birds would have homed. It was not until the conclusion of the war that I heard my good pigeon, 1100, and the other two lost with him, must have been sunk by an enemy torpedo, as the trawler, with all hands on board as well as the pigeons, was never heard of again after putting to sea.

Some of the skippers of these trawlers got very fond of the pigeons and treated them as friends, but there was sometimes a comic side to the messages sent. One skipper sent a message, 'All well, having beef pudding for dinner.' As owners had to take all messages received to the nearest Post Office, this message would pass through to the Lords of the Admiralty and then back to the base to which this particular trawler was attached. For the duration of the war, that skipper was known as 'Beef Puddings'.

One of the most fortunate and meritorious performances in the Naval Service was that of the red chequer cock known as 'Crisp VC'. When the skipper of the trawler *Nelson* was attacked by a U-boat, he defied the Germans and fought his ship to the last. Lying mortally wounded on the deck, he scribbled a hasty message, which was sent off by this pigeon. This was his last act before he died. The pigeon carried it to a vessel in the vicinity and help was sent to the gallant trawler crew. It arrived in time to save the rest of them from death. Skipper Crisp was posthumously awarded the VC.

20

THE OSMAN FAMILY

The Osman family is very well known in the world of pigeons, with three generations involved in compiling information for many splendid articles and books on the war years. We will always be grateful to Lt-Col. A.H. Osman OBE, Major W.H. Osman and Colin Osman.

On 17 August 1928, Mr Osman received a letter from his old chief whom he served under on the headquarters staff at Horse Guards. It read, 'During the war, we scarcely or properly appreciated all that pigeons did for the cause.' Mr Osman also believed that neither the general public nor the fanciers themselves realised the scope of carrier pigeons during their service in wartime. It took Mr Osman a good many years to decide to compile the details that may remove any doubt that the carrier pigeon service was a valuable one on all fronts.

He received much sympathy and help in the arduous work undertaken in connection with the service, from people such as Col. H. de Watteville, Captain Ashmead Bartlett and General Shaw. To these officers great thanks are offered for all the consideration shown to Mr Osman at all times.

THE INTELLIGENCE SERVICE

After being attached to RE Signals in the early stages of the organisation of the Carrier Pigeon Service, Mr Osman was eventually attached to the Intelligence Corps. It was here that the pigeons helped enormously in the silent and efficient messenger work they performed.

Just one of their uses involved a small balloon that was constructed with a metal bank worked by clockwork. This band was attached to a small basket containing a single pigeon with a message-holder on its leg, and to each basket was attached a small parachute. The balloons were then automatically released in favourable wind conditions at regular intervals.

These were dropped into Belgium and French territory when it was occupied by the Germans. In each basket was a request in French and Flemish to the finder to supply intelligence information that was needed. Much valuable information was obtained in this manner. This method was so successful that the Germans placed posters throughout Belgium, which read: 'The enemy is in the habit of dropping from aeroplanes little baskets containing homing pigeons, by means of which they desire to obtain information concerning this side of the line. The pigeons are placed in small baskets and marked, PLEASE OPEN. Any person who finds one of these baskets must, without tampering with it, report to the nearest Military Authorities. All persons are forbidden to open the baskets or any letters attached to them from the location they were found. Inhabitants disobeying these orders are liable to the severest punishment. If they attempt to escape they run the risk of being shot instantly. Any town in which these pigeons are secreted is liable to a fine of 10,000 to 100,000 francs.'

In addition to the issue of this proclamation, the Germans set a trap for those who might discover the birds and be tempted to use them. They removed the British pigeons and replaced them with one that would home to one of their lofts. So if anyone attached their name and address to the message, they would be arrested and shot as a deterrent. For this reason, the instructions sent a warning never to use any names. They also asked for the birds to be released at night so that they would return to Britain in the morning.

This method succeeded for a while but it was then decided to try other means, namely that our aircrews should carry a brave Belgian who would be willing to descend with a basket of pigeons by parachute at night, when a favourable position for his drop was reached. Many brave men were found for such a task.

For this service, Mr Osman designed a special basket in the shape of a fisherman's creel that strapped onto the parachutist's back. He carefully wrapped the birds in paper and packed them in straw.

This was a success, except that at the outset great difficulty was experienced in getting the man to jump from the plane at the chosen time.

A special aircraft was designed in such a fashion that the seat on which the man sat gave way automatically when the pilot moved the lever, which allowed the man to gracefully parachute to earth. In almost all cases, this scheme was successfully executed, apart from on one occasion when the aircraft crashed and one of these brave men was tragically killed . The other man released all the pigeons and news was received of the disaster.

The carrying of larger objects than the ordinary message presented some difficulty, and when Mr Osman was told about the object he decided that the tail of the bird should be used as the carrier.

The method was to thread a piece of fine wire through each side of the outside tail feathers, leaving two loose ones to come underneath. One piece of wire was then threaded through the strongest tail feathers near the root of the tail and this was repeated about two inches lower down the tail.

The package to be sent was held by two thin pieces of wire at the same distance apart and then attached to the loose wires under the tail; a whole sheet of newspaper could easily be delivered in this manner. It was certainly an ingenious method.

Behind enemy lines, our agents would flag a signal at night and relays of pigeons would be dropped. The message or parcel would then be attached to the bird, which was liberated to return to its loft the following morning.

Although the Germans boasted of their intelligence service, our Pigeon Service was as good as any used at any point during the war. Considering the extent to which Britain used pigeons for intelligence work, it is surprising that it was deemed necessary that every precaution should be taken to prevent the promiscuous release of pigeons in this country during the conflict.

On one occasion, on boarding a foreign steamer from a neutral country off Newcastle, a dozen racing pigeons were found, but the skipper had them killed and said that he always carried live pigeons to kill for food.

Mr Basil Thompson's men were a bit slow in getting hold of these birds before they were killed; we could have used them to send the enemy some 'useful' news.

The German message holders used for their service were very finely made and although we often captured pigeons, few of the holders came to the fore. When one was obtained, Mr Osman contacted Carter of Birmingham, who was able to copy them so accurately that it was impossible to tell them from the original. A trick often played on the Germans was to send them bogus messages with their own captured pigeons.

21

LETTERS

The Secretary
National Pigeon Service
22 Clarence Street
Gloucester

Headquarters
United Kingdom Base
A.P.O. 413 U.S. Army
25th August 1945

Dear Sir

On behalf of the Signals Corps, United States Army, I would like to express sincere appreciation to the members of the National Pigeon Service for the help and co-operation, which they have so generously extended.

During the operations of our forces in the European Theatre, British Pigeon Fanciers furnished 46,532 pigeons for our use. Some of these birds landed with American troops on D-Day and communication by pigeon continued until the final surrender of Germany.

We will recognise that this abundant supply of carrier pigeons would not have been possible without the splendid assistance of the many civilian breeders of your organisation, who, without cost to us, kept our needs constantly supplied.

It would be impossible to express our gratitude personally to each member of the National Pigeon Service who participated, so that I am taking this method of conveying our thanks to the entire group.

Yours very truly.

(Signed) F.S. Strong Junior
Brigadier General U.S.A. Commanding

Home Office
Whitehall
London
10th May 1945

Sir,

Now that hostilities have ceased in Europe and the immediate danger to the security of our country has been entirely removed, the Secretary of State would like to take this opportunity to express his appreciation of the co-operation given to the police by the local representatives of the National Pigeon Service throughout the war years.

From the outbreak of war, the police have been faced with many duties relating to pigeons, which have been rendered necessary in the interests of national security. The execution of these duties was no easy matter for those unfamiliar with the technicalities of pigeon flying; by generously placing their time and experience at the disposal of the police, the National Pigeon Service representatives have enabled them to carry out their tasks with a thoroughness and consideration, which would not otherwise been possible.

Although happily never called upon to assist against invasion of this country by the enemy, the readiness of the National Pigeon Service representatives help in preparations for such a contingency and to give further assistance if it were needed, was of the very greatest value to both the police and the other authorities concerned.

The Secretary of State for Scotland desires to be associated with this expression of thanks and wishes his appreciation to be conveyed to the National Pigeon Service representatives in Scotland. I am asked that you will bring the contents of this letter to all in the National Pigeon Service with a request that they will accept the grateful thanks of the Secretary of State.

22

A BRAVE AND VALIANT HEART FROM THE WEST COUNTRY

The war clouds hung in sombre hue over the British Isles in 1941. We were battered, but unbroken, and were badly prepared for total war. Planning, scheming and organisation were the order of the day while we stood fast and firm in this island fortress.

Out of this turmoil was born a service with the objective of bringing news and vital military information from the torn and bleeding heart of France, now occupied by the enemy. How was this to be accomplished? It was to be by pigeon, the courier used in so many battles and on so many occasions by warriors of the past.

A few selected lofts and groups of lofts were chosen for the task and it must be borne in mind that this service had yet to win its spurs and prove its usefulness in modern warfare. In early July of that year, a call was made for the supply of birds on the Bridgewater group of lofts operating under Pigeon Supply Officer Mr J. Seaman. As well as the men being 'up from Somerset' in answer to that Churchillian clarion call of 'blood, tears, toil and sweat', their pigeons , with steady wingbeat, were also ready to do their part for the freedom that they and we might have and hold fast that blessed state of liberty.

The early bank of Somerset pigeons arrived at headquarters on 5 July and were conveyed to an airfield known as 'up the road'. Here, each was placed in a separate cardboard container with parachute and all instructions attached. They were loaded onto the giant aircraft and headed away into the moonlight and, at her rendez-vous, the boxes at the end of the parachutes slowly made their way down to the soil of France.

Some days later, from the very midst of the enemy, a message was proudly borne aloft and our courier fought the wide expanse of the Channel and arrived at his home in Bridgewater, Somerset on 19 July, bearing one of the earliest messages brought by this means – he was a veritable pioneer. It was nearly a hundred to one chance against being released, to attempt the journey, and then the hazards encountered in flight had to be reckoned with. The casualties were heavy, but this did not deter our men and pigeons of Somerset. Our feathered hero was again floating down over France on 7 September, and he was back again with another message on 9 September. Many would have said that he had done enough.

Casualties grew higher and higher, but the information was of such importance that the task had to go on. One mission took place on 26 November, when the pigeon was released over Montagne, France. It was a cold night, so the odds were stacked against him being able to survive the freezing conditions. This brave and valiant bird fought a terrific duel, for again he conquered the Channel crossing and arrived with yet another message.

He was now a veritable 'ace' flyer, but, as with the 'Battle of Britain' pilots, there was no time to rest on laurels won, and again the call came for another trip.

Like so many of our valiant airmen, our game pigeon was reported missing on operations. Days became months, leaving an aching void in a Somerset man's heart. The pigeon joined the ranks of the brave and was posthumously awarded a medal, bearing the Royal Signals emblem, as a token of remarkable service.

Mr Bryant Snr of Bridgewater was a man with a very full heart as he received this medal from the Director of Signals on behalf of his son, who was serving his country whilst his pigeon, the blue pied cock number 6, was gaining renown for him and Somerset.

23

WHICH WAS FIRST?

Recent comments in the *Racing Pigeon* concerned the deeds of 'Section Hope', who brought information from the Normandy beaches. S. Grose of Exeter has sent more information on this topic, in which the question was asked, 'Which pigeon was the first to bring back messages from the D-Day landings?' The general opinion is that no one really knows the answer and, of course, the situation is further complicated by the fact that both paratroopers and land forces carried pigeons as part of their communication systems. Indeed, only last year, while visiting the museum situated at the Merville Battery Complex, it was obvious that pigeons had been used for message-carrying purposes during the course of the operation against the massive German gun battery.

One of the first birds known to have brought messages from Normandy was 'The Duke of Normandy', owned and bred by Gaston Noterman. After six days in a basket, the grand cock bred in 1941 was landed with special invasion paratroops deep behind the German beach defences and was liberated at 6.00 a.m. on D-Day. Despite the barrage and gunfire, he faced the northerly Channel gales and heavy rain to drop with an operational message at the home loft in London within twenty-four hours, although no specific time was given.

Included in the information sent by Mr Grose was a letter written by George Stubbs of Portsmouth dated 1969, at which time he was ninety-two years old. The letter covered many aspects of the war and started from the time he joined the Army Pigeon Service attached to Thorney Island Bomber Command, which collected the birds required from him.

When France was invaded by Germany, Winston Churchill made a broadcast to the French fleet, asking them to make for British ports. Mr Barrett, head of Army Pigeon Service, asked George if he had two pigeons that could fly 400 miles from the Continent. George had a cock that had won Twentieth Mirande N.F.C. in 1939 and a hen that had flown to Bordeaux in 1939, and he was duly advised that the APS would send for them when required. The following week, R. Byrne, later Captain Byrne, serving in the APS, called to collect the birds and advised George not to expect a pigeon for at least seven days. The second bird would follow after a further seven days and any messages received should be telephoned to Whitehall. The birds were dropped into France with two French Officers, who were subsequently captured and shot; the two birds were also destroyed. In addition, when invasion of the country was expected, George received a letter from the Air Ministry advising him that, in the case of invasion, his birds would not be destroyed, because his loft was considered a service loft.

As the war progressed, Thorney Bomber Command acquired sufficient pigeons of their own and kept them in their own lofts. When America joined the Allies, George's loft of birds was turned over to them.

On D-Day, the Americans carried sixteen of George's birds into battle with them, but, because of his duties as Air Raid Warden, George was not at the loft when the first of the birds arrived. However, he was informed that they had received the first message back in Britain from Normandy in just over two hours.

Of the sixteen birds sent, only nine returned. No doubt some of the lost pigeons were casualties of German sharp-shooters who were only too aware that pigeons in the vicinity of the battlefield invariably carried vital messages.

As the war was reaching its end, George's lofts of birds were transferred back to the Army Pigeon Service, where their next operational task was at Arnhem. The Army had seventeen pigeons from George's loft, which included the nine that returned from D-Day. Out of the seventeen, only one returned with a message and was duly named 'Arnhem Billy'. Sadly, many of the pigeons dropped at Arnhem were later found dead in their containers in the cornfields, and were only discovered when the corn was cut. 'Arnhem Billy' went on to be the first bird timed in the NFC in its first race from Bordeaux after the end of the war.

During the war George used his own family of pigeons, although he did have NPS pigeons offered to him. He had no knowledge of the conditions for applying to the Dicken Medal award, but he did know one was awarded to Thorney Island Lofts.

Only really bad weather will prevent a bird from flying. This has been proved, without any shadow of a doubt, by the use of pigeons in the services. If the sport of racing pigeons is to be used as a means to an end in finding and breeding a type of pigeon which will really race to its home, lessons should be taken from the experiences of practical fanciers in the forces.

Signalman V. Parkin, serving with Paiforce (after Ilfracombe DHS), wrote to me about pigeons in North Africa and Middle East. He refers to the pigeons recently commented upon by Signalman Cyril Fox (India). Signalman Parkin says he noticed that all the pigeons in Sollum were either blues or blue chequers.

These pigeons were like rock doves, with a very small wattle and a head like that of a thrush. They had thin primaries and plenty of space between vent and keel, and also handled like thrushes. Signalman Parkin writes that when he was in the Pigeon Service he handled plenty of real pigeons (NPS), which were almost as difficult to train. These native pigeons had red eyes and one pair had made a home in a burnt-out tank. He had five pigeons with him, two blues, a silver chequer, a pied which the Arab children gave him and one with feather legs which is 'all Tumbler'.

Signalman Parkin went on to say that 'the unions should buy up service lofts and equipment in the interests of fanciers returning from the forces, even if they do nothing about corn.'

He feared that ex-serviceman and others would stand little change of restarting unless the unions get a firm grip on things, particularly in connection with new housing schemes. He added that he was afraid the serving men would be forgotten more than ever after the victory had been gained and felt the Paiforce and Burma men had already been forgotten.

24

TONY KEHOE INVESTIGATES THE IRISH CONNECTION

Tony Kehoe was a little apprehensive as he approached the security checkpoint at Cathal Brugha Barrack in Dublin. With his ID and letter of invitation to the Military Archives at the ready, Cdr Peter Young, OIC, had informed him that they had various files on the Pigeon Service of the 1930s and 1940s which might be of interest to him. They also had Military Intelligence files for the Second World War, which listed all the fanciers in the country and the details of missing and lost pigeons.

It was Young's colleague, Cdr Victor Lang, who met Tony and had all the relevant files ready for inspection. Tony didn't go empty-handed, as he took along the book *Pigeons in Two World Wars* and a folder with details of the British Army Pigeon Service in Ireland up to 1922, which Tony know Cdr Young would be interested in. Added to that, he included a few articles such as the one by Captain E.E. Jackson from 'Squills', in 1918. In it, he highlighted his involvement with the Pigeon Service in Belgium, France and Ireland. It was evident that he had the highest regard for the Irish pigeons and found that it was much harder to fly pigeons in Ireland than on the Continent. When he left Ireland, he was replaced by Wing Commander W.D. Lea Rayner who wrote in details about the Pigeon Service.

Tony's research revealed that, early in 1923, an application was made from the Belfast HPS to the Ministry of Home Affairs of the newly-formed Irish Free State for permission to race from racepoints such as Wexford. It caused some concern for the Ministry, who in turn wrote to the Minister of Defence asking, 'Will you please state whether it is desired to prohibit or control the use of such pigeons, or is there any objection to these races being held?' Common sense prevailed; the Minister stated that he had no objections to these races and saw no reason to prohibit them.

There was nothing more about the next thirteen years and then, amazingly, Tony discovered that in 1936, the Army had had its own lofts in Curragh Camp in County Kildare. A report on the amount of corn used, number of birds in stock, young birds hatched and losses in training were sent to GHQ in Dublin.

Tony then found two beautiful catalogues of M. Renier Gurnay's sale, held in Brussels on Christmas Day in 1936. The Department of External Affairs had forwarded the catalogues to the Army with the view that the Irish Army would purchase birds to use for breeding purposes. The 1937 *Stud Book* says that Mons Gurney was Christmas World Champion for forty years, right up to 1936, when, owing to ill health and old age, his loft was disbanded. The Department certainly went for the best birds. What was surprising was that, at this point, the Second World War was still three years away, so one wonders whether they expected the worst, or at least were preparing for it.

On the other side of the Irish Sea, Lea Rayner reports that, also in 1936, the International Pigeon Board offered the services of the members of the unions, said to number 120,000, to the Under Secretary of State at the War Office in the event of hostility.

Tony also found the Military Intelligence files were an eye-opener with the information they had on the sport and it was only natural that he sought the big names. He couldn't find anything on Stewart Cant on the Dublin list but came across the name Rochcliffe & Cant, 7 Hawthorne Terrace, Church Road. Stewart lived in nearby Fairfield Avenue. Tony wondered if that racing partnership had anything to do with the fact that he came from Scotland and that Ireland was a neutral country during the war.

The control of racing and homing pigeons was taken very seriously and all unringed birds had to be wingstamped, with one number allocated to each owner and letters added to identify individual birds. Fanciers were encouraged to procure rings from Mr P.J. Maley, North Strand, Dublin, who was secretary of the Southern Provincial Council of the Irish Union.

The list of clubs given for 22 August 1944 was very interesting, as was the list of unrung birds. Kilkenny had one member and one bird. Waterford's three members had nine pigeons, Cork North's ten members had twenty-three, Dungarvan's five members had forty-two and Limerick had twelve members with ninety-one birds. There were also some clubs with membership only, such as Drogheda with twenty-three, Wexford ten and Kerry two.

In the case of a stray pigeon, whether Irish or from outside the country, a report in duplicate had to be forwarded by the District Garda Officer to the Crime Branch, Section 3 in Dublin. Birds bearing Irish rings were to be released unless the Garda had any reason to suspect that a bird was not an Irish bird, or where any such pigeon was found to be carrying a message. Non-Irish pigeons were sent by bus or train to Officer Commanding Garrison Signals Co., Portobello Barracks, Dublin.

So what happened to these pigeons, who found themselves on the wrong side of the Irish Sea in wartime? They were reported back to their owners by Denis O'Callaghan, Harolds Cross Road, Dublin, secretary of the Metropolitan RPC. What connection he had with the Army, if any, we do not know, but there is a lot of correspondence directed to him on the Army files, such as the letter from a Mr Ernest Gibson, Hetton-le-Hole, County Durham, asking him to liberate his bird and saying that it had been lost at Penzance. He then went on to say that this West Coast route had proved a disaster to the Up North Combine Fanciers and that there must be hundreds of their pigeons in Eire and Northern Ireland. Some fanciers sent postal orders for 3/6 or 4 shillings to cover the cost of returning their pigeons to England and sometimes failed to enclose an import permit, which delayed their return.

The arrival of black hen, NURP.40.NPS181, at Ballygurteen in the south of Ireland on 9 July 1944 set the alarm bells ringing when it was discovered that she was carrying a handwritten message in French. This time it went beyond the normal regulations, with both the Department of Defence and the Department of External Affairs becoming involved. In the file were six copies of the message, which was in three parts.

The black hen, along with two message carriers, was taken to Dublin, but we do not know what became of her. It appears that she had belonged to the National Pigeon Service and would have been returned.

25

RECOGNITION AT LAST FOR THE FEATHERED HEROES

BY DANNY BUCKLAND

Just as Mayor Ken Livingstone wants to banish them from Trafalgar Square, pigeons are to gain a place of honour in Whitehall on Remembrance Sunday. Today, they are regarded as airborne vermin spreading a medical dictionary of diseases, but carrier pigeons did more than their fair share to ensure this nation maintained its freedom.

The National Pigeon Service, which bred and trained up to 500,000 pigeons during both world wars, is credited with saving thousands of lives and providing key intelligence and reconnaissance photographs from double agents in Europe, yet it remained the forgotten service.

For a long time it seemed the birds' efforts would stay lost under the welter of opinion that casts pigeons as vermin. Only a concerted effort by pigeon fanciers has won the National Pigeon Service an historic spot at the Remembrance Sunday march past. A full fifty-five years after the Armistice, now at last they will receive their full official recognition.

The role of the pigeon has gone unremarked and unnoticed for too long, said leading pigeon spokesman, Derek Partridge. 'The fuss about pigeons in Trafalgar Square only reinforces the public's view that they are all horrible creatures. The truth is vastly different: pigeons were crucial in both world wars, with many thousands trained in London and flying from bases in the south'.

It is only a short flap down Piccadilly to what was once known as Wing House, an office sequestered by the Air Ministry, which installed pigeon lofts on the roof. From there, birds with capsules containing information attached to their legs were launched into the air to speed across the channel. Hitler was so worried that he ordered all troops in coastal zones to blast any bird heading for Britain out of the sky, in case it was carrying secret messages.

Barely a minute further by pigeon wing is Doughty Street, where number seventeen was National Pigeon Service HQ, a central point for the distribution of pigeons to all branches of the forces. Lofts were also kept in Horse Guards, where dispatch riders stood by to whisk messages from returning birds to Churchill's War Cabinet.

Thousands of service men owe their lives to pigeons making it through murderous fire with vital messages. Large sections of the 56th (London) Division would have been annihilated but for the mile-a-minute flight by one bird.

By 1943, the effectiveness of pigeons was so great that a scheme was devised to use them, Kamikaze-style, to smash enemy searchlights. Experiments were carried out which involved strapping two-ounce explosive charges to a bird's back so that it could fly straight into the lights, but the plan was never implemented.

In the Italian campaign, elements of the 56th (London) Division struck hard and fast into German lines. The only problem was that their advance was too fast and they reached the village of Colvi Vecciato twenty minutes ahead of an allied air strike. Without radio contact, the troops dug in, while a bird called 'GI Joe' was released in the hope that it could cover terrain that would have taken more than an hour in a jeep, in time to call off the strike. 'GI Joe' flew twenty miles in twenty minutes and certain carnage was averted.

Details of pigeon exploits have been scant for years, but the birds featured in many of the engagements of the Second World War. At Arnhem, where British paratroopers landed in the heart of German divisions, the pigeon 'William of Orange' flew sixty-eight miles to his London loft in fifty-nine minutes, carrying a key operational message.

On another mission with airborne troops, it covered 260 miles (135 miles across open seas) in four hours and twenty-five minutes. It was awarded the Dicken Medal, the animal Victoria Cross.

One of the most prolific pigeons used in the war was 'Kenley Lass'. She brought back intelligence on German troop movements, and the identities of collaborators were obtained and coded on a scrap of paper fixed to her leg. She covered 300 miles in less than seven hours to safely transmit the message.

Her triumph led to pigeons being issued to many agents dropped behind enemy lines. The files of several clandestine operations held at the Public Record Office at Kew reveal the central role pigeons played in military intelligence.

Hector Goffin, an agent codenamed 'Bracelet', was parachuted into occupied Belgium to gather photographic evidence of German positions. The mission details covered some thirty pages, but five are given over to the care of his accompanying pigeon and a range of measures to ensure it was healthy enough to carry his intelligence home.

Trained birds were supplied to the resistance movements and coded messages were sent out on BBC programmes to complete the two-way conversation. The eminent fashion designer, Hardy Amies, then a major based at Belgrave Square, was one of the liaison officers who instructed the BBC on what message to broadcast to continue a secret dialogue.

The Carol Network, which produced a steady and vital stream of information despite great danger, used pigeons to order anything from high explosives to currency.

Pigeons flew thousands of sorties in both world wars, relaying operational messages and SOS signals; some birds clocked up more than 150 'Active Service Patrols' before they retired.

These birds had no choice about going to war, yet they served with great bravery. There are many reports of pigeons being shot or becoming badly injured delivering their messages and then dying on the spot.

26

THE PILOT AND THE PIGEON

Jack Curtis wrote a short, fictional story dedicated to the fanciers of Great Britain who supplied many superb pigeons to the Armed Forces for use in the Second World War. It was also written to record the vital part played by the pigeons themselves and the many lives they saved, often under the most trying circumstances.

Ralph Punshon removed his cap and mopped his brow with his handkerchief; he then drew out his watch from his waistcoat to see that it was 10.30 a.m. The sun shone from a clear blue sky on this fine April Sunday morning and peace had settled on the land once more.

As was his wont, he had gone through his regular routine: the lofts had been scrubbed out from top to bottom with hot water plus common soda and carbolic soap, then a coating of sawdust used to absorb the moisture was taken up and replaced with a sprinkling of fresh beach sand. The water was changed, nest bowls checked and every detail completed.

This was a slow methodical approach to his pigeons. Moving to the garden seat, he watched as the cocks completed their bathing, and began to fill his pipe. As always, a coil of Rubicund twist baccy was carefully sliced with his pocket knife, rubbed between the palms of his hands, then the pipe was filled and compressed with the index finger of his right hand. The match was struck and he methodically puffed away until the tobacco was well alight. His mood was very sombre as he reflected on the past week's events. The news that he was being forced to retire came like a bolt from the blue: fifty years a diver and now with the war over he was to be let go.

He had never even considered the prospect; he had been far too busy for that. The thought of leaving the docks after twenty-eight years as port diver had left him in deep despair. He had been almost sixty-five when war was declared, but he had carried on as the young men were called up and went to fight.

At seventy-one years of age, he was still a magnificent man, tall and broad with a great hooked nose and lined craggy features. Fortunately, his loft was safe, tucked away in the corner of the blockyard at the end of the South Pier. Mr Tripp, the port engineer had given him written authority that it would remain where it stood for the rest of his life.

With unseeing eyes, he sat smoking quietly in the warm spring sunshine. Most of the eggs were chipping and his pigeons flew back and forth to the beach only a hundred yards from his loft, as they had done for three decades now. His mind wandered back to the many great races they had won, back to the cornerstone of his family. 'The Old

Light 'Un', what a pigeon he had been, and he was still fertile at eighteen years of age, bred from a half brother and sister mating from Osman's 'Forlorn Hope', six times nevers and a winner from Grantham, Arras and three times nevers. He had filled the loft with winners from every distance out to 580 miles. They had come from far and wide before the war trying to buy his bloodlines, but he had been sparing with those he allowed to go.

Then his thoughts turned to the Le Puy races of the 1920s and the superb pigeons he had bought from J.L. Baker of Sedgeley in Staffordshire. They had won two of the races for him and had crossed in well with his own stuff.

A warm smile crossed his face as he thought of those race days and the tremendous atmosphere at the lofts. 'Flonkey' Donkin with his haircutting gear and hair all over the cabin, as he cut anyone and everybody's hair for twopence a time. Dick Mitinson, George Sands, Tommy Hutchinson, Little Moir – his pumpman, who fed him his air while he was under water.

They were all great company and made the time fly so pleasantly. There had been a weekly sweep, at a tanner a man, for the first bird back to the loft, and a lot of leg-pulling went with it.

Captain Wallace was the skipper of the Lea Grange, who carried coal from the port down to Southampton week in and week out. What a friend he had turned out to be – he trained his brother-in-law's pigeons on the north road and had ended up training his for the south road, tossing them off the Thames Estuary in ones and twos and even from Southampton, singled up when required for a big one. He was a real secret weapon, and a true friend.

The smile slid from his face as he reflected on his last great champion before the war intervened. 'The York Cock', as he became known, was killed during an air raid. He had had eleven wins up to the age of three, topping the federation from nevers at his first attempt.

He was from 'The Old Light Un' and Tom Goodrum's good 'Blue Barker Hen'. Tom Goodrum had been a great man, he reflected. Their friendship had grown out of a disaster at Estington Colliery. The last thing on his mind had been pigeons when he was called to the flooded mine.

Tom had been the 'overman', delegated to look after Ralph and take him down into the mine to set up pumping-out operations. His mind saw the man quite clearly, as he relived the time they descended in that gigantic bucket down the shaft.

He remembered Tom's voice controlling the winding man's actions, one leg dangling over the side of the bucket in as relaxed a pose as he had ever seen. He had set up the diving gear in the dry, dusty seam, then had given him precise and detailed instructions of what he would find at the bottom of the shaft and how he should proceed with the work involved.

Ralph had stayed a full fortnight and Tom's home had been his home. In that time they had worked together, drunk a few pints together and surveyed Tom's lovely team of Logans and Barkers.

Tom's parting gift had been a little smokey blue Barker squeaker – what a gift she was, winning at 300 and 476 miles, then going on to breed a lot of superb winners with 'The Old Light 'Un'.

A faint smile flickered across the craggy face again as he had Tom in his mind – short and stocky in build, with his bowed, muscular legs quite distinctive in his hose and breeches, plus steel-capped pit boots. Clad in leather waistcoat and carrying his stick, he was an 'overman' without any doubt. Brooking neither delays nor slackness, he drove everyone around him with an unremitting energy and determination. Five feet nothing, he was, nevertheless, the cock of the walk and you crossed him at your peril.

His face set suddenly as he saw again the bodies that he and Tom had brought to the surface. The womenfolk had been standing bedraggled in the rain to receive their menfolk, dead, from the bowels of the earth. Death had been a common factor throughout his diving career. He had come across it often during the First World War when he worked for the British Admiralty, diving all over Europe recovering secret information, or blasting wrecks to clear harbours or rivers.

He was seventy-one years of age. The war had given him six good years of work and he had made the contribution he had felt was so important. He could look back at his life with pride, knowing full well that he answered the call in England's time of need. The future need not be bleak. Then he noticed the hens beginning to change over with the cocks; his eyes beheld the telltale quiver of their tails as they came into the garden. The creamy white droppings told him a tale also and he was satisfied that all was well for this time of the year. Their lean bright red feet and tight gathering backed up by sparkling eyes and snow-white wattle gave him a great boost. The new season beckoned full of promise, yet the dark mood and feelings remained.

His thoughts were suddenly interrupted by a rattle upon the garden latch. Swinging the gate open he was greeted by the smiling face of David Taylor, resplendent in his flight lieutenant's uniform. 'Morning, Mr Punshon', he beamed. 'To what do I owe this pleasure?' asked Ralph. 'Well, I know that you like a drink when you are finished with the pigeons and I owe you one'.

Ralph was surprised. 'Owe me one, whatever for?' 'It's a long story,' David replied, 'and a drink will certainly help me with its telling, but put your loft book in your pocket please'.

Ralph locked the loft up and left the cat bob open, picked up the book from the cabin table and then joined David. Together they strolled out of the blockyard, then over the caisson casing of the Number One Graving Dock, round the corner and across the Gladstone Bridge before climbing the banks of the docks. The King's Head stood opposite the dock gates and there they retired.

David was his youngest son's pal from schooldays and they had remained pals. He had been a constant visitor to their home and was like one of the family to him.

Jonathan was still in the Fleet Air Arm and they would both be released within the next few months. In the pub, David called in a pint for himself and a double rum for Ralph. The ritual of filling and lighting the pipe was performed and good health was drunk. The first double was replaced by a second, and then the young pilot began his story. 'Well, Mr Punshon, you may not remember that I was at your loft with Jonathan in 1941, when they came to collect a batch of baby pigeons that you had bred for War Service. Amongst them was a blue cock rung, NPS41.31121 and my birthday was 3 November 1921, so that number stood out like a beacon. In 1942 I was posted to RAF

Catfoss near York with Coastal Command. I was flying Beaufighters at that time and on one mission, as I signed for my two pigeons, guess what? There it was on the sheet, NPS41.31121. To say that I was dumbstruck is an understatement. The memories all came flooding back and it turned out to be a tremendous and lucky coincidence for me. To cut a long story short, he went with me on an attack on enemy shipping in Danish coastal waters, but remained in his container, and I brought him back home safe and sound. Back at base, I waited for the pigeon man to come and collect him after debriefing, to find that he was stationed at RAF Linton-on-Ouse.

'The next day, I borrowed a bike and cycled over to see the NCO in charge of the lofts. I told him my story and he showed me the blue cock. He named him 'The Diver' after you, and told me he was mine whenever I flew. We did over eighty missions together, along with my navigator, Jimmy Wilkinson, and the next drink is on him'. With that he went to the bar and replenished both glasses. Jimmy's health was toasted before David resumed his tale. 'We flew summer or winter, weather permitting, and The Diver went too. On one sweep we located the German liner, *Strasberg*, in broad daylight. She was protected by a heavily-armed escort and the flack was intense. Nevertheless, in we went with cannon, bombs and machine gunfire. Two direct hits were recorded and we strafed her, leaving her on fire. We lost two planes and my aircraft was hit, but not seriously. However, on return to base I found that the blue cock had been wounded. He lost a lot of blood and was out of action for two months. Later, we had a part of our tail shot away and he got out of the container. Jimmy air-released him over Holland, as he had no means of locking him up again. He was home in five hours against a south-west wind'.

Old Ralph came to life as he said 'Let me check the book, son'. The experienced hand whipped through the pages to the matings of 1941 and in box four was the significant ring number against a blue baby. 'He's out of the Arras Hen and The York Cock, the Arras Hen was a half brother and sister out of The Old Light 'Un and the York Cock was out of Tom Goodrum's hen. Of course he's a good 'un'. David sat there smiling at the excitement welling up in the old man, hardly daring to continue. 'Mr Punshon, the truth is that your cock had been trained all round the compass. He had brought messages from minesweepers from way out in the North Sea and goodness knows what before I got him, but a bottle of whisky or two ensured he was mine for keeps. He was with me when I won my DFC for blocking the Kiel Canal for two whole weeks.'

'It was really a hairy job; news came through of massive enemy barge movements through the canal. The decision was taken to send just one aircraft and I drew the short straw. I was flying Mosquitos by then and it was to be a low-level job. Jimmy and I were briefed and studied every obstacle, right down to the overhead power lines. We took off in the pre-dawn darkness and crossed the enemy coastline as the sun came up. I had flown as low as possible over the North Sea to avoid their radar, then we were over enemy territory, keeping down to less than 100 feet above ground level. Jimmy plotted our course and alerted me to the especially dangerous obstacles.

'Our route was to the south of the targets and we picked up the canal about three miles from then. I banked and turned before dropping down to within forty feet of the water, then opened the throttle to full power. We met a hail of machine-gun and ack-

ack fire, and there were about a dozen barges and tugs. We hit them with everything we had and they must have been loaded with ammunition. The havoc was tremendous; lock gates and lock houses just vanished off the face of the earth. How we escaped the blast, I will never know. I think it was the most satisfying attack I have ever carried out, but we were off on a different course as quick as lightning before the enemy fighters could pick us up, then home post-haste.'

Looking at the old man's craggy face, the younger one saw the excitement and emotion. He knew this man had faced death several times himself. As a boy, he had held him in awe when he saw him in that massive brass and copper-bound diving suit and helmet; now he knew the roles were reversed.

The old man looked long at the young man before him before he spoke, 'David, I was more proud of you than anyone when you won your DFC'. The old face wrinkled with pride as it fought to control the emotions within. 'If only your father could have lived to have seen that day'.

'You know I won a bar to my DFC, now I can tell you it was nearly posthumous. After the Kiel Canal job, I was selected for three more special tasks. We were hit several times here and there, but our luck held good, then we landed a plumb job if ever there was one. Military Intelligence was informed that the enemy had captured the leader of the Danish underground movement, he had been taken to Gestapo headquarters in Copenhagen for interrogation. Everyone knew what that meant – torture until he finally cracked and gave everything away.

I was selected to destroy their HQ in another single aircraft strike. All I was told at the time was that it was of vital importance that the HQ was completely destroyed, but not the actual reason for it. That information only came to me after the event. Jimmy and I were briefed in great detail, with a host of high-definition reconnaissance photographs and a mock-up of the area in which the HQ stood. There could be no room for error. It had to be clean, with no mistakes. Our route was worked out to avoid any enemy action as far as we could see. It was 1 November, just two days before my birthday. The time selected for the strike was a half-hour before dusk fell, as very few attacks ever took place at that time. Then we would have the benefit of the darkness to evade any enemy fighters we might encounter. We flew low level again, as by now I was quite a dab hand and Jimmy could find a tanner in a field. He is a good navigator, Mr Punshon, one of the very best, and that makes a great difference to a pilot.

'Our route had a few good landmarks and we picked our way carefully, then swept in on our final run to our designated target. It was a big house standing upon a small knoll, and Jimmy was right on it. There was no mistaking it. There were staff cars and sentries all over the place. We dropped a stick of bombs, then I turned and banked sharply before passing for the second time. The house had virtually vanished but I gave it a second stick then turned for home. Suddenly, I felt the plane shudder and I knew we had been hit. I felt the warm blood begin to run down my leg but felt no pain for a few seconds. From sheer instinct I called Jim, but there was no answer. I called again and again, and my body went cold with fear for him.

'I flew on homewards for some twenty minutes before Jimmy came round. He had been wounded but he rallied to set our course. We cleared the coast before I realised we were low on fuel. They must have damaged the tanks or the fuel lines. I had made a tourniquet for my thigh from a belt, which helped arrest the bleeding. Then I opened the throttles to maximum and went for home. Jimmy's voice broke my concentration. 'Dave, the radio's knackered, I can't get a bloody squeak out of it'. I told him we were losing fuel rapidly. After another ten minutes, the starboard engine began to splutter and cough, before it died on us completely. The port engine began to react shortly afterwards and I told Jim I would have to put her down in the drink. He wedged himself in as tightly as possible to reduce the effect of the impact.

There was a little moonlight visible through the broken cloud, and I concentrated as hard as I ever have. I kept her nose up to the right angle when the time came and put her down. The plane was nearly all wood and I was afraid the impact would break her up, but she held and floated for a while. We got the dinghy, pigeons and other bits and pieces out, then we were afloat in the total darkness. Jimmy had received a nasty wound to his right shoulder and I did my best for him with the first aid gear. The tourniquet was working on my leg and I released it every now and again to let the blood flow. We worked out our approximate position and wrote two messages out by flashlight, and fixed them to our pigeon's legs. By this time, Jimmy's shoulder was causing him severe pain and I was worried about him. Later I noticed that we were shipping water and that the pannier and pigeons were now quite wet.

'It was then that I took our lives into my hands and liberated the blue cock and his companion in total darkness. With a prayer, I closed my eyes and tried to sleep. The cold was intense and Jim had passed out. That night and the following morning are without doubt the worst hours of my life. They are a blur of pain, cold and misery that will live with me forever. Even now they bring a shudder through my body. Eventually, as if by magic, a minesweeper was towering above us. Later, we were transferred to an air rescue launch and I woke up in a warm, clean hospital bed as if from a bad dream.

'When I recovered I came home on leave for a while. It was only when I returned to the station that I learned that the blue cock had arrived back at its home loft at 9.00 a.m. that morning with his message. I went over to Linton with a bottle for my friend and to see our saviour. He stood on his perch and looked me in the eye as if to say it was nothing at all.'

David then asked: 'Could you stand another surprise this morning, Mr Punshon? A really big one, I mean'. Ralph replied: 'I could stand any bloody thing this morning, son, I feel on top of the world'. David raised his glass and said: 'To The Diver, NPS41.31121' and they drank together again.

The young pilot winked at George, the barman. With a wide smile, George reached under the bar counter and placed the small pannier on the top. There stood The Diver, a magnificent blue cock with bold crusty wattles, great thick circles of eye cere and character written all over him.

The old man found it difficult to swallow the lump which had suddenly appeared in his throat. He stood for many long moments, just looking at the pigeon before his voice would respond to his will. 'How the hell have you managed this, David?' was all he could say. 'It was very simple, Mr Punshon. Sergeant Ransome had to disband the loft and was allowed to select two pigeons for himself. He chose The Diver and sends him to you with his best wishes. There is a letter from him which you can read later'. The old man took the letter and placed it in his pocket. 'However, he also sent this for you and said that I must put it straight into your hands'. With that, he passed over a bronze medal hung by ribbon.

The old eyes blurred again as he read the inscription. It was the Dicken Medal, the animal equivalent of the VC. He turned from the bar and walked to the nearest chair, then sat down. The medal gleamed in his palm for a long while as the bowed grey head gazed in wonder and disbelief. Then he returned to the young man. 'David, lad, you don't know what you have done for me today and I thank you from the bottom of my heart'.

David continued: 'I received the bar to my DFC from the King, Mr Punshon, and he had the full report of the strike, including the part played by him', he said, pointing to the blue cock. 'We talked for a full five minutes because he has pigeons himself. I had the longest audience of the day with him, I was told, just because of The Diver.' The war was over for Ralph Punshon. He had a hero in his left hand and another one holding his right hand to steady him. There was no happier Englishman in the realm.

27

WOMEN, WARTIME AND THE FANCY

In 1947, Mrs M. Lawson wrote a wonderful article about the role of women during the war years.

Five years ago, I was a stranger to the pigeon world. Its language, like Arabic or Italian, was foreign to me. Many hundreds of women were in exactly the same position, yet, because their menfolk were called to some form of National Service, they were suddenly confronted with the task of loft management. It is for this reason that I accept so gladly the Chairman's invitation to write this article. Other women, no doubt, would express our point of view or outline our experiences more ably, but since the invitation has come to me, I will try to rise to the occasion. Let me begin at the beginning.

My brother-in-law, the Revd D.W.G. Lawson, has been an enthusiast for livestock ever since he was a child. My interests, on the contrary, lay in books, in the home and in social activities. I shuddered at the thought of keeping hens or cleaning out a poultry house. Then came the war and with it my brother-in-law's request that I should take over his pets. In a foolish moment, my husband and I agreed to do so. We are not farmers, although our house is built on the site of an old farm and we have a few acres of land. Our dreams were of rose gardens, tennis courts, a bathing pool and picturesque terraces. Instead, we began to dig for victory, and geese and ducks became the only swimmers. In place of tennis courts we had fowl pens and along the hedgeside, three pigeon lofts. What a job it was, feeding, cleaning out, breeding, separating, advertising, corresponding, training, selling, basketing, dispatching and at the time it was necessary to learn the language and the technique.

What was meant, for example, by such terms as 'squab', 'squeaker', 'young bird' or 'yearling'; what were primaries and secondaries, wattle and eye cere? What were logans and gurneys and how did they differ from Marriott's and Bricous'? Again, how did one join a club and in what way did it differ from a federation, an amalgamation or a union? How and when should one feed pigeons, what were their staple foods and how much should you give them at a time how many times a day? What was inbreeding, crossbreeding, line breeding and blending? How can you tell a cock from a hen, how many eggs were there to a nest, when would the young be hatched, how were they fed, when were they to be weaned? How can you tell a mean pigeon from an intelligent one, what was meant by an apple body, a bent keel, and a roomy hen, close in vent? What was a fret mark, what caused canker? How do you keep the records, ring the birds and prevent red mite and feather lice; what was meant by proud, sweeping, calling and driving? These and other points were as new to me as would be the science of medicine to an early caveman. Verily, I started from scratch and became a wartime fancier.

My brother-in-law was stationed in Kent for a time, and then in Scotland. We corresponded regularly and discussed pigeon problems until he went to Africa. The birds were named and paired up on paper long before the breeding season came round. Our best youngsters were weaned and sent out to the Army or Air Force, and every time the birds were dispatched, I had a two-mile walk to Thorner Station, carrying a heavy basket, sometimes in pouring rain. It seemed a thankless task until letters began to arrive expressing appreciation of our birds. The ration of priority corn was welcome but most inadequate; it also grew dearer in price and less in quantity. My work at the lofts was carried on under difficulties as the local NPS had their headquarters at my house and I was responsible for manning the telephone all day and, often, making cups of tea at night. Meanwhile, fanciers were writing for stock lists and expressing a desire to visit the lofts. It was with keen regret that I had to discourage these visits, but I just didn't have enough rations to make possible the offer of a meal. You menfolk will never know [the struggle] we women have had to contrive in order to keep things going, but we have done it with a good heart.

Of mistakes, as you may expect, there have been plenty, for we have learned our job in the costly school of experience. We did not always tell you of our losses, of the birds that were poisoned through fielding, of the old favourite killed by the rats of the prisoners lost in settling or the new generation that fell to the gun or were lost in a flyaway. We just did our best with what we had left in order that you might have a team for which to return. Try not to judge us too harshly if you feel our work lacked the perfection of your master touch. We have, at least, kept the birds together, we have kept the lofts clean, we have fed and watered, we have both lost and won. Now you are coming home, soon we will complete our task by 'handing over'. Some of you are already back, others are returning daily. What about the women whose men will never return? There are empty chairs in the home as well as empty perches in the loft. Think generously of such women; they kept the birds and while their loved ones lived and fought, the pigeons were always a welcome topic for discussion by letter.

Yes, it was good while it lasted. One by one, we are handing over to the men. I wonder what sort of job they will make of things? Well, good luck to them. We women can always put the kettle on and make them a cup of tea. Oh, and in case you have grown rusty, you menfolk just get busy with the scraper. Trace that leak in the loft top, don't forget the clean water and be sure there is no slime in the water fountain. Remember to put a little salt in the water once a week, get those birds dusted with insect powder and what about a spot of lime washing?

We've scrubbed out the nest pans for you and put all the nest box fronts away. Just make sure that all the other odd jobs are done, will you, and then when you've finished and you're thinking of taking it easy, there are some pedigrees to be brought up to date and some strays to be reported. Oh yes, you're taking over now.

A postscript and then I'm done. Just a word of gratitude to all the 'old hands', who, by kindly advice or a handful of corn, have eased the burden and proved themselves unexpected friends. Thank you, gentlemen.

28

LANCASHIRE CONSTABULARY VOLUNTARY PIGEON SERVICE

16 FEBRUARY 1945

LETTER FROM THE CHIEF CONSTABLE OF

LANCASHIRE

Sir,

The Government has recently announced substantial relaxations and modifications in many wartime restrictions, Civil Defence Services etc. In view of this, and also on the instructions of the Home Office that Police Pigeon Services should be discontinued, I have therefore decided to disband the Lancashire Constabulary Voluntary Pigeon Service as from 28 February next.

I was very pleased, naturally, that recent events in the conduct of the war have made this possible and my decision to disband the service is tinged with regret, in that the many close associations which have been formed between members of the Police Pigeon Service and other branches of the Police Service will to some extent be severed.

The service has undoubtedly been second to none in the Pigeon Services of the country, both military and civil, and many tributes have been paid to the organisation from time to time. Happily, the necessity for the full extension of the service has never arisen, but, by the efforts of the members, the service has always been maintained in a state of efficiency and ready to operate at any time and I know from my own experience that should circumstances arise in the future whereby pigeons were urgently required by the Police for communication purposes, members would only be too pleased once again to give their services.

I desire to take this opportunity of expressing my sincere thanks and the gratitude of the members of the force, to you and all other members of the Pigeon Service for your unstinting help in maintaining a means of communication during the critical years of the war through which we have passed. Last but not least, I am very grateful for the extremely generous assistance given by the fanciers to two very worthy war objects, namely, the British Red Cross Fund, which has benefited to the extent of more than £2,800 as a result of pigeon shows and races organised by the fanciers, and the Lancashire Constabulary Fighter Aircraft Fund, which received substantial support from the fanciers.

Finally, I would like to offer my very best wishes to you for the happier times, which lie ahead after the cessation of hostilities.

Yours faithfully,

Chief Constable of Lancashire.

29

EXTRACTS FROM BRITISH HOMING WORLD

22 DECEMBER 1945
BRITISH PIGEONS GIFT TO HOLLAND

Dutch fanciers recently received 2,000 British pigeons. They were presented with these pigeons as a result of negotiations by a Dutchman, Mr A.M. Doelman, an ex-NCO of the Dutch Military Pigeon Service, who approached the NPS Committee in England through the Air Ministry before Holland had been liberated. The convoy was met by Civic Officials at 'The Hook', and at Rotterdam the police and thousands of people walked in a procession accompanying the birds to the clubhouse.

The pigeons will not be sold or dealt in, but will be under control of Dutch Federations and in effect [will be] leant to the members for breeding.

7 APRIL 1945

During the past week, we heard the first weather forecast since wartime restrictions were imposed in that respect. True, it was only a warning about frost for farmers, but it was a good omen. We may look forward to weather forecasts of a more general nature in the near future.

There is no denying that weather forecasts are of great help to an intelligent convoyer. We do not advocate the holding over of pigeons unless it is absolutely necessary, but we do impress on officials the very important necessity of employing, as convoyer, a person who can make the best use of information about weather. In the past we have heard about too many convoyers who have lacked initiative, they have not liberated their pigeons simply because other convoyers had not liberated theirs, although they may have had a sound reason.

28 JULY 1945
(MENTIONED IN DISPATCHES)

In the *London Gazette*, the following Pigeon Service NCOs are named as 'Mentioned in dispatches': 1053038 A/F/Sgt H.C. Healey, RAF.V.R.; 1420448, Sgt H.W. Halsey, RAF.V.R.

A/F/T. Sgt Healey's mention was by the Air Officer Commanding-in-Chief, West Africa for his work with pigeons in that command.

Sgt Healey is now stationed at Calshot.

Sgt Healey's mention was by Air Officer Commanding, No. 16 Group, Royal Air Force and Coastal Command. Congratulations to both of these fanciers.

SERVICE DEMONSTRATIONS

Approval has been given to the public demonstration of nomadic homing by the RAF Pigeon Research Section (Sgt Sheppard), at the following shows:

Saturday 4 August, at Miles Aircraft Horticultural Show at the Recreation Ground, Woodley, Reading, Berkshire.
Wednesday and Thursday 22 and 23 August, at the Blackpool and Fylde Show at Stanley Park, Blackpool.
Saturday 8 September, at the Allied Forces Animals 'War Memorial Show' and Fête in the grounds of the Royal Hospital Chelsea.

The demonstration is of extreme interest to the orthodox pigeon fancier, as showing the degree of control which is possible. The birds, released from aircraft in an entirely strange location, will seek and find a target they have been trained to seek in the locality in which they are released, wherever that may be.

4 AUGUST 1945

We learn that the Air Ministry after 1 August 1945 will cease to control the manufacture of metal pigeon rings. Red tape had been cut at last, now we can get on with our business without outside interference.

We have made enquiries about rubber rings and it is possible we shall be in a position to supply these again, at popular prices next year. Naturally, these will be a little higher than pre-war prices, which were about nine shillings per thousand for large quantities.

7 JULY 1945
WAR PIGEONS FOR EX-SERVICEMEN

Several thousand pigeons, which have been operating with the Army, Royal Air Force and United States Army Pigeon Service, are now being made available throughout the National Pigeon Service Committee to ex-Service fanciers. These pigeons will be allocated to fanciers who were actually members of recognised clubs and who were compelled to dispose of their birds on enlistment.

Consideration will be given to the enrolling of ex-Service fanciers as members of the

NPS, in order that they may be in a position to obtain feeding stuffs for their pigeons. Ex-Service fanciers who desire to set up their lofts again and to receive a supply of surplus Service pigeons should make application to Mr J. Selby Thomas, secretary, National Pigeon Service, 22 Clarence Street, Gloucester, stating the date of their discharge and name of the club of which they were members prior to enlistment.

5 MAY 1945

Fanciers whose pigeons were accepted in some of the Wartime Services for communications, were, we understand, supplied with baskets in which to train and send their birds on different journeys. As soon as these services were discontinued, the fanciers concerned were asked to return the baskets. Would it not have been a friendly gesture on the part of the authorities to present them to the fanciers as a mark of appreciation for services rendered by them and their pigeons? It is very difficult to get baskets and they would have been a very useful present, but no, the fancier is expected to give everything for nothing and expect nothing in return and that is exactly what he gets.

We notice the N.H.U. Council on 21 April dealt briefly with the subject of overhead electric cables; this, we consider, is one of the most urgent problems fanciers have to deal with.

In one particular area near our editor's home, scores of pigeons are maimed or killed annually and that is only in the space of half a mile, so what must be the total loss of birds from these wires throughout the country? On race days when there is a strong wind blowing, hundreds of birds would be killed. This is a more serious matter than it appears. It is not only the loss of the pigeons, [as] it makes the fancier believe that the stock is not good enough and he probably disposes of the parents believing them to be incapable of racing long distances.

Besides being a disfigurement of the countryside, overhead cables are a menace to all bird life and particularly to pigeons, which fly in flocks. The first birds may clear the cables but those following have smashed into them before they are seen. We notice that the local authorities at Lowestoft are trying to get them removed and are taking the matter up with the Ministry of Town and Country Planning. Everyone agrees they disfigure the landscape and it is time they were put underground.

30

MEMORIES OF THE CHANNEL ISLANDS DURING THE WAR

In 1940, when many people left the Channel islands, Alderney, twenty miles to the north east of Guernsey, was completely evacuated. The Guernsey authorities sent a party of men to Alderney daily to clear up the island and bring back stores. These men were equipped with birds from the lofts of C.G. Lowe to release with messages if they found on arrival that the island had been occupied by German forces.

C.G. Lowe had joined the National Pigeon Service and was on a list of members that were in the hands of the Government Secretary. Soon after the Germans arrived, notices were put in the local newspapers that all pigeons had to be registered and confined to their lofts. The fanciers were not allowed to kill any birds without first obtaining permission to do so. The fanciers tried to explain that they would soon be without corn to feed their birds and were told that the Germans would supply them with some. However, on a Sunday afternoon during September, a German officer, accompanied by an interpreter, called on Mr Lowe and told him that all the pigeons had to be destroyed. When Mr Lowe said he would like to appeal to the bailiff, the officer tapped on his revolver and the interpreter said, 'This is the only appeal', so they soon got on with the job of killing the birds.

At the time, Mr Lowe had four young birds bred from his father's best birds at the loft of a fancier who did not race and were not registered. After a short while, these were handed to another friend who took them and kept them in an attic. Arriving home one day, he was told that the Germans were taking over his house the next day, so during the night, despite the curfew (which was from 10.00 p.m. until 6.00 a.m.), he took the four youngsters across some fields and hid them in a greenhouse which stood well away from the road. This went on for some time, with eventually Mr Lowe taking them back and hiding them himself. At his loft, his stock of maple peas had been used up, so he fed the birds on wheat, barley and haricot beans.

By the time D-Day arrived, Mr Lowe still had the birds, although the penalty would have been death if he had been caught with them. The islanders were expecting to be liberated at any time, but in fact hostilities had ceased before the actual day of liberation.

In August of that year, the Germans caught Mr Lowe with a radio, for which he was sentenced to twelve months in prison; however, he did manage to get a message out to a friend asking him to destroy the birds, as he knew what awful trouble it would be to obtain food and the risk he would take seeking it. At that time, the civilian population had been without bread for several weeks and it was difficult enough to get food for themselves without having to provide for pigeons. So, with the end of the war in sight, and having kept those four birds throughout the occupation years, they were finally destroyed.

The late Mr George Nicol of Pewsey, who was a close friend of Mr Lowe's father, came to Guernsey after the Germans had left to see what had happened to his hotel on the island after the occupation, which had actually been badly damaged. Mr Nicol asked Mr Lowe if he intended to start in the sport again. As his answer was yes, he gave him a pair to start the new loft.

Fred Boyle of Warrington and Jim Lowe of Lowton also sent him birds. John Taylor of Walsall, on hearing he was starting up again, also sent him pigeons. Tommy New of Ogbourne St George organised a collection of birds in the Marlborough area, to which, among others, Sir Gordon Richards contributed. As a result, other fanciers in Guernsey had a pair or two to get started again.

Fanciers in Jersey had National Pigeon Service birds sent to them, but, for some reason or other, Guernsey did not.

31

THE 34TH DICKEN MEDAL WINNER,

'TOMMY' NURP41DHZ56

During the war, the secretary of the NHU and others made an attempt to stop pigeon racing in this country. *The Racing Pigeon* opposed this and suggested that these competitions were necessary if a sound type of pigeon was to be maintained.

The strength of the argument was obvious and it seemed wrong that anyone would want to stop pigeon racing completely, although restrictions would be necessary.

The story of 'Tommy' illustrates one advantage of having pigeon racing carried on during the war, for 'Tommy' was the only pigeon not on active service to be awarded a Dicken Medal.

'Tommy' was bred by W. Brockbank of Dalton-in-Furness from a blue cock bred by himself and a mealy hen bred by Mr Jamieson of Renfrewshire. In 1941, 'Tommy' flew all stages to Mangotsfield – some 200 miles. The following year he won first place at Crewe, first at Stafford and first at Mangotsfield. He was then sent to Christchurch, where he was expected to win. He did not turn up at his loft and flew so far off course that he was found exhausted in a street in Holland. A small boy found him and gave him to a local postman, who in turn gave him to a Mr Drijver, a Dutch resistance fighter who was hiding from the Nazis.

The story of Mr Drijver indicates the danger that partisans were willing to risk by using these little message carriers. The Germans had ordered the killing of all Dutch homing pigeons when they occupied Holland; they also insisted that the metal leg ring had to be handed to the authorities.

Mr Drijver had killed all his pigeons except for two known as 'Tijger' and 'Amsterdammer' – he managed to save these by removing the rings and putting them on the legs of pigeons that had already been killed.

The local resistance forces had their headquarters at the village of Santpoort. Mr Drijver trained the birds to carry messages for them. This they did throughout September and October of 1944. It was in that year that Mr Drijver was captured by the Nazis and sent to a concentration camp in Germany. He eventually escaped by jumping from a moving train and was hidden by the partisans; the birds also remained hidden in spite of the fact that he had been captured. Unfortunately, in February of 1945 the birds met a sad end as they were caught and eaten by a cat.

It was soon after this that Mr Drijver was handed 'Tommy'. He was kept hidden for over two weeks and nursed back to health, although he could only be fed on bread and a little wheat. At that time it was not known if the bird would be able to fly, and it was to be many weeks before he could prove himself.

On 18 August 1945, the Dutch Partisan Forces received a message, which was imperative and was to be carried to the British Military Forces at the earliest possible moment. The message was fixed to Tommy's leg and he was released, but, much to the dismay of the partisans, he flew up and perched on the sails of a windmill.

It was possible that he was spotted by the Germans, as they tried to shoot him down to stop any message getting through. Eventually he flew off and headed for his home loft in England. On arrival, he was found to be very badly wounded in the breastbone.

Part of the message sent by the Partisan Forces was a request that if the message were received it would be acknowledged by a coded message on the BBC Dutch Service. On the next day, when the coded message was heard, it made all the care and attention given to this bird by Mr Drijver well worth it.

In February 1946, Tommy and Mr Drijver were reunited at the Dutch Club in London, where Tommy was presented with the Dicken Medal by Major General Van Oorshot of the Dutch Intelligence Service. Mr Drijver was presented with a pair of British pigeons to help him start up again at the end of the war.

As for Tommy, his wound healed and he spent the remainder of his life in retirement until he died in October 1952. Among his notable descendants was a granddaughter who won 1st club Rennes and 1st club Nantes in 1953.

32

PADDY MADE THE FASTEST TIME FROM NORMANDY

'Paddy', NPS439451, was bred by A.S. Hughes of Carnlough, Northern Ireland. He was one of several hundred pigeons used to carry messages in the Normandy invasion and had the distinction of making the fastest recorded time from Normandy, covering the distance to his loft on the south coast in four hours and fifty minutes.

He was bred in Northern Ireland and worked with Air Sea Rescue Units from an RAF station in Northern Ireland from May 1943 until March 1944. He was then transferred to the South Coast and within eight days was flying out of an RAF station in Southern England.

Sergeant Maclean, who was in charge of training, had a very high opinion of this bird and regarded him as the best of the batch. His breeding is from Mr Hughes's well-known Putmans, and the details are from Mr Hughes himself:

Sire red chequer pied cock 7404.41NURP.UC. Dam, dark chequer pied hen 4173.37.NURP.UC. The sire of 7404 is red chequer pied cock 32BELGE3202751, bred by and imported from M. Putman of Courtrai, Belgium. The sire of this pigeon is M. Putman's famous racer '87', which won a lot of prizes from Tours to Bordeaux. The dam is M. Putman's blue chequer hen, half sister to his Champion '42'. The dam of 7404 is blue chequer pied hen 2786.40NURP.UC. Her sire is red chequer cock 33BELGE320560, bred by M. Putman from his famous racer 'Sentinel'. And the black hen is a sister to his Champion 'Chocolate'. The dam of 2786 is blue pied hen 34BELGE3293039. Her sire is M Putman's blue 'White Feathers' from his big blue Bordeaux cock. Her dam is his good racer '31'. The dam of 9451 is dark chequer pied hen 417437NURP.UC. Her sire is red chequer pied cock 32BELGE3202751, (same sire as 7404) and her dam is red chequer hen 30BELGE3206369 bred by M. Putman from champion racer 'Red Whitehead', which was a great long-distance racer, her dam from 'Big Red' of his old strain.

Like some other Dicken Medal winners, 'Paddy' came to an untimely end. At the end of the war, he was returned to Mr Hughes by the RAF Pigeon Service. He was rested and kept for stock and up to 1954 he had sired many outstanding pigeons. In May 1954, Mr Hughes allowed his birds to have an open loft with the birds sunning themselves on the grass in front of the loft after a bath. Suddenly, a peregrine falcon swooped over the garden, scaring the birds wildly into the air. 'Paddy' and several others smashed into wires about fifty yards away from the loft and he dropped to the ground with a broken neck.

33
HEROIC JOHN SILVER

Most of the older readers of pigeon literature are familiar with the great services performed during the First World War by homing pigeons. Younger readers have digested the records of many Second World War pigeons, so this story is to acquaint those younger readers with the heroism of John Silver and to inform the older ones of John's present whereabouts.

In the Hall of Honour of the Air Force Technical Museum at Wright-Patterson Air Force Base, near Dayton, Ohio, USA, there is a pictorial history of aviation. It features pictures of contraptions which, their designers hoped, would fly. Many of them failed, but all served as foundation stones on which the first model of a successful flying machine was eventually based.

Pictured are planes which flew in the First World War. The first aerial combat was between a man with a piston in one plane and one man with a rifle in the other. Later, an ingenious English pilot mounted a machine gun in this plane and synchronised it to fire between the propeller blades. Every step of aircraft history is featured in this museum, right up to the present supersonic jet aircraft, mounted at the end of the line.

In the display rooms of the Air Force Technical Museum there are models of many types of flyable aircraft and their component parts. Returning to the Hall of Honour, we see pictures of heroes of aircraft battles and of aircraft production. The fighting McCooks are pictured in a group, with many others shown in individual portraits. The thrilling experiences of Captain Eddie Richenbacher are depicted with some of the planes he flew to glory.

As we go down the line, hero after hero is pictured and at the end is Ohio's Don Gentile, whom even the younger of readers have probably heard about.

The planes are displayed in one aisle of the hall and the heroes in the other. At the point where the isles converge, we find John Silver. John was named for the one-legged character made famous by Robert Louis Stevenson in *Treasure Island*, and somewhere along the historic line the pigeon had acquired the word 'Stumpy'. He is mounted and rehoused in a glass case with his famous message capsule near his one remaining foot. He is listed in the Hall of Honour as 'Stumpy John Silver'.

He was hatched in a dugout loft immediately behind the front lines in France in 1918, was inducted into service at a few months old and began carrying messages from the front lines to headquarters. The sound of gunfire was not new to him, for it can truthfully be said that he was hatched in the suburbs of hell.

At 2.35 p.m. on 21 October 1918, John Silver was liberated at Grand Pré in the Meuse-Argonne drive, to take a message to headquarters at Rampont, which was a distance of twenty-five miles.

The proximity of an exploding shell put considerable shrapnel in his body and machine gun fire pierced his breast and shot away his right shank and foot. Being more durable than a man, he continued on his assigned mission and, in spite of his wounds, delivered his message just twenty-five minutes after his liberation. This means that he averaged a mile a minute even though the shell and machine-gun fire undoubtedly threw him off course. Considerate care restored his health, and the shrapnel and machine gun wounds in his body healed, but his right shank and foot were gone forever.

At the conclusion of the war, John Silver was retired to Schofield Barracks at Honolulu and committee to the care of the 11th Signal Corps Company. He died on 6 December 1935, at the age of 17 years and 11 months. On each Organisation Day (Anniversary) of the 11th Signal Corps Company, the name 'Stumpy John Silver' is included in the roll call. The Senior Non-Commissioned Officer present responds: 'Died of wounds received in battle in the service of his country.'

Within a month of his death, John Silver's body was received at Wright Field (now Wright-Patterson Air Force Base), and mounted in the glass case for honourable preservation in the Hall of Honour. The portraits of human heroes hang in the hall, but only this pigeon is encased in glass, for truly no human ever performed more valiantly.

34

THE LATE STAN BRYANT OF BRIDGEWATER

AND CHEQUER HEN, DICKEN
MEDAL WINNER, NURP38BPC6

Mr Bryant of 20 Victoria Road, Bridgewater, made the journey to London to receive the Dicken Medal for gallantry which had been awarded to one of his pigeons for outstanding service during the war. Unfortunately, this pigeon died before her part in the war effort was to be recognised, probably due to strain caused through long and hazardous flights in trying conditions. This brave bird was dropped over France by parachute on three occasions, and each time was picked up by members of the French underground movement. Messages were attached to the bird, which returned to Mr Bryant's loft in Victoria Road.

The medal bears the inscription record: returned 10 July 1941 from Angers. 9 September 1941 from Chartres. 29 November 1941 from Montagne. Owner: S Bryant.

It was during the last flight from Montagne that the pigeon made its most gallant and outstanding performance, as the weather conditions at the time were appalling.

The bird had previously been sent on war service as a yearling from Berwick upon Tweed, and from Banff as a two year old; it was second best in the town from the Banff flight.

Previous to the Dicken Medal award in August 1946, she was awarded another honour while flying with the Special Section A.P.S. It too was inscribed with the best operational record returned and listed the heroic flights from Angers, Chartres and Montagne.

This award was presented to Mr Bryant while he was serving with the forces and was received by his father, Mr W.J. Bryant, on his behalf.

During Mr Bryant's absence on War Service, his parents looked after his loft and Mr W. Gratton of Bridgewater, the pigeon supply officer at the time, attended to the despatch of the messages which the bird brought from France.

About twenty other local fanciers sent birds for War Service, with many birds failing to return. Mr Bryant lost twenty of his service pigeons. Official statistics show that 16,554 birds were despatched on various flights, with only 1,842 returning. It is still quite an amazing success rate when you consider that these pigeons had only ever raced the North Road prior to the war.

The late Stan Bryant lived for the sport and was well known in the west of England for his prowess with pigeons and for his forty years as clock setter for his club and the

Stan Bryant, aged twenty-eight, outside his loft in Bridgewater in the 1930s.

THE PEOPLE'S DISPENSARY FOR SICK ANIMALS

FOUNDED 1917. OF THE POOR. INCORPORATED 1923.

Patron : H.R.H. The Duchess of Kent
Founder & Hon. Director : Mrs. M.E. Dickin, O.B.E.

Allied Forces Mascot Club.

THIS IS TO CERTIFY that *N.U.R.P. 38 B.P.6.6*

has been awarded the

DICKIN MEDAL FOR GALLANTRY

For *three outstanding flights from France*

While serving with *the Special Section, Army Pigeon Service, 11.7.41,*
9.9.44, –29.11.44

Date *August* 1946   *M.E. Dickin.*
                                    Founder.

No. *39, A.F.M.C. No. 1187*

Certificate awarded with the Dicken Medal.

Stan Bryant's magnificent awards.

National Flying Club. He was always prominent in the N.F.C. results, as in just three years he won 13th Section, 28th Section, and 48th and 147th Open Pau in 1965. He also won the 155th Open Pau, and the 3rd Open Lamballe in 1966.

These and other positions were won with a small team, and during his lifetime this modest and unassuming man spoke little of the performances of his birds, but forty years' service to the sport deserves recognition, particularly when it goes hand in hand with the successes mentioned.

35

DOVETAIL

THE STORY OF THE RAF PIGEON
WOUNDED IN A RAID OVER GERMANY

P/3579, 'Dovetail', is the first pigeon casualty of the war. [He is] owned by Mr H. Thompson of Burnholme Drive, Heworth, a well-known breeder of racing pigeons. He is at present Category E, temporarily unfit for any form of military service.

Dovetail had a very narrow escape in a bomber over Berlin. He was in a Halifax when a piece of shrapnel tore through the aircraft and pierced the pigeon container in which he was confined. Half of his beak was shot away and the lower beak was split up to the jaw – another half an inch or so and Dovetail would surely have died.

On arrival back at base, he was rushed to the emergency dressing station as he was in really bad shape. He was then returned to his owner's loft, where Mr Thompson fed him on milk and soft food. He now has a pot of his own and manages to shovel provender into his mouth.

The Squadron Commander said that he was thinking of recommending the bird in dispatches because it made no fuss and was always ready on its feet if needed for service.

In the words of his breeder, 'He is now in good heart, although he has lost a lot of weight. He comes from good stock, as his grandsire won the King's Cup in 1933. In other words, like the people of Britain, he can take it.'

As soon as Dovetail is fit again, a 'Medical Board' will regrade him and he will be back in service again. Dovetail has served both in the Army and RAF and with other birds was loaned to carry many important messages, but he wasn't too keen on the Infantry. Like all young men, he wanted to join the Air Force, so he was transferred to Bomber Command.

Dovetail had been in the news before. He won second prize in a race from Banbury to York, covering 224 miles in excellent time. Mr Thompson had been breeding pigeons for more than twenty years and was certainly doing his bit loaning his pigeons for message-carrying.

36

THE HEROES OF CORNWALL

Sandra Williams' father remembers only too well some of the names of his friends who were specially selected to keep pigeons in the war. The late Charlie Rule kept a loft at North Roskeor Road, only a stone's throw from the area where Sandra's family lived. He remembers him having the electrical wire overhead corked in some way, to protect the pigeons from flying into them.

Every pigeon was precious and had an important part to play. When a pigeon arrived with an urgent message strapped to its leg, a telephone or radio message was sent to the Air Ministry at Portreath, St Eval or St Mawgan in Cornwall. St Eval was one of the very first aerodromes ever to be built in Cornwall and also the largest. It was built in 1939 whilst Sandra's father was stationed there, before being posted to the Isles of Scilly.

Trewen Hall is where a service loft was kept full of pigeons. It is thought that a loft still stands there behind the hall, and this loft had been used regularly for some fifty years. One of the most famous pigeons was a blue chequer hen called 'Winkie', to whom the crew of the Beaufort bomber owed their lives in 1942.

Their plane was forced down in the North Sea. 'Winkie' was put in a long tube container and, with her wings clogged in oily water, she set off for home. All night the crew grew colder in the dinghy, wondering if 'Winkie' had made it back or not. Time was getting short and the crew knew only too well that their chances of survival were slim. Fortunately, an exhausted 'Winkie' was made her way home towards the Scottish coast, some 129 miles away and, just before dawn, a telephone call to the operation room at the crew's aerodrome told of her safe arrival.

She didn't carry a message but she did have a code number, which gave them some indication of the crew's whereabouts, and the crew were eventually picked up and rescued.

'Winkie' was classed as one of the bravest pigeons in the Second World War. She was awarded the Dicken Medal and attended a celebration dinner in her honour given by the crew she saved.

In the First World War, pigeons that were wounded were quickly pensioned off and became pets of the crews' aerodrome, but in the Second World War, life was rougher, and it was back to work as soon as possible whenever they recovered.

We talk about the problem we have with hawks today; the danger was even greater in the first half of the twentieth century.

Sandra mentions another brave pigeon that was also awarded the Dicken Medal,

'Mary'. This pigeon was in service from 1940 until the end of the war and ended up having twenty-two stitches in her body.

Once, she failed to· show up for a whole week but eventually arrived with her message, her neck and right breast ripped open, having been attacked by a hawk. A couple of months later, having been lost for three weeks, she arrived home with one wing shot away and three pellets in her body.

During the German raids on Exeter, a large bomb fell outside her loft, killing most of her loftmates. After a short break, 'Mary' was back at work again, but within ten days she was picked up in a field more dead than alive, as thin as a skeleton and with a large gash in her head and several wounds on her body. Her owner was a dedicated pigeon fancier, and spent weeks nursing her back to health; he also put a little leather collar around her neck for support.

On 20 November 1945, 'Mary' of Exeter was awarded the Dicken Medal by Sir James Ross of the Air Ministry. The love of home and the determination of this brave pigeon were quite incredible.

37

WHITE VISION

AN ANGEL OF MERCY

The background to the Dicken Medal story of 'White Vision' involved the Catalina Squadrons in the Shetland Isles, who patrolled the North Sea looking for U-Boats returning to Germany via the northern route. These sorties usually lasted for about twenty-two hours. Thomas Edwin Southern, of Dunham Massey near Altrincham, was an air gunner stationed in the rear bubble of the plane. Thomas was also in charge of cooking the meals, which was a bit handy, as when some of the crew were air sick he could eat what they couldn't face. Crews in those days used to take with them two pigeons on each flight in case the radio failed, or there was some other problem. As press cuttings from the time indicated, this practice was almost redundant but, fortunately, on this particular sortie they took both.

There was some very bad weather during the flight on 10 October 1943 and when the time came for them to return to base, the plane was diverted to Aberdeen, where conditions were no better. From there they were sent to Oban, where they could not land either. In the end the plane ran out of fuel and ditched in the Atlantic in storm conditions with very poor visibility. Radio contact had been lost before the plane went down, so the crew wrote down the co-ordinates and put them in the leg capsules of the two pigeons before releasing them.

The crew had two dinghies, but something went wrong and two men drifted away in the first one. This meant that there were now too many for the second dinghy, so they opted to stay with the plane. The rescue launch arrived many hours later. Just as the last man was boarding, the Catalina tipped up and sank like a stone.

In 1973, Thomas and his wife, Marjorie, attended a ceremony in Motherwell, where the RAF presented the 'White Vision Trophy' to the Dalziel Flying Club. There was a great deal of press coverage of this story and below are just a few comments at the time and since.

THE *SUNDAY POST*, 13 MAY 1973

Two English men will travel north to Motherwell in a couple of week's time to repay an old wartime debt to a pigeon. At the start of the Second World War, over 25,000 racing pigeons were presented to the RAF by fanciers all over Britain. One of them, 'White Vision', was given a commission with the Flying Boat Squadron, based in the Shetlands, when the plane with a crew of ten ditched into the sea. 'White Vision' was released sixty miles from land. For hours the bird battled into the teeth of a storm and a gale and

'*White Vision', winner of the Dicken Medal.*

finally, nearly dead with exhaustion, it arrived at its loft. These men never forgot this bird and were delighted when the Dalziel Club invited them to their Fiftieth Anniversary. These two men, Thomas Southern and Mr Carter of Bakersfield, Nottinghamshire, owe their lives to this pigeon and were now guests of honour at the presentation.

SUNDAY TELEGRAPH, 10 APRIL 1977

I must come to the defence of the much-maligned pigeon, which Doctor B. Mortimer of Epsom alleges, 'leers evilly as he prepares to wreak havoc in towns and gardens'. It is not against pigeons that Dr Mortimer should be conducting a war, he needs to be reminded of or debt to the thousands of war pigeons during the two world wars, like 'White Vision' who was instrumental in saving the lives of a ten-man crew which came down in the sea. And 'Winkie' who saved the crew of a Baltimore, and 'GI Joe' who flew twenty miles in twenty minutes from the village of Colvi, Vecchiato, to a British airstrip, just in time to stop an air strike against the village and the troops that had just captured it, the 56th London Division.

A.K.C. Hamblin, Hon. Director, Magna Carta Campaign for the Protection of the Ethos of Britain.

From: Wing Commander A Steedman AFC RAF (Ret'd)
        Staff Officer to Air Officer Scotland & N Ireland

                                    Office of
                                    Air Officer Scotland & N Ireland
                                    Royal Air Force
                                    Pitreavie Castle
                                    Dunfermline
                                    Fife
                                    0383/
AOSNI/45   Dunfermline/23436 Ext 154

Mr T E Southern
2 Raingills Cottages
Henshall Lane
Dunham Massey
Altringham
Cheshire   / May 1973

Dear Mr Southern,

    On returning from leave this morning I received a letter from your
nephew, Corporal Bowman of RAF Valley, concerning my search for the crew
members of the Catalina which ditched off the Shetlands in 1943. I was
interested to hear from him that you were an air gunner in the crew.

    I have now established most, if not all, of the facts involved in that
flight of 30 years' ago and am aware that a few discrepancies exist between
the actual incident and the report which has resulted from my search.
However, the details concerning White Vision's release, return to base and the
part which the pigeon played in the recovery of the crew are without question
and it gives the Royal Air Force (Scotland) great pleasure in presenting a
Commemorative Trophy to the Dalziel Flying Club as part of the Bi-Centenary
celebrations.

    I would be very grateful for any further background you can give me on
the incident, particularly if you have any lead on any other member of your
crew of that time. Finally, if it can be organised, would you be in a
position to come up to Motherwell in Scotland and present the Trophy in due
course? I look forward to your reply.

                                    Yours sincerely

                                    A Steedman

The reply to Mr Southern.

					Time carried forward :—	167·10	44·10

OCTOBER 1943 190 (CATALINA') SQUADRON

Date	Hour	Aircraft Type and No.	Pilot	Duty	REMARKS (including results of bombing, gunnery, exercises, etc.)	Flying Times Day	Night
		CATALINA					
10·10·43	10·55	FP 280	F/O VAUGHAN	FM A/AG	A/S PATROL. FORCED LANDING IN SEA ABANDONED AIRCRAFT IN SINKING CONDITION 0200 HRS 12·10·43	10·00	12·00

S/LDR.
FLIGHT COMMANDER, 190 SQUADRON

SUMMARY FOR OCTOBER 1943
DAY 10·00
NIGHT 12·00
TOTAL DAY 177·10
TOTAL NIGHT 56·10
TOTAL Nº SORTIES 6.

SIGNED S/LDR FLT CNDR.

SUMMARY FOR NOVEMBER 1943.
UNIT 190 SQDN.
DATE 1·12·43 DAY NIL
NIGHT NIL
SIGNATURE.

					TOTAL TIME ...	177·10	56·10

Log record for the plane which had 'White Vision' aboard.

Mrs Southern holding the White Vision Trophy for filming Animals in the War.

Thomas Edwin Southern, one of the ten airmen rescued due to the bravery of 'White Vision'.

EVENING NEWS, 9 APRIL 1973

The RAF at Pitreavie Castle, Dunfermline, are trying to trace an ex-officer or any member of the crew of a Catalina Flying Boat, [which was] involved in a wartime incident which resulted in a carrier pigeon being awarded the animal VC. The aircraft was piloted by Flying Officer Vaughan, a member of the 190 Squadron, stationed at Sullom Voe in 1943, who had to ditch the plane due to engine trouble. The crew were rescued because of a pigeon called 'White Vision' that was being carried in the aircraft and released with an SOS message attached to its leg.

DAILY TELEGRAPH – PIGEON THAT SAVED TEN WAS 'UNAUTHORISED'

'White Vision', an RAF pigeon which saved the ten-man crew of a ditched Catalina aircraft thirty years ago by flying sixty miles to alert rescuers, was an unauthorised passenger on the plane, it was disclosed yesterday. Coastal Command decided pigeons should not be carried anymore but ignored orders and gave two to the crew, said Mr

George Thick, who was in charge of the Pigeon Section at the Catalina's base at Sullom Voe, Shetland at the time. 'It was a fantastic piece of luck really, because this particular Catalina was the only crew to take them; the other crews regarded them as further encumbrance.'

This new light on the famous wartime incident involving the bird (number 3089) has been provided by Mr Thick in a search by the RAF for the surviving members of the crew.

They want the former captain of the Catalina or a member of the crew to present a trophy to 'White Vision's' former owners, the Dalziel Flying Club of Motherwell, commemorating the bird's epic flight for which she was awarded the animal VC.

Mr Thick, aged fifty-two, and now a landscape gardener of High Wycombe, Bucks, volunteered for the Pigeon Service during the war because of his experience as a fancier. He said, 'I saw the crew after they had been rescued and they were overjoyed about the pigeon.'

The Commanding Officer of the Coastal Command asked me to give it a name, so I settled on 'White Vision' because it was a pure white hen.

Thomas Southern was not flying with his usual crew, but on the picture of 'White Vision' all the rescue crew have signed it. Thomas told his wife that while the diversions were being made he had fallen asleep and woke up as they were about to land, thinking they were about to touch down safely. The tremendous crash which followed convinced him that something indeed had gone very wrong. Thomas used to say that concrete would break up if a plane hit it, but sea water doesn't, hence landing in the sea is always extremely dangerous. The outcome was that one bird was lost, but 'White Vision' returned home, albeit minus lots of feathers.

38

'DATELINE ...
ROYAL AIR FORCE'

NO. 178, 19 APRIL 1973

SEARCH LAUNCHED – THIRTY YEARS AFTER!

The Northern Rescue Co-ordination Centre at RAF Pitreavie Castle in Scotland has launched an unusual search mission – for the crew of a plane which ditched thirty years ago.

The Royal Air Force in Scotland is trying to trance an ex-Officer or any member of the crew of a Catalina flying boat who were involved in a wartime incident.

The aircraft was piloted by Flying Officer Vaughan, a member of number 190 Squadron stationed at Sullom Voe during 1943. They had to ditch under adverse conditions because of engine failure and owe their survival to the homing instincts of a pigeon. Pigeons were carried as standard procedure in operating aircraft of that day.

Following the ditching, the pigeon was released with a message capsule giving the estimated position.

Despite very bad weather conditions, this pigeon made it back to base with the information, which saved the crew from almost certain death from exposure.

Subsequently, the pigeon, named 'White Vision', was awarded the Animal VC.

The club which presented 'White Vision' to the RAF at the outbreak of war – Dalziel Flying Club (Racing Pigeons) of Motherwell, Lanarkshire, is celebrating its bicentenary this year and the Royal Air Force in Scotland is presenting a trophy in commemoration of its most famous pigeon.

Wing Commander Alex Steedman, Staff Officer to the Air Officer Scotland and Northern Ireland, at Pitreavie Castle, near Dunfermline, Fife, has been trying to locate ex-Flying Officer Vaughan or a member of the crew to present the trophy, but his searches have so far drawn a blank. 'It would be a nice gesture if one of the original crew members could make the presentation'. He said, 'I have been following a tentative lead which established the address of the Captain, who is now out of the Service, [and living] around the Southampton area. But I have come up against a dead end. I would be grateful if anyone could put me in touch with any member of the crew'

Further information can be obtained from the Strike Command Public Relations Officer at Pitreavie Castle, telephone Dunfermline 23436 Ext. 198

39

INTERESTING FACTS ABOUT PIGEONS

Little pigeon statues have been found, which were made 5,000 years before our era. The statues have a striking resemblance to modern race birds. Greek and Roman writers and historians mention pigeons. Throughout history, pigeons have informed the home front on the victories and defeats of kings and generals.

Pigeons were the carriers of news between Iraq and Syria in the twelfth century. The Sultans built pigeon houses, and Belgium and Dutch newspapers relied upon pigeons to bringing information. Napoleon's defeat in the battle of Waterloo was reported to England by Nathan Rothschild's pigeons.

During the First World War, some action was undertaken after the Forces were informed that photos had been taken by military pigeons. German forces took possession of more than one million Belgium racing pigeons. A war memorial in Brussels is a reminder of the military pigeons and their fanciers who died during the war. There is also a war memorial in Lille in France that remembers more than 20,000 military pigeons killed during the war. Planes and warships were always accompanied by military pigeons.

Military pigeons brought 717 tidings of crashed aircraft at sea. Ninety-five per cent of the military birds returned from their mission. All seventy-two pigeons returned to their destination during the offensive of Aisne-Marne. They brought back seventy-eight important tidings. 442 pigeons were used during the offensive of Mense-Argonne, bringing back 403 messages.

Many birds were badly injured during these conflicts. Some of the most famous military pigeons were: 'Cher Ami', 'President Wilson', 'Big Tom', 'Colonel's Lady', 'Steady', 'Lord Adelaine', 'The Mocker' and 'Spike'.

'Cher Ami' was the last hope of a New York battalion when many pigeons had already been killed. 'Cher Ami' reached his loft although he was wounded very badly. He saved 194 lives of the 'Lost Battalion'. Once in America, he became the mascot of the Department of Service.

'The Mocker' was born in 1917. He was wounded on his fifty-second mission. He lost his left eye and part of his cranium. 'The Mocker' died on 15 June 1937.

'President Wilson', lost his foot on 5 November 1918. It seemed impossible that the bird could reach his destination, but he saved the lives of many American infantrymen who were surrounded by enemies. 'Wilson' died on 8 June 1929.

'Spike' was born in January 1918. He flew fifty missions and was never injured. 'Spike' died on 11 April 1935.

Many pigeons moved to America after the war. One of the most famous German pigeons was 'The Kaiser'. He was born in 1918 and was trained for special missions. 'The Kaiser' was captured in 1918 by American forces in the battle of the Meuse. He was a very clever and beautiful bird and had many descendants who proved their intelligence in races. 'The Kaiser' lived to an incredible thirty-two years of age.

British and American museums are full of memories of our flying heroes. Some of them were decorated and buried with military honours. Visitors can admire military pigeons such as 'Lord Adelaide', 'President Wilson', 'Julius Caesar', 'Lady Astor', 'Jungle Joe' and 'Burma Queen'. There were more than 3,000 soldiers and 150 officers of the United States Pigeon Service taking care of 54,000 military pigeons.

Some of these pigeons were trained to fly at night and were taken on service with the field post, paratroopers and submarines, where they took photographs that were returned by the birds, giving positions of enemy fleets, troops and targets for air attacks.

The Royal Canadian Air Force had two successful military pigeons, '10601' and '120'. The '10601' was born in 1928 and flew its missions mostly from submarines. He accomplished all his missions, but sadly was killed by a bird of prey.

The '120' flew from Sasaginigek lakes in very bad circumstances and struck a radio wire.

'Snow White' had a successful flight in Berlin during heavy bombardments. She flew from Hamburg to different lofts; later on she flew missions in Italy. 'Snow White' was honoured with the Military Cross.

H.M. Queen with the Royal Pigeon.

154

40

ROYAL OPENING

The Royal Family has been very involved in pigeon racing for many years. Even today, the Queen takes great interest in the Royal Lofts at Sandringham and is Patron of the Royal Pigeon Racing Association.

Her Majesty visited the Regimental Headquarters of the Royal Army Veterinary Corps at Melton Mowbray on 28 June 1996. After a wet start to the day, the weather had considerably improved and it was dry by the time Her Majesty arrived at 2.30 p.m. The radiance of the Queen's smile and her obvious enjoyment of the visit was, however, more than fair compensation for the indifferent weather.

A very tight Royal programme, with only ninety minutes allocated to the visit, meant that Her Majesty's tour of the Defence Animal Centre facilities was confined to the Equine and Veterinary Divisions, with the Canine Division presentation taking place on the 14 acre field between the two. On arrival, Her Majesty released a pigeon which carried a message of the occasion back to the Royal Lofts at Sandringham.

An old comrade, Dennis Sanders, after speaking to the Queen about his charitable work with 'Stephanie', a pigeon given to him from the Royal Lofts three years ago, was given permission to release five pigeons carrying messages from the five Corps Units.

This was possibly the first occasion that a carrier pigeon had been released from a military unit since the last war and certainly the first released by a monarch in such circumstances.

The Queen seemed amused when the first pigeon paused to consider the situation before taking flight after some encouragement from the director, but, having shown the way, the flight of five required no assistance in taking to the air in style.

41

'STEPHANIE' ATTRACTS CROWDS TO COUNTY SHOW

One Bank Holiday in 1997 saw an estimated 30,000 people attending the Leicestershire County Show held at Dishley Grange near Loughborough. The attendance for this annual event was boosted this year because a Royal celebrity would be at the centre of an official opening at midday on the Sunday.

'Stephanie', one of Queen Elizabeth II's racing pigeons, was the star attraction and for the first time ever, a racing pigeon stand was set up at the show. This was organised by Loughborough Premier South Road Club under the guidance of club chairman, Jim Smelt, who was assisted by club members.

Dennis Sanders travelled up from Birmingham with 'Stephanie', a five-year-old light blue chequer hen that was obtained from the Royal Loft Manager after Dennis had made enquiries about promoting the sport. Dennis is himself a keen fancier, but has not raced for some time due to his heavy workload, attending shows and other events. These events included the VE Day celebrations at the Birmingham Hall of Memory, where forty-nine white pigeons and a dark blue pigeon were released to fly back to different parts of the UK. The dark pigeon was again from the Royal Loft and was chosen so that it could be easily picked out by the watching crowds.

A pigeon racing stand was set up in the marquee that housed the main attractions and was decked out with posters and books. As well as show pigeons, pens were supplied by Nottingham Show Fanciers Club. Many people enquired about the sport, especially about their involvement during the Second World War.

42

AT LAST – A SALUTE FOR OUR WINGS

The year 2000 saw pigeon fanciers countrywide rejoice and celebrate Remembrance Sunday, when, for the first time in this historical event, carrier pigeons were finally commended in a true, honourable fashion.

Veterans countrywide made the journey to the Lion Brewery, Ash, Surrey, where Mike and Susan Armitage had great pleasure meeting these interesting and eager people.

Mr Keith Sandbach, a keen fancier, was amongst those to participate in the march to the Cenotaph. Keith who has been racing pigeons for almost forty years, flies with the Kersal Vase H.S. and makes a yearly appearance alongside the Royal British Legion, of which he is an avid supporter. Keith also very generously donated some of his pigeon winnings, which was much appreciated.

A communications man, Mr Jack Porter from Stalmine, served with the Royal Signals during the forties and was responsible for training the forces pigeons. He initially trained nearby in Aldershot and then went on to the Shetlands, Scotland, where he continued training. After the war, Jack and his wife ran a little Post Office, which had been a family business for over 100 years and continues to be run by his family.

Eddie Gilbert and Porter were joined in camaraderie. They had been signalmen in the 1940s in the depths of Maadi and trained pigeons in South Africa for the National Pigeon Service. Aldershot was the training area, and they then moved further north to Bishop's Monkton. It was near here that many lofts were erected. Eddie went on from there with his dear comrade Jack Porter to Egypt and set up the headquarters in Maadi, where they were responsible for training the birds over the desert. This pigeon HQ was a little nondescript, with lofts erected in the Syrian hills, attached to the Arab Legion. So things were pretty tricky to say the least and they finished up at Damascus in a mobile loft. In 1944, they, along with the birds, were taken to Turkey, where of course war was not an issue.

Also in the party was a gentleman from Stockington, Mr Frederick Dyke, who was allocated through the Special Sections Home Guard Unit and was a member of the National Pigeon Service. Frederick bred in the region of fifty to sixty birds for the forces.

Carrier pigeons played an enormous part in the war, particularly in Germany where Churchill's secret army sought out concentration camps, Hitler's flying bomb production sites and the like. Once located, the birds were liberated and returned to the UK and thus divulged the vital location points in Germany.

The RAF successfully bombed Peenamunde. Frederick said that many of our pigeons, along with thousands from the occupied countries, were eventually shot or captured by the Germans. Despite this, Britain replaced those birds for the Belgians.

43

ANIMALS IN THE WAR MEMORIAL FUND

In early 1998, a group of like-minded individuals discussed the possibility of erecting a monument dedicated to the millions of animals who have served unswervingly alongside the British and Commonwealth forces during the conflicts of the twentieth century. Coming from such diverse worlds as the arts, animal welfare, television, the services and politics, this group formed a board of trustees to begin the long process of selecting a sculptor, a site and planning the complex route of fundraising to make the dream a reality.

The committee were chaired by Major-General Peter Davies, Director General of the RSPCA, and supported by figures such as Brigadier Andrew Parker-Bowles, Jilly Cooper, Joanne Lumley and Kate Adie. The initial selection of sculptor began in April 1998. Since that time, the board has been joined by another patron, The Duke of Wellington, and most recently, as chief Patron of the project, Her Royal Highness The Princess Royal.

At all times, the trustees have worked with the local council to ensure a suitable choice of both artist and site. From an initial list of forty artists, twelve were asked to produce sketches of their proposed work and a final four were asked to produce a maquette.

After many hours of deliberations, celebrated sculptor David Backhouse was chosen for attaining the closest representation of the vision and meaning behind the Animals in War project.

Running parallel to artistic considerations were those of the selection of the site. As a monument of significant interest to animal lovers, the forces, the art community and the general public as a whole, the selection of the site had to be carefully considered.

Several sites in central London were looked at and after considerations of planning permission, accessibility and suitability, the Park Lane site at Brook Gate was chosen.

During some of the most violent conflicts of the twentieth century, animals were chosen for a variety of their natural instincts. Dogs accompanied troops into the jungle combat as their sense of smell easily identified ambush parties, often hugely increasing the survival rates of British troops entering unknown territory. Dogs were also widely used in the First World War to run messages through the trenches.

Homing pigeons were often used when troops were dropped behind enemy lines in order to communicate the position of the enemy. Pigeons were also taken on flights and released if a plane was hit and was going down. When the pigeon returned to base, the home team could work out an estimate of where the plane went down by calcu-

The model of the war memorial.

Artist's impression of the war memorial in London.

lating flight times and so ensure a better chance of rescuing the crew.

In addition, there were many millions of horses used for transport as well as donkeys, mules, camels and elephants, a great many of which did not survive. All of these creatures, both great and small, valiantly played a part in some of the bloodiest conflicts of history, giving their support and often their lives as part of their loyalty to their masters. This monument will be our way of paying service to their efforts.

LAUNCH OF THE ANIMALS IN THE WAR MEMORIAL FUND
15 FEBRUARY 2001, LONDON HILTON, PARK LANE.

Best-selling author Jilly Cooper hosted a star-studded reception to officially launch the Animals in War Memorial Fund, joined by other trustees of the fund such as Joanna Lumley, Kate Adie, Nicholas Soames and with the backing of well-known personalities such as Simon Weston and Angela Rippon. Jilly outlined the project for

The founder members of the War Memorial Committee. From left to right: Brian Newsome, Garry McCafferty, Ken Smith and Derek Partridge.

Simon Weston and party at the war memorial event in London, 15 February 2001.

London's newest monument.

She said: 'Countless millions of innocent animals served and died terrible deaths beside of British and Commonwealth armies during the twentieth century. They had no idea why they had been drawn into our conflicts and acted solely out of loyalty and love. It is a national disgrace that Great Britain is the only Commonwealth country not to honour such selfless heroism. The Animals in the War Memorial Fund will redress the balance by building a beautiful monument in Park Lane as a constant reminder of the debt we owe our animal allies. Remember them all, they had no choice.'

Corporate sponsor Petplan, the UK's largest pet insurance company, generously sponsored the reception as well as lending administrative support to the fund.

In addition to the long list of celebrity names backing the project, the reception will also host the official announcement of Her Royal Highness The Princess Royal as Patron of the trust and the Duke of Wellington as Vice-Patron.

Simon Weston, veteran of the Falklands War, marked the beginning of fundraising in earnest by presenting a cheque for £10,000 on behalf of the Sport of Racing Pigeons to Jilly Cooper, the vice-chairman of the fund. Amongst other guests present was one of London's most ardent supporters of these birds, The Right Honourable Tony Banks MP

Over the past six months, pigeon fanciers from all over the United Kingdom have organised events to support their fundraising campaign. One of the most prestigious of these held so far has been a unique auction of racing pigeons, including one of the Queen's prize birds from the Royal Loft at Sandringham. Other celebrities such as football stars Gerry Francis and Duncan Ferguson also gave birds to be auctioned.

The involvement of the sport will for the first time officially recognise the exceptional role that racing pigeons played in the war, primarily in communications and rescue efforts. Thirty-one pigeons have been awarded Dicken Medals, the animal equivalent of a Victoria Cross, for their efforts during the Second World War, more than any other animal. Many of the ancestors of those brave birds now race from those original releasing grounds of France, Spain and Germany, purely for the fun and sport.

Amongst the guests at the Hilton were Mrs M. Southern and Mrs M. Blyth from Scotland, who fully appreciated this vital role. A pigeon called 'White Vision', bred by Mrs Blyth's late father, rescued Mrs Southern's late husband, Ted, along with the crew of his plane during the Second World War. The crew was part of a squadron that patrolled the North Sea looking for U-boats.

On 10 October 1943, the plane ditched in the Atlantic in storm conditions. The crew wrote down the co-ordinates and put them in the leg capsules of the pigeons on the plane. 'White Vision' made it back to base and alerted the rescue launches, which saved every man.

Derek Partridge, PR for the Sport of Racing Pigeon War Memorial Fund said, 'We are delighted to be part of the fundraising for this tremendous monument and will continue with our efforts throughout 2001. We believe our sport should be a major player for the fund due to the heroic efforts so many birds made in communicating vital information from behind enemy lines and also in the rescue of countless of our men such as Ted Southern.'

To date, the War Memorial Fund of Pigeon Racing has donated £20,000 to the cause.

44

THE WORTHING MEMORIAL

Racing pigeon trainer and stonemason, Stewart Earl, could not bear to see the sad state of a memorial to carrier pigeons during the Second World War. He decided to give the unique tribute a face-lift to mark the sixtieth anniversary of the conflict which saw these birds on active service.

The two stones on the mound in Worthing's Beach House Park are thought to be the only such monument in the country. The inscription quotes the book of Ecclesiastes, 'A bird of the air shall carry the voice and that which hath wings shall tell the matter'. As we have mentioned, during the war, pigeons were used for a number of different purposes and military lofts were set up, with the birds ferrying messages and reports because it was unsafe to use the radio. They were also dropped into Belgium and France in the hope that civilians could use them to attach details of enemy movements.

The War Memorial at Worthing.

The beautiful flower design at the Worthing War Memorial.

The heartfelt words on the stones at the Worthing Memorial.

As well as these uses, all pilots carried pigeons in their aircrafts in case they ditched into the sea.

However, not a great deal is known about the Worthing Memorial, but we do know that it was unveiled in 1951 by the Duke and Duchess of Hamilton, and originally consisted of stone pigeon statues. These were vandalised a number of times over the years and had not been replaced.

Mr Earl, co-owner of the monument company, became aware of the stones when he was commissioned by the council to clean them. He decided to adopt them permanently and is now keen to find out more about their history. He said, 'It needs cleaning with an anti-algae chemical, then the cut lettering needs to be repaired and repainted'.

Nancy Price (in the next extract) established a number of animal sanctuaries; perhaps she had a relative in the Pigeon Service.

45

A TELEGRAM GIRL
REMEMBERS NANCY PRICE

In 1917, I was a telegram girl. I was thirteen years old and can remember delivering several telegrams to the home of Nancy Price; her married name was Mrs Maude. She was a tall skinny lady, plain looking with absolutely straight hair. She had one daughter, Joan, and possibly another daughter, I'm not quite sure. She lived in a house in Marine Parade, opposite the bandstand; it was called Montague Cottage. I recall delivering telegrams (the quickest means of communications in those days) and then waiting for the answers.

I would wait in a small hall, where I was fascinated by a beautiful painting of a Victorian lady dressed in a black dress with the finest lace collar. Nancy Price was a West End actress and later appeared in films. She appeared in the film *Mandy*, about little deaf children, where she played a doctor.

I can hear her now talking about her 'warrior birds', as she called the pigeons. She was always very concerned when she spoke of them; she hated to hear of them being shot down. The local newspapers were often reporting her concerns; all of this was during the First World War.

Even before the memorial was built in Beach House Park, she asked for a stone basin of water to be placed on the mound so that all birds could have a drink. It was arranged that the water from the pool would trickle down the mound.

During the Second World War, she moved to High Salvington but never forgot her 'warrior birds'.

46

MEMENTO FOR THE QUEEN'S MUSEUM

Six men who served in the Middle East Pigeon Service in the Second World War met annually at the Old Comrades show. One of the six was Bill Button, who is now eighty-one years old and emigrated to Australia in 1979.

Bill had raced his pigeons in the Ipswich Flying Club with the Essex and Suffolk Border Federation and was 'Scribe' under the name of 'Uno Solo'. Before emigrating, Bill went to the Old Comrades for the last time and was presented with a memento, a shield, by the other five servicemen who were: J. Crossland, R. Ebdon, J. Ambler, J. Errant and Eddie Gilbert; all six names were inscribed on the shield.

Bill, who lives in Adelaide, decided when his daughter Lydia and grandson Edward were planning a holiday to England that the pigeon world shouldn't forget these six men who served in the Middle East. So Lydia and Edward came over with the shield.

They wanted to contact Eddie Gilbert, whose name and address was on the back of the shield, hoping that he might be able to get the shield into the Queen's Museum at Sandringham, as he lived nearby at King's Lynn in Norfolk. Unfortunately, before they could contact him, he sadly died, a couple of days before Christmas. They then got in touch with her Majesty the Queen's Loft Manager, Carlo Napolitano, who in turn contacted the Queen, who was delighted to have the shield in her museum.

Lydia and Edward then went to the Royal Lofts at Sandringham and presented the shield to Carlo.

If any of the old members would like to contact Bill, his address is: Unit One, 34 Harvey Street, Nailsworth 5081, South Australia.

47

THE DICKEN MEDAL AWARDS

The Dicken Medal was instituted by Mrs Maria Dicken, the founder of the People's Dispensary for Sick Animals (PDSA). It was awarded to animals that showed gallantry and devotion to duty while serving with any section of the armed forces or civil defence sections during the Second World War and afterwards. The award was made only upon official recommendation and was exclusive to the United Kingdom.

The bronze medal bears the initials 'PDSA' at the top and the words 'For Gallantry' in the centre. It has the words 'We also serve' below, all within a laurel wreath. The reverse was left blank for details of the recipient. The medal ribbon is green, dark brown and pale blue, representing water, earth and air to symbolise the Naval, Military, Civil Defence and Air Forces. Fifty-three Dicken Medals were awarded – eighteen to dogs, three to horses, one to a cat and thirty-one to pigeons.

The following are some details of the brave birds that were awarded this outstanding honour.

NURP41SBS219 COCK 'DUKE OF NORMANDY' (Award 8 January 1947)
For being the first bird to arrive with a message from Paratroopers of the 21st Army Group behind enemy lines on D-Day, 6 June 1944, while serving with the APS.

NURP43CC2418 (Award 8 January 1947)
For the fastest flight with a message from the 6th Airborne Division in Normandy on 7 June 1944 while serving with the APS.

NURP36JH190, 'KENLEY LASS', DARK CHEQUER HEN
She was the thirteenth Dicken Medal winner and was the first pigeon to carry messages out of enemy-occupied France. The secret agent was dropped into enemy territory with the pigeon attached to him and he had to cover nine miles on foot before dawn without being discovered. The agent then had to arrange for the pigeon to be hidden for eleven days until the required information could be obtained. In all this time the bird was in the care of someone who only had very brief instructions in looking after pigeons.

She was released at 8.20 a.m. on 20 October 1940 and reached Kenley, Shropshire at 3.00 p.m., a distance of over 300 miles.

On 16 February 1941 she performed a similar task, except that she was only kept hidden for four days.

The Dicken Medal.

She was bred by W.H. Torkington of Pointon, Lancashire, and trained by R.W. Beard of Kenley. Details of the bird appeared in the sale list printed after the death of Beard in 1942. It appears as number twenty-four and was sold for £3 to Don Cole of Cirencester. H.E. Whitworth of Peterborough visited Don Cole several times while he was stationed at Cirencester during 1944 to 1945 and described her as being 'a lovely hen', very slightly pied.

The last news heard was that the breeder, Mr Torkington, wanted the pigeon back again, but no further information is available since Mr Torkington and Mr Cole are now dead.

Mr Cole had a loft manager who helped him, but we understand that he was not well versed in the handling of pen or pencil and consequently further information has been lost.

A granddaughter of 'Kenley Lass' was presented to H.E. Whitworth and from her he bred a blue chequer cock, which flew 525 miles in one day as a yearling; another granddaughter won 17th section N.R.C.C. 1954.

'GI JOE', USA43SC6390 (Award August 1946)
This bird is credited with making the most outstanding flight by a USA army pigeon in the Second World War. It made the twenty-mile flight from British 10th Army HQ in the same number of minutes. It brought a message which arrived just in time to save the lives of at least 100 Allied soldiers from being bombed by their own planes.

'PADDY', NPS439451 (Award 1 September 1944)

For the best recorded time with a message from the Normandy operations while serving with the RAF in June 1944.

'ALL ALONE', NURP39SDS39 (Award February 1946)

For delivering an important message in one day over a distance of 400 miles, while serving with the NPS in August 1943.

'PRINCESS', 43WD593 (Award May 1946)

Sent on a special mission to Crete, this pigeon returned to her loft (RAF Alexandria) having travelled about 500 miles, mostly over sea, with highly valuable information. One of the finest performances in the war record of the Pigeon Service.

'MERCURY', NURP37CEN335 (Award August 1946)

For carrying out a special task involving a flight of 480 miles from Northern Denmark while serving with the Special Section Army Pigeon Service in July 1942.

NURP38BPC6 (Award August 1946)

For three outstanding flights from France while serving with the Special Branch Section Army Pigeon Service. 11 July 1941, 9 September 1942, 29 November 1941.

NU41HQ4373 BLUE COCK, 'BILLY'

Released with a message from a forced landed Bomber crew in the Netherlands at 10.00 a.m. on 21 February 1942 and delivered its message the following day at 1.40 p.m. in a state of complete collapse. The weather conditions could hardly have been worse – a gale-driven storm (snow). 'Billy' was eleven months old at the time and the distance was approximately 250 miles.

Bred and trained by J. Greenwood, Bathurst, Moor Lane, Hykeham, Lincoln. RAF Station, Waddington.

NEHU40NS1, BLUE CHEQUER HEN, 'WINKIE'

On 23 February 1942, a damaged Beaufort ditched suddenly whilst returning from a strike off the Norwegian coast and partially broke up on heavy impact, 120 miles from the Scottish coast. This pigeon accidentally escaped from the container in the crash and fell into the oily sea before struggling clear. The distance to base was 129 miles, the nearest land 120 miles, and there were one-and-a-half-hours of daylight left. The pigeon homed soon after dawn the next morning, exhausted, wet and oily. The air search for the crew on a very poor radio fix up to them had been unsuccessful.

Sergeant Davidson, RAF Pigeon Service, deduced from the arrival of the pigeon, its condition and other circumstances, that the area of search was incorrect. The search was redirected in accordance with his advice and fifteen minutes later the crew was located and rescue action taken. This was the first rescue during the Second World War attributable to a pigeon. The rescued crew gave a dinner in honour of the pigeon and her trainer at which they christened the pigeon 'Winkie' because she appeared to be winking at them – in fact, the unusually slow reaction of the eyelid would be due to the after-effects of extreme fatigue.

'Winkie' was bred by NPS member A.R. Colley, Whitburn, Sunderland. She was trained by NPS members Ross and Norris, 88 Long Lane, Broughty Ferry, Angus, Scotland. RAF Station, Leuchars.

NURP38EGU142, RED CHEQUER COCK, 'COMMANDO'

On three occasions, namely in June 1942, August 1942 and September 1942, this bird was sent with agents into occupied France and on each occasion returned with valuable information on the day of release. The conditions in which this pigeon had to operate on two occasions were exceptionally adverse.

Bred and trained by NPS member S.A. Moon, Haywards Heath.

NURP39NRS144, RED COCK, 'COLOGNE'

This pigeon had been on over 100 operational Bomber sorties and had homed from diverted or force-landed aircraft from widely separated positions in Great Britain at various times. On 29 June 1943, its aircraft was lost over target (Cologne) and there was no news of the aircraft crew. On 16 July, this pigeon homed with severe injuries, including a broken breastbone which had healed and over which the feathers had regrown, showing that the injury was at least two weeks old.

Bred and trained by NPS member W.H. Payne, 8 Frederick Avenue, Nottingham. RAF Station, Bottesford.

NURP40GV1S453, BLUE COCK, 'ROYAL BLUE'

This was the first pigeon during the last war to bring a message from a force-landed aircrew on the continent. On 10 October 1940, this young bird was released in Holland, approximately 120 miles from base at 7.20 a.m. and arrived at Sandringham at 11.30 a.m. the same day with information regarding the situation of the crew.

'Royal Blue', the King's racing pigeon sent on war service in 1940, has won fame as a carrier pigeon and was presented with the Dicken Medal for outstanding achievement.

The official Air Ministry citation states: 'This was the first pigeon during the present war to bring a message from a force-landed aircrew on the Continent. On 10 October 1940, this young bird was released in Holland, approximately 120 miles from base at 7.20 a.m. and arrived at Sandringham at 11.50 a.m. on the same day with information regarding the situation of the crew.

The presentation was made by Rear Admiral R.M. Bellairs, C.B.C.M.G. at the 'To Victory With The RAF' exhibition organised by the *Daily Herald* at Dorland Hall, Regent Street, SW1.

Rear Admiral Bellairs decorated five other pigeons, which had won war honours. The award had been made on nineteen previous occasions to twelve pigeons and seven dogs.

After the ceremony, two carrier pigeons from the Royal Lofts were released from the entrance, in front of the statue, 'The Winged Victory of Samothrace'.

These birds carried a message to the King from the Allied Mascot Club, asking His Majesty to accept the Dicken Medal on behalf of 'Royal Blue'. A reply was received later in the day to say that the King had been graciously pleased to accept.

'Royal Blue' was bred and trained by the King at Sandringham. RAF Station, Bircham Newton.

NURP41A2164, 'DUTCH COAST'

On 13 April 1942, this pigeon was released by a ditched aircrew from their dinghy off the coast of Holland at 6.20 a.m. with a message giving their position. The pigeon delivered the message at 1.50 p.m. that day, a distance of 288 miles in seven and a half hours under conditions that were by no means favourable.

Bred and trained by NPS member J. Flowers, Radcliffe-on-Trent. RAF Station, Syerston.

SURP41L3089, WHITE HEN, 'WHITE VISION'

This pigeon was carried in a Catalina flying boat which, owing to engine failure, had to ditch into a rough sea in Northern Waters at approximately 8.20 a.m. on 11 October 1943. Owing to radio failure, no SOS was received from the aircraft and no fix obtained. As the aircraft was overdue and suspected to be in difficulties, rescue searches were made but were limited owing to the severe weather conditions. No aircraft was permitted to take off. At 5.00 p.m., 'White Vision' arrived with a message giving the position and other information concerning the aircraft and crew. The time of origin of this message was 8.20 a.m.

As a result, the sea search was continued in the direction indicated and at five past midnight the following morning the aircraft was sighted by HSL and the crew rescued. The aircraft had to be abandoned and sank. Weather conditions were: visibility at place of release of pigeon, 100 yards. Visibility at base when pigeon arrived, 300 yards. Head wind for pigeon, 25 miles per hour.

'MARQUIS', NPSNS36392 (Award October 1945)

For bringing important messages three times from enemy-occupied country. May 1943 (Amiens), February 1944 (Combined Operations) and in June 1944 (French Marquis) while serving with the Special Service from the Continent.

NPS42NS7524 (Award October 1945)

For bringing important messages three times from enemy-occupied country. In July 1942, May 1943 and July 1943, while serving with the Special Service from the Continent.

MPS42NS278 (Award October 1945)

For bringing important messages three times from enemy-occupied country in July 1942, August 1942 and April 1943, while serving with the Special Service from the Continent.

'BROAD ARROW' 41BA2793 (Award October 1945)

For bringing important messages from enemy-occupied country three times in May 1943, June 1943 and August 1943, while serving with the Fifth Special Service from the Continent.

'MARY', NURP40WCE249 (Award November 1945)

For outstanding endurance on War Service.

'TOMMY', NURP41DHZ56 (Award February 1946)

For delivering valuable messages from Holland to Lancashire under difficult conditions, while serving with the NPS, July 1942.

NPS41NS2862, BLUE COCK, 'NAVY BLUE'

This pigeon had an excellent flying record in the RAF on Air and Sea Rescue Service and was selected for a special task in connection with a seaborne landing by a small reconnaissance party on the west coast of France, some 200 miles from Plymouth. The pigeon was issued on 15 June 1944, in a small container, but the operation did not take place until the night of 17 June. The message did not state time of release, but was of immense value to the Intelligence Branch concerned. The pigeon was injured, but managed to reach Plymouth where it was picked up at 2.45 p.m. on 19 June, when its message was delivered.

NPS41NS4230, 'BEACHCOMBER'

One of a pair released from the beachhead during the Dieppe raid, his companion was killed by enemy fire.

Owned by W.H. Tompkins, 5/9 Stratford Road, Wolverton, Bucks. Bred by W. Lane, 61 Allen Road, Ipswich. Trained by Army Pigeon Service.

NPS42NS15125, MEALY COCK, 'WILLIAM OF ORANGE'

During training flew sixty-eight miles in fifty-eight minutes while on service with airborne troops at Arnhem. Was liberated at 10.30 a.m. on 19 September 1944, returned to loft in 4 hours 25 minutes, distance 260 miles, of which 135 miles was across open sea.

'William of Orange' was bred and owned by W. Proctor Smith, Bexton House, Bexton, Knutsford. Trained by Army Pigeon Service.

NPS4221610, BLUE CHEQUER HEN, 'SCOTCH LASS'

Her service commenced at RAF Wick and continued in 1943 at RAF Felixstowe and included forty-three flights from small naval craft in the North Sea. She was dropped with an agent in Holland in September 1944 and, although injured by hitting telegraph wires in semi-darkness when released in early dawn, she successfully delivered her message and photo films on the same day. Distance was approximately 260 miles.

Bred by Collins & Son, 68 Whitecraig Crescent, Whitecraig, Musselburgh. Trained at RAF Station, Felixstowe, Suffolk.

NPS4231066, GRIZZLE COCK, 'GUSTAV'

This pigeon was the first to arrive with information concerning the Normandy landings on D-Day. He carried the message from a Reuter's correspondent from landing craft standing off the beach during the first landings. The weather was adverse and Gustav's time was 5 hours 16 minutes. During his two years of RAF service, Gustav had built up a reputation for reliability.

Bred by NPS member F.E. Jackson, 5 Windsor Road, Cosham. Trained by RAF Thorney Island.

NPS42NS44802, DARK CHEQUER COCK, 'FLYING DUTCHMAN'

In addition to a great many flights from light naval craft in the North Sea, this pigeon was dropped with an agent at various points on the continent on three occasions, in March, May and June of 1944. Distance travelled was between 150 and 250 miles and on one occasion the bird delivered valuable information on the day of release. In August 1944, this pigeon was sent for the fourth time on a similar task, but sadly did not return.

Bred by NPS member E.G. Forster, 67 Castleton Road, Walthamstow, London. Trained by RAF Station, Felixstowe.

NPS4329018, DARK CHEQUER COCK, 'RUHR EXPRESS'

After two years' consistently good work in ASR and Emergency Intercommunication Service, this pigeon was dropped by parachute within the enemy lines more than 300 miles from base and brought very valuable information in the best time recorded in this operation. It was one of the best performances of its kind on record.

Bred by RAF Station, Detling and trained by the same station.

MEPS431263, RED CHEQUER COCK, 'GEORGE'

On 22 June 1943, this pigeon was carried in a Baltimore, which ditched in the Mediterranean, 100 miles from base. Search for the dinghy on poor radio was unsuccessful, visibility two miles. The pigeon was released with information about their position. It homed successfully to Berka, although it was twice accidentally dropped into the sea. The crew of four was rescued as a result of the message.

Bred by M.E.P.S. Cairo, from British and South African stock. Bred by RAF Station, Berka.

NEHU393738, BLUE CHEQUER HEN, 'BOUNCER'

Whilst on operations in a bomber, the bird was hit by enemy fire; three bullets passed through the pigeon container, one through the bird's tail and one scalped her head. She homed to her loft normally.

'Bouncer' was bred by NPS member T. Chisman. Trained at RAF Station, Middleton.

NURP39DX4038

On 13 August 1941, the aircraft in which this pigeon was serving was damaged and had to make a hurried forced landing in darkness on Thetford Heath. This pigeon and its companion were released with a message, giving this information at 2.00 a.m., and arrived at 1.45 p.m. the same day, a distance of 110 miles; the other pigeon also arrived, but two days later. This was the first RAF release in complete darkness.

Bred and trained by NPS members Hodges and son, Moor Ends, Doncaster. RAF Station, Lindholme.

NURP40PPC488, BLUE CHEQUER PIED HEN

In the course of her career, this hen took part in fifty operational sorties with flying boats. On 28 May 1942, for test purposes, she was air-released from base at 12.08 p.m. Her message was delivered at 1.30 p.m., 86 miles in 82 minutes, velocity YPM 1843. On 28 May 1943, this pigeon carried a message from the Chancellor of the Exchequer in London to the Mayor of Plymouth in connection with the 'Wings for Victory' publicity campaign.

Bred by S. Leeman, 72 Dunford Street, Plymouth. Trained by RAF Station, Mount Batten.

NURP40PDF175, BLUE CHEQUER COCK

This pigeon was the first in the last war to deliver a message from a ditched aircrew in their dinghy. They were 115 miles from Base and the message was delivered in just under three hours on 17 August 1941.

'175' was bred and trained by NPS member Mr Mantle, Beaumont Fee, Lincoln. RAF Station, Scampton.

NU40HHK180, MEALY COCK

This pigeon went on many flights from light naval craft in the North Sea off Dutch and Danish coasts and carried important messages from agents in enemy-occupied Holland. On 10 September 1944 it did so after being dropped by parachute at night with an agent.

Bred by J. Ward, 8 Silverdale Terrace, Highley, Kidderminster. Trained by RAF Station, Felixstowe.

NU41TDS38

This pigeon was released by a force-landed aircrew during a heavy snowstorm, 120 miles from base, and arrived the following day, 29 January 1942.

Bred by NPS members Pugh Brothers, 39 Vermaiden Road, Moorends, Doncaster. RAF Station, Lindholme.

NU42D670, BLUE CHEQUER COCK

This pigeon was aboard a homeward bound naval MGB off the enemy coast when the ditched crew of five of an RAF Sterling were sighted in a dinghy. The crew were picked up with serious injuries. Wireless silence was being maintained. This pigeon was released with a message requesting an ambulance at the dockside and the MGB proceeded to base, about 100 miles away, at full speed. The pigeon homed in a little over two hours and on the arrival of the MGB, an ambulance and a surgeon were at the dockside, on 11 September 1942.

Bred by Mr Pole of Gloucester. Trained by RAF Station, Felixstowe.

NUHW39PPC592, BLUE HEN

On 8 May 1943, this pigeon was supplied to an Intelligence Section and was dropped with an agent in France. It was released at dawn on 16 May in the French interior, and it delivered its message on 18 May, in spite of injuries probably received soon after liberation. This pigeon was subsequently sent on another similar mission, but was killed when the aircraft was destroyed by enemy action.

Bred and trained by NPS member S.A. Moon, Haywards Heath.

NUHW40SNR116, BLUE COCK

On 3 November 1941, this pigeon was released 170 miles at sea off the west of Scotland in a 50mph unfavourable gale and homed successfully the same day. During service the following year, he was killed when his Sunderland flying boat crashed with the loss of all crew.

Bred by NPS member Major Rodgers of Sheringham. Trained by RAF Station, Oban.

NUHW42E4221, BLUE COCK

He made a large number of North Sea flights from light naval craft and twice carried important messages and photographic film from agents in the Netherlands, arriving on the day of release in both cases. His longest flight was 360 miles.

Bred by NPS members Hall and Minns, 29 Gordon Road, Harrow.

NURP35SHD71, BLACK HEN

During the night of 23 June 1943, the aircraft in which this pigeon was serving disappeared on operations, presumably in Germany; she arrived back at base at 5.30 p.m. on that day.

Bred and trained by Mr MacLean, 7 The Avenue, Lincoln. RAF Station, Scampton.

NURP30TZ219, MEALY HEN

This was a very reliable pigeon with over fifty operational sorties to her credit. In the course of her experience, she homed from 200 miles south, 300 miles south-west, 300 miles north and 150 miles south-east.

Bred and trained by NPS members Jackson and Webb, 476 Hazel Road, Moorlands, Doncaster. RAF Station, Lindholme.

NURP37DX616

This pigeon homed at dawn with a message from the Polish crew of a crashed Wellington, giving their position on a lonely moor and particulars of their casualties and requesting an ambulance. They were only twenty miles from the base and an ambulance was dispatched in thirty minutes.

Bred and trained by NPS member H. Knapper, Moorends, Doncaster. RAF Station, Lindholme.

NURP38CAR21 DARK CHEQUER COCK

This pigeon survived over 100 operational bomber sorties. In the course of his service, he homed successfully from diverted or force-landed aircraft on two occasions from 200 miles and two other occasions from approximately 250 miles in various directions.

On 22 March 1943, its aircraft force landed 360 miles from base and the crew released him at 8.30 a.m. in unfavourable weather. He homed in 8 hours 5 minutes.

Bred and trained by NPS member W.H. Payne, 8 Frederick Street, Nottingham. RAF Station, Bottesford.

NURP39BFF2178 RED CHEQUER COCK

On 13 June 1944, this pigeon carried a message from the US Army in Normandy in good time on the day of release.

Bred by E. Brown, 6 Boreley Lane, Creekmore, Poole. Trained by RAF Station, Hamworthy.

NURP41PST86 BLUE CHEQUER HEN

On 27 January 1942, the aircraft in which this pigeon was serving got into difficulties on returning from a strike, running into a severe east-south-east gale with snow and sleet (surface wind 50mph). The pigeon was liberated seventy miles from base with this information. The pigeon homed to base in three hours. (The crew eventually baled out successfully on Dartmoor).

Bred and trained by NPS member G. Hood, 13 Mountgold Crescent, Plymouth. RAF Station St. Eval.

NURP41NRH135, PIED COCK

This bird was bred in September 1942 and on 23 March 1943 was released by a crew of a diverted aircraft, 360 miles from its base Lossiemouth in a direction in which it had not been trained. The pigeon homed in eight and a quarter hours; the weather conditions were a north-east wind with occasional drizzle.

Bred by NPS member A.W. Jacks, Curzon Avenue, Carlton or RAF Station, Bottesford.

NURP41GMN199, BLUE HEN

On one of her 64 operational sorties, this pigeon was air-released from a Beaufighter over the Bay of Biscay, 200 miles from base. The Beaufighter is a difficult aircraft from which safely to release a pigeon and this bird was evidently injured in the release. It still managed to reach South Wales and was picked up in Llanelli on the same day, when its message was transmitted by the police.

Bred by NPS member W. Hamlyn, Steam Mills, Midsomer Norton, Bath. Trained by RAF Station, Chivenor.

NURP41KB343, BLUE CHEQUER COCK, 'CHIEFY'

On 14 November 1942, this pigeon was released from an aircraft 150 miles from base. In semi-darkness, with visibility about 100 metres, it homed with its message in five hours. On 15 May 1943, this bird was released from a diverted aircraft in Northern Ireland 400 miles from base in a direction remote from that for which the pigeon had been trained. It was liberated at 10.35 a.m. with a shoulder wind all the way; she made it home at 8.45 a.m. the following morning. 'Chiefy' made sixty-one operational trips over enemy territory and made many more excellent performances.

Bred by NPS member E. Renshaw, 31 Mill Street, Sutton in Ashfield. Trained by RAF Station, Thornley Island.

NURP43CC2418 BLUE CHEQUER HEN

This was the only pigeon to home from British airborne troops or paratroopers in the Normandy operation within twenty-four hours. The weather was extremely adverse and the birds were detained for six days in small containers. She was released with a message at 8.37 a.m. on 7 June, arriving home at 6.41 a.m. on 8 June (23 hours 4 minutes, including some flight in darkness). This pigeon was subsequently lost in a further flight from France.

Bred by NPS member T. Markham, Chain House, Bonningate, Kendal. Trained by RAF Station, Thornley Island.

NPS41NS8638, GRIZZLE COCK

For more than two years, this pigeon worked consistently in a district where the flying conditions were such that comparatively few birds stood up to it. Among his best performances were 200 miles from a northerly point and 200 miles from a southerly point from aircraft, and later from a force-landed aircraft in Northern Ireland under extremely bad weather conditions with visibility only 300 yards, homing on the morning following liberation. Unfortunately, this bird was killed by a falcon while at exercise on 13 March 1943.

Bred by NPS member H.G. Smith, 1,091 Dumbarton Road, Whiteinch, Glasgow. Trained by RAF Station, Oban.

NPS41NS8895, GRIZZLE HEN (GRAND DAM OF 'PER ARDUA', NPS4417264)

Having built up a reputation for reliability on normal RAF Service, this pigeon was selected for a special task for an intelligence branch. Dropped with an agent in the Netherlands, she delivered her message on the same morning she was released, 10 September 1944, a distance of approximately 200 miles, liberated in darkness before dawn. She was lost in operations in 1945.

Bred by NPS member M. Kemp, 16 Grange Drive, Falkirk. Trained by RAF Station, Gillingham.

NPS41NS9979 BLUE CHEQUER HEN

During five years in RAF Service, this hen was never late, even though on one occasion an encounter with a hawk necessitated thirteen stitches. On one task under favourable conditions she homed at a mile a minute. In 1945, she was prepared for a task of special hazard and dropped by parachute in enemy-occupied territory, more than 300 miles distance and made it back successfully after several days' detention under conditions of hardship. Trained by RAF, Detling.

NPS426746 RED CHEQUER COCK 'LAST HOPE'

This was a very consistent pigeon whose best performances were 230 miles (north) in 6 hours 51 minutes. 130 miles from the Cherbourg peninsular, under difficult conditions, in 5 hours 10 minutes and again a similar distance from France in 4 hours 52 minutes.

Bred by J. King, 75 Cuthiel Crescent, Stoneyburn, West Lothian. Trained by RAF Station, Thornley Island.

NPS4213694, BLUE CHEQUER COCK

In the course of his service, which included ninety-five operational sorties, chiefly with light naval craft in the North Sea, this pigeon delivered an urgent operational message from an MTB in close action off the enemy coast during wireless silence on 14 September 1943. The distance travelled was approximately 120 miles, flying time 3 hours 40 minutes.

Bred by R. Rowell, Peterborough. Trained by RAF Station, Felixstowe.

NPS4230865 DARK CHEQUER PIED HEN

In the course of her service, which included over fifty operational sorties, this pigeon was air-released in darkness at 11.00 p.m. on 11 January 1943, forty miles from base, and she made it home successfully at 9.00 a.m. next morning.

Bred by NPS member T. Morgan, 43 Woodland Avenue, Airdrie, Scotland. Trained by RAF Station, Leuchars.

NPS4330825 BLUE CHEQUER PIED HEN

On 26 August 1943, this pigeon was air-released 25 miles from base at 4.20 p.m. and delivered its message at 4.45 p.m., (25 miles in 25 minutes). On another occasion, it was air released 50 miles from base at 2.20 pm and arrived at 3.30 pm, (50 miles in 1 hour 10 minutes). On 14 June 1944, carried a message from USA troops in Normandy, it was released in late afternoon and made it back early dawn next morning at 5.15 am B.D.S.T.

Bred by NPS member J. Waite, 53 Pickwick Road, Corsham Wilts. Trained by RAF Station, Hamworthy.

NPS4246991

This pigeon was liberated by American troops in Normandy at dusk on 14 June 1944 and delivered its message soon after dawn on 15 June at 6.55 a.m. (B.D.S.T.)

Bred by NPS member Blumberg, 290 Tiverton Road, Selly Oak, Birmingham. Trained by RAF Station, Hurn.

NPS4349818 MEALY COCK

On 13 October 1943, this bird was released by a force-landed aircrew, 160 miles from base in adverse weather conditions, including thick fog and drizzle and delivered its message in six hours.

Bred by NPS member T. Forster, 67 Castleton Road, Walthamstow. Trained by RAF Station, Beaulieu.

NPS 4343843 BRONZE PIED COCK

On three occasions this pigeon was air-released in the Channel with messages, including one on 23 August 1943, 150 miles from base, all of which were delivered successfully.

Bred by NPS member W. Maddock, Tutts Clump, near Reading. Trained by RAF Station, Hamworthy.

NU40BDF156 BRONZE COCK

Air released over the Bristol Channel on a moonlight night at 1.50 a.m. on
13 June 1943, 130 miles from base, homed in 8 hours 10 minutes.

Bred and flown by Mr Walton, Emsbury Park, Bournemouth. Trained at RAF Station, Hamworthy.

NU41NS469 BLUE CHEQUER COCK

This bird made many operational flights from aircraft and from the continent, including one of 230 miles in 6 hours 27 minutes and two from the south of Cherbourg Peninsular, in 5 hours 10 minutes and 4 hours 52 minutes respectively, during the Normandy operations.

Bred by RAF, Calshio. Trained by RAF, Thornley Island.

NU41NS2456 BLUE HEN

Her best performance was when air-released at sea 100 miles from base on 12 July 1943, in extreme adverse weather conditions; she homed in seven and a half hours.

Bred by NPS member F.W. Read, Wendover, Western Road, Long Ashton, Bristol. Trained by RAF Station, Carew Cheriton.

NU41NS2897 BLUE CHEQUER COCK

Was released at the same time as 2456 above on the same task and arrived at the same time.

Bred by NPS member S.P. Griffiths, Broken Cross, Northwich. Trained by RAF Station, Carew Cheriton.

NU41NS3546 BLUE COCK

During the period of the Normandy operations and up to August 1944, this pigeon flew over 2,000 miles in total, including one flight on 17 June 1944, of 387 miles at over 50mph and another flight of 450 miles, arriving on the day of release.

Bred by NPS member H. Grocott, 24 Bruton Crescent, Sneyd Green, Stoke on Trent. Trained by RAF Station, Deling.

NU42G7746 RED CHEQUER COCK

This pigeon homed in excellent time on two occasions from south of the Cherbourg Peninsular, and also flew 260 miles in 6 hours 32 minutes.

Bred by Trefrell Brothers, Acklington. Trained by RAF Station, Thornley Island.

NU42E8554 RED COCK

This pigeon took part in over fifty Bomber operations. On one occasion, when released from a force-landed aircraft 360 miles from base, it homed with its message in 8 hours 30 minutes on 14 April 1943.

Bred and trained by NPS member W.H. Payne, 8 Frederick Street, Nottingham. Trained by RAF Station, Bettesford.

NU43A4013 BLUE CHEQUER

4013 was taken on Service, 1 June 1944 by the US Army to Normandy. Time of release was not given, and it arrived home on 15 June 1944.

Bred by G. Lillyer, 43 George Street, Devonport. Trained by Mr Pitt, Plymouth.

NEHU38M9909 BLUE CHEQUER COCK

This bird carried message from an aircraft in distress at sea off the Scottish coast, 150 miles against a head wind in six and a half hours on 2 April 1943.

Bred by NPS member R. Squires, 29 Landsdowne Road, Middlesbrough. Flown by Jackson and Pyman, 12 St John's Grove, Redcar. RAF Station, Thornaby.

NEHU41B2378 RED CHEQUER HEN

Released by a force-landed aircrew 260 miles from base on 19 June 1943 and made it back home in five and a half hours.

Bred by NPS member E. Oxley, Neasham Road, Darlington. RAF Station, Middleton.

NEHU42B7031 BLUE CHEQUER PIED COCK

Liberated from an aircraft on sea search, 200 miles at sea. Homed in eight hours against a strong north-west wind on 23 June 1943.

Bred by NPS member B. Llewellyn, 3 Stockton Terrace, Drinkfield, Darlington. RAF Station, Middleton.

NEHU42B9549 BLUE CHEQUER COCK

Released by a force-landed aircraft crew 260 miles from home, flying the distance in five and a half hours, 19 June 1943.

Bred by NPS members Oxley and Garter. RAF Station, Middleton.

NUHW37EGU248 COCK

This pigeon was engaged on the same task as HUHW38EGU139 and also reached England with its message.

Bred and trained by NPS member S.A. Moon, Haywards Heath.

NUHW38EGU139 COCK

Before dawn on 31 May 1942, this pigeon was released in darkness in the French interior eight days after its issue for the task. It arrived with the most valuable information on the same day, inspiring a special letter of appreciation from the Intelligence Service.

Bred and trained by NPS member S.A. Moon, Haywards Heath.

NUHW39CEH342

This pigeon was dropped in Germany on a Special Service mission during the night of 11 April. It was released with a message at Brunswick at 11.40 a.m. on 18 April. Homed with a message at 7.45 p.m. on 30 April 1945.

Bred by J. Gould, 115 Belverdere Road, Ipswich. Trained by the Ipswich Group NPS, Mr Gould.

NUHW41LDS75 BLUE CHEQUER COCK

In March 1942, this pigeon was dropped with an agent in France and returned with its message on the day of release; it was subsequently lost on a similar operation.

Bred and trained by S.A. Moon, Haywards Heath.

NUHW41WB119 MEALY HEN

In the course of her service, this hen had flown over 400 miles in 11 hours 50 minutes, and a few weeks later approximately 500 miles in 13 hours 50 minutes.

Bred by NPS member W. Astell, 13 Westmorland Road, Wallasey. RAF Station, Gillingham.

NUHW41PHN156 BLUE CHEQUER

This pigeon was taken on service on 1 June 1944 by US Army, Normandy, and it arrived home on the same day; the time of release was unknown.

Trained by Mr Gregory, Plymouth.

NUHW41PSJ242

Taken on active service 1 June 1944 by the US Army, Normandy, this bird homed on 16 June; time of liberation was unknown.

Bred and trained by Mr Woodman, Plymouth.

NUHW42B229 BLUE CHEQUER

This bird was taken on service on 1 June 1944 by the US Army, Normandy. It arrived back home on 3 June – time of release unknown.

Bred by Dr D.J. Buckley, Southfield House, Bramcote. Trained by Mr Gregory, Plymouth.

NUHW42E6641 DARK CHEQUER COCK

In the course of his service, this pigeon twice flew 360 miles and twice over 400 miles on the day of release.

Bred by NPS members Marsh and Baily, Derby Road, Swanwick, Alfreton. Trained by RAF Station, Felixstowe.

NUHW43P1 RED

Taken on service 1 June 1944 by US Army, Normandy, this bird homed on 8 June; time of liberation is unknown.

Bred and trained by Taw, Doidge and Woodman, Plymouth.

NUHW43P12

Taken on service 1 June 1944 by US Army, Normandy, this pigeon arrived home on 7 June with a message, time of release unknown.

Bred and trained by Taw, Doidge and Woodman, Plymouth.

NUHW43P22 DARK CHEQUER

This pigeon was taken on service 1 June 1944 by US Army, Normandy. Homed on 13 June 1944, liberation time not given.

Bred and trained by Mr Ham, Plymouth.

NUHW43P26 RED

This bird was taken on service 1 June 1944 with the US Army, Normandy. Time of release was not given.

Bred and trained by Mr Ham, Plymouth.

NUHW43P361 BLUE CHEQUER

Taken on service 1 June 1944 by US Army, Normandy, the time of release is not known, but it arrived back at its loft on 13 June.

Bred by Mr Redmore, Plymouth.

NUHW43P405 BLACK PIED

Taken on service 1 June 1944 by US Army, Normandy, this bird homed on 5 June, time of liberation not known.

Bred by T. Moore, 229 Genville Road, Plymouth. Trained by Mr Partridge, Plymouth.

NUHW43P413 BLUE CHEQUER

Taken on service 1 June 1944 by the US Army, Normandy, this pigeon returned home on 3 June, time of release unknown.

Bred and trained by Mr Partridge, Plymouth.

NUHW43P696 RED

Taken on service 1 June 1944 by US Army, Normandy, this bird returned home on 8 June, time released unknown.

Bred and trained by NPS members Taw, Doidge and Woodman, Plymouth.

NUHW43P715 GRIZZLE

This pigeon was taken on service on 1 June by US Army, Normandy. It arrived home on 9 June, time of liberation not known.

Trained by Mr Partridge, Plymouth.

NUHW43W2944 BLUE CHEQUER

Taken on service on 1 June 1944 by US Army, Normandy, this bird homed on 9 June, time of release not known.

Bred and trained by Revell and Ellis, Plymouth.

NUHW43X8059 BLUE

Taken on service on 1 June 1944 by US Army, Normandy, this pigeon returned on 3 June, release time unknown.

Bred and trained by Mr Metherall, Plymouth.

NUHW44U579 RED CHEQUER COCK

On 9 September 1944, this young bird made the fastest time in a test flight of 298 miles, recording a velocity of 1171ypm.

Bred and trained by RAF Station, Felixstowe.

NUHW44V1592

Dropped into Germany on a Special Service mission on the night of 12 April 1945, the pigeon returned with a message at 5.45 p.m. on 5 May 1945.

Bred by F.W. Bugg, Royal William, London Road, Ipswich. Trained by Ipswich Group NPS, Mr Bugg.

NUHW44E8679

Dropped into Germany on a Special Service mission on the night of 12 April 1945, this bird arrived home at 20.00 hours on 27 April.

Bred by Gent and Leak, 419 Edge Road, Stonebroom, Derby. Trained by NPS Pigeon Group Ipswich, Mr Bugg.

NURP34SVS402 RED CHEQUER HEN

Was detailed for the same tasks as NURP36JH190 and arrived with a duplicate of 190's messages within a minute of 190 on 20 October 1940. 401 was unfortunately lost on a similar task.

Bred and trained by R.W. Beard of Kenley.

NURP36RWM107 RED CHEQUER COCK

On 26 May 1943, this pigeon was released in darkness from an aircraft at 8,000 feet at 3.45 p.m., 100 miles from base and arrived back at 10.20 p.m.

Bred and trained by NPS member G.W. Kettlewell, 43 Murray Street, York. RAF Station, Linton.

NURP37PPC496

On 21 May 1942, this pigeon was air-released from a Sunderland aircraft 120 miles from base. The bird had been in a small container for thirteen and a half hours. It delivered its message in 4 hours 5 minutes.

Bred and trained by NPS member C. Bygraves, 24 Greville Road, Plymouth. RAF Station, Mount Batten.

NURP37DX3628

The aircraft in which this pigeon was serving was lost on the night of 28 March 1942, about 300 miles from base. The pigeon arrived at 11.30 hours on 30 March, being the second arrival from the missing aircraft. It was injured and had no tail, and there was no other news of the crew.

Bred by NPS member P. Maltby, 7 Dunholme Crescent, Moorends. Trained by RAF Station, Lindholme.

NURP38CHC22 GRIZZLE

Taken on service 1 June 1944 by US Army, Normandy, this bird returned on 12 June, time of liberation not known.

Trained by Mr Partridge, Plymouth. Bred by G. Senior, 72 Elm Street, Holyland Common.

NURP38EGU125 RED CHEQUER COCK

125 returned on the same day it was sent with a message. In May 1943 this pigeon was lost on a similar mission, presumably in enemy action.

Bred and trained by NPS member S.A. Moon, Haywards Heath.

NURP38EGU142

In July 1942, this bird homed from France with information from an agent, having been dropped from an aircraft for that purpose.

Bred and trained by S.A. Moon, Haywards Heath.

NURP389849 RED COCK

His best performance on service was on 22 May 1942 when air-released with a message 120 miles from base; he delivered the message in three hours.

Bred by NPS member Mr Chudley Swilly. Trained by RAF Station, Mount Batten.

NURP39PSJ112 RED

Taken on service 1 June 1944 by US Army, Normandy, this pigeon homed on 11 June with a message, time of release not known.

Owner Mr Goffin, Plymouth. Bred by Thomas and Son, Washington Inn, Millbay, Plymouth.

NURP39PHN249 BLUE CHEQUER

Taken on service on 1 June 1944 by US Army, Normandy, this pigeon homed on 3 June, time of liberation not given.

Owner Mr Metherall, Plymouth.

NURP39HQ605

Sole survivor of an aircraft lost on the night of 16 August 1941. This bird arrived home a month later with its message carrier removed.

Bred and trained by NPS member J. Jones, 219 Broadway, near Doncaster. RAF Station, Lindholme.

NURP39T1209 GAY PIED COCK

Carried a message from Normandy on the 13 June 1944 in good time on day of release.

Bred by NPS member Courtney, Brailswood Road, Poole. Trained by RAF Station, Hamworthy.

NURP39DX1695

The aircraft in which this pigeon was serving was lost on operations during the early morning of 20 June 1942, about 300 miles from base. The pigeon returned home on 22 June with a message, no other information received.

Bred by NPS member P. Rimmington, 2 Millfield Road, Thorne, Doncaster. Trained by RAF Station, Lindholme.

NURP39DX4141

The aircraft in which this pigeon was serving was lost on operations on the night of 16 December 1942. The weather was extremely bad with thick fog and intense cold. The pigeon homed on 18 December and was the only communication of any kind received from the aircraft.

Bred and trained by NPS member C. Ross, 31 Grange Road, Moor Ends, Doncaster. RAF Station, Lindholme.

NURP39DX4204

The aircraft in which this bird was serving was lost on operations during the night of 28 March 1942. The pigeon returned to its loft at 2.00 p.m. on 29 March, but without a message; there was no other news of the crew. It is thought that the aircraft was lost near a target approximately 300 miles from base.

Bred and trained by NPS members Hodges and Son, 7 Park Road, Moor Ends, Doncaster. RAF Station, Lindholme.

NURP39HQP6679 RED CHEQUER COCK

This pigeon survived more than sixty Operational Bomber Sorties and in the course of its service homed from 300 miles north and south-west of base.

Bred and trained by Jackson and Webb, 47 High Hazel Road, Moor Ends, Doncaster. RAF Station, Lindholme.

NURP40AWM153 GRIZZLE HEN

On 14 April 1943, this pigeon was released by the crew of a force-landed aircraft 300 miles from base, arriving back home in twelve hours.

Bred and trained by NPS member G.W. Kettlewell, 43 Murray Street, York. RAF Station, Linton.

NURP40PDF175 BLACK CHEQUER COCK

This pigeon was the first in the late war to deliver a message from a ditched aircrew in their dinghy. They were 115 miles from base and the message was delivered in just under three hours on 17 August 1941.

Bred and trained by NPS member Mr Mantle, Beaumont Fee, Lincoln. RAF Station, Scampton.

NURP40PPC458 PIED HEN

This pigeon's best performance was to deliver a meteorological message when air-released eighty miles from base in eighty-two minutes.

   Bred by G. Masters, 36 Cremyle Street, Plymouth. Trained by RAF Station, Mount Batten.

NURP40BED654 RED CHEQUER COCK

654 was the sole survivor of an aircraft, which crashed on the beach, killing the crew. The pigeon escaped from the broken container and from the aircraft wreck and homed normally.

   Bred by NPS member E. Crosbie, 8 Vanderbyl Avenue, Spittal, Wirral. RAF Station, Hooten Park.

NURP40DX1806 MEALY HEN

Took part in fifty operational Bomber sorties and in the course of her service homed from 300 miles north and 300 miles south-west of her base.

   Bred and trained by NPS members Jackson and Webb, 47 High Hazel Road, Moor Ends, Doncaster. RAF Station, Lindholme.

NURP41BHP17 BLUE COCK

In the course of its service this pigeon homed in bad weather from a position over 450 miles from its base, on 5 July 1944.

   Bred by NPS member R. Worton, Burton Lofts, Christchurch, Hants. RAF Station, Detling.

NURP41WMK64 BLUE COCK

This pigeon was dropped in Germany on Special Service during the night of
14 April and homed with a message at 9.30 p.m. on 2 May 1945.

   Bred by A. Izzard, Buling, West Malling. Trained by NPS Group West Malling, Mr Izzard.

NURP41POP98 RED

Taken on service 1 June 1944 by US Army, Normandy, this bird homed on 7 June, time of release unknown.

   Bred and owned by Hawing & Wall, Plymouth.

NURP41WE122

122 was dropped in Germany on Special Service during the night of 14 April 1945 and returned to its loft at 9.00 p.m. on 16 May.

   Bred by F.C. Brame, 63 Kelly Road, Ipswich. Trained by NPS Group Ipswich, Mr Brown.

NURP41QDS222, BLUE COCK, 'BLUE PETER'

His best performance was approximately 380 miles in 6 hours 40 minutes. Lost on operations in Germany April 1945, he was the sire of NPS4417276, 'Junior Miss'.

   Bred by NPS member Col. Best, 2 Southbank, Queensbury, Bradford. Trained by RAF Station, Gillingham.

NURP41APC235 MEALY COCK

His best performances were approximately 400 miles in 12 hours 5 minutes and approximately 500 miles in 14 hours.

Bred by NPS member R. Jones, Lower Panty, Pwdyn Road, Abertillery, Mon. Trained by RAF Station, Gillingham.

NURP41EAN385, DARK CHEQUER PIED COCK, 'NEILSON'

A most consistent and reliable performer on service for five years, prior to 1945 he had flown from distances between 300 and 500 miles in good time on five occasions. In 1945 he was selected for a very hazardous task; he was dropped by parachute in the Ruhr Pocket more than 300 miles away and, after several days' detention, homed successfully, being one of the earliest arrivals.

Bred by J. Cowles, 122 Beecheno Road, Norwich. Trained by RAF Station, Gillingham.

NURP41C531 BLUE HEN

Her best performances were 380 miles in 6 hours 40 minutes, 300 miles under difficult conditions in 8 hours 56 minutes and 400 miles in 11 hours 13 minutes.

Bred by H. Houghton, Hill Crest, Southlingborough Road, Finedon. Trained by RAF Station, Gillingham.

NURP41S1409

Was released from an aircraft in the Atlantic 110 miles from base at 4.15 pm on 15 March 1942 and arrived in two and a half hours.

Bred by NPS member W. Partridge, 5 Portland Place, East Plymouth. Trained by RAF Station, Mount Batten.

NURP41L6451

On 9 June 1942, this pigeon was released at 1.35 p.m. in the Atlantic in very bad weather, 221 miles from base. It returned home at 8.45 a.m. the following morning. It was subsequently lost on operations.

Bred and trained by RAF Station, Mount Batten.

NURP42P2101 BLUE CHEQUER

Taken on service on 1 June 1944 by US Army, Normandy, 2101 homed on 20 June, time of release unknown.

Bred and owned by M. Bishop, Plymouth.

NURP42Q2511

Taken on service on 1 June 1944 by US Army, Normandy, this bird returned home on 20 June, time of liberation not known.

Bred and owned by Mr Smith, Plymouth.

NURP42Q2960 DARK CHEQUER

This bird was taken on service on 1 June 1944 by the US Army, Normandy. It homed on 13 June with a message, time of release unknown.

Owner, Mr Earle, Plymouth.

NURP42R3287 BLUE CHEQUER COCK

In the course of its service, this pigeon twice flew over 350 miles on the day of release.

Bred by NPS member, R. Rowell, 6 Clare Road, Peterborough. Trained by RAF Station, Felixstowe.

NURP42A4708 MEALY HEN

The best performances during the course of her service were 200 miles in 5 hours 19 minutes, 320 miles in 9 hours 18 minutes and 380 miles in 6 hours 40 minutes.

Bred by NPS member H.R. Veal, Basingstoke, Hants. Trained by RAF Station, Gillingham.

NURP42N4971 BLUE CHEQUER

Taken on service on 1 June 1944 by the US Army, Normandy, this pigeon returned on 13 June, time of liberation not given.

Bred and owned by Mr Thorne, Plymouth.

NURP42H5041 BLUE CHEQUER HEN

5041 was serving on an aircraft lost on operations during the night of 24 June 1943. No information as to the fate of the crew or the aircraft had been received when the pigeons homed, recovering from wounds, on 16 July. The message carrier had been removed.

Bred by NPS member Mr Blackburn, Short Street, Grimsby. Trained by RAF Station, Binbrook.

NURP42H5095 BLUE CHEQUER HEN

This bird was serving in an aircraft which went missing during the night of 3 July 1943 and was presumed to have been brought down near a target in Germany. This pigeon arrived back at nightfall on 4 July but carried no message.

Bred by NPS member C.A. Dixon, O'Clee, Cleethorpes. Trained by RAF Station, Binbrook.

NURP42B5937 DARK CHEQUER COCK

In the course of its service, this pigeon flew 360 miles and 420 miles on the day of release.

Bred by NPS member B. Pole, 'Rosedene', Longford Lane, Gloucester. Trained by RAF Station, Felixstowe.

NURP42Y6262 RED CHEQUER COCK

On 15 July 1943, the aircraft in which this pigeon was serving crashed on return from operations, some of the crew bailing out, about forty miles from base. This pigeon was injured but returned home in 1 hour 42 minutes.

Bred by NPS member A.J. Canter, 8 Council Houses, Great Summerford. Trained by RAF Station, Holme.

NURP42A6832 BLUE CHEQUER WHITE FLIGHTED HEN

A very consistent pigeon, this bird was sent to compete against 395 civilian pigeons in a race over a distance of 418 miles, for test purposes, on 19 July 1943. The weather conditions were rather difficult and this pigeon completed the journey on the day of release with a velocity of 92ypm, beating all the civilian competitors.

Bred by NPS member F. Harmer, 7 Grand Avenue, Pakefield, Lowestoft. Trained by RAF Station, Felixstowe.

NURP42Z7618 RED CHEQUER HEN

7618 was flown from a light naval craft operating off the coasts of Holland and Denmark. During her service, on 1 September 1944, she was dropped with an agent in the Netherlands and delivered an extremely important message on the day of release – approximate distance 200 miles.

Bred by NPS member Mr Forster, 67 Castletown Road, Walthamstow. Trained by RAF Station, Felixstowe.

NURP42F8167 BLUE CHEQUER

Taken on service by the US Army, Normandy, on 1 June 1944, 8167 homed on 13 June. Time of release not known.

Bred and trained by NPS member J. Pitt, Randwick House, Plymstock.

NURP42D8371 DARK CHEQUER PIED

Taken on service on 1 June 1944 by the US Army, Normandy, this pigeon returned to its loft on 15 June, time of liberation not known.

Bred and trained by NPS member J. Pitt, Plymstock.

NURP42C8705 BLUE HEN

In the course of her service, this pigeon homed from an aircraft 200 miles from base on 20 August 1942. She was subsequently lost with her aircraft in enemy action on 16 May 1943.

Bred by NPS members Bullock & Sons, Macclesfield. Trained by RAF Station, Pembroke Dock.

NURP43Q187 RED

Taken on service on 1 June 1944 by the US Army, Normandy, this red bird turned up at its loft on 6 June; time of release was not known, but it returned with a message.

Bred and owned by Mr Bygraves, Plymouth.

NURP43R1540 GRIZZLE

Taken on service on 1 June 1944 by the US Army, Normandy, 1540 homed on 9 June with a message, the time of liberation unknown.

Owned by Mr George, Plymouth. Bred by H. Perrett, 24 Molesworth Road, Plympton.

NURP43F2714 BLUE CHEQUER

Taken on service on 1 June 1944 by the US Army, Normandy, this blue chequer homed on 9 June, time of release not known.

Bred and owned by Mr Partridge, Plymouth.

NURP43N4362 GRIZZLE

Taken on service on 1 June 1944 by the US Army, Normandy, 4362 homed on 9 June, time of release not known.

Bred and owned by Mr Partridge, Plymouth.

NURP43BB7771 DARK CHEQUER PIED COCK

This bird carried a message from the US forces in Normandy, despite being released very late in the day, at 8.00 p.m. on 11 June 1944 (British Daylight Saving Time). It arrived home at 6.48 a.m. on 12 June to deliver its message.

Bred by NPS member A. Bridle, 105 Stewarts Road, Bournemouth. Trained by RAF Station, Hurn.

NURP43E7877 BLACK COCK

This pigeon's best performance was to home 94 miles in two and a quarter hours in poor visibility when released off Fishguard from an aircraft. Sadly, he was killed by a falcon on a later flight.

Bred by Veal Brothers, 326 Walkden Road, Worsley. Trained by RAF Station, Penrhos.

NURP44G1980

This pigeon was dropped in Germany on Special Service during the night of 19 April 1945 and returned to its loft at 11.30 a.m. on 27 April.

Bred by F. Jenkins, 81 Morse Avenue, South Stafford. Trained by Essex Group NPS, Mr Jenkins.

NURP44W4891

This bird was dropped in Germany on Special Service on the night of 13 April 1945 and homed at 11.00 a.m. on 20 April.

Bred by F. Bugg, Royal William, London Road, Ipswich. Trained by Ipswich Group NPS, Mr Bugg.

SU442191 BLUE CHEQUER HEN

In the course of her training, as a young bird, this pigeon homed from over 290 miles on the day of release.

Bred by NPS member W. Watson, 17 Broomhill Avenue, Aberdeen. Trained by RAF Station, Felixstowe.

SHU38ML4341 BLUE CHEQUER HEN

On 29 July 1943, this pigeon was released in the Atlantic, 250 miles from base, under adverse weather conditions and returned home on the same day. It was carried on over fifty operational sorties.

Bred by NPS member G. Shanks, Johnstone Road, Balerno. Trained by RAF Station, Oban.

SHU41AN212 BLUE HEN

212 carried an SOS message from an aircraft 110 miles from base at 12 noon on 1 October 1942, arriving at 4.20 p.m. – the weather conditions were not favourable.

Bred and trained by J. Bruce, High Street, Inverurie. RAF Station, Dyce.

SHU41AN213 BLUE HEN

This hen carried the duplicate of the SOS message referred to in 212 above, and arrived at 5.30 p.m.

Bred and trained by J. Bruce, High Street, Inverurie. RAF Station, Dyce.

SHU41AN223 BLUE CHEQUER COCK

On 22 September 1941, this pigeon carried an SOS message from an aircraft approximately 100 miles from base. It was released at 9.00 a.m. and arrived home at 1.05 p.m. Fog and rain were encountered en route.

Bred and trained by William Anderson, 57 Middlefield Terrace, Aberdeen. RAF Station, Dyce.

SHU42A4042 BLUE COCK

On 2 April 1943, the plane in which this pigeon was serving crashed in the Faroe Islands. The bird escaped from the container at 4.00 p.m. that day and made it back over 200 miles of open sea at 3.15 p.m. on 4 April.

Bred and trained by W. Gun, 20a Henrietta Street, Wick. RAF Station, Wick.

SURP42L2702, BLACK PIED HEN, 'MISS MAJOR'

A most consistent pigeon, her best performance during a good service was 200 miles when air-released from an aircraft in 3 hours 30 minutes.

Bred by NPS member J. Francis, 31 Victoria Road, Fauldhouse, West Lothian. Trained by RAF Station, Thornley Island.

SURP42A5931 BLUE CHEQUER HEN

On 10 August 1943, this pigeon was released from a force-landed aircraft 200 miles from base in a direction quite unfamiliar to the pigeon. The weather was extremely adverse but the bird arrived home on the day of release. This pigeon was later lost with its aircraft on operations.

Bred by NPS member T. Mitton, 90 Neilston Road, Paisley. Trained by RAF Station, Pocklington.

SURP42B8884 BLUE CHEQUER PIED COCK

In the course of its service, this bird homed from a light naval aircraft operating at the southern end of the North Sea and on 5 September 1944, it brought back an important message from an agent in the Netherlands with whom the pigeon had been dropped overnight.

Bred by G. Gass, Sherwood Park, Annan. Trained by RAF Station, Felixstowe. It was one of the few to complete four years' operational service with the RAF. This bird was flown from all points of the compass and returned from numerous aircraft releases of the south-west coast of England. Trained by RAF Station, St Eval. Bred by J. Hendrie, 17 Port Buchan, Broxburn.

NPS41NS4958 RED HEN

On 26 June 1942, this pigeon was released for test purposes from an airborne aircraft, forty-five miles due east of base and delivered the test message in forty-five minutes.

Bred by NPS member T.S. Clark, 33 Union Street, Market Rasen. Trained by RAF Station, Scampton.

NPS41NS5626 BLUE CHEQUER HEN

The aircraft in which this pigeon was serving was compelled to land at another station owing to adverse weather conditions. The weather continued to be bad and all aircraft remained grounded. Two days later this pigeon was released by mistake at 10.30 a.m. on 26 January 1942 in a heavy snowstorm. The bird homed to base at 11.20 a.m. the same day and, although the distance was only about 20 miles, the impossible flying conditions render the performance noteworthy.

Bred by NPS member C. Brodie, 115 Glasgow Road, Bathgate. Trained by RAF Station, Wick.

NPS41NS5704 MEALY HEN

This pigeon carried an SOS message from an aircraft approximately 100 miles from base under conditions of fog and almost continuous rain in eight hours on 22 September 1941.

Bred by NPS member T. Hardie, 26 Edinburgh Road, Bathgate. Trained by RAF Station, Dyce.

NPS41NS7102 BLUE HEN

During the night of 11 June 1943, the Halifax Bomber on which this pigeon was serving was lost on operations, presumably near a target in Germany. The pigeon returned home on 16 June with an incomplete SOS message and, judging by the condition of the bird on arrival, it is likely that it was released by a member of the crew at large in enemy territory on that day. The target was approximately 400 miles from its base.

Bred and trained by NPS member H.D. Summers, 34 Lombard Street, Newark. RAF Station, Snaith.

NPS41NS9535

On 30 January 1942, this pigeon was released by the crew of a force-landed aircraft 120 miles from base in a heavy snowstorm and homed on the day.

Bred and trained by NPS member G. Harper, Hatfield Woodhouse, Doncaster. RAF Station, Lindholme.

NPS41NS12075 RED CHEQUER COCK

After four days' detention, this pigeon was released at 7.30 a.m. on 31 July 1943, 375 miles from its base, after which the weather deteriorated to a gale and thunderstorms. The pigeon arrived at 8.20 p.m., after 12 hours 50 minutes.

Bred by NPS member A. Pays, Micham. Trained by RAF Station, Calshot.

NPS41NS13022 RED CHEQUER HEN

On 15 May 1943, this hen was released at 10.35 a.m., 400 miles from base in an unfamiliar direction. It arrived at 8.45 a.m. the next day; weather conditions were not favourable.

Bred by H. Summers, 34 Lombard Street, Newark. Trained by RAF Station, Thornley Island.

NPS41NS13115 BLUE CHEQUER HEN

On 15 May 1943, this pigeon was released from a diverted aircraft 400 miles from base and returned home on the same day, in 10 hours 10 minutes. The bird had no previous experience in that direction and the flight included a sea crossing.

Bred by NPS member, L.G. Colebourne, 19 Burns Avenue, Mansfield, Woodhouse. Trained by RAF Station, Thornley Island.

NPS41NS13290

On 15 May 1943, the aircraft in which this pigeon was serving was diverted to a Northern Island Station 400 miles from base, in a direction with which the pigeon was entirely unfamiliar. The bird was released at 10.35 a.m. and homed at 9.15 p.m., taking 11 hours 20 minutes. It had no previous training in a north-west direction.

Trained by RAF Station, Thornley Island.

NPS41NS18836 BLUE CHEQUER

Taken on service on 1 June 1944 by the US Army, Normandy, its time of liberation is not known, but it homed on 5 June.

Trained by Messrs Hobbs and Jefford, Plymouth. Bred by J. McJoer, 67 Church Street, Trenant.

NPS42NS523 SMOKEY HEN

Her best performance was when released from a force-landed aircraft, 240 miles from home at 11.00 a.m. with much fog prevalent en route; she homed at 7.30 p.m.

Bred and trained by RAF Station, Snaith.

NPS42NS4555 BLUE CHEQUER

Taken on service on 1 June 1944 by the US Army, Normandy, this bird homed on 6 June, time of release was not given.

Owned by Mr Shepherd, Plymouth. Bred by Mr Knowlson, 8 Bowles Street, Marchay, Derby.

NPS42NS4550 BLUE CHEQUER

Taken on service by the US Army, Normandy, its time of release is unknown. It returned home on 10 June with a message.

Owned by Mr Shepherd, Plymouth. Bred by Mr Knowlson, 8 Bowles Street, Marchay, Derby.

NPS42NS5313 BLUE CHEQUER COCK

This bird made many flights from light naval craft in the North Sea. On 9 September 1943, it was dropped with an agent in the Netherlands, 280 miles from base. After three days' detention, it homed on the day of release with an important message, at 9.45 p.m. in darkness.

Bred by NPS members Marsh and Baily, Swanwick. Trained by RAF Station, Felixstowe.

NPS42NS13094 'STUMPY'

Continuous A.S.R. work from 1942 occupied this pigeon, which flew from Normandy beaches after D-Day, but returned to its loft minus a foot.

Bred by I. Weaver, 22 Bathurst Road, Gloucester. Trained by RAF Station, St Eval.

NPS42NS14425 BLUE CHEQUER HEN

On 15 June 1942, this bird was released from an aircraft 150 miles from base and delivered its message in four hours; sadly, it was lost on a later operation.

Bred by NPS member A. Robinson, 140 Knighton Road, Southampton. Trained by RAF, Mount Batten.

NPS4213689 MEALY COCK

On 11 September 1942, the M.G.B. on which this pigeon was serving picked up the crew of a RAF Stirling from their dinghy. They were badly injured. The M.G.B. was maintaining radio silence close to the enemy coast. This bird was released with a message requesting a clear berth and an ambulance. The M.G.B. then proceeded at full speed for home. The pigeon beat its ship by a sufficient margin for the message to be complied with and the ambulance was standing by at the vacant berth. The distance travelled was 100 miles.

Bred by NPS member R. Rowell, Peterborough. Trained by RAF Station, Felixstowe.

NPS4214991 BLUE COCK

Released from a dinghy off the Scilly Isles, this pigeon delivered its message over 180 miles in 5 hours 5 minutes on 26 September 1943.

Bred by NPS member J. Byron, 21 Low Albion Street, Witton Park, Auckland. Trained by RAF Station, Pembroke Dock.

NPS42NS15241, 'TIGER TIM'

Several times released from aircraft over the sea, and always making good time to the loft, this pigeon was also used by the US Army in Normandy.

Bred by W.T. Rimer, Corbridge, Newcastle. Trained by RAF Station, St Eval.

NPS42NS16542 RED HEN

Released from a force-landed aircraft ninety-five miles from base in thick mist, this red hen arrived home after 3 hours 30 minutes on 12 March 1943.

Bred by NPS member H.V. Douglas, 32 Great Dockway, Penrith. Trained by RAF Station, Carew Cheriton.

NPS42NS18425 BLUE COCK

This pigeon had many flights from light naval craft in the North Sea and on two occasions was dropped with agents in the Netherlands. Firstly, on 12 April 1944, a distance of 180 miles, homing on the same day with a message; secondly, on 11 May 1944, after a period of detention, it carried photographic film just over 200 miles, arriving on the day of liberation.

Bred by NPS member J. Haworth, 330 Willow's Lane, Accrington. Trained by RAF Station, Felixstowe.

NPS42NS18976 RED CHEQUER COCK

In the course of his service with light naval craft, this bird delivered an operational message from an M.T.B. in action during wireless silence off the enemy coast. It flew approximately 120 miles in 3 hours 50 minutes on 30 October 1942.

Bred by NPS member T. Ray, Middlesex. Trained by RAF Station, Felixstowe.

NPS42NS19730 RED CHEQUER HEN

After three years of consistently good work in the RAF service, including one flight of 350 miles in eight and a half hours, this pigeon was dropped by parachute in German-occupied territory over

300 miles from base and homed successfully after several days' detention in a small container.

Bred by A.J. Board, Mitcham. Trained by RAF Station, Gillingham.

NPS42NS19786 RED GRIZZLE COCK

During the invasion operations, on 7 June 1944, this pigeon was released in Normandy at 8.00 p.m. (B.D.S.T.), when it was almost dusk, and homed with his message at 6.48 a.m. the following morning, 8 June.

Bred by J.J. Gardner, 43 Milliken Drive, Milliken Park, Renfrewshire. Trained by RAF Station, Hurn.

NPS4221311 BLUE CHEQUER COCK

On 11 June 1944, this pigeon carried a message from the US Army in Normandy in 6 hours 48 minutes.

Bred by Philbin & Dunlevy, 45 Fontford Road, Cowdenbeach, Fife. Trained by RAF, Hurn.

NPS4221612

On 26 August 1943, the aircraft in which this pigeon was serving crashed fifty miles from base. The container in which the bird was carried was badly damaged and the pigeon badly injured. It was released by a local doctor attending the crew, and in spite of its injuries homed to base three days later.

Bred and trained by NPS member D. Swanson, 6 Coach Road, Wick for RAF Station, Wick.

NPS4221921, RED COCK, 'RED LION'

This bird was released from an aircraft in the Atlantic 100 miles from land and returned home the same day, the time of release unknown.

Bred by NPS member A.B. Dennis, 73 Eastland Road, Neath. Trained by RAF Station, St. Eval.

NPS4222501 RED CHEQUER HEN

Many flights from small naval craft on operations in the North Sea. On 14 June 1944, she was dropped with an agent on the Continent and delivered her message the same day. Time of distance flown, and of liberation, unknown. Trained by RAF Station, Felixstowe.

NPS4222685 BLUE CHEQUER HEN

This pigeon arrived at the same time as 22679 with a duplicate message.

Bred by J. Guthrie, 10a King Street, Galashiels, Selkirk. Trained by RAF Station, Hurn.

NPS4222679 RED CHEQUER PIED HEN

In the course of her service, this pigeon carried a message from US troops in Normandy and arrived in semi-darkness at 10.05 p.m. (B.D.S.T.) on the day of release. The time of liberation is not known, but the date was 14 June 1944.

Bred by J. Guthrie, 10a King Street, Galashiels, Selkirk. Trained by RAF Station, Hurn.

NPS42NS22876 DARK CHEQUER COCK

On 16 June 1943, this bird was released from a dinghy in the Atlantic, approximately 100 miles from the coast, and homed to its base in 1 hour 10 minutes with its message.

Sadly, he was later lost in its aircraft by enemy action on 13 July 1943.

   Bred by NPS member W. Bryne, 20 North Side Road, Houghton le Spring. Trained by RAF Station, Pembroke Dock.

NPS42NS23182 DARK CHEQUER HEN

The bomber in which this pigeon was serving was lost, on an operation during the night of 11 June 1943, and no information was received as to the fate of the crew. The pigeon returned to its loft on 12 June without a message. It is possible that the aircraft was lost near its target in Germany, about 300 miles from base.

   Bred and trained by H. Brown, 1 Church Street, Arnold, for RAF Station, Bottesford.

NPS4224415 BLUE COCK

Released by the crew of a flying boat, 100 miles out to sea in fog on 7 June 1942, this pigeon homed to base in five hours.

   Bred by NPS member, Mr Greenaff, Gateshead on Tyne. Trained by RAF Station, Pembroke Dock.

NPS4224662 BLUE CHEQUER HEN

In the course of her service, this pigeon carried a message from the US Forces in Normandy, on 13 June 1944, arriving at its loft at 16.49 p.m. (B.D.S.T.) on the same day, time of liberation not known.

   Bred by W. McLuckie, Parkhill Cotts, Shieldhill. Trained by RAF Station, Hurn.

NPS4224662 BLUE CHEQUER HEN

On 14 June 1944, this bird delivered a message from the US Troops in Normandy in semi-darkness on the evening of the day of release, the time of liberation not known.

   Bred by W. McLuckie, Parkhill Cotts, Shieldhill. Trained by RAF Station, Hurn.

NPS4225794 BLUE HEN

On the night of 19 September 1942, the Lancaster in which this pigeon was serving was lost on operations over Germany. From approximately 250 miles from base, the pigeon homed at 6.40 p.m. on the same day with its message. Sadly, the bird was later found shot dead in England in the course of a flight from a force-landed aircraft on 15 January 1943.

   Bred and trained by RAF Station, Coningsby.

NPS426557 MEALY COCK

In the course of his service, the bird was released with a message by US troops in Normandy at 8.00 p.m. (B.D.S.T.) on 11 June 1944. This was too late for the pigeon to cross the Channel before darkness, but it delivered its message at 7.13 a.m. the following morning.

   Bred by J. Morrison, 292 Cambuslang Road, Eastfield, Cambuslang, Lanark. Trained by RAF Station, Hurn.

NPS4228342 MEALY

Taken on service by US Army, Normandy, 1 June 1944, its time of liberation is not known, but it returned home on 13 June 1944 with a message.

Trained by Mr George, Plymouth. Bred by T Gover, 17 Rose Gardens, Bournemouth.

NPS4229015 RED CHEQUER HEN

This pigeon was sent on a special mission with the US Airborne Troops on 4 June 1944, to a point well to the south of the Cherbourg Peninsula. It was released with an important message at 6.30 a.m. (B.D.S.T.) on 8 June, having been in a container for four days. The weather conditions were extremely adverse and the distance of about 220 miles was mostly over the sea. In spite of the conditions, the pigeon arrived at 8.59 a.m. on 9 June with its message.

Bred by A. Cooper, 178 Rhodeswell Road, London, E14. Trained by RAF Station, St Eval.

NPS4229248 BLUE CHEQUER HEN

In the course of her service, this hen homed many times from light naval craft in the North Sea. On 13 January 1944, she delivered a message from an agent in Holland with whom she had been dropped the previous night.

Bred by NPS member Mr Ellason, 30 Kingsway, Alverton. Trained by RAF Station, Felixstowe.

NPS4230264 BLUE CHEQUER PIED HEN

On 2 December 1942, this bird was released by the crew of a Liberator, eighty miles north of base at sea and delivered its message in 2 hours 40 minutes. On 24 December 1942, she was released ninety miles north-west of base at sea late in the afternoon, arriving at its base at dusk in 2 hours 30 minutes.

Bred and trained by RAF Station, Limavady.

NPS4230621 GRIZZLE HEN

On 14 June 1944, this pigeon was released by US troops in Normandy and delivered its message in semi-darkness on the evening of the same day, though time of release is not known.

Bred by RAF Station, Wick. Trained by RAF Station, Hurn.

NPS4230687

On 23 March 1943, this bird was released from an aircraft eighty miles out in the North Sea at 2.55 p.m. It delivered its message at 4.30 p.m. (eighty miles in one and a half hours).

Bred and trained by RAF Station, North Luffenham.

NPS4230704 DARK CHEQUER COCK

On 23 March 1943, this bird was released from an aircraft 80 miles out in the North Sea at 3.00 p.m. and delivered its message at 4.28 p.m. (eighty miles in 1 hour 28 minutes).

Bred and trained by RAF Station, Luffenham.

NPS4230712 BLUE CHEQUER PIED HEN

On 21 July 1943, this hen was released by an aircrew 176 miles north of base at 5.30 a.m. In spite of a headwind, she arrived at 9.35 a.m., beating her companion with a duplicate message by thirty-nine minutes (176 miles in 4 hours).

Bred and trained by RAF Station, Luffenham.

NPS42316 BLUE COCK

In the course of its service, this pigeon was air-released seventy miles from base and arrived at its loft in 1 hour 34 minutes. Sadly, it was shot on another flight in England, on 10 August 1943.

Bred and trained by RAF Station, Mount Batten.

NPS423118 RED HEN

In the course of her service, this hen was released by US troops in Normandy on 13 June 1944 and returned with her message at 4.05 p.m. on the same day, time of release not known.

Bred by RAF Station, Mount Batten. Trained by RAF Station, Hurn.

NPS4231404 RED COCK

On 24 March 1943, this bird was released from a flying boat 180 miles from base and returned with its message in 4 hours 20 minutes. Sadly, on 16 May it was lost with its aircraft on operations.

Bred by NPS member Mr Hammond, Durham. Trained by RAF Station, Pembroke Dock.

NPS4232695 BLUE COCK

On 30 May 1943, this pigeon was air-released ninety miles from its base and homed in two and a half hours.

Bred by NPS members Bannister & Son, 4 Club House, Market Street, Cudworth. Trained by RAF Station, Mount Batten.

NPS4234437 RED COCK 'RELIANCE'

The aircraft in which this pigeon was serving was damaged and the crew bailed out about fifty miles from base in darkness at 2.00 a.m. After releasing the pigeon, whose wing was injured in the release, homed successfully the same morning.

Bred by NPS member W.T. Carr, 73 Avondale Road, Harringay. Trained by RAF Station, St Eval.

NPS4234510 BLUE CHEQUER HEN

At 2.45 p.m. on 18 August 1943, this pigeon was released by a force-landed aircrew 130 miles from base, under very adverse weather conditions. The bird homed at noon the following day.

Bred by NPS members Gilbert and Son, 16 Bridge Street, Bingley. Trained by RAF Station, Leeming.

NPS4234510 BLUE WHITE FLIGHTED HEN

Released by a force-landed aircrew 130 miles from base at 2.45 p.m. on 18 August 1943, with a duplicate message of 34510's message and arrived home at 3.00 p.m. next day under very adverse weather conditions.

Bred by NPS members Gilbert & Son, 16 Bridge Street, Bingley. Trained by RAF Station, Leeming.

NPS4234550

In the course of its service, this bird was released by US Forces in Normandy on 11 June 1944 and arrived home at 6.00 p.m. on the same day. Unfortunately, its message carrier was missing.

Bred by T. Preece, 66 Moat Road, Walsall. Trained by RAF Station, Hurn.

NPS4234704 RED PIED COCK

In the course of its eighty-six operational sorties, this pigeon was released by a force-landed aircrew 145 miles from base and homed in 2 hours 40 minutes on 4 April 1943.

Bred by NPS member E. Bowden, 49 Celtic Street, Stockport. Trained by RAF Station, Chivenor.

NPS4235902 BLUE CHEQUER HEN

In the course of her service, this hen was released by a diverted aircrew 200 miles from home at 2.00 p.m. under adverse weather conditions. She arrived with a message at 8.00 p.m. (200 miles in six hours).

Bred and trained by RAF Station, Snaith.

NPS4236094 RED CHEQUER COCK

In the course of its service, this bird delivered an operational message from an M.T.B. in action of the enemy coast, while maintaining wireless silence. It delivered its message in good time on 20 October 1942. On 8 May 1943, it delivered an important message from an agent with whom it was dropped on the Continent. Arriving on the day of release, the actual time of liberation is not known.

Bred by NPS member H. Harrison, West Hendon. Trained by RAF Station, Felixstowe.

NPS4236871 BLUE CHEQUER HEN

On 18 September 1942, this young bird was air-released from a Sunderland west of the Scilly Isles, 120 miles from base, and homed with a message in 135 minutes.

Bred by NPS member Mr Hully, 236 Lythals Lane, Coventry.

Trained by NPS members Messrs Taw, Doidge and Woodman, 128 King Street, Plymouth for RAF Station, Mount Batten.

NPS4237192 DARK CHEQUER COCK

In the course of his service, he was released in France 210 miles from home at 2.00 p.m. on 31 August 1944 with a message. The weather conditions were adverse, with rain over most of the route. He arrived at 1.10 p.m. on 1 September 1944.

Bred and trained by RAF Station, Gillingham.

NPS4237739 BLUE CHEQUER COCK 'CHIEFTAIN'

This was a consistently reliable pigeon, particularly under adverse weather conditions. During three years' service, among his best performances were 80 miles in one and a half hours, 150 miles in three and three quarter hours, 200 miles in four and a half hours and 350 miles in eight and a half hours.

Bred by T. Bennett, 22 Lomeshaye Road, Nelson. Trained by RAF Station, Gillingham.

NPS4238855 BLACK CHEQUER COCK

The best performances of this bird were 350 miles on 14 hours 15 minutes and 450 miles in 14 hours.

Bred by NPS member B.F. Pye, 12 Bungalow, New Ollerton. Trained by RAF Station, Gillingham.

NPS4239464 BLUE CHEQUER HEN

This bird went on many flights from light naval craft in the North Sea. In May 1944, she was dropped with an agent on the Continent and brought back an important message on 8 May, on the day of release.

Bred by NPS members, Hudson and Torsey, 20 Bessie Terrace, Blaydon Burn. Trained by RAF Station, Felixstowe.

NPS4240624

This pigeon was dropped in Germany on a special mission during the night of 25 April 1945, more than 300 miles from base and homed at 1.00 p.m. on 28 April. The time and date of release are not known.

Bred by H. Leamon, 64 Lawson Road, Norwich. Trained by RAF, Thornley Island.

NPS4242004 BLUE CHEQUER HEN

In the course of her service, this bird was released in France 210 miles from her base at 2.00 p.m. on 31 August 1944 with a message. The weather conditions were adverse with low cloud and rain. The pigeon arrived home at 2.25 p.m. on the following day.

Bred by NPS member T.H. Solomon, Edgehill, 40 Sutherland Street, Liverpool. Trained by RAF Station, Gillingham.

NPS4242005 BLUE CHEQUER COCK

In the course of his service, this pigeon flew 350 miles in 14 hours 30 minutes and later in 1943, 450 miles in 14 hours and 8 minutes.

Bred by NPS member T.H. Solomon, Edgehill, 40 Sutherland Street, Liverpool. Trained by RAF Station, Gillingham.

NPS4242997 BLUE CHEQUER PIED COCK

This bird accompanied many flights from light naval craft in the North Sea. In August 1944, it was selected for a special task and dropped with an agent overnight on the Continent about 200 miles from base. On 1 September 1944, this pigeon was released with important information, which he delivered the same day; the time of liberation is not known.

Bred by NPS member J. Caldon, 4 Croombe Road, W4. Trained by RAF Station, Felixstowe.

NPS4243037

This pigeon carried a message for American troops from Normandy on 13 June 1944, arriving home at 4.31 p.m. on that day; the time of release is not known.

Bred by G. Davidson, 48 Gorgrave Place, Broadway, Lupsett, Wakefield. Trained by RAF Station, Hurn.

NPS4243373 BLUE CHEQUER HEN

In the course of her service, which included fifty RAF operational sorties, she was released 120 miles from base, over sea, and returned in 2 hours 50 minutes.

Bred and trained by RAF Station, Mount Batten.

NPS4244773 BLUE CHEQUER COCK

A very consistent worker on service, this bird's best performance was 387 miles at a speed of 1,694 yards per minute.

Bred by NPS member J. Rivenell, 148 Eastcourt Road, Fulham, London. Trained by RAF Station, Detling.

NPS4245021 BLUE HEN

In the course of her service, which included 74 operational sorties, this hen was released with a message by a ditched aircrew in the Atlantic, 135 miles from base. She arrived home in 3 hours 5 minutes on 27 August 1943.

Bred by NPS member A. Macintosh, Windsor Road, Slough. Trained by RAF Station, Chivenor.

NPS4245382 RED GRIZZLE COCK

This bird had over ninety operational trips over enemy territory and twice flew from occupied France.

Bred by NPS member Chervis Dale, Meadowside, Plumbley, Knutsford. Trained by RAF Station, Thornley Island.

NPS4247257 BLUE CHEQUER COCK

A very consistent service record for this bird included 230 miles in 6 hours 31 minutes, 130 miles in 5 hours 10 minutes and 130 miles in 4 hours 52 minutes from France.

Bred by NPS member Thomason, Manchester. Trained by RAF Station, Thornley Island.

NPS4246261 BLUE COCK

This pigeon's best performances were 230 miles in 6 hours 54 minutes, 130 miles in 5 hours 10 minutes and 130 miles in 4 hours 51 minutes from France.

Bred by NPS member Thomason, Manchester. Trained by RAF Station, Thornley Island.

NPS4247262, BLUE CHEQUER COCK, 'WINSTON'

In the course of his service, Winston had 53 operational trips over enemy territory. Among his performances were the following: air-released seventy miles from base, homed in two hours. Air-released ninety miles from base, homed in 1 hour 57 minutes. Air-released 145 miles from base, returned home in 5 hours 6 minutes. Air-released 200 miles from base, homed in 4 hours 48 minutes. He also flew forty miles in 13 and a half hours. These flights were from all directions.

Bred by NPS member Mr Thomason, 35 Lancaster Road, Cadishead, Manchester. Trained by RAF Station, Thornley Island.

NPS4247263 BLUE COCK

In the course of his service, this pigeon flew 230 miles in 6 hours 18 minutes, 130 miles in 5 hours 10 minutes and a similar distance in 4 hours 51 minutes from France.

Bred by NPS member Mr Thomason, Manchester. Trained by RAF Station, Thornley Island.

NPS4247544 BLUE CHEQUER HEN

This hen was released by US troops in Normandy on the evening of 14 June 1944 and delivered her message at 6.55 a.m. next morning. Exact time of liberation not known.

Bred by NPS members Roberts and Son, 130 Great King Street, Macclesfield. Trained by RAF Station, Hurn.

NPS4247879 BLUE HEN

Many flights from light naval craft in the North Sea were undertaken by this bird. In February 1944, she was selected for a special mission and dropped on the continent with an agent approximately 200 miles from base. Released on 1 March 1944, she delivered her message on the same day. Again in May of that year, she was dropped overnight with an agent and delivered her information on the same day, again covering approximately 200 miles.

Bred by NPS member H. Taylor, 18b Marinefield Road, S.W.6. Trained by RAF Station, Felixstowe.

NPS4248159 BLUE CHEQUER COCK

On 6 March 1943, this bird was released from an aircraft 180 miles at sea and homed with its message on the same day. On 5 May of that year, it was sadly killed in an aircraft crash.

Bred by NPS member C. Livingstone, Willowholme Crescent, Belfast. Delivered by RAF Station, Limavady.

NPS4249832 RED CHEQUER HEN

In the course of her service, this hen was released by an aircrew, eighty miles at sea, with a message and homed in 3 hours 15 minutes, under adverse weather conditions.

Bred by NPS member W. Thompson, Stormong, Ballygomartin Road, Belfast. Trained by RAF Station, Limavady.

NPS4248259 BLUE CHEQUER COCK

On 13 September 1942, this bird was released by an aircraft sixty miles out at sea under very bad weather conditions. Eighteen hours later, the following morning, the pigeon arrived home having been struck by a hawk. On 6 March 1943, it was released from an aircraft 180 miles out at sea and arrived back in 14 hours, again badly injured by a hawk. On 5 May 1943, this pigeon was killed when its aircraft crashed.

Bred by NPS member N. Corry, Terrycalf, Finaghy Road, South Belfast. Trained at RAF Station, Limavady.

NPS4248710 DARK CHEQUER COCK

In the course of its service, this bird was released by an aircrew approximately 180 miles out at sea on 10 September 1942, under extremely stormy conditions. It arrived at its base twelve hours later, injured and exhausted.

Bred by NPS member D. McAllister, Millar Bungalow, Coast Road, Ballycarry. Trained by RAF Station, Limavady.

NPS4249114 BLUE CHEQUER COCK

In the course of its service, this pigeon was released by a force-landed aircrew in South West England, 350 miles from its base in Northern Ireland. The wind was northerly and the weather stormy. The pigeon arrived with its message twenty-four hours later.

Bred by NPS member J. Nicholson, Drumero, Marslin, Lurgan. Trained by RAF Station, Nutts Corner.

NPS433870

On 13 June 1944, this bird carried a message for US troops in Normandy and arrived at 3.45 p.m. that day.

Bred by A. Chalcroft, 14 Sultan Road, Emsworth. Trained by RAF Station, Hamworthy.

NPS4250650 BLUE CHEQUER HEN

This hen went on many flights from light navel on operations in the North Sea. In October 1943, she was dropped on the Continent with an agent and on 9 October delivered an important message from him on the day of liberation, a distance of approximately 250 miles.

Bred by NPS member R. Rosewell, 9 Watson Street, Stoke Newington. Trained by RAF Station, Felixstowe.

NPS4251085 BLUE CHEQUER HEN

In the course of her service, this bird was released with a message from a diverted aircrew in Northern Ireland, 400 miles from base in a direction over which the pigeon had no training or experience. It arrived home in 10 hours 10 minutes with a shoulder wind on 15 May 1943.

Bred by NPS member W. Hogg, 27 Holding, Domhead, Lothianburn. Trained by RAF, Thornley Island.

NPS4251162

This pigeon was dropped in Germany on a special mission during the night of 25 April 1945 and homed at 1.25 p.m. on 4 May 1945. Time and date of release are not known.

Bred by Mr Swain, 31 Northwick Road, Evesham. Trained by RAF, Felixstowe.

NPS4251347

During the afternoon of 14 June 1944, this pigeon carried a message from US troops in Normandy and delivered it at 10.05 p.m. in darkness on the day of release. The exact time of release is not known.

Bred by NPS member J. Wilson, 70 Drummond Place, Milngavie. Trained by RAF Station, Hurn.

NPS425034 BLUE CHEQUER COCK

In the course of his service, this pigeon flew 300 miles in 9 hours 17 minutes on 5 June 1943, and on 19 June 1943 approximately 400 miles in 12 hours 17 minutes.

Bred by NPS member W. Proctor Smith, Knutsford. Trained by RAF Station, Gillingham.

NPS4252527 BLUE COCK

In the course of its service, which included 89 operational sorties, this bird was released with a message on 19 May 1943, from a force-landed aircrew 120 miles from base and delivered it in four hours under adverse weather conditions (thick mist), which rendered its base unserviceable for aircraft for that day.

Bred by NPS member S.O. Spriggs, 17 Priory Avenue, High Wycombe. Trained by RAF, Chivenor.

NPS4253944 BLUE CHEQUER PIED COCK

On 23 June 1943, this bird was released under adverse conditions with a message 200 miles at sea and returned home in eight hours.

Bred by NPS member J. Johnson, 5 Tweed Street, Easington Lane, Hetton le Hole. Trained by RAF, Middleton.

NPS4254261 BLUE CHEQUER HEN

On 10 August 1943, this hen was released with a message, 220 miles from base, in stormy weather, by a force-landed aircrew, and delivered its message in nine and a half hours.

Bred by NPS member F.W. Campbell, Cheadle, Staffs. Trained by RAF, Pocklington.

NPS4256414 BLUE CHEQUER COCK

This pigeon carried a message from Normandy for US troops on 11 June 1943 and homed in 6 hours 25 minutes.

Bred by B. Gallagher, 47 Hammond Road, Southall.

NPS431129 RED CHEQUER COCK

On 8 September 1943, the aircraft in which this young bird was serving ditched suddenly seventy miles from base. It was released from a dinghy by the aircrew with an SOS message, which it delivered in ninety minutes. (The crew were rescued independently of the pigeon's message, as it happened, as they were observed by another aircraft).

Bred by NPS member C. Manley, 60 Rhymney Street, Cardiff. Trained by RAF, Hooton Park.

NPS432336 BLUE CHEQUER COCK

On 28 August 1943, this young bird was air-released ninety miles from base and delivered its message in 2 hours 30 minutes.

Bred by NPS member E. Newton, 6 Glebe Road, Clevedon Trained by RAF Station, Hamworthy.

NPS432437 BLUE HEN

On 10 June 1944, this hen was sent to US troops in Normandy and on the evening of 14 June she was released with a message. There was insufficient daylight for channel crossing and she delivered her message at 7.25 a.m. the next morning.

Bred by NPS member G. King, The Grove, Nailsea. Trained by RAF, Hamworthy.

NPS432503 RED CHEQUER HEN

This hen was released by US troops in Normandy during the afternoon of 14 June and arrived in semi-darkness at 10.05 p.m. (B.D.S.T.) the same day. Exact time of liberation not known.

Bred by S. Travis, Shipham, Winscombe. Trained by RAF, Hurn.

NPS422600 BLUE CHEQUER HEN

This pigeon was released by US troops in Normandy with a message during the afternoon of 14 June and arrived at dusk at 9.45 p.m. (B.D.S.T.) the same day.

Bred by F.L. Doll, 47 Broadway, Frome. Trained by RAF Station, Hamworthy.

NPS432834 BLUE CHEQUER PIED HEN

On 23 August 1943, this bird was air-released at 10.15 a.m. and arrived back at 2.25 p.m., a distance of sixty miles in a head wind.

Bred by NPS member C. Grainger, 32 Horton Street, Frome. Trained by RAF, Hamworthy.

NPS433028 BLUE CHEQUER HEN

This hen was released in Normandy by US troops with a message on 13 June 1944 and arrived at 4.05 p.m., exact time of release unknown.

Bred by T. Moore, 229 Glenville Road, Prince Rock, Plymouth. Trained by RAF Station, Hamworthy.

NPS433031 BLUE CHEQUER COCK

In the course of its service as a young bird, he was air released at sea on three occasions and delivered the message in good time on each occasion. On 22 August, the air release was at a point 120 miles from a base in mid-Channel, and he arrived home in 4 hours 55 minutes.

Bred by NPS member T. Moore, 229 Glenville Road, Prince Rock, Plymouth. Trained by RAF Station, Hamworthy.

NPS433032 BLUE CHEQUER PIED COCK

On 2 August 1943, this young bird was air-released forty-five miles from base and homed in one hour.

Bred by NPS member T. Moore, 229 Glenville Road, Prince Rock, Plymouth. Trained by RAF Station, Hamworthy.

NPS433307

On 13 June 1944, this pigeon carried a message from US troops in Normandy and arrived at 4.05 p.m. on the same day. The time of release is not known.

Bred by H.E. Pooley, 16 Fore Street, Blazey. Trained by RAF, Hamworthy.

NPS433870

On 13 June 1944, this bird carried a message for US troops in Normandy, arrived back at 3.45 p.m. on the same day.

Bred by A. Chalcroft, 14 Sultan Road, Emsworth. Trained by RAF, Hamworthy.

NPS434112 BLUE CHEQUER PIED HEN

During the evening of 16 September 1944, this hen was released from a dinghy of ditched aircraft in position 49-15 N, 04-33 W, about 100 miles from base, with an SOS message, which she delivered next morning. The crew was rescued; the pigeon arrived back wet and smeared in oil.

Bred by C.H. Hector, Thelms, Southleigh Road, Emsworth. Trained by RAF Station, Mount Batten.

NPS434507

This pigeon carried a message from Normandy for US troops on 14 June 1944 and arrived back home at dusk at 9.05 p.m. on the day. Time of release not known.

Bred by V. Robinson, 55 Weston Lane, Woolston, Hants. Trained by RAF, Holmsley.

NPS435550 BLUE CHEQUER COCK

This pigeon was sent to rendez-vous with SAS troops on 7 June 1944 and returned from near the Swiss border on 29 June after being in a small container for twenty days.

Bred by NPS member Doe and Skinner, 92 Friendly Street, Deptford, S.E.8. Trained by Army Pigeon Service, London.

NPS438208 BLUE HEN

This hen went on many flights from light naval craft during operations in the North Sea. In September 1944, she was dropped with an agent in Holland and was released carrying a photographic film on 10 September, arriving on the same day, a distance of over 200 miles.

Bred and trained by RAF Station, Felixstowe.

NPS438226 BLUE COCK

In August 1944, this bird was dropped with an agent on the continent and was released with a message at dawn on 6 August 1944, which it delivered the same morning.

Bred and trained by RAF, Felixstowe.

NPS438231 BLUE CHEQUER HEN

Many flights from light naval craft on operations in the North Sea had thid bird on board. In August 1944, she was dropped with an agent in the Netherlands and released with a message at dawn on 3 August, which she delivered the same day, a distance of over 200 miles.

Bred and trained by RAF, Felixstowe.

NPS4310025

This pigeon carried a message from Normandy for US troops on 13 June 1944, arriving home at 5.00 p.m. that day.

Bred by H.C. Putt, 29 Larkfield Road, Kenton. Trained by RAF, Holmsley.

NPS4311147 RED COCK

On 17 August 1943, this pigeon was released with a message 122 miles from base by a force-landed aircrew at 2.50 p.m. and arrived back at 5.02 p.m.

Bred by NPS members Godfrey & Son, McCauley Drive, Lincoln. Trained by RAF Station, North Luffenham.

NPS4311459 BLUE CHEQUER COCK

This bird carried a message from Normandy for US troops on 13 June 1944, which it delivered the same afternoon; the time of release is not known.

Bred by J.B. Robinson, Hawthorne Cottage, Grange Laural, Wickham. Trained by RAF Station, Hamworthy.

NPS4312830 BLUE CHEQUER

Taken on service on 1 June 1944 by US Army, Normandy, the time of release was not given. The bird returned home on 15 June 1944.

Bred by M. Tomlin, 6 Cowley Road, Great Birmingham. Trained by Mr Mears, Plymouth.

NPS4313695 BLUE CHEQUER HEN

On 24 October 1943, this hen was air-released at sea in the Channel, 150 miles from base and delivered its message in 5 hours 20 minutes. On the afternoon of 14 June 1944, it carried a message from the US troops in Normandy and arrived in darkness at 10.25 p.m. (B.D.S.T.) that evening.

Bred by NPS member W.J. Kibbey, 167 Ashton Drive, Ashton Vale, Bristol 3. Trained by RAF Station, Hamworthy.

NPS4314316 BLUE CHEQUER HEN

In the course of its service, this hen was air-released 120 miles from base in mid Channel on 22 August 1943 and homed in 5 hours 35 minutes.

Bred by NPS member R.E. Gowden, 26 Brunswick Street, St Thomas, Exeter. Trained by RAF, Hamworthy.

NPS4314465 BLUE CHEQUER HEN

On 19 August 1943, this hen was air-released 120 miles from base, mid-Channel, and delivered its message in four hours. On 14 June 1944, it was released in Normandy during the late afternoon by US troops and arrived at dawn at 5.15 a.m. (B.D.S.T.) the next morning.

Bred by NPS member H.L. Brown, Phillips Avenue, Exmouth. Trained by RAF, Hamworthy.

NPS4315121 BLUE CHEQUER HEN

On 13 October 1943, this hen was released by a force-landed aircrew, 160 miles from base under adverse weather conditions, fog and drizzle. It delivered its message in six hours.

Bred by NPS members Homer and Randell, 16 Newton Avenue, Gloucester. Trained by RAF Station, Beaulieu.

NPS4315333 MEALY HEN

This pigeon was released with a message by US troops in Normandy during the afternoon of 14 June 1944 and arrived at dawn at 05.15 hours (B.D.S.T.)

Bred by Tozer and Hooper, 28 Coventry Close, Piston Lane, Churchdown, Gloucester. Trained by RAF Station, Hamworthy.

NPS4315574 MEALY HEN

This pigeon carried a message from US troops in Normandy on 13 June 1944, which it delivered at 19.12 hours on that day.

Bred by T. Roberts, Southview Brangreen, Redmorley, Gloucester. Trained by RAF Station, Hamworthy.

NPS4316304 MEALY COCK

On 11 August 1943, this pigeon was air-released in the Atlantic, fifty miles from base and arrived in fifty minutes. On 22 October 1943, he was sadly killed by a falcon while on exercise.

Bred by NPS member J. Grieve, Viola Cottage, Station Road, Armadale, West Lothian. Trained by RAF Station Stornaway.

NPS4317906 RED

Taken on service 1 June 1944 by US Army, Normandy, the bird's time of release is not known. It homed on 3 June 1944.

Bred by A. Thompson, 3 Mons Street, Kellsbank, Kirkconnel, Dumfries. Trained by Mr Metherall, Plymouth.

NPS4319312

This pigeon was released in Normandy with a message from US troops during the afternoon of 14 June 1944 and arrived at 06.55 hours (B.D.S.T.) the next morning.

Bred by R. Todd, 43 Boyd Street, Kilmarnock. Trained by RAF Station, Hurn.

NPS4319337 BLUE COCK

On 30 July 1943, this bird was released over 150 miles from base on an unfamiliar route by a force-landed aircrew. The weather conditions were terrible, yet it homed with its message in seven and a half hours.

Bred by NPS member W. Strickland, 1 Templeton Place, Auchinleck. Trained by RAF Station, Benbecula.

NPS4320732 BLACK COCK

On 9 August 1943, this pigeon was released by force-landed aircrew, 380 miles from base on an unfamiliar course, and it delivered its message in nine hours.

Bred by NPS member A. Spillett, 17 Belmont Rise, Maidenhead. Trained by RAF Station, Cranage.

NPS4321900 DARK CHEQUER COCK

On 31 August 1944, this pigeon was released on the continent 210 miles from base at 2.00 p.m. under adverse weather conditions, low cloud, headwind and rain. It arrived home at 8.25 a.m. the next morning.

Bred by A. Clark, 56 Northbrook Road, West Croydon. Trained by RAF Station, Gillingham.

NPS4321940 MEALY COCK

After two years' consistently good work, including one service flight of 250 miles in five and a half hours, this bird was dropped on service by parachute in Germany in 1945. It was released more than 300 miles from base and homed successfully after several days' detention in a small container.

Bred by E. Edgington, Godalming. Trained by RAF Station, Gillingham.

NPS4324495 BLUE CHEQUER PIED HEN

Carrying a message from Normandy for US troops on 13 June 1944, this hen delivered it the same afternoon.

Bred by Mr Hicks, 19 Alexander Road, Barnstable. Trained by RAF, Hamworthy.

NPS4324548 MEALY COCK

On 26 August 1943, this pigeon carried a message from a force-landed aircraft, ninety-five miles from base, in eighty-eight minutes. On 5 October 1943, it carried a message from a point 145 miles from base in 2 hours 50 minutes.

Bred by NPS member A. Mathews, 2 Council Houses, Upper Summer Street, Stroud. Trained by RAF Station, Chivenor.

NPS43NS26790

On service with both Bomber and Coastal commands, this pigeon returned to its loft from operational work three times from approximately 270 miles.

Bred by J. Curtis, Bridge House, Dunston, Lincoln. Trained by RAF Station, St Eval.

NPS4326858 RED CHEQUER HEN

This hen was released with a message in Normandy by US troops during the afternoon of 14 June 1944 and homed in semi-darkness at 10.05 p.m. (B.D.S.T).

Bred by E. Lowcock, Woodlands, Settle. Trained by RAF Station, Hurn.

NPS4327912 BLUE CHEQUER HEN

In the course of its service, this hen was released from an aircraft with an emergency message, off the Scilly Isles, 200 miles from base on 28 August 1943. It arrived home after 6 hours 15 minutes. In September 1944, on a test flight when air-released 140 miles from base in an unfamiliar direction, it homed in 3 hours 5 minutes. She was a most consistent worker throughout her service.

Bred by NPS member W. Walker, 3 Maundetts Park Street, Somerford. Trained by RAF Station, Hamworthy.

NPS4328458 BLUE HEN

On 31 August 1944, this blue hen was released on the Continent 210 miles from base at 2.00 p.m.; under adverse weather conditions, it arrived at 8.10 a.m. the following morning.

Bred and trained by RAF, Gillingham.

NPS4328791 BLUE COCK

This pigeon was released by US troops at 2.35 p.m. on 11 June 1944 and homed in darkness at 10.29 p.m. (B.D.S.T.) that day with a message.

Bred by RAF Station, Wattisham. Trained by RAF Station, Hurn.

NPS4328902 BLUE CHEQUER HEN

In October 1943, this young bird was released by a force-landed aircrew, 230 miles from base in a heavy gale, and delivered its message the next morning.

Bred by NPS member Bernard, Scarborough. Trained by RAF Station, Pocklington.

NPS4329022 BLUE CHEQUER HEN

For two years, this hen maintained a reputation for consistent performance. In 1945, she had the ill luck not to be picked up for several days after being dropped by parachute; nevertheless, she struggled home ten days later from a distance over 300 miles away in German-occupied territory.

Bred and trained by RAF Station, Detling.

NPS4330072 GRIZZLE COCK

This pigeon carried a message from Normandy for US troops on 13 June 1944, arriving the same afternoon.

Bred by H. Elkins, 61 Vicarage Road, Warminster. Trained by RAF Station, Hamworthy.

NPS4330071 BLUE HEN

This pigeon was released with a message by US troops, Normandy, during the afternoon of 14 June 1944 and homed at dusk at 10.07 p.m. (B.D.S.T.) that night.

Bred by H. Elkins, 61 Vicarage Road, Warminster. Trained by RAF Station, Hamworthy.

NPS4330075 BLUE HEN

On 23 August 1943, this pigeon was air-released at sea, 150 miles from base at 4.30 p.m. and delivered its message at 8.30 a.m. the next morning. On 14 June 1944, during the afternoon, this pigeon was released in Normandy by US troops with a message, which it delivered in darkness at 10.46 p.m. (B.D.S.T.) that night.

Bred by H. Elkins, 61 Vicarage Road, Warminster. Trained by RAF Station, Hamworthy.

NPS4330800 BLUE CHEQUER HEN

On 2 August 1943, this hen was air-released forty-five miles from base and homed in 1 hour 15 minutes. On 13 June, she carried a message for the US troops from Normandy, and delivered it the same afternoon.

Bred by T. New, 3 The Ferns, Ogbourne St George. Trained by RAF Station, Hamworthy.

NPS4331185 BLUE COCK

On 19 August 1943, this pigeon was air-released 120 miles at sea and homed in 4 hours 10 minutes.

Bred by NPS member F. Golding, Silver Street, Potterne, Devizes. Trained by RAF Station, Hamworthy.

NPS4331186 RED CHEQUER HEN

On 25 October 1943, this hen was air-released at 2.45 p.m., 90 miles from base and homed at 5.45 p.m. as darkness fell.

Bred by NPS member F. Golding, Silver Street, Potterne, Devizes. Trained by RAF Station, Hamworthy.

NPS4331683 BLUE CHEQUER PIED COCK

This pigeon was released with a message by US troops in Normandy during the afternoon of 14 June 1944 and homed in darkness at 10.46 p.m. (B.D.S.T.) that night.

Bred by C. Timberlake, 14 Cranbourne Crescent Close, Slough. Trained by RAF Station, Hamworthy.

NPS4331727 BLUE COCK

This pigeon went on many flights from light naval craft on operations in the North Sea. In September 1944, it was dropped with an agent in the Netherlands and on 6 September delivered an important message dispatched at dawn that day.

Bred by NPS member P. Taylor, 2 Goodriche Street, Melton Mowbray. Trained by RAF Station, Felixstowe.

NPS4332334 BLUE CHEQUER COCK

On 23 September 1943, this bird was released by a force-landed aircrew with a message, 220 miles from base at 3.00 p.m., arriving home at 9.05 a.m. next morning. The weather conditions were unfavourable.

Bred by NPS member T. Redferne, Anchor Inn, Retford. Trained by RAF Station, Linton.

NPS4332997 BLUE CHEQUER PIED HEN

On 17 August 1943, this pigeon was released with a message 122 miles from base at 2.55 p.m., arriving back at 5.10 p.m.

Bred by NPS member Mr Price, 9 Brewery Street, Kimberley. Trained by RAF Station, North Luffenham.

NPS4334101 BLUE HEN

This pigeon was on several flights from light naval craft on operations in the North Sea. In July 1944, it was dropped with an agent in the Netherlands and released with a message on 23 July which it delivered the same day, approximately 200 miles away.

Bred by NPS member A. Brett, 27 Upper Strood Street, Sandwich, Kent. Trained by RAF Station, Felixstowe.

NPS4333161

This pigeon carried a message for the US troops in Normandy on 13 June 1944, which it delivered the same afternoon.

Bred by R. Scott, 13 Percival Street, Worksop. Trained by RAF Station, Holmsley.

NPS4334437 RED COCK

This pigeon was released from a distressed aircraft in darkness at 2.00 a.m., fifty miles from base, although its wing was damaged. It successfully homed the same morning.

Bred by W.T. Carr, 73 Avondale Road, Harringay. Trained by RAF Station, St Eval.

NPS4334766 BLUE CHEQUER PIED COCK

On 19 September 1943, this bird was air-released 180 miles from base at 3.30 p.m. and delivered its message the next morning, the weather conditions were adverse. On 13 June 1944, it carried a message from Normandy for US troops that it delivered the same afternoon.

Bred by A. Ford, 22 Malvern Street, Cheltenham. Trained by RAF Station, Hamworthy.

NPS4334773 BLUE CHEQUER COCK

On 13 June 1944, this pigeon carried a message for US troops from Normandy, which it delivered the same afternoon.

Bred by A. Ford, 22 Malvern Street, Cheltenham. Trained by RAF Station, Hamworthy.

NPS4337922 RED CHEQUER HEN

On 13 June 1944, this hen carried a message from US troops in Normandy, which it delivered the same afternoon.

Bred by T. Murdock, 130 Lochend Road, Gartcosh. Trained by RAF Station, Holmsley.

NPS4337925 RED CHEQUER COCK

On 30 July 1943, this pigeon was released by a force-landed aircrew, 150 miles from base on a route that was unfamiliar for this pigeon and under very adverse weather conditions. He covered the flight in seven and a half hours.

Bred by NPS member T. Murdock, 130 Lochend Road, Gartcosh. Trained by RAF Station, Holmsley.

NPS4341615 BLACK

Taken on service on 1 June 1944 by US Army, Normandy, its time of release is unknown, but it returned on 7 June.

Bred by Southern Command, Army Pigeon Service. Trained by Harding and Wall, Plymouth.

NPS4341925 DARK CHEQUER PIED COCK

On 29 July 1943, this bird was released at sea by a ditched aircrew during the afternoon. It arrived the next morning covered in oil and with eight of its twelve tail feathers missing.

Bred by A. Wright, 66 Carrington Lane, Ashton on Mersey. Trained by RAF Station, Jurby, Isle of Man.

NPS4341946 BLACK HEN

On 5 September 1943, she was air-released with an emergency message at 4.20 p.m., seventy-four miles from base and arrived at 6.50 p.m. The message it carried informed the base that the aircraft was landing elsewhere owing to bad visibility and strong headwind, conditions that made the pigeon's task an extremely difficult one.

Bred by J. Johnson, Nant View, Nant Marr, Buckley. Trained by RAF Station, Llandwrog.

NPS4343842 RED CHEQUER COCK

On 14 June 1944, this pigeon carried a message from US troops in Normandy, which it delivered in darkness at 10.25 p.m. (B.D.S.T.) that day.

Bred by W. Maddock, Tutts Clump, near Reading. Trained by RAF Station, Hamworthy.

NPS4344515 BLUE CHEQUER COCK

On 13 October 1943, this pigeon was released by a force-landed aircrew, 160 miles from base under adverse conditions, including thick fog and drizzle. It delivered its message in six and a half hours.

Bred by NPS member H. Mycroft, 9 Brindle Lane, Seabrooks. Trained by RAF Station, Beaulieu.

NPS4348767 RED

Taken on service on 1 June 1944 by US Army, Normandy, this bird's time of release is not known, but it homed on 8th June.

Bred by E. Smith, 25 Peel Brow, Ramsbottom, Manchester. Trained by Mr Metherall, Plymouth.

NPS4350087

On 13 June 1944, this bird carried a message for US troops in Normandy, which it delivered the same afternoon.

Bred by T. Spencer, Gyldart, Middleton, Wirksworth, Derby. Trained by RAF Station, Hamworthy.

NPS4350502 RED CHEQUER COCK

On 11 June 1944, this bird carried a message from Normandy for US troops and arrived at 9.50 p.m. (B.D.S.T.) that evening.

Bred by Dr J. Buckley, Southfield, Bramcote, Notts. Trained by RAF Station, Hurn.

NPS4351906 DARK CHEQUER PIED HEN

On 13 June 1944, this hen carried a message from Normandy for US troops that it delivered the same afternoon.

Bred by S. Clarke, 13 Sydney, Kimberley. Trained by RAF Station, Hurn.

NPS4353555

On 14 June 1944, this pigeon carried a message for US troops at Normandy, arriving at dusk at 10.00 p.m. (B.D.S.T.) that same evening.

Bred by J. Bailey, 61 Prue Street, South Moor, Durham. Trained by RAF Station, Holmsley.

NPS4353739

On 13 June 1944, this bird carried a message for US troops in Normandy, which it delivered the same afternoon.

Bred by J. Jeffrey, 177 North Seaton Road, Ashington. Trained by RAF Station, Holmsley.

BPS4354292 BLUE CHEQUER HEN

On 13 June 1944, this bird carried a message for US troops in Normandy, which it delivered the same afternoon.

Bred by W Reddle, 1 Kings Row, High Spen, Rowland Gill, Durham.

NPS4355095 RED CHEQUER HEN

On 13 June 1944, this pigeon carried a message for US troops in Normandy and delivered it the same afternoon.

Bred by J. Maddock, 380 Stenson Road, Derby. Trained by RAF Station, Hurn.

NPS4355605 GAY PIED COCK

On 13 June 1944, this bird carried a message for US troops in Normandy, which it delivered the same afternoon.

Bred by H. Evans, 50 Brandon Village, Brandon, Durham. Trained by RAF Station, Hamworthy.

NPS4356275

On 13 June 1944, this bird carried a message for US troops in Normandy, which it delivered at 9.00 p.m. (B.D.S.T.) that evening.

Bred by J. Tierney, 36 Durham Street, Wallsend. Trained by RAF Station, Holmsley.

NPS4356455 BLUE PIED HEN

On 13 June 1944, this hen carried a message for US troops in Normandy, which it delivered the same afternoon.

Bred by D. Taylor, Eastnor, Crabtree Road, Stocksfield. Trained by RAF Station, Hurn.

NPS4356657 MEALY COCK

On 12 June 1944, this bird delivered a message for US troops in Normandy in 6 hours 32 minutes.

Bred by Gorton and Bell, 67 Forth Street, Blackhall, Durham. Trained by RAF Station, Hurn.

NPS4357196 BLUE COCK

In the course of its service, this pigeon delivered a message from a diverted aircrew 160 miles from base under very adverse weather conditions in six and three-quarter hours.

Bred by NPS member T. Laws, Cowarth Road, Sunningdale, Berks. Trained by RAF Station, Beaulieu.

NPS4357221

On 13 June 1944, this bird delivered a message from US troops in Normandy the same afternoon.

Bred by A. Horner, 172 Ashley Road, South Shields. Trained by RAF Station, Holmsley.

NPS4357231

On 13 June 1944, this pigeon carried a message for US troops in Normandy, which it delivered the same afternoon.

Bred by A. Horner, 172 Ashley Road, South Shields. Trained by RAF Station, Holmsley.

NPS4358968 BLUE CHEQUER HEN

On 14 June 1944, this pigeon carried a message from US troops in Normandy, which it delivered in semi-darkness at 10.05 p.m. (B.D.S.T.) that evening.

Bred by RAF Nutts Corner. Trained by RAF Station, Hurn.

NPS4359438

In the course of its service as a young bird, this pigeon was released by a force-landed aircrew 230 miles from base, on a route unfamiliar to the pigeon and it still delivered its message the same day. It was later lost with its aircrew on operations.

Bred by NPS member L. Gerard, 209 Easter Grove, Morecambe. Trained by RAF Station, Pocklington.

NPS4364638 RED CHEQUER COCK

On 11 June 1944, this red chequer was released with a message by US troops in Normandy at 8.00 p.m. (B.D.S.T). – too late to make the Channel crossing that night. It delivered its message at

10.26 a.m. the next morning.

Bred and trained by RAF Station, Hurn.

NPS4364651

On 11 June 1944, this pigeon was released in Normandy with a message from US troops, too late in the evening to cross the channel that night. It delivered its message at 9.02 a.m. (B.D.S.T.) the next morning.

Bred and trained by RAF Station, Hurn.

NPS4364659 RED PIED COCK

On 11 June, this pigeon was released in Normandy by US troops, too late in the evening to make the Channel crossing, and delivered its message at 9.02 a.m. (B.D.S.T.) next morning.

Bred and trained by RAF Station, Hurn.

NPS4364661 GRIZZLE HEN

On 14 June 1944, this pigeon carried a message for US troops from Normandy, which it delivered in semi-darkness at 10.05 p.m. (B.D.S.T.) that night.

Bred and trained by RAF Station, Hurn.

NPS4364662 RED CHEQUER COCK

On 11 June 1944, this pigeon was released in Normandy at 10.30 a.m. by US troops, and arrived back at base at 4.00 p.m.

Bred and trained by RAF Station, Hurn

NPS4364947

This bird flew many times from light naval craft operating in the North Sea. On 30 September 1944, this pigeon was selected and dispatched on a special task involving dropping with an agent at night in Holland, where it was released on 2 October and homed with its message the same day. The distance was approximately 200 miles; the time of release is not known.

Bred and trained by RAF Station, Felixstowe.

NPS4364992 BLUE CHEQUER COCK

After several flights from light naval craft in the North Sea, in August 1944, this pigeon was dropped with an agent in the Netherlands and on 1 September was released with a message and returned the same day.

Bred and trained by RAF Station, Felixstowe.

NPS4366019 BLACK CHEQUER COCK

On 25 October 1943, this young bird was released with an emergency message 104 miles from base at sea at 10.30 a.m. It delivered its message at 2.41 p.m., (104 miles in 4 hours 11 minutes) in adverse weather conditions.

Bred by Baker and Hare, 128 Hurst Street, Southport. Trained by RAF Station, Llandwrog.

NPS4369609 BLUE CHEQUER HEN

On 30 November 1943, this young bird was released by a force-landed aircraft under extreme adverse weather conditions, 150 miles from base. It may be noted that no flying was permitted at the base on that day or the next owing to low cloud, rain and fog. The pigeon home in 4 hours 40 minutes.

Bred by J. Beswick & Son, 97 Egertion Terrace, Knutsford. Trained by RAF Station, Llandwrog.

NPS4373382 WHITE

Taken on service on 1 June 1944 by the US Army, Normandy. Time of release is not known, but it homed on 12 June with a message.

Bred by W. Wright, 9 Broughton End, Lidlington. Trained by Mr Crabb, Plymouth.

NPS4417262 BLUE PIED HEN 'LITTLE MISS'

This young pigeon completed her operational training at four months old. A month later, she delivered a message over 190 miles in four hours under conditions that were not favourable. She was then sent for test purposes with a civilian open race from Penzance 280 miles, homing in six hours, beating all the civilians and only being beaten by one RAF pigeon.

Bred and trained by RAF Station, Gillingham.

44WD1063

This pigeon first saw service with the Army Pigeon Service in North Africa, returning with the unit to the United Kingdom.

It was then sent to the European theatre of war. Resettled at Bayeaux for service, it carried important messages from the Falaise pocket during the action. After this, it was again resettled for service in Belgium.

Bred and trained by the Army Pigeon Service.

AUSTRALIAN ARMY SIGNAL CORPS

DD43Q879

During the fight for Manus Island, the US Marines sent a patrol to the village of Dravito. The patrol was strongly attacked by Japanese soldiers. Whilst returning with the information that a strong counter-attack was in preparation, the patrol's radio was rendered inoperative during the action, so two pigeons were released warning HQ of the impending attack. These pigeons were shot down immediately as the Japanese intensified their efforts to annihilate the patrol. This left one pigeon – DD43Q879 – which was the sole remaining means of contact with headquarters. It was released during a temporary lull and, despite heavy fire, immediately directed at it. It reached headquarters thirty miles away in difficult country in forty-six minutes. As a result, Dravito was heavily bombed and the patrol extricated from its perilous position.

Bred by the Australian Voluntary Pigeon Service. Trained by the 7th Australian Pigeon Service Section whilst attached to the United States 6th Army.

DD43T139 BLUE COCK

During an exceptionally heavy tropical storm in June 1945, army boat 1402 foundered on Wadou Beach in the Huon Gulf. This pigeon was released with the following message: – 'Engine failed, washed on beach Wadou owing to heavy seas. Send help immediately. Craft rapidly filling with water.' The pigeon homed to Madang through heavy rain, a distance of forty miles in fifty minutes.

As a result, a rescue ship was sent and the craft, together with its valuable cargo of ammunition and stores was salvaged. This pigeon had flown a total of twenty-three operations totalling a distance of 1,004 miles.

Bred by the Australian Voluntary Pigeon Service. Trained by the 1st Australian Pigeon Service, (operating with 1st[t] Australian Water Transport Group).

DD443863

In July 1945, during the operations on Bougainville, an infantry company of the 3rd Australian Division was pinned down and surrounded by superior enemy forces. All means of communication with headquarters had been cut off or destroyed, with the exception of two pigeons. This particular pigeon was sent with an urgent call for reinforcements and artillery support.

Despite heavy tropical rain and heavy fire directed on the pigeon by sixty or seventy Japanese on release, which wounded the bird, it flew the twenty-two miles back to base in three hours, arriving in a state of exhaustion. As a result, the necessary artillery support was given and the company safely withdrew with its woundedbefore dark.

Bred by the Australian Voluntary Pigeon Service. Trained by 1st Australian Pigeon Section, (operating with the 1st Australian Water Transport Group).

QPS411382 BLUE COCK

In March 1945, Water Transport Group Headquarters at Madang received the following message by pigeon: – 'Steer cable broke, am in middle of Rasch Passage, send urgent help.' A rescue craft was sent immediately and reached the helpless barge just in time to prevent it from being washed onto the reef. The saving of this barge loaded with valuable equipment was due principally to the speed with which the message for assistance was delivered – four miles in five minutes. This pigeon had previously flown thirty-one operational flights totalling 1,257 miles.

Bred by the Australian Voluntary Pigeon Service. Trained by 1st Australian Pigeon Section, (operating with the 1st Australian Water Transport Group).

THE COMPLETE LIST OF PIGEONS AWARDED THE DICKEN MEDAL

NEHU40NS1, BLUE CHEQUER HEN, 'WINKIE'

MEPS431263, RED CHEQUER COCK, 'GEORGE'

SURP41L3089, WHITE HEN, 'WHITE VISION'

NPS41NS4230, 'BEACHCOMBER'

NPS4231066, GRIZZLE COCK, 'GUSTAV'

NPS4394451, DARK CHEQUER COCK, 'PADDY'

NURP36JH190, DARK CHEQUER HEN, 'KENLEY LASS'

NURP38EGU242, RED CHEQUER COCK, 'COMMANDO'

NPS42NS44802, DARK CHEQUER COCK, 'FLYING DUTCHMAN'

NURP40GVIS453, BLUE COCK, 'ROYAL BLUE'

NURP41A2164, 'DUTCH COAST'

NPS41NS2862, BLUE COCK, 'NAVY BLUE'

NPS42NS15125, MEALY COCK, 'WILLIAM OF ORANGE'

NPS4329018, DARK CHEQUER COCK, 'RUHR EXPRESS'

SPS4221610, BLUE CHEQUER HEN, 'SCOTCH LASS'

NU41HQ4373, BLUE COCK, 'BILLY'

NURP39NRS144, RED COCK, 'COLOGNE'

NPS4236392, 'MARQUIS'

NPS42NS7542

41BA2793, 'BROAD ARROW'

NURP39SDS39, 'ALL ALONE'

NURP37CEN335, 'MERCURY'

NURP38BPC6

DD43T139

DD43Q879

NURP41SBC219, 'DUKE OF NORMANDY'

NURP43CC2418, BLUE CHEQUER HEN

NURP40WLE249, 'MARY'

NURP41DHZ56, 'TOMMY'

42WD593, 'PRINCESS'

USA 43SC6390, 'GI JOE'

MERITORIOUS
PERFORMANCE LIST

The following pigeons were all used on particularly hazardous tasks, as they were dropped by parachute in single bird containers into occupied territory in Europe, with instructions to the finders to answer a questionnaire and return it using the pigeon. Obviously, many dropped birds would be found by the enemy and some would not be found at all. In most cases, the date of release of the pigeons which returned was not known and for this reason the particulars given below, under the heading 'Date Sent', indicates the date on which the pigeon was dropped.

'Date Returned' signifies the date of the arrival of the pigeon at its home loft in England and 'Place' indicates the area in which the pigeon was dropped. The birds were supplied by the National Pigeon Service 'Special Section' groups.

Reinforcements of these Special Section groups were provided by NPS breeders in other parts of the country.

Some 27,000 birds were maintained and trained for this task and approximately 17,000 were actually dropped on these operations during the war. A number of the arrivals survived two such tasks and three of them succeeded three times. The breeders, where known, are indicated.

Ring No.	Date Sent	Date Returned	Place	Owner/NPS Group	Bred By
IU.41.NS.771	24/6/42	29/6/42	France	Bridgewater	F.J. McConkey, 63 High Street, Bangor, Co. Down
NUHP31.BN.4919	21/6/45	7/8/42	Belgium	Folkestone	J. Banks, Teddars Lees, Folkestone
NU.34.HQ.8758	25/8/42	8/9/42	Dives	Folkestone	A Caller, The Chalet, Dargate Road, Yorklett, Faversham, Kent
NU.36.D.22	11/6/41	28/6/41	Caen, Brittany	Folkestone	J. Banks, Teddars Lees, Folkestone
NU.35.D.22	7/5/41	28/5/41	W. Flanders	Folkestone	G. Hardy, 17 Broadway, Denscroft, Hatfield, Doncaster
NU.35.PHS.10	5/3/44	14/4/44	Guise	Bournemouth	R.L. Cobb, 6 St. Mary's Road, Poole
NU.38.BRP106	21/10/43	20/3/44	Belgium	Thames Estuary	J. Clements, 12 Western Road, Burnham-on-Crouch
NU.38.GFS.197	28/8/42	3/9/42	Amiens	Ipswich	W. Grantham, 290 Wherstead Road, Ipswich
NU.38.PHC.61	12/8/43	22/8/43	France	Thames Estuary	Mrs H. Bridge, White House, Kiln Road, Thundersley
NU.38.PHC.61	22/2/44	26/2/44	Combined Ops	Thames Estuary	
NU.38.WE.857	20/5/43	22/6/43	Belgium	Ipswich	
NU.38.WE.859	20/5/43	21/6/43	Belgium	Ipswich	
NU.38.WHF.700	27/5/44	29/5/44	France	Shepherd's Bush	S. Griffin, 3 St James's Street, London, W6
NU.39.DUN.173	7/9/41	9/9/41	France	Bridgewater	A. Pople, Brick House, Puriton, Bridgewater
NU.39.H.949	14/9/43	26/9/43	France	Isle of Wight	
NU.39.HHS.396	14/3/43	19/3/43	France	Bridgewater	E.J. Hooper, 10 Horston Road, Highbridge
NU.39.HQA.927	13/7/43	15/7/43	Mesnil Simon	Harrow	A. Cain, 125 Long Elms, Harrow Weald
NU.39.HQD.6729	6/8/44	25/8/44	Ferrières	Folkestone	J. Banks, Teddars Lees, Folkestone

Ring No.	Date Sent	Date Returned	Place	Owner/NPS Group	Bred By
NU.39.PHC.68	23/8/43	1/9/43	Mayenne	Thames Estuary	Mr & Mrs J. Rasfield, 20 Station Avenue, Prttlewell, Southend-on-Sea
NU.39.SOS.173	25/8/44	25/8/44	Gelderland	Thames Estuary	G. Davis, Silverdale Avenue, Westcliff-on-Sea
NUHW.40.CEN.263	12/6/43	24/6/43	France	Ipswich	B. Westcott, 27 Campbell Road, Ipswich
NU.40.NNK.313	25/6/42	28/6/42	Elbeuf	Bognor	
NU.40.NNK.336	14/3/43	8/3/43	Vimoutiers	Bognor	
NU.40.NNK.392	20/3/43	25/3/43	France	Bognor	
NU.40.PT.143	28/7/42	23/8/42	France	H. Whitley, Paignton	H. Whitley, Primby, Paignton
NU.40.PT.255	22/1/43	27/1/43	Auxi Le Château	H. Whitley, Paignton	H. Whitley, Primby, Paignton
NUHW.41.CEN.239	10/6/43	20/8/43	France	Ipswich	H.E. Keys, 51 Belvedere Road, Ipswich
NU.41.GHS.18	28/8/44	15/9/44	Holland	Chatham	J. Carter, The Hope, Wigmore, Gillingham
NU.41.GHS.36	22/7/43	26/7/43	Lisieux	Chatham	C. Clout, 190 Castle Road, Chatham
NU.41.NS.1311	25/6/42	25/6/42	Falaise	Chard Junction	
NU.41.PHC.47	14/4/44	10/8/44	Seine Inférieure	Bexleyheath	J. Ellis, 26 Eastern Avenue, Southend-on-Sea
NU.41.PHC.168	7/8/44	15/8/44	Geldermalsen	Thames Estuary	J.B. Atkinson, Post Office, Church End, Paglesham
NU.41.RD.22	14/9/43	4/10/43	France	Isle of Wight	R.N. Daish, Homelands, 51 John's Wood Road, Ryde
NU.41.WU.188	18/5/43	23/5/43	Authis	Walthamstow	F. Baltrop, 22 Beulah Road, Walthamstow, E17
NU.41.WU.378	16/8/43	19/8/43	France	Walthamstow	W. Dell, 49 Lymouth Road, Walthamstow, E17
NU.42.A3120	1/5/44	22/5/44	Belgium	Weymouth	G. Lovell, 3 May Terrace, Chickerell, Weymouth

Ring No.	Date Sent	Date Returned	Place	Owner/NPS Group	Bred By
NU.42.A.3124	8/8/44	10/8/44	Seine Inférieure	Weymouth	G. Davis, 8 Wenham Drive, Westcliff-on-Sea
NU.42.B.928	30/4/44	5/5/44	Bonnetable	Thames Estuary	C. Jackson, 7 Waverley Road, London, E17
NU.42.B.5349	6/1/43	9/1/43	France	Walthamstow	C. Jackson, 7 Waverley Road, London, E17
NU.42.B.5349	5/7/44	9/7/44	Seine Inférieure	Walthamstow	L.H. Turner, West View, High Cross Road,
NU.42.B.6817	20/3/43	25/3/43	Orne	Bognor	Poulton, Blackpool
NU.42.C.63	17/9/43	April 44		Walthamstow	F. Hudson, 77 Waterside Road, Barton-on-Humber, Lincs.
NU.42.C.1202	5/7/44	July 44	Caux	Walthamstow	J & G Brown, Fran Hor, Chearsby, Aylesbury
NU.42.C.1163	18/9/43	15/4/44	France	Walthamstow	G. Sutherland, 44 Lennox Road, Walthamstow, E.17
NU.42.D.1260	28/8/42	3/9/42	Wieringermeer	Ipswich	W. Westcott, 10 Ruskin Road, Ipswich
NU.42.D.1403	18/5/43	30/5/43	Doullens	Ipswich	F. Vince, "Lerwick", Humber Douchy Lane, Ipswich
NU.42.D.1475	16/8/43	1/9/43	Hesdin	Ipswich	J. Catchpole, 170 Cemetery Road, Ipswich
NUHW.42.E.4353	15/8/43	20/8/43	Aunay-sur-Odon	Ipswich	Sparry Bros., 17 Hitchman Street, Stambormell, Stourbridge
NU.43.E.4713	22/6/44	15/6/44	Orne, France	Lyme Regis	W. Bailey, 31 Alma Street, Weston-super-Mare
NU.42.F.7829	20/3/43	5/5/43	Fougères	H. Whitley, Paignton	H. Whitley, Paignton
NU.42.G.4761	12/6/43	16/6/43	Pas de Calais	Ipswich	H.E. Kemp, Belvedere Road, Ipswich
NU.42.G.4790	18/5/43	21/5/43		Ipswich	C.H. Folkhan, "Overlette", Hadleigh Road, Ipswich
NU.42.H.1968	20/3/43	15/4/43	Vimoutiers	H. Whitley, Paignton	H. Whitley, Paignton
NPS.42.17430	27/10/42	9/11/42	St Lô	A. Chester Beatty	F. Lewry, 117 Maybury Road, Woking

Ring No.	Date Sent	Date Returned	Place	Owner/NPS Group	Bred By
NU.43.A.9504	6/8/44	8/8/44	Dorceau	Thames Estuary	Gray & Son, "Violet Villa", Kiln Road, Thundersley
NURP.43.AA.883	5/5/44	7/8/44	France	Thames Estuary	G. Messett, 21 Arkwright Road, Tilbury Dock
NU.43.C.7989	29/6/44	9/8/44	France	Isle of Wight	J. Gordon Hammond, Wyke House, Trowbridge
NURP.43.L.7149	30/4/44	2/5/44	La Flèche	Thames Estuary	A. Moss, Anchor Inn, Hullbridge
NS.40.711	12/6/43	14/6/43	Lorient	Gen. Sir H. Jackson	Army Pigeon Service
NPS.41.NS.2308	16/10/43	18/10/43	France	Sir E. Debenham, Dorchester	J. Gordon Hammond, Trowbridge
NPS.41.NS.2322	23/6/42	25/6/42	Falaise	Mottistone Manor	J. Gordon Hammond, Trowbridge
NPS.41.NS.2329	1/6/42	4/6/42	Normandy	Mottistone Manor	J. Gordon Hammond, Trowbridge
NPS.41.NS.2523	23/3/42	6/4/42		Weston-super-Mare	J. Gordon Hammond, Trowbridge
NPS.41.NS.2529	30/7/42	31/7/42	France	Mottistone Manor, Isle of Wight	J. Gordon Hammond, Trowbridge
NPS.41.NS.2543	26/9/42	14/10/42	France	Mottistone Manor, Isle of Wight	J. Gordon Hammond, Trowbridge
NPS.41.2805	18/1/43	25/1/43	France	Sir Ernest Debenham, Dorchester	G. Graham, 76 Queen's Crescent, Chapelhall, Audris
NPS.41.2856	18/1/43	24/1/43	Caen	Sir Ernest Debenham, Dorchester	RAF, St Eval, Cornwall
NPS.41.NS.2902	30/7/42	4/8/42	Normandy	Mottistone Manor, Isle of Wight	G. Braithwaite, Brownberry Manor, Horsforth, Leeds
NS.42.NPS.503	14/7/43	18/7/43	Alençon	Mottistone Manor, Isle of Wight	J. Bawn, 3 Myrtle Avenue, Whitburn

Ring No.	Date Sent	Date Returned	Place	Owner/NPS Group	Bred By
NPS.41.NS.507	12/6/43	14/6/43	France	Mottistone Manor, Isle of Wight	J. Bawn, 3 Myrtle Avenue, Whitburn
NPS.41.NS.957	7/10/43	11/10/43	Florennes	Shepherd's Bush	Dr W. Anderson, Armadale, West Lothian
NPS.41.NS.1518	25/6/42	5/7/42	France	Bognor Loft	S. Griffin, 3 St. James's Street, London, W.6
NPS.41.NS.2493	27/4/42	1/5/42	Manche	Weston-super-Mare	J. Gordon Hammond, Trowbridge
NPS.41.NS.2499	28/6/42	1/7/42	Mortrée	Weston-super-Mare	J. Gordon Hammond, Trowbridge
NPS.41.3339	15/2/43	22/2/43	Belgium	Bognor Loft	F. Smyth, 2 Newton Park, Belfast
NPS.41.NS.9529	24/7/42	28/7/42	France	Weston-super-Mare	
NPS.41.NS.9670	23/7/42	26/7/42	Lison	Mottistone Manor, Isle of Wight	
NPS.41.NS.10824	26/9/42	28/9/42	Voorne	Mottistone Manor, Isle of Wight	B. Coleman, Ellel Hill, Bay Horse, Lancaster
NPS.41.10896	31/7/42	31/7/42	Condroz	Chard Junction	H. James & Son, Sagebury Terrace, Stoke Works, Broomsgrove
NPS.41.10896	24/6/42	6/7/42	Navarre-Evreux	Chard Junction	H. James & Son, Sagebury Terrace, Stoke Works, Broomsgrove
NPS.41.NS.11226	30/7/42	31/7/42	Calvados	Mottistone Manor	J. Shaw & Son, 18 Grahamsdyke Road, Scabegs, Bonnybridge, Stirling
NPS.41.NS.11345	28/8/42	21/9/42	Turnhout	Mottistone Manor	Gorkstone & Son, 44 Thistle Street, Cowdenbeath
NS.41.11390	16/6/43	22/6/43	Triequeville	Fuller Isaacson	J. Mackie, Black Faulds, Fauldhouse
NPS.41.NS.11743	24/6/42	29/6/42	Belgium	Bognor Loft	J. Scally, 4 Mint Cottages, Cardenden, Fife
NPS.41.NS.12284	3/7/44	7/7/44	Le Mage	Maidstone	
NPS.41.NS.15156	23/6/42	29/6/42	Lison	Mottistone Manor	Gilmour & Grieve, West Coattown

Ring No.	Date Sent	Date Returned	Place	Owner/NPS Group	Bred By
NPS.41.NS.15168	23/7/42	2/8/42	Caen	Mottistone Manor	Balgonie, Markinch, Fife
NS.41.15204	14/4/43	27/4/43	France	Bognor Loft	R. Littlejohn, Basin Station, Kirkintilloch
NPS.41.NS.15438	28/7/42	13/8/42	Belgium	Mottistone Manor	J. McIvor, 67 Church Street, Tranent, E. Lothian
NPS.41.NS.19661	18/8/43	6/9/43	France	Sir E. Debenham, Dorchester	J. Gordon Hammond, Trowbridge
NPS.41.NS.19669	14/6/43	2/7/43	Sebourg	Folkestone	J. Gordon Hammond, Trowbridge
NPS.41.NS.19674	24/10/42	31/10/42	Belgium	Folkestone	J. Gordon Hammond, Trowbridge
NPS.41.NS.19680	16/4/43	3/5/43	Crèvecoeur	Folkestone	J. Gordon Hammond, Trowbridge
NPS.42.NS.62	25/7/42	6/8/42	France	Lyme Regis	F.L. Coles, 84 Larnbrook Road, Taunton
NPS.42.NS.75	24/10/42	28/10/42	Belgium	Lyme Regis	F.L. Coles, 84 Larnbrook Road, Taunton
NS.42.75	12/6/43	14/6/43	Orne	Gen. Sir H. Jackson	
NPS.42.NS.79	23/7/42	20/8/42	France	Sir Ernest Debenham	F. Cudland, 42 Parr Street, Exeter
NPS.42.NS.311	28/6/42	15/7/42	France	Lyme Regis	W. Low, 52 Brook Street, West Reading, Berks.
NPS.42.NS.907	15/1/43	20/1/43	France	Lyme Regis	W.T. Hitchcock, 57 Hutland Road, Ipswich
NPS.42.G.1151	22/6/43	16/7/43	Belgium	Plymouth	The late Over Dix, Pensford, Bristol
NPS.42.NS.1496	26/9/42	8/10/42	Belgium	Gen. Sir H. Jackson	D. Evans, 5 Jones Street, Treherbert
NS.40.1791	10/8/44	25/8/44	Montluçon	Portsmouth	H. Hammond, 11 Nile Street, Emsworth
NPS.42.NS.1818	12/6/43	14/6/43	Lorient	A. Hewitt, Horsley	A. Hill, 27 Belvoir Street, Ilkeston
NPS.42.NS.2099	25/7/42	18/8/42	France	Lyme Regis	J.A. Albert, 140 Bright Street, Sheffield
NS.40.2308	12/6/43	14/6/43	France	Gen. Sir H. Jackson	Army Pigeon Service
NPS.42.NS.2546	24/10/42	31/10/42	Belgium	Lyme Regis	S.W. Thorne, 15 The Barracks, High Wycombe

Ring No.	Date Sent	Date Returned	Place	Owner/NPS Group	Bred By
NS.40.2643	12/6/43	16/6/43	Loudéac	Gen. Sir Henry Jackson	Army Pigeon Service
NPS.42.2736	29/7/44	10/8/44		Lyme Regis	Miller & Sims, 54 Hele Road, St. Mary Church, Torquay
NPS.42.NS.2780	23/7/42	25/7/42	Constance	Sir Ernest Debenham, Dorchester	B. Powell, 61 Penngrove, Hereford
NPS.42.NS.2780	27/8/45	27/8/45	Belgium		
NPS.42.NS.2780	15/4/43	16/4/43	France		
NPS.42.NS.3722	28/6/42	2/7/42	Nevilly	Lyme Regis	H.R. Heath, Station Road, Tean, Stoke-on-Trent
NPS.42.NS.3803	18/9/42	21/9/42	St Pol	A. Chester Beatty	J. Dobson, 83 Parker Street, Derby
NS.42.3827	15/7/42	18/7/42	Fosses (Namur)	Mottistone Manor	R.L. Donaldson, 122 High Street, Dunbar
NPS.42.NS.3827	16/4/43	20/4/43	Tillières	Mottistone Manor	R.L. Donaldson, 122 High Street, Dunbar
NPS.42.NS.4125	23/7/42	7/8/42	France	Sir Ernest Debenham, Dorchester	O.W. Walls, Vale House, Chester Road, Sutton Coldfield, Birmingham
NPS.42.NS.4340	28/7/42	31/7/42	Condroz	Gen. Sir Henry Jackson	Doughty & Griffiths, 25 Claenowen Terrace, Tynewydd, Treherbert, Glamorgan
NPS.42.NS.4340	21/10/42	30/10/42	French Coast		
NPS.42.NS.4977	18/9/42	28/9/42	Assen	Folkestone	J.H. Finney, 83 Portland Avenue, Gravesend
NPS.42.NS.5103	11/4/43	13/4/43	France	Chard Junction	W. Harrell, "Hampton", Old Butt Lane, Talke, Stoke-on-Trent
NPS.42.NS.5354	18/5/43	21/5/43	France	Mottistone Manor	E. Griffiths, "Glenola", Park Avenue, Cheadle
NPS.42.NS.6248	4/8/44	10/8/44	Tourouvre	Oxford	J. Kendall, 9 Crockland Avenue, Dalton-in-Furness

Ring No.	Date Sent	Date Returned	Place	Owner/NPS Group	Bred By
NPS.42.NS.6261	24/8/42	26/8/42	St Pol	A. Chester Beatty	F.R. Hayman, 5 St. George's Square, Maidstone
NPS.42.NS.6455	16/5/43	18/5/43	France	Mottistone Manor	W.H. Bishop, 1 Rock Terrace, Crawshawbooth, Rossendale
NPS.42.6462	19/9/43	?		Plymouth	C. Pallet, 1 Dirredor View, Hunderton Road, Hereford
NPS.42.NS.6851	27/10/42	1/11/42	France	Mottistone Manor	Moore & Son, 14 Harthorne Bank Altham, Accrington
NPS.42.NS.7524	23/7/42	28/7/42	Brittany	Lady Mary Manningham-Buller	C. Dyson, 12 Station Road, Worsboro Dale, Barnsley
NPS.42.NS.7524	10/5/43	17/5/43	France		
NPS.42.NS.7524	227/43	26/7/43	France		
NPS.42.NS.7730	27/9/42	9/10/42	Belgium	Gen. Sir Henry Jackson	T. Marks, 86 Arnstead Road, Beighton, Sheffield
NPS.42.NS.8305	24/2/43	26/2/43	France	H. Whitley, Paignton	T.F. Robertson, 18a Exchange Street, Jedburgh
NPS.42.NS.9697	11/4/43	15/4/43	Rennes	Chard Junction	Gregory & Trenfield, 35 High Street, Gloucester
NPS.42.NS.9697	10/6/43	20/7/43	France	Chard Junction	
NPS.42.9758	21/2/43	2/3/43		Weston-super-Mare	H.S. Pegler, 124 Coney Hill, Gloucester
NPS.42.NS.9846	24/8/42	26/8/42	Lille	A. Chester Beatty	P. Hale, 53 Portman Road, Scunthorpe
NPS.42.NS.9986	14/4/43	17/4/43	Eure et Loire	Bognor Loft	S.J. Wood, 10 Wellesley Street, Gloucester
NPS.42.NS.10616	18/9/42	26/5/42	Vire	Weston-super-Mare	R. Maitland, 26 Hables Street, Daisy Hill, Westhoughton, Bolton

Ring No.	Date Sent	Date Returned	Place	Owner/NPS Group	Bred By
NPS.42.NS.11244	23/7/42	25/11/42	France	Sir Ernest Debenham, Dorchester	W.J Cannam, Ullesthorpe, Rugby
NPS.42.NS.11542	27/8/42	12/9/42	Amiens	Bognor Loft	G.A. Cross, 82 Queen's Road, Slough
NPS.42.11648	27/10/42	6/11/42	N. V. Holland	Clacton	E. Watson, 46 Bramford Road, Ipswich
NPS.42.NS.12040	26/9/42	28/9/42	Belgium	Bognor Loft	E. Dellow, 22 Clifton Square, Corby, nr Kettering
NS.42.12046	15/1/43	21/1/43	Carfour St Jean	Clacton	R.S. Bliss, 118 Usher Road, Bow, London, E3
NPS.42.12857	18/1/43	20/1/43	France	Clacton	C.H. Peppiatt, 20 Haverstock Hill, London
NS.42.12872	17/6/43	21?/7/43	France	Lady Mary Manningham-Buller	
NPS.42.NS.12883	27/10/42	31/10/42	Holland	Gen. Sir Henry Jackson	
NPS.42.NS.13394	21/10/42	24/10/42	French Coast	A. Chester Beatty	Mr & Mrs Lowes, Tower House, Arcadian Gardens, Hadleigh
NPS.42.13435	23/9/42	3/10/42	N. France	Mottistone Manor	J.C. Haslam, 412 Rippponden Road, Oldham
NPS.42.NS.13547	27/8/42	29/9/42	Amiens	A. Chester Beatty	J. Paxton, 54 Highway Road, Maidenhead
NPS.42.NS.13770	4/6/44	9/6/44		Maidstone	J. Bloor, 88 Park Street, Uttoxeter
NS.42.14524	13/4/43	23/4/43	Belgium	Folkestone	V. Woodbush, 11 Stanley Street, Ulverston
NPS.42.NS.15080	27/8/42	19/9/42	Amiens	A. Chester Beatty	Laws & Son, 17/3 Single Row, nr Seaton Colliery, Ashington
NPS.42.15555	19/2/43	24/2/43	Hambye	Bognor Loft	Gibbons & Sons, 23 Rutland Street, Maidenhead
NPS.42.NS.15833	27/9/42	12/10/42	Pas de Calais	A. Chester Beatty	N. Tidd, 14 Paddock Street, Norwich
NPS.42.16022	22/1/43	2/2/43	France	Isle of Wight	F. Bryant, 2 Hewers Road, Plymouth

Ring No.	Date Sent	Date Returned	Place	Owner/NPS Group	Bred By
NPS.42.NS.16223	20/11/42	2/12/42	France	A. Hewitt	Hearman, 4 Norfolk Park Cottages, Maidenhead
NPS.42.NS.16247	23/9/42	30/9/42	N. France	Sir Ernest Debenham, Dorchester	J. Bowes, 23 Dunn Terrace, Harthill, Lanark
NPS.42.NS.16247	15/4/43	15/4/43	France	Bognor Loft	T. Irving, 8 Church Street, Dearham, Maryport
NS.42.17114	28/2/44	4/3/44			
NPS.42.NS.17384	28/7/42	31/7/42	Marche	Bognor Loft	S. Sewell, East Longton, Market Harboro', Leicester
NPS.42.NS.17395	27/8/42	30/8/42	Arras	Bognor Loft	W. Buckley, 7 Summerhill, Mossley, Manchester
NPS.42.NS.17780	20/8/42	3/9/45	Dieppe	A. Chester Beatty	Harley Bros, 23 Ivy Avenue, Bath
NPS.42.NS.17805	24/8/42	28/8/42	Bapaume	Chard Junction	
NPS.42.NS.17805	17/7/43	3/8/43	Elbeuf	Chard Junction	
NPS.42.NS.18033	12/4/43	16/4/43	France	Chard Junction	S. Wheeler, 78 Exchange Street, Round Oak, Brierley Hill
NS.42.18558	22/7/43	18/7/43	France	Lady Mary Manningham-Buller	W. White, New Gilston, Leven, Fife
NPS.42.NS.18742	20/8/42	30/8/42	Dieppe	Mottistone Manor Weston-super-Mare	R. Richardson, 31 Poplar Street, Ashington
NPS.42.18756	13/7/43	30/7/43	France		S. Parrett, 49 Rocking Road, Weston-super-Mare
NPS.42.NS.18800	26/9/42	7/10/42	Belgium	Bognor Loft	P.R. Timms, 69 Clarendon Road, Hove
NS.42.19675	16/4/43	18/4/43	Belgium	Folkestone	WE. Partington, 28 Panton Street, Horwich, Bolton
NPS.42.NS.19708	17/7/42	20/7/43	France	Chard Junction	T. Bailey, 144 Black Road, Macclesfield

Ring No.	Date Sent	Date Returned	Place	Owner/NPS Group	Bred By
NPS.42.NS.19713	10/6/43	13/6/43	France	Chard Junction	
NPS.42.20092	27/10/42	2/11/42	France	H. Whitley, Paignton	
NPS.42.20093	27/10/42	30/10/42	France	H. Whitley, Paignton	Muir Bros, Railway Cottage, Fergushill, nr Kilwinning
NPS.42.20093	11/4/43	13/4/43	France	H. Whitley, Paignton	
NPS.42.NS.20157	31/7/42	15/8/42	Belgium	A. Chester Beatty	
NPS.42.NS.21057	24/8/42	3/9/42	Belgium	A. Chester Beatty	Knight, Church Bungalow, Church Lane, Oulton Road, Lowestoft
NS.42.NS.20164	18/9/42	26/9/42	Hesdin	Lyme Regis	H. Hay, Cairnfield Avenue, Maybole, Ayrshire
NPS.42.20443	15/1/43	17/1/43	France	Lyme Regis	E. Hardy, Victoria Inn, Chickerall, Weymouth
NPS.42.20644	24/9/42	25/9/42	Brittany	Mottistone Manor	
NPS.42.20656	27/10/42	30/10/42	France	Mottistone Manor	
NPS.42.21168	19/2/43	24/2/43	Manche	Bognor Loft	C. Abbot, 115 Sturgess Avenue, London, NW4
NPS.42.21178	14/4/43	16/4/43	France	Bognor Loft	
NPS.42.NS.21328	24/8/42	22/9/42	Frevent	A. Chester Beatty	A. Tinker, Ivy Cottage, Jackson Bridge, Huddersfield
NPS.42.21964	18/1/43	21/1/43	France	Lyme Regis	E. J. Spare, Fiar Park Villa, Crankhall Lane, Wednesbury
NPS.42.22489	26/9/42	27/9/42	Belgium	Mottistone Manor	H. Donachy, 5 Wellington Road, Wanstead, London, E11
NPS.42.NS.23159	31/7/42	15/7/42	Belgium	A. Chester Beatty	Naylor Bros, Redbourne, Bentley, Doncaster
NPS.42.NS.23213	27/8/45	21/9/45	Amiens	A. Chester Beatty	W. Hutchinson, 10 Belmont Avenue, Calcut, Knaresborough

Ring No.	Date Sent	Date Returned	Place	Owner/NPS Group	Bred By
NPS.42.23407	14/4/43	17/4/43	Fermenville	Bognor Loft	G. Storey, 7 Victoria Street, Hoyle Hill Road, Stairfoot, Barnsley
NPS.42.NS.23525	24/8/42	27/8/42	Amiens	A. Chester Beatty	R. Sims, Hussar Hotel, Garbinge, Margate
NPS.42.NS.23528	24/8/42	28/8/42	Monchy-Breton (Pas de Calais)	A. Chester Beatty	
NPS.42.NS.23690	27/8/42	29/8/42	Amiens	A. Chester Beatty	J. Wolfenden, 13 Emily Street, Burnley
NPS.42.NS.23693	24/8/42	7/9/42	Belgium	A. Chester Beatty	
NPS.42.23953	14/3/43	4/4/43	France	Lady Mary Manningham-Buller	T. Andrews, 39 Wren Street, Burnley
NPS.42.NS.24043	23/8/42	24/8/42	Tréport	Mottistone Manor	H. Sartin, 17 Hillgrove Avenue, Yeovil
NPS.42.24070	27/10/42	28/10/42	France	H. Whitley; Paignton	G. Douglas, 11 South Street, Cupar, Fife
NPS.42.NS.24076	28/8/42	5/9/42	Brittany	H. Whitley; Paignton	G. Douglas, Fife
NPS.42.24398	16/11/42	25/11/42	Cormont	A. Chester Beatty	R. Keen, Pond Bungalow, Fifield, Maidenhead
NPS.42.24503	18/9/42	26/9/42	Holland	A. Chester Beatty	Fisher & Mason, 34 Furlong Street, Arnold
NPS.42.25287	10/6/43	21/6/43	Argentan		
NPS.42.25287	29/4/44	2/5/44	Le Bény Bocage	Chard Junction	G. Long, 20 Waylands Avenue, Conisboro, Doncaster
NPS.42.25290	11/4/43	14/4/43	France		
NPS.42.25290	11/7/43	1/8/43	Rennes		
NPS.42.25454	17/10/42	Jan. 1943		Weston-super-Mare	H. Nippen Uvington, Bristol
NPS.42.25780	19/2/43	1/3/43	Canisy	Bognor Loft	J. Fletcher, 48 Liverpool Road, Huyton, Liverpool
NPS.42.26235	15/1/43	20/1/43	Manche	Whetstone	N. Atkinson, 8 Percy Street, Wheeler Street, Hull

Ring No.	Date Sent	Date Returned	Place	Owner/NPS Group	Bred By
NPS.42.25242	15/1/43	18/1/43	Avranches	Whetstone	W. Barber, 39 Caroline Street, Irlam, Manchester
NPS.42.27142	15/7/43	27/7/43	Chimay	Mottistone Manor	P. Evans, 3 Clifton Road, Llandudno
NPS.42.28791	18/1/43	21/1/43	Arras	Bognor Loft	G. Hodgson, 101 Drip Road, Raploch, Stirling
NPS.42.28962	3/5/44	5/5/44	France	Isle of Wight	
NPS.42.NS.28969	20/8/42	24/8/42	Dieppe	Mottistone Manor	G. Hodgson, Raploch, Stirling
NPS.42.29363	12/7/43	15/7/43	Fougères	Plymouth	J. Barnes, 94 Regent Street, Gloucester
NPS.42.31242	16/4/43	21/4/43	Belgium	Folkestone	J. Gordon Hammond, Trowbridge
NPS.42.32833	19/2/43	26/2/43	Granville	Bognor Loft	H. Gobbold, 8 Avondale Road, Lowestoft
NPS.42.32921	20/12/42	19/4/43	Belgium	Bognor Loft	Chadcerton & Son, 122 Turf Lane, Hollinwood, Oldham
NPS.42.33785	20/5/43	5/7/43	Belgium	Folkestone	J. Mackie, Blackfaulds, Fauldhouse
NPS.42.34190	17/8/43	19/8/43	Havrincourt	Chatham	S.J. Scott, 48 Franklin Road, Gillingham
NPS.42.35362	23/8/42	12/9/42	Hesdin	Bognor Loft	G. Purbrick, 21 Sidney Road, Staines
NPS.42.35740	12/4/43	13/4/43	Pontivy	Sir Ernest Debenham, Dorchester	T. Robson, 83 Station Road, Easington, Durham
NPS.42.35741	12/6/43	16/8/43	France	Sir Ernest Debenham, Dorchester	T. Robson, Easington, Durham
NPS.42.NS.36151	24/8/42	28/8/45	Belgium	A. Chester Beatty	E.H. Moates, Prospect Road, Scholes Green, Norwich
NPS.42.NS.36159	31/7/42	5/9/42	Belgium	A. Chester Beatty	E.H. Moates, Norwich
NPS.42.36258	15/1/43	24/1/43	Belgium	Folkestone	J. McDougal, "Dalvavey", Cash Pens, Strathniglo, Scotland

Ring No.	Date Sent	Date Returned	Place	Owner/NPS Group	Bred By
NPS.42.36423	27/10/42	30/10/42	Le Torigni	Mottistone Manor	F. Jones, Alma Inn, Victoria Street, Gloucester
NPS.42.36423	15/7/43	30/7/43	Boue (Aisne)	Mottistone Manor	P Irvine, 142 Stoneyburn, West Lothian
NPS.42.36962	14/6/43	16/6/43	Valenciennes	Folkestone	
NPS.42.36967	24/10/42	26/10/42	France	Folkestone	
NPS.42.36967	6/8/44	15/8/44	La Selle sur la Bied et Courtemaux		
NPS.42.37336	17/4/43	23/4/43	Pottes	Folkestone	Fling, Whinburn, Watnall Road, Hucknall
NPS.42.NS.37394	31/7/42	15/8/42	Belgium	A. Chester Beatty	R. Tower & Son, 27 Horn Park, Lee, London
NPS.42.37800	6/6/44	8/6/44	Emanville	Maidstone	Gray Bros, 22 Whitehouse Road, Wallsley, Sheffield
NPS.42.38022	12/7/43	1/8/43	France	Sir E. Debenham, Dorchester	A. Broomhead, 1 Lansdown Street, Macclesfield
NPS.42.38162	15/2/43	18/2/43	Belgium	Clacton	H.S. Holden, 118a Northgate, Bury St. Edmunds
NPS.42.38181	12/6/43	14/6/43	Merdrignac	Mottistone Manor	E.A. Ball, 76 Sackup Lane, Darton, Barnsley
NPS.42.38181	15/7/43	28/7/43	Belgium	Mottistone Manor	
NPS.42.39256	17/12/42	20/12/42	France	Weston-super-Mare	F.L. Brown, 1 Upper Denmark Road, Ashford
NPS.42.39340	27/8/42	30/8/42	Pas de Calais	A. Hewitt Bridgewater	A. Winster, 46 Mills Road, Wolverhampton
NPS.42.40187	14/4/43	14/5/43	Gisors	Lady Mary Manningham-Buller	Brookham & Barker, 18 Gray Street, Cardiff
NPS.42.NS.40359	26/7/42	26/7/42	Brittany		
NPS.42.NS.40360	23/7/42	25/7/42	Avranches	Lady Mary Manningham-Buller	J.H. Dobbs, Keys House, Dinnington, Sheffield

Ring No.	Date Sent	Date Returned	Place	Owner/NPS Group	Bred By
NPS.42.40647	13/4/43	17/4/43	St Lô	Chard Junction	J. Beveridge, Bar Crescent Cottages, Clackmannan
NPS.42.40650	24/9/42	28/9/42	Jamelles	Chard Junction	J. Beveridge, Clackmannon
NPS.42.40923	16/7/43	21/7/43	Couvin	Weston-super-Mare	P.J. Parrett, 49 Locking Road, Weston-super-Mare
NPS.42.40955	7/8/44	14/8/44	France	Weston-super-Mare	P.J. Parrett, Weston-super-Mare
NPS.42.41053	15/5/43	19/5/43	Rouen	Weston-super-Mare	P.J. Parrett, Weston-super-Mare
NS.42.42143	16/4/43	21/4/43	Belgium	Folkestone	C. H. Peppiatt, 20 Haverstock Hill, London, N.W.3
NPS.42.42150	10/5/43	1/6/43	Quoeux	Folkestone	C.H. Peppiatt, London, NW3
NPS.42.43120	18/9/42	21/9/42	Flenu (Belgium)	Folkestone	A. Pattman, 87 Clova Road, Forest Gate, London
NPS.42.43142	24/9/42	27/9/42	N. France	Folkestone	Moore, 5 Keith Grove, London W12
NPS.42.43554	17/12/42	21/12/42	France	A. Chester Beatty	Newton, 36 Forest Lane, Leytonstone, London
NPS.42.43621	15/5/43	19/5/43	Mortain	Sir E. Debenham, Dorchester	H. Thomson, 4 Ritchie Street, West Kilbride
NPS.42.43642	14/7/43	20/8/43	France	Sir E. Debenham, Dorchester	R.R. Hunter, 43 High Street, Tilicoultry, Clackmannan
NPS.42.43647	17/7/43	19/7/43	France	Chard Junction	
NPS.42.44447	18/9/42	26/9/42	France	Weston-super-Mare	S. Travis, Shipham, Winscombe
NPS.42.44454	21/10/42	25/10/42		Weston-super-Mare	S. Travis, Shipham, Winscombe
NPS.42.44731	23/3/43	5/5/43	France	W. Hardcastle, Whetstone	A. Thomas, 60 Buckingham Avenue, Whetstone, London, N10

Ring No.	Date Sent	Date Returned	Place	Owner/NPS Group	Bred By
NPS.42.45104	12/7/43	3/8/43	France	Staines	G. Palmer, Coal Exchange, Emsworth
NPS.42.45611	7/6/44	10/6/44	Montreuil-sur-Brèche	Gravesend	W. McIntyre, 21 The Grove, Kilbarcham, Scotland
NPS.42.45823	13/6/43	6/7/43	France	Lady Mary Manningham-Buller	P. H. Freeman, 4 Balmoral Drive, Caversham, Reading
NPS.41.46148	15/1/43	25/2/43	Belgium	Folkestone	J. Townsley, 13 Archer Street, Harrington, Cumberland
NPS.42.46149	15/1/43	16/1/43	France	Folkestone	
NPS.42.46684	13/7/43	29/7/43	Montaigu	Weston-super-Mare	A. Robson, 16 Ribblesdale View, Chatburn, Clitheroe
NPS.42.46719	14/7/43	17/7/43	Nogent le Rotrou	Folkestone	W. Creber & Sons, 49 Dalton Lane, Dalton Brook, Rotherham
NPS.42.NS.47334	18/9/42	22/9/42	Zeeland	Mottistone Manor	A. Cornley, 65 Robinhood Street, Gloucester
NPS.42.48097	24/9/42	30/9/42	Brittany	Mottistone Manor	
NPS.42.48190	24/9/42	12/10/42	Brittany	Mottistone Manor	
NPS.42.48714	15/4/43	18/4/43	St Martin de Blangy	Sir E. Debenham, Dorchester	
NPS.42.NS.49620	16/4/43	21/4/43	France	Mottistone Manor	
NPS.42.49676	11/4/43	14/4/43	Giberville	Mottistone Manor	
NPS.42.49676	15/7/43	18/7/43	Busigny	Mottistone Manor	
NPS.42.49730	26/2/43	25/3/43	France	Mottistone Manor	
NPS.42.50238	13/7/43	9/8/43	France	Weston-super-Mare	H. Gale, 27 Prince Albert Square, Earlswood
NPS.42.50728	24/9/42	4/10/42	Caen	Mottistone Manor	W. Taylor, 9 Highland Terrace, The Broan, Ferryhill

Ring No.	Date Sent	Date Returned	Place	Owner/NPS Group	Bred By
NPS.42.50829	20/4/43	30/4/43	Brimeux	Ipswich	H.R. Keer, 27 Stoke Street, Ipswich
NPS.42.50888	24/10/42	31/10/42	Belgium	Lyme Regis	W. Brown, Sunnybank, Liverpool Road, Aughton
NPS.42.50891	18/1/43	27/1/43	Orne	Lyme Regis	V.Hancock, Hornington,
NPS.42.50983	20/3/43	25/3/43	Orne	Sir E. Debenham, Dorchester	Lawrence Grove, Kingshill, Dursley
NPS.42.50990	19/2/43	23/2/43	France	Sir E. Debenham	V.Hancock, Dursley
NS.42.51558	14/6/43	24/6/43	France	Folkestone	P.J. Huxford, 89 Summer Street, Stroud
NPS.42.51818	24/2/44	24/5/43	France	Fuller Isaacson	J.T. Edwards, 61 Warrenhurst Road, Fleetwood
NPS.42.52539	18/1/43	20/1/43	France	Lyme Regis	J.Smith, 69 Crofton Street, St Helens
NPS.42.52539	20/10/43	6/11/43	France	Sir E. Debenham	
NPS.42.52793	14/3/43	4/4/43	France	Bognor	J.Pottinger, 232 Bollo Bridge Road, Acton, London, W3
NPS.43.2139	16/8/43	6/9/43	Loperec	Mottistone Manor	W. Luik, The Cottage, Bellingbear Park, Wokingham
NPS.43.2292	11/8/43	22/8/43	Breux	A. Hewitt	E. Brock, Laurel Farm, Nailsea, Bristol
NPS.43.2292	30/4/44	4/5/44	La Ferte Mace	A. Hewitt	
NPS.43.3317	30/4/44	3/5/44	France	A. Hewitt	W.C. Artus, 170 Painswick Road, Gloucester
NPS.43.4545	13/10/43	17/10/43	France	Isle of Wight	W.H. Tainsh, 3 Haitlands Road, Fareham
NPS.43.4577	11/8/44	27/8/44	La Fermettée	Catford	R.T.A. Shepherd, 63 Biockhurst Road, Gosport
NPS.43.15031	8/5/44	11/5/44	France	Lyme Regis	G. Clements, Down Hatherley, Glos.
NPS.43.15031	5/6/44	6/7/44	Chouze	Lyme Regis	

Ring No.	Date Sent	Date Returned	Place	Owner/NPS Group	Bred By
NPS.43.15272	6/6/44	9/6/44	France	Chard Junction	G.A. Perkins, 62 Northfields Road
NPS.43.17016	8/9/43	28/9/43	France	Enfield	R.R. Leslie, 158a Main Street, Townhill, Dunfermline
NPS.43.17588	7/10/43	3/11/43	Valenciennes	Weston-super-Mare	J. Warrender, 64 Haughgate Street, Leven, Fife
NPS.43.20200	11/8/43	11/9/43	Belgium	Muswell Hill	W.J. Chidgey, 172 Milton Road, Swanscombe, Kent
NPS.43.20880	9/4/44	18/5/44	Coulommiers	Folkestone	H. Hoad, Church Farm Lofts, Lower Beeding, Horsham
NPS.43.20977	15/9/43	25/9/43	France	Tottenham	J. Buckland, 34 Durnsford Road, Wimbledon, London
NPS.43.21508	11/8/43	20/8/43	France	Tottenham	W. Kenward, 63 Ludlow Road, Guildford
NPS.43.21919	11/8/43	1/9/43	France	Tottenham	A. Ford, 117 Pendle Road, Streatham, London, SW16
NPS.43.22654	6/6/44	29/6/44	Touraine	Folkestone	A. Purnnell, 18 Walnut Tree Close, Guildford
NPS.43.22749	12/8/43	1/9/43	France	A. Hewitt	A. Willmott, 4 Ashford Place, Portishead
NPS.43.23346	12/7/43	18/8/43	France	A. Hewitt	A. Bobwell, 6 Mount Pleasant Row, Bath
NPS.43.23346	30/4/44	7/5/44	Flers	A. Hewitt	
NPS.43.24557	7/5/44	10/5/44	France	Isle of Wight	A. Wheatley, 38 Chapel Street, Stroud
NPS.43.24560	9/8/44	26/8/44	Loiret, France	Weymouth	
NPS.43.24714	7/10/43	17/10/43	Braine Le Chateau	Lady Mary Manningham-Buller	G. Bloodworth, 16 Union Street, Dursley
NPS.43.25291	5/5/44	9/5/44	Grace le Merlerault	Catford	F. Landgrab, 38 Knighthill, West Norwood, London, SE7

Ring No.	Date Sent	Date Returned	Place	Owner/NPS Group	Bred By
NPS.43.26924	8/9/43	17/9/43	Flers	Tottenham	H. Webster, Thornton Heath Lodge, Grangewood Park, South Norwood, SE25
NPS.43.27557	11/8/43	18/9/43	Vire	Sir E. Debenham, Dorchester	C. Brewer, 58 West Street, Exeter
NPS.43.27670	21/10/43	24/10/43	France	Sir E. Debenham	D. Kirwin, 31 Horse Road, Hilperton Marsh, Trowbridge
NPS.43.29004	8/8/44	12/8/44	Bacqueville	Sir E. Debenham	Air Ministry Pigeon Service
NPS.43.31030	7/5/44	10/5/44	France	Weymouth	A. Perry, 45 Rounds Pounds, Melksham
NPS.43.33525	8/8/44	20/8/44	Elbeuf	Weymouth	F. E. Jackson, 5 Windsor Road, Cosham
NPS.43.33657	10/1/44	18/1/44	Chievre, Belgium	Harrow	A. Haines, 29 Jubilee Road, Toots Cray, Sidcup
NPS.43.34292	29/6/44	13/7/44	France	Tottenham	A. Burrow, 19 King's Road, Aylesham, Canterbury
NPS.43.34294	13/10/43	16/10/43	France	Tottenham	R. Harris, Park Silverton, Exeter
NPS.43.34734	3/7/44	6/7/44	France	Sir E. Debenham	F. Skoulding, Police Station, Norwich Road, Wisbech
NPS.43.34781	30/3/44	1/4/44	Belgium	Folkestone	
NPS.43.35326	16/8/43	20/8/43	France	Mottistone Manor	R. Crouch, Newlands, Upper Mill Hill Road, Cowes, Isle of Wight
NPS.43.36580	13/10/43	15/10/43	France	Old Ford	D. Gillespie, 33 Burns Crescent, Audris
NPS.43.37089	15/9/43	19/9/45	Torigny	Tottenham	J. Harrower, Kennels Coltness Estate, Wishaw, Lanarks
NPS.43.37902	11/8/43	27/10/43	Caen	Enfield	Robertson & Watson, 31 Dunrobin Road, Airdrie

239

Ring No.	Date Sent	Date Returned	Place	Owner/NPS Group	Bred By
NPS.43.29421	16/10/43	20/10/43	Mayenne	Kingston	A. Wilton, c/o Taylor, 2 Miller Street, Clydebank
NPS.43.40808	20/10/43	29/10/43	Nogent le Rotrou Mitcham		Watt & Son, 67 Main Street, Longriggend, Lanarks
NPS.43.45138	10/7/44	18/7/44	Masle	Folkestone	Challen & Sons, 168 Elmshott Lane, Chippenham, Slough
NPS.43.45376	3/5/43	9/5/43	Brittany	Enfield	S. Rowbotham, 14 Gresham Road, Drayton Estate, Norwich
NPS.43.45429	10/4/44	12/4/44	Belgium	Folkestone	W. Goodson, 51 Appleyard Cres., Mile Cross, Norwich
NPS.43.45729	3/5/44	7/5/55	Orléans	Tottenham	Army Pigeon Service (Eastern Command)
NPS.43.45854	4/6/44	6/7/44	France	Margate	
NPS.43.45857	10/12/43	15/12/43	Amiens	Margate	
NPS.43.46142	13/10/43	15/10/43	France	Old Ford	J. Godbold, 8 Avondale Road, Lowestoft
NPS.43.46259	15/11/43	5/5/44	Vire	Folkestone	E. Smith, Sedge Fen, Lakenheath, Suffolk
NPS.43.46261	10/4/44	21/4/44	Neuville sous Arzillières		Folkestone
NPS.43.46467	13/10/43	17/10/43	Dozule	Folkestone	T. James, 16 Garlic Row, Cambridge
NPS.43.46725	7/10/43	9/10/43	Belgium	Tottenham	J. Mugglestone, 56 Tunbridge Avenue, Luton
NPS.43.48134	18/10/43	3/11/43	Hastière, Belgium	Chatham	S. Banford, 136 Shear Brow, Blackburn
NPS.43.48257	9/8/44	19/9/44	France	Sir E. Debenham Mottistone Manor	W. Boldsworth, 19 Albert Street, Bury
NPS.43.48881	15/9/43	19/10/43	France	Folkestone	R. Scholes, 1 Co-op Houses, Cliviger, Burnley
NPS.43.49102	3/5/44	18/5/44	France	Folkestone	T. Franklin, 18 Gresham Road, Drayton Estate, Norwich

Ring No.	Date Sent	Date Returned	Place	Owner/NPS Group	Bred By
NPS.43.50524	7/5/44	14/5/44	Couvron	Weymouth	L. Dangerfield, New Inn, King's Stanley, Stonehouse
NPS.43.51489	5/5/44	22/5/44	Fleury-en-Bière	Sir E. Debenham	J. Taylor, 10 Elm Cotts., Fairfield Parade, Cheltenham
NPS.43.56770	10/12/43	18/12/43	Vouchelles, Abbeville	Lady Mary F.W. Hale, Manningham-Buller	"Leabrooks", Shield Row, Stanley
NPS.43.56865	28/5/44	4/6/44	St. Leonard	Maidstone	Capt. J.S. Thompson, School House, Denham
NPS.43.59141	6/6/44	14/6/44	Montereau	Chard Junction	W. Knight, 3 Moorland Road, Taunton
NPS.43.59141	8/8/44	15/8/44	Carignan	Chard Junction	
NPS.43.60033	6/6/44	13/6/44	Coulommiers	Chard Junction	G. Jones, 34 Chadwick Road, Eastleigh
NPS.43.60709	13/10/43	20/10/43	France	Harrow	A. Cooper, 178 Rhodeswell Road, Limehouse, London, E 14
NPS.43.61054	4/6/44	8/6/44	Orne	Margate	R. E. Butler, 46 Telford Road, West Hendon, NW9
NPS.43.61308	7/5/44	14/5/44	Fougères	Weymouth	C. W. Butt, 87 Oxford Street, Burnham-on-Sea
NPS.43.61308	8/8/44	9/8/44	Seine Inférieure	Weymouth	
NPS.43.63543	7/11/43	27/8/44	Belgium	Northfleet	Mr & Mrs Dasfield, 20 Straton Avenue, Prittlewell, Southend-on-Sea
NPS.43.70696	10/3/44	22/6/44	France	Catford	S. Clark, Rayner, Freelands Road, Cobham, Surrey
NPS.43.73806	7/6/44	17/6/44	Marne	Thames Estuary	A. King, 32 Puckwillow Road, Ely
NPS.43.88612	30/3/44	1/4/44	Schelde	Folkestone	L.J. Verney, 68 Churchfields Road, Beckenham

Ring No.	Date Sent	Date Returned	Place	Owner/NPS Group	Bred By
NPS.43.91562	2/6/44	4/6/44	France	Isle of Wight	R. Crouch, "Newlands", Upper Mill Hill Road, Cowes, Isle of Wight
NPS.43.92852	4/8/44	8/9/44	France	Mitcham	Chivers Bros, 53 Chilcompton Road, Midsomer Norton, Bath
NPS.43.93294	3/7/44	12/7/44	France	Weymouth	L. Dove, High Street, Upton, Pontefract
NURP31.J.7436	27/8/42	30/8/42	Valenciennes	Folkestone	M.F. Teague, 11 Carbeny Road, Upper Norwood, SE19
NUHW.34.DNS.181	17/11/42	5/12/42	Belgium	Folkestone	T. Bartlett, Little Evenden, Alkham, Dover
NUHW.35.CEN.10	24/8/42	27/8/42	Belgium	Ipswich	W.G. Blake, 20 Schrieber Road, Ipswich
NUHW.35.CEN.10	20/12/42	22/12/42	Belgium	Ipswich	
NUHW.36.CEN.83	3/8/41	17/8/41	Flanders	Ipswich	J. Catchpole, 170 Cemetery Road, Ipswich
NUHW.36.CEN.83	5/5/44	16/5/44	Finistère	Ipswich	
NUHW.36.U.1580	31/8/44	11/9/44	France	Wolverhampton	J.R. Squire, 505 Stafford Road, Fordhouses, Wolverhampton
NUHW.37.BVM.70	13/10/43	18/10/43	France	Folkestone	J. Catchpole, Ipswich
NUHW.37.CEN.335	26/7/42	30/7/42	Denmark	Ipswich	C. Hayward, High Street, Saxmundham
NUHW.37.LDC.260	28/7/42	5/8/42	Belgium	Ipswich	Breme Bros., 49 Kelly Road, Ipswich
NUHW.37.WE.142	31/7/42	3/8/42	Amiens	Ipswich	W. Baldry, 15 St. Aubyn's Road, Ipswich
NUHW.38.CEN.106	13/8/43	25/8/43	Angoulême	Ipswich	R. W. Payne, 59 Schrieber Road, Ipswich
NUHW.38.CSR.145	24.4.42	28/4/42	Cambrai	Ipswich	F. Bartlett, "Valley View", Alkham, Dover
NUHW.38.FE.160	28/7/42	7/9/42	Amiens	Folkestone	E. Carter & Son, 14 Barr Street, Lower Gorral, Dudley
NUHW.38.FE.167	21/6/42	23/6/42	Belgium	Folkestone	
NUHW.38.LG.276	31/8/44	18/9/44	France	Wolverhampton	

Ring No.	Date Sent	Date Returned	Place	Owner/NPS Group	Bred By
NUHW.38.M.2	7/6/41	28/5/41	W. Flanders	Folkestone	G. Marwood, 10 West Street, Morley, Leeds
NUHW.38.W.361	28/7/42	3/8/42	Belgium	Trowbridge	J.G. Hammond, Trowbridge
NUHW.38.WE.857	28/7/42	2/8/42	Dinant	Ipswich	C.W. Marshall, 42 Anglesea Road, Ipswich
NUHW.38.WE.859	23/7/42	2/9/42	Holland	Ipswich	B. Mayled, Riverton House, Cross
NUHW.38.WV.112	6/5/44			Lyme Regis	
NUHW.39.CDM.54	14/6/43	16/6/43	France	Clacton	WB. Black, 19 Coppins Road, Clacton-on-Sea
NUHW.39.CEN.342	20/4/43	23/4/43	Aubigny	Ipswich	E.J. Gould, 115 Belvedere Road, Ipswich
NUHW.39.CEN.353	24/5/42	28/5/42	Capelle	Ipswich	J.F. Tillett, Belle Vue Road, Ipswich
NURP.39.CSR.262	1/6/44	5/6/44	Calvados	Ipswich	
NUHW.39.CSR.631	5/5/44	21/5/44	Loire	Ipswich	A.W. Keeble, Fen Farm, Burstall, Ipswich
NUHW.39.DCF.4	1/9/44	12/9/44	Holland	Woverhampton	E. Carter, 25 Wolverhampton Road, Bentley, Walsall
NUHW.39.DSS.69	7/11/41	10/11/41	Holland	Folkestone	A. Ruddick, 15 Winchelsea Street, Dover
NUHW.39.DSS.159	3/10/41	21/10/41	N. France	Folkestone	Clark & Crascall, 62 Clarendon Place, Dover
NUHW.39.EE.533	24/6/42	27/6/42	Belgium	Ipswich	W. Eley, 97 Camden Road, Ipswich
NUHW.39.EE.553	24/5/42	27/5/42	Bertincourt	Ipswich	
NUHW.39.EE.554	24/4/42	27/4/42	Valenciennes	Ipswich	
NUHW.39.EKP91	24/8/42	28/8/42	Belgium	Folkestone	D. Herd, Warren Road, Littlestone
NURP.39.FOL.143	8/11/41	11/11/41	Belgium	Folkestone	J. W. Gambrill, 47 Cheriton Road, Folkestone
NUHW.39.HHS.228	16/11/42	24/1/43	France	Bridgewater	E. J. Hooper, 10 Worston Road, Highbridge
NUHW.39.TTT.126	31/7/42	16/8/42	Belgium	Ipswich	J. W. Hobines, 91 Derby Road, Ipswich
NUHW.39.V.842	9/8/44	13/8/44	Coulonges	Horsham	H. Hoad, Church Farm Lofts, Lower Beeding, Horsham
NUHW.39.WE.57	24/5/42	3/6/42	Cambrai	Ipswich	G. Marriot, 1 Handford Place, Ipswich

Ring No.	Date Sent	Date Returned	Place	Owner/NPS Group	Bred By
NUHW.39.WE.871	31/7/42	13/2/43	Belgium	Ipswich	J. Gordon Hammond, Trowbridge
NUHW.39.WW.444	27/8/42	30/8/42	Vire	Trowbridge	J. Gordon Hammond, Trowbridge
NUHW.39.WW.455	24/6/42	3/7/42	Namur	Trowbridge	
NUHW.40.CCC.11	16/7/43	19/7/43	Esqucheries, Aisne	Colchester	A. A. Finch, 12 Speedwell Road, Old Heath, Colchester
NUHW.40.A.610	24/8/42	25/8/42	Belgium	Ipswich	H. Holden, 118a Northgate, Bury St Edmunds
NUHW.40.A.615	27/8/42	6/4/43	Amiens	Ipswich	
NUHW.40.CCC.277	18/8/43	25/9/43	Montaigu	Colchester	W. T. King, Swan Hotel, Maldon, Essex
NUHW.40.CEN.6	17/8/43	20/8/43	Auxi Le Château	Ipswich	H. E. Keys, 51 Belvedere Road, Ipswich
NUHW.40.CEN.47	20/4/43	6/5/43	St Pol	Ipswich	
NUHW.40.CSS.84	20/4/43	6/5/43	St Pol	Ipswich	R. W. Payne, 59 Schrieber Road, Ipswich
NUHW.40.CEN.54	20/4/43	8/5/43	Buissenal	Ipswich	
NUHW.40.CEN.98	24/4/42	14/5/42	Friesland	Ipswich	E.J. Gould, 115 Belvedere Road, Ipswich
NUHW.40.CEN.160	2/6/42	4/6/42	Holland	Ipswich	W.T. Fowkes, Albion Mills, Ipswich
NUHW.40.CEN.202	1/3/42	3/3/42	Belgium	Ipswich	W. Sheppard, 3 Turner's Place, St Helen's Street, Ipswich
NUHW.40.CEN.223	26/6/42	29/6/42	Belgium	Ipswich	J. Catchpole, 170 Cemetery Road, Ipswich
NURP.40.CSR.23	15/5/43	18/5/43	Ange	Ipswich	A.W. Keeble, Fen Farm, Burstall, Ipswich
NURP.40.CSR.23	28/8/42	31/8/42	Amiens	Ipswich	
NUHW.40.CSR.634	2/6/42	10/6/42	N.E. Holland	Ipswich	
NUHW.40.CSS.68	20/12/42	24/12/42	Belgium	Ipswich	
NUHW.40.DC.30	25/7/43	29/7/43	France	Ipswich	
NUHW.40.M.686	7/9/41	10/9/41	Holland	Ipswich	B. Upton, 139 Robech Road, Greenwich Estate, Ipswich

Ring No.	Date Sent	Date Returned	Place	Owner/NPS Group	Bred By
NUHW.40.TTT.1	2/6/42	4/6/42	N.E. Holland	Ipswich	R.J. Saul, 11 Hamilton Road, Ipswich
NUHW.40.TTT.139	20/4/43	25/4/43	Ronse	Ipswich	W.C. Eley, 97 Camden Road, Ipswich
NUHW.40.TTT.144	24/8/42	25/8/42	Belgium	Ipswich	
NUHW.40.WD.136	25/7/43	1/8/43	France	Walthamstow	K. Eaton, 31 Lower Park Road, Loughton, Essex
NUHW.40.WE.229	24/5/42	22/6/42	Cambrai	Ipswich	W. Westcott, 10 Ruskin Road, Ipswich
NUHW.40.WE.312	2/6/42	5/6/42	Medemblik	Ipswich	C.H. Folkard, Oll Yetts, Hadleigh Road, Ipswich
NUHW.40.WE.414	9/8/41	23/9/41	Belgium	Ipswich	
NUHW.40.WE.634	1/4/42	19/4/42	Cherbourg	Ipswich	
NUHW.40.WE.795	1/4/42	4/4/42	Cherbourg	Ipswich	
NUHW.40.WHS.318	21/6/44	22/6/44	N. France	Isle of Wight	
NUHW.40.WHS.333	30/4/42	29/5/42	Versailles	Isle of Wight	
NUHW.40.WHS.334	30/4/42	6/6/42	Anquers	Isle of Wight	
NUHW.40.336	23/6/42	24/6/42	France	Isle of Wight	H. Tong, "Llwyn", Llanfair, Co. Montgomery
NUHW.40.WHS.341	23/5/42	25/5/42	France	Isle of Wight	
NUHW.40.WHS.388	30/4/42	4/5/42	S. France	Isle of Wight	
NUHW.40.WW.90	23/8/43	11/9/43	France	Isle of Wight	G. Barry, The Avenues, Totland, I.o.W.
NUHW.40.FE.199	19/8/44	28/8/44	Loiret, France	Chatham	J. Scott, 48 Franlin Road, Gillingham
NUHW.41.ALD.173	31/8/44	11/9/44	France	Wolverhampton	H.G. Miller, Station Road, Aldridge, Walsall
NUHW.41.ANR.81	16/5/43	18/5/43	France	Shepherd's Bush	A.A. Finch, 12 Speedwell Road, Old Heath, Colchester
NUHW.41.BHS.301	31/8/44	15/9/44	Ryen Tilbury	Wolverhampton	W. Hurley, Highbridge Road, Burnham-on-Sea

Ring No.	Date Sent	Date Returned	Place	Owner/NPS Group	Bred By
NUHW.41.BPC.85	27/8/42	30/8/42	Vire	Bridgewater	H. Templeman, 92 Rhode Lane, Bridgewater
NUHW.41.CEN.28	22/6/42	24/6/42	Holland	Ipswich	E.J. Gould, 115 Belvedere Road, Ipswich
NUHW.41.CEN.243	20/3/43	25/3/43	Orne	Ipswich	H.E. Keys, 51 Belvedere Road, Ipswich
NUHW.41.CEN.252	20/4/43	22/4/43	Rollancourt	Ipswich	
NUHW.41.CEN.264	24/8/42	1/9/42	Belgium	Ipswich	W. Fowkes, Albion Mills, Woodbridge Road, Ipswich
NUHW.41.CEN.270	18/5/43	22/5/43	Authie	Ipswich	
NUHW.41.CEN.271	30/6/42	3/7/42	Holland	Ipswich	
NUHW.41.CEN.287	20/4/43	24/4/43	France	Ipswich	H.E. Keys, 51 Belvedere Road, Ipswich
NUHW.41.CEN.292	24/4/42	28/4/42	Capelle	Ipswich	E. A. Robinson, 39 Reading Road, Ipswich
NUHW.41.CCC.51	18/10/43	18/12/43	Selvignes	Colchester	A.A. Finch, 12 Speedwell Road, Old Heath, Colchester
NUHW.41.CH.35	?	15/8/44	?	Lyme Regis	W. Huiley, Highbridge Road, Burnham-on-Sea
NUHW.41.CPC.37	23/7/42	26/7/42	St. Lô	Isle of Wight	Lt-Col. C.W. Brannon, MC, OC, 530 Coast Regt. R.A., Warden Fort, Totland, I.o.W.
NUHW.41.36	12/6/43	16/6/43	France	Colchester	
NUHW.41.F.30	28/8/42	30/8/42	Arras	Folkestone	R.L. J. Taylor, 8 Mailer Road, Folkestone
NUHW.41.G.511	20/5/43	23/5/43	Feignies	Tottenham	A.A. Fitzpatrick, 240 Phillips Lane, Tottenham, London, N.15
NUHW.41.N.451	24/5/42	26/5/42	Bapaume-Berticourt Somme	Ipswich	W. Westcott, 10 Ruskin Road, Ipswich
NUHW.41.N.541	22/6/43	5/7/43	Ath, Belgium	Woking	Gunner Bros., Rose Bank Cottages, Westfield, Kingfield, Woking

Ring No.	Date Sent	Date Returned	Place	Owner/NPS Group	Bred By
NURP.41.P.4504	2/6/44	5/6/44	France	Woking	D. Wells, "Lavande", Loop Road, Kingfield, Woking
NUHW.41.PPC.8	30/7/44	24/8/44	Sable (Sarthe)	Isle of Wight	T. Moore, 229 Grenville Road, Plymouth
NUHW.41.RAC.28	24/6/42	26/6/42	France	Bridgewater	S. Cornish, 2 Athlone Road, Bridgewater
NUHW.41.SP194	2/5/44	5/5/44	Sarthe, France	Ponders End	E. Seal, 131 Raynham Road, Edmonton, N.18
NUHW.41.TTT.147	16/8/43	18/8/43	Hesdin	Ipswich	J. Catchpole, 170 Cemetery Road, Ipswich
NUHW.41.TTT.219	18/1/43	21/1/43	Wavre	Ipswich	W.C. Eley, 101 Camden Road, Ipswich
NUHW.41.TTT.251	31/7/42	3/8/42	Amiens	Ipswich	W. Westcott, 10 Ruskin Road, Ipswich
NUHW.41.TTT.343	25/7/43	11/8/43	St Pierre de Cormielles	Ipswich	C. Bassingwaighte, 25 Penhurst Road, Ipswich
NUHW.41.WE.122	15/5/43	7/6/43	France	Ipswich	A.W. Keeble, Fenn Farm, Burnstall, Ipswich
NUHW.41.WHZ.30	27/11/42	29/11/42	France	Weston-super-Mare	R.E. Jones, Homestill, Cheddar
NUHW.41.WHZ.34	22/10/42	25/10/42		Weston-super-Mare	R.E. Jones, Cheddar
NUHW.42.A.491	22/8/43	3/9/43	Vendôme	Shepherd's Bush	W. Lloyd, 72 Carlisle Avenue, East Acton, W3
NUHW.42.A.1264	31/8/44	12/9/44	Nièvre	Wolverhampton	W. Slater, 71 Broadway W., Walsall
NUHW.42.A.3651	5/5/44	12/5/44	Sars-Poteries	Ponders End	H. Beavis, 78 Welbourne Road, Tottenham, N17
NUHW.42.B.529	4/8/44	23/8/44	Boury-en-Vexin Oise	Bournemouth	H. Woodford, 55 Heaton Road, Bournemouth
NUHW.42.B.3310	31/8/44	11/9/44	France	Wolverhampton	Bradbury & Wiley, 103 Church Street, Bloxwich
NUHW.42.B.5266	4/8/44	6/8/44	France	Bournemouth	W. Hughes, 15 Weir Cotts., Hanwood, Salop
NURP.42.B.9596	31/8/44	16/9/44	France	Wolverhampton	F. Broadbent, New Road, Netherton, Dudley
NUHW.42.C.2601	6/8/44	14/8/44	France	Thames Estuary	E.J. Hardwicke, Sunnyheath, Perry Street, Billericay
NUHW.42.C.3138	9/8/44	14/8/44	St Pancras,	Ipswich	A.W. Keeble, Fenn Farm, Burstall, Ipswich

Ring No.	Date Sent	Date Returned	Place	Owner/NPS Group	Bred By
NURP.42.C.5237	1/9/44	17/9/44	Holland	Wolverhampton	S. Armstrong, 182 Marche End, Wednesfield
NUHW.43.D.783	11/7/44	25/7/44	Siqloy	Ipswich	H.E. Keys, 51 Belvedere Road, Ipswich
NURP.42.D.1350	20/4/43	23/4/43	France	Ipswich	S. Garrard, 21 Fitzmaurice Road, Ipswich
NURP.42.D.1491	20/4/43	23/4/43	Pas de Calais	Ipswich	B. Upson, 139 Roebuck Road, Ipswich
NUHW.42.D.1874	31/8/44	12/9/44	Limbourg (Holland)	Wolverhampton	Beckley Bros., 70 Bromley Pensnett, Brierley Hill
NUHW.42.D.3134	24/10/42	1/11/42	Belgium	Lyme Regis	G. Stocker, 12 Sherbourne Lane, Lyme Regis
NUHW.42.D.3209	16/7/43	25/7/43	St Philbert	Chard Junction	H.R. Fowler, Valley View, Westford, Chard Junction
NUHW.42.D.3230	6/6/44	19/6/44	Montigny	Chard Junction	H. Whitley, Primley, Paignton
NUHW.42.D.9608	14/4/43	21/4/43	Normandy	Paignton	W. Grantham, 290 Wherstead Road, Ipswich
NUHW.43.E.1310	9/5/44	11/5/44	Belgium	Ipswich	H. Whitley, 3 Greenbank Terrace, Totnes Road, Paignton
NUHW.42.E.1515	20/12/42	9/3/43	France	Paignton	
NUHW.42.E.3013	4/8/44	21/12/44	?	Lyme Regis	C. Franklin, Fearnville Estate, Clevedon
NUHW.42.F.1183	20/5/43	24/5/43	Belgium	Folkestone	
NUHW.42.F.1187	20/5/43	24/5/43	Belgium	Folkestone	R.L.J. Taylor, 8 Marler Road, Folkestone
NUHW.42.F.1187	15/9/43	16/10/43	Orléans	Folkestone	
NUHW.42.F.2193	6/5/44	8/5/44	Lokeren	Woking	J. Chantry, 4 New Forest Cotts., Kingfield, Woking
NURP.42.G.6916	31/8/44	13/9/44	France	Wolverhampton	A. Heeley, Coppice Road, Walsall-Wood
NUHW.42.H.2132	24/10/42	31/10/42	Montreuil	Paignton	H. Whitley, 3 Greenbank Terrace, Totnes Road, Paignton
NUHW.42.H.2141	27/10/42	29/10/42	France	Paignton	H. Whitley, Paignton

Ring No.	Date Sent	Date Returned	Place	Owner/NPS Group	Bred By
NUHW.42.2164	26/2/43	5/3/43	France	Paignton	H. Whitley, Paignton
NURP.42.H.6101	31/8/44	12/9/44	France	Wolverhampton	E. Salt, Selmans Hill, Little Bloxwich
NURP.42.H.6162	31/8/44	1/9/44	Aalst (Holland)	Wolverhampton	S. Foxall, 38 Barnes Lane, Rushall
NUHW.42.L.886	14/3/43	25/3/43	France	Tackley	S. Gibbs, Dakola, Beaminster
NUHW.42.L.917	30/3/43	25/3/43	Orne	Lyme Regis	J.C. Curtis & Son, 10 Monmouth Street, Lyme Regis
NUHW.42.L.934	8/5/44	25/8/44	France	Lyme Regis	H. Sexton, 19 Sherbourne Lane, Lyme Regis
NUHW.42.L.948	11/4/43	15/4/43	Boissey	Lyme Regis	A.W. Hewitt, Field House, Hursley, Winchester
NUHW.42.L.1456	17/11/42	26/11/42	Calvados	Hursley	
NUHW.42.L.1466	4/5/43	15/5/43	Mayenne, France	Hursley	T. Bartlett, Valley View, Alkham
NURP.42.M.8550	10/6/43	12/6/43	Holland	Folkestone	T. Burns, 27 Passfield Road, Lea Hall, Birmingham, 26
NUHW.43.N.48	6/8/44	23/8/44	Montargis	Folkestone	
NUHW.42.N.256	16/4/43	19/4/43	Belgium	Folkestone	J. Banks, Teddars Lees, Folkestone
NUHW.42.P411	12/7/43	15/7/43	Cormeilles	Plymouth	W. Partridge, 5 Portland Place, Plymouth
NUHW.42.P.1152	20/4/43	23/4/43	Hesdin	Ipswich	B. Upson, 132 Roebuck Road, Ipswich
NUHW.42.P.1306	20/4/43	21/4/43	St Pol	Ipswich	S. Garrard, 21 Fitzmaurice Road, Ipswich
NUHW.42.R.201	31/8/44	7/9/44	France	Thames Estuary	L. Duke, Shelford
NUHW.42.S.4101	16/10/43	19/10/43	France	Walthamstow	K. Eaton, 31 Laver Park Road, Loughton
NUHW.42.V.735	27/10/42	26/11/42	Brittany	Paignton	H. Whitley, Primley, Paignton
NUHW.42.W.103	1/6/44	7/6/44	France	Woking	Mr & Mrs Watts, 145 Walton Road, Woking
NUHW.42.W.3826	22/11/42	25/11/42	France (Calvados)	Paignton	H. Whitley, Primley, Paignton

Ring No.	Date Sent	Date Returned	Place	Owner/NPS Group	Bred By
NUHW.42.W.3987	31/8/44	18/9/44	Ruages Nièvre	Wolverhampton	W. Allport, The Forge Hotel, Plack Road, Walsall
NURP.43.A.A.883	?	7/8/44	Loir et Cher	Thames Estuary	G. Messett, 21 Arkwright Road, Tilbury Dock
NUHW.43.C.1090	30/7/44	10/8/44	France	Colchester	A.A. Finch, 12 Speedwell Road, Old Heath, Colchester
NUHW.43.C.1113	5/3/44	10/5/44	Aisne	Colchester	A. Goodings, 4 Foresight Road, Old Heath, Colchester
NUHW.43.C.1116	5/11/43	10/11/43	France	Colchester	A. Goodings, Old Heath, Colchester
NUHW.43.C.1213	30/7/44	10/8/44	France	Colchester	F. Hamm, 20 Vint Crescent, Colchester
NUHW.43.C.1277	5/7/44	23/7/44	Seine Inférieure	Colchester	W.T. Calver, 20 Gilberd Road, Colchester
NUHW.43.C.1323	7/1/44	9/5/44	France	Colchester	G. Nunn, 267 Harwich Road, Colchester
NUHW.43.D.761	11/7/44	18/7/44	Somme	Ipswich	H.E. Keys, 51 Belvedere Road, Ipswich
NUHW.43.D.3019	13/10/43	15/10/43	France	Isle of Wight	C. Cook, Almgrove, Mill Hill Cowes, I.o.W.
NUHW.43.E.1460	8/8/44	9/8/44	Belgium	Ipswich	R.W. Payne, 59 Schrieber Road, Ipswich
NUHW.43.G.1952	30/5/44	8/6/44	Sarthe	Woking	J. Henderson, 66 Beckenham Road, Guildford
NUHW.43.D.8763	5/5/44	9/5/44	France	Catford	S.A. Bayley, 2a Merchiston Road, Catford, London, SE6
NUHW.43.K.1033	6/8/44	8/8/44	Montdidier, Somme	W. Malling	W.E. Hickmott, Woodlands, London Road, West Malling
NUHW.43.K.1757	7/7/44	2/8/44	France, Pas de Calais	Folkestone	A. Howland, 3 Thanet Gardens, Folkestone
NUHW.43.L.2703	9/8/44	24/8/44	France	Horsham	H. Hoad, Church Farm, Lower Beeding, Horsham
NUHW.43.M.2566	8/8/44	23/8/44	Belgium	Folkestone	J.W. Gambrill, 47 Cheriton Road, Folkestone

Ring No.	Date Sent	Date Returned	Place	Owner/NPS Group	Bred By
NUHW.43.M.2579	11/7/44	18/7/44	Mayenne	Folkestone	J. Banks, Teddard Lees, nr Folkestone
NUHW.43.N.9	11/7/44	16/7/44	Mayenne	Folkestone	
NUHW.43.N.2360	8/8/44	8/9/44	Moislains	Plymouth	R. Mears, The Old Vicarage, Modbury, S. Devon
NURP.43.N.3001	11/7/44	9/9/44	Eryon	Harrow	Chalkley & Son, The Forge, The Hyde, Hendon, London, NW9
NUHW.43.P1050	8/8/44	20/8/44	N. of Seine	Plymouth	R.C. Stephens, 40 Station Road, Keyham, Devonport
NUHW.43.P1233	8/8/44	16/8/44	St Pierre	Plymouth	S. Williams, 29 Northdown Gardens, Devonport
NUHW.43.S.1322	29/6/44	7/7/44	Marsac-sur-Don	Shepherds Bush	S. Griffin, 3 St James's Street, London, W6
NURP.43.S.8337	2/6/44	4/6/44	Sees (Orne)	Woking	D. Wells, Lavande, Loop Road, Kingfield, Woking
NUHW.43.T.3951	13/10/43	15/10/43	France	Isle of Wight	S.R. Crisp, Victoria House, Norton Green, Freshwater, I.o.W.
NUHW.43.V.1086	4/8/44	9/9/44	Le Couray	Enfield	P. Cornell, 96 Galliard Road, Lower Edmonton, London, N9
NUHW.43.V.1146	?	1/5/43	Calvados	Thames Estuary	J.B. Atkinson, Church End, Paglesham, Rochford
NUHW.43.W.3974	3/5/44	9/5/44	Sarthe	Isle of Wight	Dayer, Ocean View Cottages, Freshwater Bay, Isle of Man
NURP.31.A.4496	29/6/42	3/7/42	Melon	Folkestone	F. Webster, 3 Alexandria Drive, St. Annes-on-Sea
NURP.31.BM.4919	7/5/41	21/5/41	Ypres	Folkestone	J. Banks, Teddars Lees, nr Folkestone

Ring No.	Date Sent	Date Returned	Place	Owner/NPS Group	Bred By
NURP43.B.61	1/6/44	6/6/44	France	Woking	Halse & Gerrish, 32 Richmond Place, Bath
NURP33.FOL.4	1/10/41	21/10/41	Brussels and Ghent	Folkestone	
NURP33.W.225	5/6/44	8/7/44	France	Woking	R. Willett, 18 Lime Grove, Westfield, Woking, Surrey
NURP34.WE.86	26/6/42	7/8/42	Belgium	Ipswich	Rampling & Son, King's Head, Sproughton, Ipswich
NURP35.BHB.1361	30/3/44	21/4/44	Antwerp	Dagenham	G. Pearman, 51 Meadow Road, Dagenham
NURP35.FOL.4	7/5/41	19/9/41	W. Flanders	Folkestone	
NURP35.ONR.120	11/8/44	25/8/44	France	Oxford	H. Weller, The Garage, New Marston, Oxford
NURP35.SAT.240	18/8/43	23/8/43	France	East London	
NURP35.SET.241	18/8/43	30/8/43	St Georges, De Montaigu	East London	
NURP35.TTT.366	24/4/42	25/4/42	Wieringerwaard	Ipswich	H. Burton, 22 Clapgate Lane, Ipswich
NURP35.WSM.139	4/7/41	10/7/41	W. of Calvados	Weston-super-Mare	J. Dunstone, 11 Milton Rise, Weston-super-Mare
NURP36.A.2353	24/7/42	28/7/42	France	Weston-super-Mare	W. Bailey, 31 Alma Street, Weston-super-Mare
NURP36.A.2353	20/11/42	24/11/42	Vire	Weston-super-Mare	
NURP36.BAN.386	4/6/44	8/6/44	Boane (Loir et Cher)	Oxford	W.J. Merry, 20 Burdell Avenue, Headington, Oxford
NURP36.CAH.3	31/7/42	5/8/42	Somme	Shepherds Bush	G.H. Ransley, 38 Cardross Street, Hammersmith, London, W6
NURP36.CHC.307	16/7/43	1/8/43	Belgium	Plymouth	G. Hobbs, 33 Fore Street, Saltash, Cornwall

Ring No.	Date Sent	Date Returned	Place	Owner/NPS Group	Bred By
NURP36.ETC.650	18/5/43	14/7/43	?	Enfield	W. Taylor, 65 Third Avenue, Bush Hill Park, Enfield
NURP36.FOL.255	7/5/41	7/5/41	Coutrai	Folkestone	J. Banks, Teddars Lees, nr Folkestone
NURP36.HWD.274	13/7/43	15/7/43	France	Harrow	P. Hawes, 27 Whitby Road, South Harrow
NURP36.LRC.162	13/4/42	25/4/42	N. France	Lyme Regis	S.W. Gibbs, Netherbury, Beaminster
NURP36.POR.137	29/4/44	10/5/44	Bourbon Lanoy	Romford	C. Hollington & Son, 3 Manor Road, Romford
NURP36.T.1558	7/9/41	17/9/41	Holland	Folkestone	R.J. Cartwright, 18 Clarendon Street, Dover
NURP36.TBD.370	16/7/43	9/8/43	France	East London	H. Thacker, 36 Crediton Road, Tidal Basin, London, E16
NURP36.WCE.356	24/6/42	26/6/42	De Laigle	Honiton	H. Record, New Street, Honiton, Devon
NURP36.WCE.488	24/5/42	27/5/42	Argentan	Honiton	
NURP36.WSM.306	5/7/41	22/7/41	Normandy	Weston-super-Mare	J. Dunstone, 11 Milton Rise, Weston-super-Mare
NURP36.WSM.306	5/8/41	16/8/41	Calvados	Weston-Super-Mare	
NURP36.WWP97	23/6/42	29/6/42	Bayeux	Trowbridge	J. Gordon Hammond, Wyke House, Trowbridge
NURP36.WWP.127	29/7/42	31/8/42	France	Trowbridge	
NURP37.A.91	15/7/43	17/8/43	Nogent le Rotrou	Plymouth	W. Hardcastle, Grove House, High Road, London, N20
NURP37.BDH.209	?	15/4/42	?	?	
NURP37.BDH.267	29/5/42	3/6/42	Belgium	?	G. Fry, 84 Polden Street, Bridgewater
NURP37.BNX.508	25/6/42	17/8/42	France	Bridgewater	Crossman Bros., 59 Polden Street, Bridgewater
NURP37.BNX.535	7/9/41	20/9/41	France	Bridgewater	

Ring No.	Date Sent	Date Returned	Place	Owner/NPS Group	Bred By
NURP37.C.6921	2/6/41	4/6/41	?	Chard Junction	H. Fowler, Valley View, Westford, Chard
NURP37.CE.134	7/6/44	14/6/44	Cuigneres	Walthamstow	G. White, 53 Garage Road, Walthamstow, London
NURP37.EE.230	16/4/43	21/5/43	France	Enfield	Parker & Saunders, 23 Eastfield Road, Enfield
NURP37.EE.343	28/4/42	18/5/42	Belgium	Enfield	Capt. W.H. Stevens, The Cottage, Little Park, Enfield
NURP37.FOL.41	7/5/41	9/5/41	W. Flanders	Folkestone	J. Banks, Teddars Lees, nr Folkestone
NURP37.GD.235	?	?	?	Gravesend	Finney & Son, 83 Portland Avenue, Gravesend
NURP37.LRV.61	2/6/41	4/6/41	?	Chard Junction	H.R. Fowler, Valley View, Westford, Chard
NURP37.PWE.516	16/7/43	12/8/43	Belgium	East London	G. Bandy, 17 Melford Road, London, E13
NURP37.SBC.801	1/5/42	30/5/42	Nr Paris	Shepherds Bush	A. Gillman, 152 Percy Road, London, W12
NURP37.SDS.179	15/7/43	29/7/43	Belgium	Staines	J.W. Paulger, Blue Anchor, Staines
NURP37.SOS.37	22/2/44	28/2/44	Combined Ops.	Thames Estuary	G. Davis, 20 Silverdale Road, Westcliff-on-Sea
NURP37.W.1133	5/5/44	?	?	Woking	F. Lewry, 117 Maybury Road, Woking
NURP37.WE.287	16/5/43	19/5/43	Merleraut	Colchester	W.J. Cooksey, 28 Victor Road, Colchester
NURP37.WPW.175	23/6/42	26/6/42	Alencon	Trowbridge	J. Gordon Hammond, Wyke House, Trowbridge
NURP37.WPW.249	29/6/42	2/7/42	Bayeux	Trowbridge	E. Tancock, 3 Ewart Road, Weston-super-Mare
NURP37.WS.8	24/5/42	27/5/42	Havre	Weston-super-Mare	
NURP38.A.1004	16/7/43	12/8/43	France	Chard Junction	R. Fowler, Valley View, Westford, Chard
NURP38.AYM.88	27/4/42	21/5/42	Rouen	Folkestone	W. Cullimore, 22 King's Road, Aylesham, Kent
NURP38.AYM.99	27/4/42	25/5/42	Rouen	Folkestone	J. Williams, 54 King's Road, Aylesham

Ring No.	Date Sent	Date Returned	Place	Owner/NPS Group	Bred By
NURP.38.BC.708	27/8/42	31/8/42	Amiens	Fordingbridge	H. Tillyer, Edensor, Whitsbury Road, Fordingbridge
NURP.37.BPC.6	7/9/41	9/9/41	France	Bridgwater	S.J. Bryant, 20 Victoria Road, Bridgewater
NURP.38.C.9606	2/6/41	26/6/41	Caen	Chard Junction	H.R. Fowler, Valley View, Westford, Chard
NURP.38.CAH.734	27/8/42	4/9/42	Valenciennes	Shepherd's Bush	G.H. Ransley, 38 Cardross Road, London, SW6
NURP.38.CAH.744	24/6/42	27/6/42	Belgium	Shepherd's Bush	
NURP.38.CEN.359	28/8/42	3/9/42	St Quentin	Ipswich	H.E. Keys, 51 Belvedere Road, Ipswich
NURP.38.CPC.1260	9/4/44	16/4/44	Mayenne	Isle of Wight	G. Wright, Glengarry, Newport Road, Cowes, Isle of Wight
NUHW.38.CSR.145	22/6/42	24/6/42	Holland	Ipswich	R. W. Payne, 59 Schrieber Road, Ipswich
NURP.38.D.3383	7/9/41	28/9/41	France	Folkestone	W. Reason, 39 Union Road, Dover
NURP.38.DNS.1440	7/5/44	18/5/44	Holland	Dagenham	W. Wills, 69 Rogers Road, Dagenham
NURP.38.DNS.1440	5/7/44	20/7/44	Gournay	Dagenham	
NURP.38.EE.1069	17/4/43	21/4/43	France	Enfield	B. Davis, 55 Halifax Road, Enfield
NURP.38.F.2023	3/10/41	14/10/41	Belgium	Muswell Hill	S. Fuller Isaacson, Minden, Woodside Avenue, Muswell Hill, London, N.10
NURP.38.F.2080	2/8/41	5/8/41	Belgium	Muswell Hill	
NURP.38.F.4053	28/7/42	10/8/42	Belgium	St Albans	T. Wiggins, St. Julian's Road, St Albans
NURP.38.F.4056	28/7/42	2/9/42	Belgium	St. Albans	
NURP.38.F.7659	17/8/43	9/9/43	Cambrai	Woking	Seaman Bros., Westfield, Woking
NURP.38.F.451	16/8/43	20/8/43	Loperec	Folkestone	
NURP.38.FOL.989	18/8/44	7/8/44	Dordrecht	Folkestone	J. Banks, Teddars Lees, nr. Folkestone
NURP.38.FSR.130	11/7/44	11/8/44	France	Mill Hill	Alexander, 63 Marsh Lane, Mill Hill, London
NURP.38.GD.264	15/9/43	19/9/43	Belgium	Gravesend	Shields & Martin, 7 Castle Street, Swanscombe

Ring No.	Date Sent	Date Returned	Place	Owner/NPS Group	Bred By
NURP.38.GD.302	30/3/44	1/4/44	France	Gravesend	A. Springett, 280 Rochester Road, Gravesend
NURP.38.GFS.197	15/7/43	17/7/43	Belgium	Ipswich	H. Beaumont, 33 Palmerston Road, S. Stifford
NURP.38.GHG.91	6/1/44	14/1/44	Calvados	Thames Estuary	G. Bath, 33 Hurstfield Crescent, Hayes
NUHW.38.GNS.263	16/6/43	19/6/43	France	Harrow	Jackson, 78 Staines Road, Hounslow
NURP.38.H.412	17/8/43	30/8/44	Charleroi	Woking	E. Hedges, Church Lane, Old Headington, Oxford
NURP.38.HHC.391	30/7/44	15/8/44	Totnes (Seine Inf)	Oxford	
NURP.38.LRC.216	19/5/43	24/5/43	Soligny	Lyme Regis	R. Winscombe, 48 Church Street, Lyme Regis, Dorset
NURP.38.LRC.335	29/4/44	2/5/44	Connerre	Lyme Regis	H. Sexton, 19 Sherbourne Lane, Lyme Regis
NURP.38.MMA.462	19/5/43	31/5/43	Vaires	Tottenham	Noonan Bros, 25 White Hall Street, London, N17
NURP.38.NW.7878	5/6/44	11/6/44	Bréhal	West Malling	
NURP.38.RY.215	28/5/44	2/6/44	France	Isle of Wight	Mochard, 11a West Street, Ryde, I.o.W.
NURP.38.SFA.9	27/8/42	31/8/42	Brittany	Fordingbridge	H. Tillyer, Edensor, Whitsbury Road, Fordingbridge
NUHW.38.SFC.383	27/8/42	29/8/42	Brittany	Fordingbridge	Arden & Houghton, 76 Lowndes Lane, Stockbridge
NURP.38.WA.133	22/7/44	?	?	Walthamstow	A. E. Sheppard, Sundridge, Horn Lane, Woodford Green, Essex
NURP.38.WAC.524	16/10/43	20/10/43	Mayenne	Walthamstow	L. Loxdale, 49 Grange Road, Walthamstow, London
NURP.38.WDS.72	10/8/44	16/3/45	France	Bexleyheath	W. H. Green, 49 The Quadrant, Bexleyheath

Ring No.	Date Sent	Date Returned	Place	Owner/NPS Group	Bred By
NURP.38.WDS.127	6/8/44	16/8/44	Hangest en Sautenne, Somme	West Malling	A. R. Hancock, Mountain Villa, Burrage Road, London, S.E.18
NURP.38.WPN.310	22/8/43	1/9/43	France	Isle of Wight	Gilbert, Padarn, The Avenue, Freshwater, I.o.W.
NURP.38.WS.55	4/7/41	6/7/41	Caen (Isigny)	Weston-super-Mare	J. Hazel, Beach Farm, Sand Bay, Kewstoke, Weston-super-Mare
NURP.38.WS.579	5/8/41	9/8/41	Caen / Calvados	Weston-super-Mare	P. Parrett, 49 Locking Road, Weston-super-Mare
NURP.38.WS.585	?	?	?	Weston-super-Mare	P. Parrett, Weston-super-Mare
NURP.38.WS.586	9/7/41	21/7/41	Brittany	Weston-super-Mare	P. Parrett, Weston-super-Mare
NURP.38.WS.683	5/8/41	21/8/41	Caen	Weston-super-Mare	W. E. Thomas, Ardnave Farm, Kewstoke, Weston-super-Mare
NURP.38.WS.941	24/7/42	23/8/42	France	Weston-super-Mare	J. Hazel, Beach Farm, Sand Bay, Kewstoke, Weston-super-Mare
NURP.38.WSM.39	4/7/41	12/7/41	Cully le Patrie	Weston-super-Mare	
NUNF.39.A.29	31/9/41	4/10/41	?	Muswell Hill	S. Fuller Isaacson, 84 Woodside Avenue, Muswell Hill, London, N10
NURP.39.A.43	3/10/41	29/10/41	Belgium	Muswell Hill	
NURP.39.A.92	12/6/41	22/7/41	N.E. Holland	Muswell Hill	
NURP.39.ANR.33	14/3/43	22/3/43	Sonnerville	Shepherds Bush	R. Gillman, 152 Perry Road, London, W12
MURP.39.AYM.9	24/7/42	31/7/42	France	Folkestone	Phillips & Son, 19 Burges Road, Aylesham, Kent
NURP.39.B.9650	5/4/44	18/4/44	Bagnoles	Kings Cross	R. Morrison, 141 Price of Wales Road, London, NW5

Ring No.	Date Sent	Date Returned	Place	Owner/NPS Group	Bred By
NURP.39.BA.279	27/4/42	30/4/42	Belgium	Folkestone	Walters, Rose Bank View, Wingerworth, Chesterfield
NURP.39.BKR.1	27/8/42	16/9/42	Brittany	Thames Estuary	W. Tillyer, Edensor, Whitsbury Road, Fordingbridge
NURP.39.GEN.172	3/8/41	6/8/41	Belgium	Ipswich	W.T. Towkes, Albion Mills, Ipswich
NURP.39.DSS.230	7/5/41	28/5/41	W. Flanders	Folkestone	Clark & Small, 62 Clarendon Place, Dover
NURP.39.DSS.230	27/4/42	29/4/42	Belgium	Folkestone	
NURP.39.EHC.83	13/7/43	13/7/43	Lisieux, France	East London	F. Pennell, 90 Talbot Road, East Ham, London, E6
NURP3.EHD.578	22/6/43	4/7/43	Belgium	Enfield	A.J. Speller, 51 Catisfield Road, Enfield Wash, London
NUHW.39.FE.249	30/4/42	3/5/42	Belgium	Folkestone	T. Highland, Kenneldene, Capel, Folkestone
NURP.39.FOL.1	7/9/41	24/9/41	France	Folkestone	T.G. Wellard & F. Oliver, Radiguard House, Hawkinge
NURP.39.FOL.67	16/8/43	25/8/43	Loperec	Folkestone	J.W. Gambrill, 47 Cheriton Road, Folkestone
NURP.39.FOL.173	24/8/42	28/8/42	Belgium	Folkestone	D. Heard, Warren Road, Littlestone, Folkestone
NURP.39.FSR.561	1/5/42	13/5/42	Bauva's	?	W. Hardcastle, Grove House, High Road, Whetstone, London, N30
NURP.39.GHN.545	5/5/44	13/5/44	Mayenne	Chatham	Eldridge, 26 Dagmar Road, Chatham
NURP.39.GS.99	3/8/41	8/8/41	Flanders	Ipswich	J. Edmondson, Barngarth, Carthnel
NURP.39.HQB.188	4/7/41	3/8/41	Brittany	Weston-super-Mare	E.J. Palmer, 13 Winscombe Road, Weston-super-Mare
NURP.39.KES.77	8/5/44	15/8/44	St Cyr	Plymouth	J. & E.W. Horsfield, Royal Oak Hotel, Kelsall, Chester

Ring No.	Date Sent	Date Returned	Place	Owner/NPS Group	Bred By
NURP39.LRC.41	6/8/41	17/8/41	Calvados	Lyme Regis	Stocker Bros., 12 Sherbourne Lane, Lyme Regis
NURP39.LRC.216	11/6/41	17/6/41	Caen, Normandy	Lyme Regis	G. Snell, High Cliff Hotel, Sidmouth Road, Lyme Regis
NURP39.LRC.290	2/9/41	12/8/41	?	Chard Junction	H.R. Fowler, Valley View, Westford, Chard Junction
NURP39.LRC.303	6/8/41	6/10/41	France	Lyme Regis	H. Sexton, 19 Sherbourne Lane, Lyme Regis
NURP39.LRC.415	6/8/41	14/8/41	Calvados	Lyme Regis	Stocker Bros., 12 Sherbourne Lane, Lyme Regis
NURP39.LRC.554	11/6/41	13/6/41	Caen, Normandy	Lyme Regis	
NURP39.LPC.566	6/8/41	17/8/41	France	Lyme Regis	
NURP39.LU.239	10/8/44	22/8/44	France	Bexleyheath	C. Chatton, 49 Erith Road, Bexleyheath
NURP39.NEL.219	13/7/43	16/8/44	France	Walthamstow	G. Andrews, 171 Francis Road, Leyton, London, E10
NURP39.NRS.383	3/8/41	17/8/41	Flanders	Ipswich	
NURP39.POR.489	29/4/44	10/5/44	Bourbon Lanoy	Romford	Mansfield & Son, 16 Roslyn Gardens, Gidea Park, Romford
NURP39.PSJ.89	12/7/43	3/8/43	France	Plymouth	Goffin, Cape Cottage, Woolster, Plymouth
NURP39.PPC.286	9/8/44	16/8/44	Bienville	Plymouth	M. Smith, 19 Desborough Road, Plymouth
RP.39.RAY.75	9/4/44	12/4/44	France	Thames Estuary	A. Moss, Anchor Inn, Hullbridge, Hockley
NURP39.SAC.77	31/7/42	8/8/42	Amiens	St. Albans	T. Wiggins, St. Julian's Road, St Albans
NURP39.SBC.50	1/5/42	17/6/42	Paris	Shepherd's Bush	Lovegrove Bros., 212 Latimer Road, London, W10

Ring No.	Date Sent	Date Returned	Place	Owner/NPS Group	Bred By
NURP.39.SDS.39	13/8/43	17/8/43	Vienne (S. of Lyon)	Staines	J. Paulger, Blue Anchor, Market Square, Staines
NURP.39.SFA.35	27/8/42	30/8/42	Brittany	Fordingbridge	H. Tillyer, Edensor, Whitsbury Road, Fordingbridge
NURP.39.SSR.219	30/7/44	4/8/44	Cleres (Seine Inf.)		Woolston
NURP.39.SVS.268	2/6/44	6/6/44	Beavais	Croydon	H. Myers, 31 Sanderstead Road, South Croydon
NURP.39.SWD.712	7/6/44	27/6/44	Bresles	Thames Estuary	J. Barker, Meadow Lane, Linton
NURP.39.TSR.73	?	6/11/43	Valenciennes	Thames Estuary	C. H. Lawrence, 78 Montreal Road, Tilbury
NURP.39.TTT.175	3/8/41	9/8/41	Flanders	Ipswich	Talbot & Son, 10 Alan Road, Ipswich
NURP.39.TTT.208	5/7/41	7/7/41	S. of Ghent	Ipswich	
NURP.30.TTT.210	5/7/41	7/7/41	S. of Ghent	Ipswich	
NURP.30.TTT.219	5/7/41	8/7/41	Ardoye	Ipswich	Margetts & Routh, 58 Lattice Avenue, Ipswich
NURP.39.TTT.219	3/8/41	12/8/41	Coutrai	Ipswich	
NURP.39.TTT.242	5/7/41	7/7/41	Ypres	Ipswich	F. Vince, Lerwick, Humber Doucy Lane, Ipswich
NURP.39.TTT.250	3/8/41	6/8/41	Belgium	Ipswich	
NURP.39.TTT.262	5/7/41	7/7/41	Westroosebeke	Ipswich	C. Bassingwaite, 25 Penshurst Road, Ipswich
NURP.39.TTT.262	24/8/42	28/8/42	Belgium	Ipswich	
NURP.39.TTT.306	3/8/41	6/8/41	Belgium	Ipswich	W. Thompson, The Croft, Kanball Street, Ipswich
NURP.39.TTT.872	5/7/41	3/7/41	S. of Ghent	Ipswich	

Ring No.	Date Sent	Date Returned	Place	Owner/NPS Group	Bred By
NURP.34.V.1146	9/4/44	1/5/44	France	Thames Estuary	Standley Bros, 22 Auckland Road, Sparkbrook Road, Birmingham
NURP.39.W.405	13/7/43	14/7/43	France	Woking	Mr & Mrs Watts, 145 Walton Road, Woking
NURP.39.WAC.137	16/7/43	26/7/43	Cambrai	Willesden	H. George & Son, 26 Windsor Avenue, Walthamstow, London
NURP.39.WB.161	18/5/43	24/5/43	Famechon	Walthamstow	Perowne & Son, 24 Cambridge Road, London, E17
NURP.39.WD.116	29/6/44	4/8/44	France	Woolston	F. Farr, 79 Markhouse Avenue, London, E17
NURP.39.WE.139	22/6/43	22/7/43	Belgium	Ipswich	C. Folkhard, Oll Vette, Hadleigh Road, Ipswich
NURP.39.WE.142	28/8/42	31/8/42	Doullens	Ipswich	A.W. Keeble, Fen Farm, Burstall
NUHW.39.WE.378	3/8/41	5/8/41	Belgium	Ipswich	H. Steward, 65 Roslyn Road, London, N15
NURP.39.WGF.230	15/5/43	21/5/43	Falaise	Tottenham	
NURP.39.WGF.230	19/6/43	8/7/43	France	Tottenham	
NURP.39.WS.50	5/8/41	10/8/41	Caen	Weston-super-Mare	J. Hazell, Beach Farm, Sand Bay, Kewstoke, Weston-super-Mare
NURP.39.WS.156	5/8/41	19/8/41	Caen	Weston-super-Mare	G.J. Williams, Hurst, High Street, Worle, Weston-super-Mare
NURP.39.WS.1147	4/7/41	7/7/41	Cotentin, Vire	Weston-super-Mare	W. Parker, 77 Langford Road, Weston-super-Mare
NURP.39.WS.1215	20/5/43	25/5/43	La Hestre	Weston-super-Mare	W. Tanner, Jnr, 11 Meadow Villas, Weston-super-Mare
NURP.40.A.218	2/8/41	5/8/41	Belgium	Muswell Hill	S. Fuller Isaacson, 84 Woodside Avenue, Muswell Hill, London, N.10

Ring No.	Date Sent	Date Returned	Place	Owner/NPS Group	Bred By
NURP.40.A.220	13/5/41	16/5/41	?	Muswell Hill	
NURP.40.A.235	30/9/41	10/10/41	Belgium	Muswell Hill	
NURP.40.A.238	12/6/41	18/6/41	Caen (Brittany)	Muswell Hill	
NURP.40.A.256	2/8/41	8/8/41	Belgium	Muswell Hill	
NURP.40.A.256	21/6/42	26/6/42	Opbrackel	Muswell Hill	
NURP.40.A.260	3/11/41	17/11/41	Belgium	Muswell Hill	
NURP.40.A.262	3/11/41	10/11/41	Belgium	Muswell Hill	S. Fuller Isaacson, 84 Woodside Avenue, Muswell Hill, London, N.10
NURP.40.A.263	3/11/41	15/11/41	Belgium	Muswell Hill	
NURP.40.A.263	30/5/42	15/6/42	Belgium	Muswell Hill	
NURP.40.A.272	30/9/41	3/10/41	Belgium	Muswell Hill	
NURP.40.A.273	3/11/41	13/11/41	Belgium	Muswell Hill	
NURP.40.A.279	13/5/41	15/5/41	?	Muswell Hill	
NURP.40.A.286	2/8/41	5/8/41	Belgium	Muswell Hill	
NURP.40.A.289	2/8/41	7/8/41	Belgium	Muswell Hill	
NURP.40.A.299	13/5/41	7/6/41	Reville-Barfleur	Muswell Hill	
NURP.40.A.311	2/8/41	28/8/41	?	Muswell Hill	
NURP.40.A.314	13/5/41	3/7/41	N.E. Holland	Muswell Hill	
NUR.A.P40.43175	1/6/44	4/6/44	Sarthe	Ramsgate	
NURP.40.ANR.236	27/8/42	31/8/42	Frevent St. Pol	Shepherds Bush	A. Gillman, 152 Percy Road, Shepherds Bush, London, W12
NURP.40.AVM.99	30/6/42	4/7/42	Romorantin	Folkestone	T. Lancashire, 2 The Crescent, Snowdown, Dover

Ring No.	Date Sent	Date Returned	Place	Owner/NPS Group	Bred By
NURP.40.B.2877	16/10/43	1/11/43	Nogent le Rotrou	Thames Estuary	R. Lowes, Tower House, Arcadian Gardens, Hadleigh
NURP.40.BD.201	16/8/43	18/8/43	Jugon	Margate	H. Wilson, 20 St James Road, Blackburn
NURP.40.BMP15	30/4/44	20/8/44	Belgium	West Malling	Bowaters Paper Mill, Northfleet
NURP.40.BMP37	2/3/44	3/4/44	Aisonville – Bernoville	West Malling	West Malling
NURP.40.BPM.37	6/8/44	9/8/44	Villers Bretonneux		
NURP.40.BRP119	7/6/44	11/6/44	France	Thames Estuary	
NURP.40.CAN.231	24/7/42	30/7/42	Lisieux	Shepherds Bush	M. Maloney, 116 Cathays Terrace, Cardiff
NURP.40.CDM.106	31/7/42	15/8/42	Amiens	Clacton-on-Sea	?
NURP.40.CDM.211	15/8/42	25/8/42	Amiens	Clacton-on-Sea	
NURP.40.CDM.213	31/7/42	3/8/41	Amiens	Clacton-on-Sea	
NURP.40.CDM.215	31/7/42	1/9/43	Amiens	Clacton-on-Sea	
NURP.40.CDM.245	24/6/42	3/7/42	Namur	Clacton-on-Sea	
NURP.40.CDM.250	26/5/42	?	?	Clacton-on-Sea	
NURP.40.CH.324	6/5/44	13/5/44	France	East London	Mackay & Son, 23 Hartington Road, Custom House, London, E16
NURP.40.CNC.108	4/1/44	20/1/44	Vire	Croydon	B. G. Revell, 94 George Street, East Croydon
NURP.40.CPC.183	7/4/44	8/5/44	France	Isle of Wight	?
NURP.40.CPC.356	19/8/43	2/9/43	Cravenchon	Isle of Wight	
NURP.40.CRS.88	18/8/43	5/9/43	Montaigne	Colchester	S. Smith, The Haven, Port Lane, Colchester
NURP.40.CRS.88	1/5/44	9/5/44	Beaumont	Colchester	
NURP.40.CRS.105	?	?	?	Colchester	T. Kettle, 37 Scarletts Road, Colchester
NURP.40.CSL.292	6/8/44	8/8/44	France	Folkestone	J. Banks, Teddars Lees, Folkestone

Ring No.	Date Sent	Date Returned	Place	Owner/NPS Group	Bred By
NURP.40.DSR.65	3/10/41	4/10/41	Bruges	Folkestone	R. Hough, 61 John Street, Derby
NURP.40.DSS.34	21/6/42	23/6/42	Belgium	Folkestone	F. Bartlett, Little Everton, Alkham
NURP.40.DSS.39	14/9/43	30/9/43	Conde-sue-Noireau	Folkestone	
NURP.40.DUK.57	6/6/44	8/7/44	France	Thames Estuary	
NURP.40.DWC.126	30/3/44	13/4/44	Zoetenaye (Belgium)	Dagenham	W. A. Willis, 69 Rogers Road, Dagenham
NURP.40.E.2420	18/9/43	7/10/43	Domfront	East London	A. R. Hill, 116 Claude Road, Upton Park, London, E.13
NURP.40.EE.21	11/5/43	18/5/43	?	Enfield	W. Love & Son, 36a Windmill Hill, Enfield
NURP.40.EHD.486	18/5/43	?	Soligny, France	Enfield	Watson Bros., 59 Jasper Road, Enfield
NURP.40.F.1407	24/5/42	27/5/42	Caen	Folkestone	Gasking & Son, 3 Hillside Road, Dover
NURP.40.F.1572	?	21/8/44	St Jean Du Woolston	Cardonnay	
NURP.40.FOL.646	24/8/42	27/8/42	Belgium	Folkestone	E. Partridge, Pretoria Street, Buckland, Dover
NURP.40.FS.66	27/3/42	1/4/42	?	?	
NURP.40.FSR.48	11/8/43	19/8/43	Belgium	?	W. Hardcastle, Grove House, High Road, Whetstone, London, N.12
NURP.40.EE.358	24/6/42	30/7/42	Orne	Honiton	
NURP.40.GD.116	2/2/44	3/3/44	?	Gravesend	
NURP.40.GD.122	14/12/43	22/12/43	Caen	Gravesend	D. Port, 34 Thong Lane, Gravesend

Ring No.	Date Sent	Date Returned	Place	Owner/NPS Group	Bred By
NURP.40.GHS.266	15/8/43	19/9/43	Cambrai	Chatham	E. Knight, Norfolk Cot., Maidstone Road, Chatham
NURP.40.H.263	21/6/43	18/7/44	Belgium	Woking	H. Holgate, Downham Road, Chatburn, Clitheroe
NURP.40.HAD.149	22/2/44	27/2/44	Combined Ops.	Thames Estuary	J. Lowes, Tower House, Arcadian Gardens, Hadleigh
NURP.40.HQ.5655	27/4/42	3/6/42	Rouen	Folkestone	F. Carter, 20 Granville Street, Dover
NURP.40.HWD.282	?	?	Mesnil Simon	Harrow	F. Henson, 76 Hamilton Road, Harrow Weald
NURP.40.JB.84	20/6/43	22/6/43	Airaines	Mitcham	S. Clark, 47 Aberdeen Road, Merton, London, SW19
NURP.40.L.115	21/1/44	6/10/44	St Omer	Woking	Miss Bates, The Shielding, Halfpenny Lane, Guildford
NURP.40.L.552	17/3/43	21/3/43	French Coast	Lyme Regis	J. Curtin & Son, 10 Georges Square, Lyme Regis
NURP.40.L.676	23/4/42	27/4/42	Caen	Lyme Regis	J. Sexton, 19 Sherbourne Lane, Lyme Regis
NURP.40.ML.49	5/9/44	15/9/44	Pas de Calais	Worcester	B.L. Sparrey, Link Elm, Church Road, Malvern
NURP.40.ML.40	5/9/44	15/9/44	Pas de Calais	Worcester	
NURP.40.N.378	11/8/44	17/8/44	Nevers	Bexleyheath	
NURP.40.NPK.102	3/5/44	11/6/44	Congrier	Northfleet	A. Russell, 15 Acacia Road, Stone, Northfleet
NURP.40.NPS.181	19/6/43	26/6/43	Aisne	Tottenham	H. Crossman, 133 Clyde Road, Tottenham, London, N15
NURP.40.OH.103	5/9/44	22/9/44	Nièvre	Worcester	

Ring No.	Date Sent	Date Returned	Place	Owner/NPS Group	Bred By
NURP.40.PDC.278	16/7/43	30/7/43	Belgium	East London	Offord & Baker, 30 Atlas Road, Plaistow, London
NURP.40.RAY.5	9/4/44	12/4/44	La Thierache	Thames Estuary	A. Moss, The Anchor Inn, Hullbridge
NURP.40.SC.505	6/8/44	10/8/44	Lyons la Forêt (Eure)	East London	W. Squill, 109 Chestnut Avenue, London, E7
NURP.40.SDS.71	10/6/43	14/7/43	Holland	Staines	F. Levy & Sons, Sunnydene, Railway Terrace, Staines
NURP.40.SDS.134	12/6/43	14/7/43	France	Staines	G. Purbick, 21 Sidney Road, Staines
NURP.40.SDS.196	11/7/43	18/7/43	Beuvron en Auge	Staines	J.H. Huxley, Bell Yard, Church Street, Staines
NURP.40.T.1795	29/12/43	10/4/44	Dieppe	Tottenham	H.J. Humphrey, 124 Roslyn Road, Tottenham, N15
NURP.40.TTT.36	24/8/42	6/9/42	St. Pol	Ipswich	S. Garrard, 21 Fitzmaurice Road, Ipswich
NURP.40.TTT.194	This Pigeon, whose owner was not a member of the Ipswich Group, was sent to a race from Durham on 29 May 1942. Returned on 14 June 1942 with message from Holland tucked in its ring. Passed to MI14				C. Symonds, 15 Coniston Square, Ipswich
NURP.40.TTT.248	31/7/42	14/8/42	Belgium	Ipswich	J. Holmes, 91 Derby Road, Ipswich
NURP.40.TTT.339	16/8/43	17/8/43	Hesdin	Ipswich	F. Vince, Lerwick, Humber Doucy Lane, Ipswich
NURP.40.W.333	5/7/41	?	Calvados	Weston-super-Mare	J.R. Brian, Lynton Dartnell Park, West Byfleet
NURP.40.WKE.14	5/8/44	?	?	Plymouth	Sugden & Crowther, 3 Ashfield Terrace, Wilson Road, Wyke, Bradford
NURP.40.WPC.324	15/7/43	?	Sains Du Nord	Willesden	W. Clare, 49 Marion Way, London, NW10

Ring No.	Date Sent	Date Returned	Place	Owner/NPS Group	Bred By
NURP.40.WS.152	?	?	?	Weston-super-Mare	J. Hazell, Beach Farm, Kewstoke, Weston-super-Mare
NURP.40.WS.158	27/8/41	10/12/41	Auxerre	Weston-super-Mare	E. Tancock, 3 Ewart Road, Weston-super-Mare
NURP.40.WS.327	5/8/41	11/8/41	Caen, Calvados	Weston-super-Mare	
NUHW.40.WHS.318	18/5/43	23/5/43	France	Mottistone Manor, Isle of Wight	T.H. Tong, Llwyn Oun., Llanfair, Co. Mont
NURP.40.WPC.333	14/8/43	6/10/43	Domfront	Willesden	Bunker & Lane, 2 Yewfield Road, Willesden, London, NW2
NURP.41.A.409	30/9/41	4/10/41	?	Muswell Hill	J.H. Hill, 45 Warburton Road, Twickenham
NURP.41.R.3841	6/8/44	11/8/44	Meharicourt	Southampton	A. Small, 38 Foundry Lane, Millbrook, Southampton
NURP.41.R.6306	11/8/44	15/8/44	Mer	Portsmouth	H.H. Jones, St Annes, Paulsgrove, Cosham
NURP.41.AB.272	14/7/43	19/7/43	Nogent le Rotrou	East London	W. Allen, 18 Pond Road, West Ham, London, E15
NURP.41.ANR.65	5/5/42	7/5/42	Évereux	Shepherd's Bush	A. Gillman, 152 Percy Road, Shepherd's Bush, London, W12
NURP.41.AVM.2	4/6/44	9/6/44	Verneuil le Chateau	Folkestone	
NURP.41.AVM.66	25/8/42	27/8/42	France	Folkestone	
NURP.41.AVM.10	29/6/42	1/7/42	France	Folkestone	
NURP.41.BCE.386	23/7/42	27/7/42	France	Dorchester	
NURP.41.BCE.386	24/8/42	29/8/42	Villers Bretonneux	Dorchester	

Ring No.	Date Sent	Date Returned	Place	Owner/NPS Group	Bred By
NURP.41.BPK.78	9 or 16/4/44	20/4/44	Belgium	Barking	F. Leader, 156 King Edward's Road, Barking, London
NURP.41.CV.63	22/6/43	1/8/43	Ath, Belgium	Mitcham	C. Langley, 29 Spencer Road, Beddington Corner, Mitcham
NURP.41.CV.180	15/6/43	21/6/43	Rouillac	Mitcham	
NURP.41.E.382	31/10/41	2/11/41	S. of Amiens	Hursley	
NURP.41.E.1009	?	?	France	Harrow	
NURP.41.E.2542	15/8/43	30/9/43	Belgium	Chatham	R. Perrin, 262 Luton Road, Luton, Chatham
NURP.41.EE.123	2/6/44	?	Mortagne Av., Perche	Enfield	R. Glover, 105 Hood Avenue, Old Southgate, London
NURP.41.EHD.174	6/8/44	27/8/44	Belgium	Ponders End	R. Lazell, 82 Northfield Road, Enfield
NURP.41.ETC.16	16/4/43	16/4/43	Châteadun	Enfield	F. Love, 36a Windmill Hill, Enfield
NURP.41.EW.18	24/6/42	3/7/42	France	Honiton	H. W. Record, New Street, Honiton, Devon
NURP.41.2990	?	?	Belgium	Harrow	G. Stubbs, Jubilee Villas, Hassall, nr. Sandbach
NURP.41.FTC.104	16/4/43	21/4/43	France	Enfield	
NURP.41.G.284	4/3/44	20/4/44	Orne	Gravesend	A. Springett, 280 Rochester Road, Gravesend
NURP.41.G.288	23/8/43	2/9/43	?	Gravesend	D. Port, 34 Thong Lane, Gravesend
NURP.41.HH.102	4/7/44	25/7/44	Hargicourt-Pierrepont	Birmingham	T. J. Casey, Stonehurst, Garret's Green Lane, Sheldon, Birmingham
NURP.41.HQ.1677	29/12/43	2/1/44	France	East London	J. Squibb, 12 Forest Street, Forest Gate, London, E7
NURP.41.HQ.2377	5/5/44	15/5/44	France	Dorchester	C. Williams, 24 Austey Street, Easton, Bristol
NURP.41.HQ.2918	5/5/44	10/5/44	Tully-sur-Loire	Dorchester	J. Hurren, 24 Richmond Road, Queen Street, Exeter

Ring No.	Date Sent	Date Returned	Place	Owner/NPS Group	Bred By
NURP.41.HQ.2919	12/6/43	4/7/43	France	Dorchester	
NURP.41.HQ.2919	5/5/44	11/5/44	France	Dorchester	
NURP.41.HQA.5826	14/7/43	28/8/43	France	Dorchester	
NURP.41.HQA.5826	16/10/43	17/10/43	France	Dorchester	A.J. Morris, Chobham Place Cottage, Burrow Hill, Woking
NURP.41.L.552	29/7/42	10/8/42	France	Lyme Regis	H. Sexton, 19 Sherbourne Lane, Lyme Regis
NURP.41.L.662	15/5/42	11/6/24	?	Chard Junction	H.R. Fowler, Valley View, Westford, Chard Junction
NURP.41.L.2527	24/8/42	27/9/42	Frevent	Ipswich	J. Tillet, 68 Belle Vue, Ipswich
NURP.41.L.3262	28/8/42	11/9/42	Arras	Folkestone	A. Ruddick, 15 Windlesea Street, Dover
NURP.41.L.4673	25/8/42	30/8/42	Valenciennes	Clacton	Major E. Collins, Marine Hotel, Clacton-on-Sea
NURP.41.L.4695	24/6/42	4/7/42	Hyot, Belgium	Clacton	
NURP.41.L.4708	29/6/42	12/7/42	Holland	Clacton	
NURP.41.L.4711	25/8/42	11/9/42	Solesmes	Clacton	
NURP.41.L.6095	23/7/42	27/7/42	France	Weston-super-Mare	C. Smith, 3 The Square, Worle, Weston-super-Mare
NURP.41.IV.230	16/7/43	?	?	Walthamstow	Bailey Bros, 55 Leasowes Road, Leyton, E10
NURP.41.IV.234	19/7/43	2/8/43	Calvados	Walthamstow	
NURP.41.03869	14/7/43	14/7/43	France	Isle of Wight	S.B. Wynne, 39 Finlay Road, Gloucester
NURP.41.03869	3/8/44	11/8/44	Meny Le Tol	Isle of Wight	
NURP.41.03871	12/6/43	14/6/43	St. Hiliare, Du Harcouet	Isle of Wight	
NURP.41.03872	14/7/43	29/7/43	France	Isle of Wight	

Ring No.	Date Sent	Date Returned	Place	Owner/NPS Group	Bred By
NURP41.OFS.285	17/6/43	21/6/43	Vimoutiers	Old Ford	R. Bliss, 118 Usher Road, Bow, London, E3
NURP41.P283	2/6/44	25/8/44	Chaumont-en-Vixen	Woolston	J. Clark, 25 Sholing Road, Hitchin
NURP41.P283	?	25/8/44	St Laurent Des Mortiers	St Laurent Des Mortiers	Woolston
NURP41.P365	?	4/8/44	St Laurent Des Mortiers	St Laurent Des Mortiers	Woolston R. C. Marshall, 5 Tranby Road, Hitchin
NURP41.P5127	14/10/43	19/10/43	France	Walthamstow	H. Donachy, 5 Wellington Road, Wanstead
NURP41.PB.139	16/7/43	21/8/43	Belgium	East London	Golby Bros., 83 Chesterton Road, London, E13
NURP41.PDC.41	12/8/43	14/9/43	France	East London	D.R. Murphy, 116 Long Lane, Bexleyheath
NU.41.PHC.47	11/8/44	14/8/44	Seine Inférieure	Bexleyheath	H. Whitley, Primley, Paignton
NURP41.PT.39	21/10/42	20/11/42	Isigny	Paignton	E. Lyon, 180 St Barnabas Road, Woodford Green, London
NURP41.Q.625	22/7/43	?/4/44	?	Walthamstow	
NURP41.Q.1592	23/8/43	3/9/43	Saumur	Thames Estuary	H. Wood, 70 Eastern Crescent, Chelmsford
NURP41.R.1952	23/8/43	29/8/43	France	Thames Estuary	L.A. Fulcher, Cock and Bull, Writtle, Chelmsford
NURP41.R.3015	7/5/?	10/5/?	Avenses-sur-Helpe	Tottenham	J. Down, Challacroft, Guildford Road, Little Bookham
NURP41.R.6414	12/6/43	4/7/43	France	Dorchester	G. Guy, Braemar, Southleigh Road, Emsworth
NURP41.R.6415	12/7/43	14/7/43	Lisieux	Walthamstow	
NURP41.R.9719	17/8/43	2/9/43	St. Brieux	East London	W. Read & Sons, 52 Malmsley Road, Canning Town, London, E.16
NURP41.RA.106	15/8/43	26/8/43	Cambrai	Chatham	S.J. Sealey, 97 Rochester Avenue, Rochester

Ring No.	Date Sent	Date Returned	Place	Owner/NPS Group	Bred By
NURP.41.SBC.70	30/6/42	5/7/42	Belgium	Shepherd's Bush	F. Herman, 11 Shepherd's Bush Place, London, W12
NURP.41.SBC.329	30/6/42	8/8/42	Holland	Shepherd's Bush	S.R. Rogers, 36 Halfacre Road, Hanwell
NURP.41.SBC.349	31/7/42	7/8/42	Belgium	Shepherd's Bush	A. Rose, 21 Avondale Park Road, London, W11
NURP.41.T.1	23/8/42	13/9/42	France	Weston-super-Mare	W.E. Thomas, Ardnave Farm, Kewstoke, Weston-super-Mare
NURP.41.T.3163	17/8/43	2/9/43	St. Brieux	East London	S. Mantel & Son, 63 Altmore Avenue, East Ham, London, E6
NURP.41.TTT.198	27/11/42	12/4/43	Holland	Ipswich	Talbot & Son, 10 Alan Road, Ipswich
NURP.41.TTT.200	26/7/42	9/8/42	Denmark	Ipswich	
NURP.41.TTT.205	24/4/42	8/6/42	Amsterdam	Ipswich	
NURP.41.V.1024	?	15/7/43	Lisieux	Harrow	A. Cain, 125 Long Elms, Harrow Weald
NURP.41.W.340	?/6/43	?/6/43	Belgium	Woking	H.G. Willett & Son, 10 Lime Grove, Westfield, Woking
NURP.41.W.415	16/8/43	24/9/43	Belgium	Woking	Mr and Mrs Watts, 145 Walton Road, Woking
NURP.41.WAC.76	21/6/43	8/7/43	Belgium	Walthamstow	W. Webster, 36 Lloyd Road, Walthamstow, London
NURP.41.WE.120	30/6/42	1/7/42	Holland	Ipswich	
NURP.41.WE.122	28/8/42	31/8/42	Avesnes	Ipswich	
NURP.41.WE.122	17/7/43	25/7/43	Les Andelys	Ipswich	F.C. Brame Bros, 63 Kelly Road, Ipswich
NURP.41.WE.132	23/7/42	19/8/42	Holland	Ipswich	
NURP.41.WGF.140	13/6/43	16/6/43	France	Tottenham	W. Smith, 74a Summerhill Road, Tottenham, London, N15

Ring No.	Date Sent	Date Returned	Place	Owner/NPS Group	Bred By
NURP.41.WHZ.30	24/11/42	27/11/42	France	Weston-super-Mare	R.E. Jones, Homestill, Cheddar
NURP.41.WMK.126	2/1/44	6/1/44	France	Gravesend	G.A. Hooker & Son, 244 Rochester Road, Chalk, Gravesend
NURP.41.WPC.74	13/8/43	21/9/43	Mayenne	Willesden	W. Bishop, 19 Cainfield Avenue, Cricklewoood, London, NW
NURP.41.WPC.214	16/8/43	3/9/43	Vendée	Willesden	Langley & Beagley, 12 Dryfield Close, Willesden, London, NW1
NURP.41.WPC.333	13/8/43	?	Cabourg	Willesden	
NURP.41.WS.113	26/7/42	25/8/42	France	Weston-super-Mare	R. Jennings, The Holmes, Sand Bay, Kewstoke, Weston-super-Mare
NURP?WV81	26/7/42	15/8/42	France	Weston-super-Mare	
NURP.41.WU.270	16/7/43	18/8/43	Belgium	East London	
NURP.41.WV81	23/8/42	2/9/42	Lille	Weston-super-Mare	
NURP.41.WV.135	22/10/42	3/11/42	?	Weston-super-Mare	W. Brooks, Wrington, nr. Bristol
NURP.41.X.414	21/6/42	26/6/42	Belgium	Muswell Hill	S. Fuller Isaacson, 84 Woodside Avenue, London, N10
NURP.41.X.465	21/6/42	14/7/42	Belgium	Muswell Hill	
NURP.41.X.491	21/6/42	26/7/42	Belgium	Muswell Hill	
NURP.41.XEB.24	11/8/44	19/8/44	Châteauroux Indre	Bexleyheath	J. Deaville, 259 Long Lane, Bexleyheath
NURP.41.XEB.224	11/8/44	11/9/44	France	Bexleyheath	J. Addis, 39 Sesley Crescent, Welling
NURP.41.Y.13	?	?	?	Clacton	
NURP.42.A.1293	4/3/44	17/3/44	St Loup De Fribois	East London	G. Weller, Rumbeans Farm, Ewhurst Green, Guildford

Ring No.	Date Sent	Date Returned	Place	Owner/NPS Group	Bred By
NURP.42.A.2081	2/6/44	12/6/44	?	Lyme Regis	H. Cole, The Bungalow, Old Junction Road, Hutton, Weston-super-Mare
NURP.42.A.2110	12/7/43	30/7/43	?	Lyme Regis	J. Hazell, Beach Farm, Sand Bay, Kewstoke, Weston-super-Mare
NURP.42.A.2176	15/5/43	28/7/43	France	Weston-super-Mare	E. Hutchings, 9 Kewstoke Road, Worle, Weston-super-Mare
NURP.41.A.2263	16/8/43	22/8/43	Morbiham	Lyme Regis	W. Thomas, Ardnave Farm, Kewstoke, Weston-super-Mare
NURP.42.A.8941	10/1/44	31/1/44	Belgium	Old Ford	R. Bliss, 118 Usher Road, Roman Road, Bow, London, E3
NURP.42.B.1095	11/8/44	1/9/44	France	Bexleyheath	W. May, 139 Manor Road, Erith
NURP.42.C.1564	13/7/43	29/7/43	Saumur	Folkestone	C. Clare, 28 Maynard Terrace, Clutton, nr Bristol
NURP.42.C.4650	11/8/44	17/8/44	Chateauneuf Loiret	Bexleyheath	J. L. Deaville, 259 Long Lane, Bexleyheath
NURP.42.C.8210	16/10/43	20/10/43	Nogent le Rotrou Harrow	Harrow Weald	W. Savage, 840 Kenton Lane, Harrow Weald
NURP.42.C.9717	26/8/44	15/9/44	?	Gravesend	C. Wake, 42 Augistine Road, Drayton, Cosham, Hants
NURP.42.D.1461	13/7/43	16/7/43	France	Weston-super-Mare	G. Noterman, 85 Frithville Gardens, Shepherd's Bush, London, W12
NURP.42.D.3348	11/8/43	15/8/43	?	Staines	W. Lewry, 16 Railway Terrace, The Hythe, Staines
NURP.42.D.6297	12/6/43	16/6/43	Honfleur	Dorchester	E. Jeffries, 2 The Nurseries, Henbury Road, Hanham, Bristol

Ring No.	Date Sent	Date Returned	Place	Owner/NPS Group	Bred By
NURP.42.D.6518	23/7/43	20/8/43	France	East London	H. Coe, 76 Blammerle Road, New Eltham, London, SE9
NURP.42.E.634	8/5/44	11/5/44	Etreux	Walthamstow	E. B. Lyon, 180 St. Barnabas Road, Woodford Green, London
NURP.42.E.3876	23/7/43	8/8/43	Flers, France	Waltamstow	T. Dell, 30 Livingstone Road, Leyton, London, E17
NURP.42.E.4066	16/7/43	23/7/43	Avesnes	Weston-super-Mare	Marsh & Bailey, Derby Road, Swanwick, Alfreton
NURP.42.E.4308	22/6/43	24/6/43	Belgium	Ipswich	H. Mycroft, Birdle Lane, Leabrooks, Alfreton
NURP.42.E.5010	18/8/43	11/9/43	Montaigu	East London	King & Judd, 126 Chobham Road, London, E15
NURP.42.E.6779	26/4/44	1/5/44	?	Woking	J. Henderson, Beckenham Road, Guildford, Surrey
NURP.42.E.6803	?/5/44	8/5/44	Sarthe (Lemans)	Woking	H.H. Boshier, Galloway, Llanaway Road, Godalming
NURP.42.F.11	22/1/43	29/1/43	Beaulieu	Muswell Hill	S. Fuller Isaacson, 84 Woodside Avenue, Muswell Hill, London
NURP.42.F.2292	20/6/43	22/6/43	Hallencourt	Mitcham	C. Langley, 29 Spencer Road, Beddington Corner
NURP.42.F.5886	11/5/43	16/5/43	Meaulte	Enfield	J. Squires & Hill, 68 Templeton Road, Tottenham, N15
NURP.42.F.7418	11/5/43	21/5/43	Pas de Calais	Enfield	B. Davies, 55 Halifax Road, Enfield
NURP.41.F.7423	7/9/43	15/9/43	France	Enfield	
NURP.42.F.7454	20/6/43	26/6/43	Hallencourt	Enfield	J. Love, 36a Windmill Hill, Enfield

Ring No.	Date Sent	Date Returned	Place	Owner/NPS Group	Bred By
NURP42.G.1099	16/8/43	31/8/43	France	Folkestone	W. Cullimore, 9 Shieldon Close, Aylesham, Kent
NURP42.G.1195	22/6/43	24/6/43	Dour, Belgium	Folkestone	J. Williams, 54 King Road, Aylesham, Kent
NURP42.G.1196	14/7/43	187/43	France	Folkestone	
NURP42.G.1196	4/6/44	6/6/44	France	Folkestone	
NURP42.G.2198	14/4/43	20/4/43	France	Tottenham	A. Clarke, 36 Glenwood Road, Harringay, London, N15
NURP42.G.2490	13/8/43	17/8/43	Mayenne	Willesden	F. Wardle, 36 Clifford Way, London, NW10
NURP42.G.5344	5/7/44	26/8/44	Blois (Loir et Gher)	Dagenham	Woodward, 58 Vincent Road, Barking
NURP42.G.5882	20/8/42	24/8/42	Somme	A. Chester Beatty	A. Robinson, Ribblesdale Avenue, Chatburn, Clitheroe
NURP42.H.2175	27/8/42	16/9/42	Amiens	Shepherd's Bush	Rose, 21 Avondale Road, London, W11
NURP42.H.2334	11/4/43	15/4/43	Laval	Shepherd's Bush	O'Connor & Russell, 206 Latimer Road, London, W10
NURP42.H.3898	11/8/44	19/8/44	France	Woolston	Stokes & Son, 22 Shaw Avenue, Warrington
NURP42.J.6040	5/5/44	9/5/44	Merlerault	Thames Estuary	Barker & Fulcher, 65 Palmerston Road, South Stifford, Grays
NURP42.J.6150	6/1/44	12/1/44	Orne	Thames Estuary	Roberts Bros., 23 Foxton Road, South Stifford, Grays
NURP42.J.6150	2/6/44	13/6/44	Châteaulin	Thames Estuary	
NURP42.K.638	11/8/43	6/9/43	Loudon	Staines	G. Sharrock, Post Office, Haskayne, Ormskirk
NURP42.K.954	11/7/43	14/7/43	Lisieux	Staines	

Ring No.	Date Sent	Date Returned	Place	Owner/NPS Group	Bred By
NURP.42.K.1003	16/7/43	26/7/43	Montlucon, France	Walthamstow	W. Webster, 36 Lloyd Road, Walthamstow, London
NURP.42.K.4426	30/5/44	19/6/44	Belgium	Romford	V. Alderson, 40 Clifton Road, Romford, Essex
NURP.42.K.6054	8/5/44	24/6/44	France	Thames Estuary	R. Boatman, Debden, Saffron Walden
NURP.42.L.39	30/5/44	4/6/44	France	Woking	Miss Bates, The Shielding, Halfpenny Lane, Guildford
NURP.42.L.2147	15/8/43	18/10/43	Doullens	Chatham	W. Doust, 144 Rainham Road, Chatham
NURP.42.L.2195	15/8/43	31/8/43	Hainaut	Chatham	E. West, 43 Clarence Road, Chatham
NURP.42.L.4056	4/4/44	8/4/44	Tully-sur-Loire	Woking	Seaman Bros., Westfield, Woking
NURP.42.L.4327	13/7/43	1/8/43	France	Woking	Mrs & Miss Micklen, Long Cross House, Chertsey, Surrey
NURP.42.L.5031	17/10/43	8/11/43	Bayeux	East London	
NURP.42.L.5615	13/7/43	15/7/43	Mezidon	East London	
NURP.42.C.5861	2/5/44	19/5/44	Bonnetable (Sarthe)	Barking	A. Nugent, 25 Shaw Avenue, Barking
NURP.42.M.3017	9/4/44	12/4/44	Romily-sur-Siene	Thames Estuary	A. Moss, Anchor Inn, Hullbridge, Essex
NURP.42.M.4749	10/9/43	16/9/43	France	Enfield	L. Mold, 12 Alexandra Road, Waltham Abbey
NURP.42.M.6290	13/10/43	23/10/43	Laignes	Gravesend	D. Port, 24 Thong Lane, Gravesend
NURP.42.M.6310	15/9/43	17/9/43	Belgium	Gravesend	D. Port, Gravesend
NURP.42.M.9267	16/8/43	23/9/43	Charlot	Folkestone	F.A. Stoker, 302 London Road, Dover
NURP.42.M.9543	5/11/43	8/11/43	France	Northfleet	W. Parker, 21 High Street, Northfleet
NURP.42.N.972	21/10/43	29/10/43	Sable	Dorchester	S. Baines, 17 Towngate, Mapplewell, Barnsley
NURP.42.N.4848	5/8/44	18/8/44	N. of Seine	Plymouth	W.J. Skelley, 2 Seaton Place, Devonport

Ring No.	Date Sent	Date Returned	Place	Owner/NPS Group	Bred By
NURP.42.N.19379	10/6/43	14/8/44	France	Walthamstow	Wright Bros, 57 Linford Road, Walthamstow, E17
NURP.42.NS.10421	23/1/43	26/1/43	France	Clacton-on-Sea	W. Perkins, 3 Beadon Road, Taunton
NURP.42.O.2132	29/6/44	13/7/44	France	Tottenham	H. Crossman, 133 Clyde Road, Tottenham, London, N17
NURP.42.O.3312	27/4/44	?	?	Clacton	Major Collins, Marine Hotel, Clacton-on-Sea
NURP.42.P2110	13/7/43	30/7/43	France	Weston-super-Mare	S.J. Ham, 2 Waltacre, Yealmton, nr. Plymouth
NURP.42.P8574	8/5/44	26/5/44	Brancourt le Grand	Thames Estuary	W. C. Morgan, 48 New Road, Sawston, Cambridge
NURP.42.Q.1902	19/7/43	28/7/43	Flers	Chatham	A. Goodacre, 44 Seymore Road, Chatham
NURP.42.Q.2482	16/7/43	19/7/43	Nogent le Rotrou	East London	F.H. Clark, 51 Livingstone Road, Stratford, London
NURP.42.Q.2925	5/8/44	10/8/44	?	Plymouth	Radmore & Counter, 55 Knighton Road, Plymouth
NURP.42.Q.3377	25/8/43	7/9/43	Wallonne	Harrow	Berryman, 16 Collins Avenue, Stanmore
NURP.42.Q.9281	5/7/44	8/7/44	Seine Inférieure	Chadwell Heath	WJ. Newton, 95 Sixth Avenue, Manor Park, London, E12
NURP.42.R.7423	10/8/44	25/8/44	Nevers	Margate	
NURP.42.R.7544	9/8/44	18/8/44	Terres	Ramsgate	
NURP.42.R.7567	16/7/43	29/7/43	France	Ramsgate	
NURP.42.R.7573	20/8/43	20/8/43	Belgium	Ramsgate	
NURP.42.R.8544	19/7/43	27/7/43	Flers (Orne)	Chatham	W. Withyman, 109 Gordon Road, Chatham
NURP.42.SDS.3348	11/7/43	14/7/43	?	Staines	

Ring No.	Date Sent	Date Returned	Place	Owner/NPS Group	Bred By
NURP.42.T.393	5/4/44	12/5/44	?	Lyme Regis	Carpenter Bros, 7 Bank Street, Newport, Mon.
NURP.42.T.2490	7/5/44	17/5/44	Oise	Tottenham	
NURP.42.U.40	23/3/43	16/3/43	France	Whetstone	W. Hardcastle, Grove House, High Road, London, N20
NURP.42.U.3407	5/9/44	22/9/44	Authiou	Worcester	
NURP.42.V.224	9/8/44	31/8/44	France	Oxford	A. Green, 49 Muscliffe Lane, Throop, Bournemouth
NURP.42.W.1270	5/7/44	8/7/44	Gisors	Oxford	D. Towner, 27 Cleveland Drive, Cowley, Oxford
NURP.42.W.4672	7/9/43	10/9/43	Valenciennes	Thames Estuary	H. Newton, Homeslaw Lane, Haslington, Crewe
NURP.42.X.1312	11/8/44	13/8/44	Seine Inf.	Woolston	A. Poore, 5 Freemantle Common Road, Woolston, Southampton
NURP.42.X.1327	2/6/44	7/6/44	Manche, France	Woolston	W. Williams, 131 Manor Road, Woolston, Southampton
NURP.42.X.1397	29/6/44	1/7/44	France	Woolston	J. Clark, 2 Scholing Road, Woolston, Southampton
NURP.42.X.1423	2/6/44	4/6/44	France	Woolston	J. Hodder, Windgarth, Kaneshill, Bitterne, Southampton
NURP.42.X.1425	30/7/44	5/8/44	Chemire	Woolston	
NURP.42.X.6363	29/6/44	8/8/44	France Sarthe	Shepherd's Bush	W. Tagg, 7 Inverness Road, Southall
NURP.42.X.6740	?/6/44	?/6/44	Ile et Vilaine	Shepherd's Bush	

Ring No.	Date Sent	Date Returned	Place	Owner/NPS Group	Bred By
NURP42.Y.1817	5/6/44	9/6/44	Nuebourg	Walthamstow	W. Herson, 205 Colchester Road, Leyton, London, E10
NURP42.Y.2868	5/4/44	23/4/44	Le Ronssey	Thames Estuary	Mr & Mrs Harwicke, Sunnyheath, Perry Street, Billericay
NURP42.Z.905	?	19/7/43	Lisieux	Clacton	Major E. Collins, Marine Hotel, Clacton-on-Sea
NURP42.Z.908	?	17/6/43	Valenciennes	Clacton	
NURP42.Z.929	?	30/8/43	France	Clacton	
NURP42.Z.943	?	13/5/43	France	Clacton	
NURP42.Z.950	?	?	St. Hilaire Du Harcourt	Clacton	
NURP42.Z.952	?	12/6/43	Mayenne, France	Clacton	
NURP42.Z.954	?	24/6/43	Bordeaux	Clacton	
NURP42.Z.1797	13/7/43	15/7/43	Mezidon	East London	
NURP42.Z.1797	6/8/44	17/8/44	La Mothe St Herage	East London	
NURP42.Z.535	8/5/44	17/5/44	Aisne	Thames Estuary	
NURP42.Z.7527	16/12/43	24/12/43	Canisy	Walthamstow	W. Webster, 36 Lloyd Road, Walthamstow, London
NURP42.Z.7796	20/4/43	23/4/43	Pas de Calais	Shepherd's Bush	Tedder, 16 Dalgarno Gardens, London, W10
NURP42.Z.8414	5/7/44	7/7/44	?	Chadwell Heath	A. Harris, 1 Lewisham Street, West Bromwich
NURP42.Z.9811	2/6/44	30/6/44	Manche	Woolston	S. Arrowsmith, Commercial Inn, Bitterne, Southampton
NURP43.A.9428	11/8/44	27/8/44	Châteauroux	Bexleyheath	Murphy & Son, 166 Long Lane, Bexleyheath

Ring No.	Date Sent	Date Returned	Place	Owner/NPS Group	Bred By
NURP43.A.9439	2/6/44	6/6/44	France	Thames Estuary	Murphy & Son, 166 Long Lane, Bexleyheath
NURP43.AA.884	2/6/44	10/6/44	France	Thames Estuary	G. Messett, 21 Arkwright Road, Tilbury Docks
NURP43.B.8796	30/7/44	4/8/44	Ile et Vilaine, France	Colchester	S. Game, 20 Recreation Road, Colchester
NURP43.BH.100	29/7/44	?/9/44	France	Plymouth	
NURP43.C.7803	2/6/44	6/6/44	Manche	Ipswich	R.W. Payne, 59 Schrieber Road, Ipswich
NURP43.C.7853	1/6/44	5/6/44	La Haye Descartes	Folkestone	W.T. Fowkes, Woodbridge Road, Ipswich
NURP43.C.9678	6/5/44	12/6/44	Mamer	Folkestone	G. Phillips, 19 Burgess Road, Aylesham, Kent
NURP43.C.9786	6/5/44	9/5/44	Mamer	Folkestone	
NURP43.C.9792	4/6/44	28/6/44	France	Folkestone	T. Lancashire, 2 The Crescent, Snowden, Kent
NURP43.C.9830	4/6/44	8/6/44	Argentan	Folkestone	A. Coles, 32 King's Road, Aylesham, Kent
NURP43.CC.7916	30/3/44	1/4/44	East Flanders	Tottenham	A. Clarke & Son, 36 Glenwood Road, N15
NURP43.CC.8795	5/8/44	11/8/44	Marne	Weston-super-Mare	F.G. Wells, Florence Villa, Worlebury, Weston-super-Mare
NURP43.D.2621	11/7/44	10/9/44	Orne	Feltham	G. Best, Bedfont House, Bedfont Lane, Feltham
NURP43.D.2959	9/5/44	12/5/44	Gournay	Feltham	B. Reynolds, 38 Westbury Road, Hansworth
NURP43.D.3550	9/8/44	14/8/44	France	Chatham	C. Clout, 190 Castle Road, Chatham
NURP43.D.3722	1/7/44	26?/7/44	Lille	Chatham	E. Knight, Norfolk Cott., Maidstone Road, Chatham
NURP43.D.3781	1/7/44	7/7/44	Athies, Somme	Chatham	G. Goodacre, 44 Seymour Road, Chatham
NURP43.D.3801	1/7/44	5?/7/44	Somme	Chatham	C. West, 43 Glencoe Road, Chatham

Ring No.	Date Sent	Date Returned	Place	Owner/NPS Group	Bred By
NURP.43.D.3803	3/5/44	11/5/44	Le Horps Mayenne	Chatham	C. West, 43 Glencoe Road, Chatham
NURP.43.D.4004	28/6/44	8/7/44	St Anne sur Vilaine	Kingsland	D. Davies, 14 Fassett Road, London, E8
NURP.43.D.4485	4/8/44	9/8/44	Durtal-sor-Loire (Maine et Loire)	Kingsland	T. Warrington, 14 Mildmay Street, London, N1
NURP.43.D.4684	28/6/44	26/7/44	Derval	Kingsland	G. Burton, 1 Benyon Road, London, N1
NURP.43.D.4758	2/6/44	5/6/44	Belgium	Thames Estuary	Connor Bros, Button, 45 Lawns Crescent, Little Thorock, Grays
NURP.43.D.9626	28/6/44	6/7/44	Nort-sur-Erdre	Woking	F. Seaman, Westfield, Woking
NURP.43.DD.5319	2/6/44	14/6/44	Bailleul	Ramsgate	G.A. Russell, 52 Alexandra Road, Ramsgate
NURP.43.DD.6219	9/5/44	13/5/44	Maurepos	Thames Estuary	Barker & Son, Outwood Common, Billericay
NURP.43.DD.6261	9/5/44	13/5/44	Esqueheires	Thames Estuary	Mr & Mrs Hardwicke, Perry Street, Billericay
NURP.43.E.1500	5/3/44	10/3/44	Belgium	Thames Estuary	W. Bundock, Gt. Baddow, Chelmsford
NURP.43.E.8152	4/4/44	8/4/44	Somme	Enfield	W. Baker, 68 Tickfield Road, Enfield
NURP.43.G.9	26/4/44	12/5/44	France	Woking	Seaman Bros, Westfield, Woking
NURP.43.G.59	30/5/44	3/6/44	Sarthe	Woking	J. Henderson, 68 Beckenham Road, Guildford
NURP.43.G.1245	2/6/44	7/6/44	Louviers	Thames Estuary	G. Merrett, 21 Arkwright Road, Tilbury
NURP.43.G.8845	9/8/44	13/8/44	Senwy	Folkestone	E. Pope, 323 London Road, Dover
NURP.43.H.3787	29/6/44	24/7/44	France	Woolston	G. Whitlock, 6 Botany Bay Road, Sholing, Southampton
NURP.43.H.3856	11/8/44	14/8/44	France	Woolston	A. Robinson, Knighton Road, Woolston, Southampton

Ring No.	Date Sent	Date Returned	Place	Owner/NPS Group	Bred By
NURP.43.H.6988	6/8/44	6/9/44	Romilly-sur-East Seine, Caubey	London	Nash & Son, 1 Woodside Road, London, E13
NURP.43.K.1927	1/6/44	3/6/44	Chasse (Sarthe)	Folkestone	T. Coupleditch, 4 The Parade, Ichenham Road, Middlesex
NURP.43.K.7527	9/8/44	31/8/44	Bressuire	Oxford	R.M. Antingham, 54 Mowell Avenue, Oxford
NURP.43.L.283	7/10/43	13/10/43	Mons	Tottenham	A. Clarke, 36 Glenwood Road, N15
NURP.43.L.2717	15/3/44	26/3/44	Asche, Belgium	?	W. Hardcastle, 150 High Street, Whetstone, N20
NURP.43.L.6810	9/5/44	13/5/44	Gouy	Ipswich	J. Rampling, Racecourse Hotel, Nacton Road, Ipswich
NURP.43.L.9132	7/10/43	13/10/43	Braine Le Château		Clacton
NURP.43.L.9148	13/12/43	16/12/43	Laval	Clacton	
NURP.43.L.9154	13/12/43	23/12/43	Caumont	Clacton	
NURP.43.L.9155	27/4/44	3/5/44	Chanties (Calvados)	Clacton	
NURP.43.L.9156	5/10/43	11/10/43	Soignies (Belgium)	Clacton	Major E. S. Collins, Marine Hotel, Clacton-on-Sea
NURP.43.M.3954	5/5/44	10/5/44	Gace Le Merlerault		Mitcham G. Gilbert, 109 Hydethorpe Road, Balham, London
NURP.43.M.5422	10/10/43	10/10/43	Holland	Mitcham	M. Scholfield, 30 Eve Road, Leytonstone, E11
NURP.43.M.5456	6/5/44	15/5/44	Mamers	East London	King & Judd, 126 Chobham Rd, Stratford, E15
NURP.43.M.6903	6/11/43	10/11/43	France	Walthamstow	M. Whitehead, Braeburn, Meadowcourt Road, Leicester
NURP.43.N.1373	?	16/8/44	France	Barking	R. Kreager, 54 Romford Street, Barking

Ring No.	Date Sent	Date Returned	Place	Owner/NPS Group	Bred By
NURP.43.N.7223	14/10/43	24/10/43	Laiglo	Lyme Regis	H. Sexton, 19 Sherborne Lane, Lyme Regis, Dorset
NURP.43.N.7343	27/4/44	5/7/44	France	Lyme Regis	S. Stocker, 12 Sherborne Lane, Lyme Regis
NURP.43.N.7378	27/4/44	531/5/33	Vay (Loire Inf.)	Lyme Regis	R. Wiscombe, 48 Church Street, Lyme Regis
NURP.43.N.7648	26/4/44	19/5/44	Sees (Orne)	Chard Junction	H.R. Fowler, Valley View, South Chard
NURP.43.N.7476	4/6/44	8/7/44	France	Chard Junction	
NURP.43.N.7521	4/6/44	15/6/44	Seine et Marne	Chard Junction	
NURP.43.N.7533	4/6/44	20/6/44	Bateilhue	Chard Junction	
NURP.43.P3342	16/12/43	19/12/43	Laval	Ramsgate	T. Richardson, 49 St Andrew's Road, Ramsgate
NURP.43.P3439	9/8/44	23/8/44	France	Ramsgate	T. Wesley, Deaville, St James Avenue, Ramsgate
NURP.43.P.3467	1/6/44	5/6/44	Essay	Ramsgate	W. Trew, 20 St. David's Road, Ramsgate
NURP.43.P.8389	2/6/44	4/6/44	France	Folkestone	Mr Webster, Thornton Heath Grange, Grange Wood, South Norwood
NURP.43.P.9050	18/9/43	24/9/43	Cericy La Salle	East London	Lebden H.S. Sec., 60 Packham Road, Lebden, Blackburn
NURP.43.P.9288	21/10/43	26/10/43	Lisieux	East London	Johnson & Son, 11 Blyth Road, London, E15
NURP.43.Q.4038	3/7/44	7/7/44	France	Muswell Hill	S. Fuller Isaacson, 84 Woodside Avenue, London, N10
NURP.43.Q.4040	3/7/44	8/7/44	Seine Inférieure	Muswell Hill	
NURP.43.Q.4047	?	7/7/44	?	Muswell Hill	
NURP.43.Q.4057	5/8/44	15/8/44	Chalons-sur-Marne	Muswell Hill	

Ring No.	Date Sent	Date Returned	Place	Owner/NPS Group	Bred By
NURP.43.Q.4083	3/7/44	?/7/44	France	Muswell Hill	
NURP.43.Q.4085	3/7/44	8/7/44	France	Muswell Hill	
NURP.43.Q.5237	13/10/43	16/10/43	Nogent le Rotrou	Tottenham	B. Hammond, 37 Durham Road, Tottenham
NURP.43.RR.9534	4/7/44	7/7/44	Nogent le Rotrou	Chatham	No Ring Issued
NURP.43.S.2492	20/8/44	22/9/44	Montmille	Margate	H.J. Fuller, St Helen's Royal Esplanade, Margate
NURP.43.S.2566	8/8/44	26/8/44	Bressuire	Romford	R.E. Blazsby, 38 Heaton Close, Romford
NURP.43.S.4889	18/10/43	24/10/43	?	Woking	G. Legg, 26 St George's Road, New Malden
NURP.43.S.8300	5/6/44	15/8/44	St Cyr du Gault, Loir et Cher	Woking	Seaman Bros, Westfield, Woking
NURP.43.S.8411	5/5/44	8/5/44	Bombrugge-Burst Holland	Woking	Mr & Mrs Micklin, Long Cross House, Chertsey
NURP.43.T.446	29/4/44	4/4/44	Chartres	Chadwell Heath	V. Plumell, 103 Woodlands Road, Ilford
NURP.43.T.1523	4/8/44	26/8/44	?	Lyme Regis	G. Williams, Hurst, High Street Worle, Weston-super-Mare
NURP.43.T.1564	29/7/44	10/8/44	?	Lyme Regis	P. Crandon, Ashdene Road, Weston-super-Mare
NURP.43.T.1673	29/7/44	6/8/44	?	Lyme Regis	H. Cole, The Bungalow, Old Junction Road, Hutton, Weston-super-Mare
NURP.43.T.5937	30/4/44	13/5/44	France	East London	Barton Bros., 32 Dacre Road, London, E13
NURP.43.T.6119	9/4/44	23/4/44	Caen	East London	Byatt & Son, 67 Jersey Road, London, E16
NURP.43.U.2863	6/7/44	7/6/44	Couterne	East London	A. Baker, Atlas Road, London, E13
NURP.43.U.3026	18/8/43	2/9/43	France	Weston-super-Mare	J. Hazell, Beach Farm, Kewstoke, Weston-super-Mare

Ring No.	Date Sent	Date Returned	Place	Owner/NPS Group	Bred By
NURP.43.V.401	5/5/44	10/5/44	Lokeren	Woking	F. Lewry, 117 Maybury Road, Woking
NRP.42.V.8838	18/5/43	21/5/43	Mealute	Ipswich	R.W. Payne, 59 Schrieber Road, Ipswich
NURP.43.W.748	5/4/44	?	Orne	Woking	E. Wells, Lavande, Loop Road, Kingsfield, Woking
NURP.43.W1643	28/5/44	31/5/44	Ile et Vilaine	Southampton	W. Cass, Scudon Street, Southampton
NURP.43.W.9310	2/6/44	17/6/44	Brasparts	Thames Estuary	Crussell & Williams, 7 Kent Terrace, West Thurrock, Grays
NURP.43.W.9605	7/6/44	26/6/44	Beauvais	Thames Estuary	P. Cope, Duxford, Cambs
NURP.43.X.2760	1/6/44	9/6/44	France	Ramsgate	G.A. Russell, 52 Alexandra Road, Ramsgate
NURP.43.X.4964	6/5/44	15/5/44	Couterne (Orne)	East London	Yarranton & Chamberlain, 44 Stirling Road, London, E13
NURP.43.X.6995	30/4/44	3/5/44	Bauge	East London	Walbis & Son, 71 Brooks Road, London, E13
NURP.43.Y.107	25/5/44	3/6/44	Nouans	Romford	T. Green & Son, 33 Dell Avenue, Grimethorpe, Barnsley
NURP.43.Y.2567	9/4/44	14/4/44	Hirson	East London	W. Nunn, 232 Grange Road, Plasitow, London, E13
NURP.43.Y.4516	?	5/8/44	France	Plymouth	R.A. Stephens, 40 Station Road, Keyham, Devonport
NURP.43.Z.973	18/5/43	24/5/43	France	Ipswich	A. Soden, 2 Forum Way, Edgware
NURP.43.Z.2506	9/4/44	24/4/44	Bayeux	Clacton	Major E. S. Collins, Marine Hotel, Clacton-on-Sea
NURP.43.Z.2511	?	?	?	Clacton	
NURP.43.Z.2546	6/4/43	24/4/43	Bayeux	Clacton	
NURP.43.Z.8313	3/5/44	8/5/44	France	Chatham	Bowyer, 155 Luton Road, Chatham

Ring No.	Date Sent	Date Returned	Place	Owner/NPS Group	Bred By
SURP.41.L.2690	30/7/42	31/7/42	Calvados	Mottistone Manor, Isle of Wight	
SURP.41.RF.1159	5/5/42	12/5/42	Evreux	Muswell Hill	
SURP.42.A.5530	17/7/43	17/8/43	France	Chard Junction	
SURP.42.A.9049	5/6/44	10/6/44	France	West Malling	
SURP.43.C.2293	9/4/44	12/4/44	Bayeux	Mitcham	
SHU.41.M.80	2/7/42	27/7/42	France	Isle of Wight	
SHU.41.WI.1744	24/6/42	28/6/42	Belgium	Bognor Loft	

BRED BY THE ARMY PIGEON SERVICE

41.BA.1067	22/1/43	26/1/43	Argences	Isle of Wight
41.BA.1093	16/5/43	19/5/43	Livarot	Isle of Wight
41.BA.1093	15/7/43	22/8/43	Belgium	Isle of Wight
41.BA.1105	18/5/43	8/6/43	Crecy	Isle of Wight
41.BA.1105	14/7/43	19/7/43	Nogent le Rotrou	Isle of Wight
41.BA.2324	16/11/42	8/12/42	France	A. Chester Beatty
41.BA.2324	20/3/43	24/3/43	Orne	A. Chester Beatty
41.BA.2364	24/10/42	2/11/42	Holland	A. Chester Beatty
41.BA.2389	24/10/42	3/11/42	Holland	A. Chester Beatty
41.BA.2418	24/10/42	22/10/42	W. Bravant	A. Chester Beatty
41.BA.2447	12/6/43	14/6/43	France	Gen. Sir H. Jackson
41.BA.2759	16/5/43	23/5/43	France	Dorchester
41.BA.2786	14/5/43	19/5/43	Vire	Dorchester
41.BA.2787	16/5/43	19/5/43	Caen	Dorchester
41.BA.2793	14/5/43	19/5/43	Vire	Dorchester
41.BA.2793	18/8/43	20/8/43	France	Dorchester
41.BA.2793	12/6/43	17/6/43	St Sever	Dorchester
41.BA.2813	8/8/44	13/8/44	Biourge (Orego) Les Betrix	Dorchester
41.BA.2840	15/4/43	18/4/43	Pontivy	Dorchester
41.BA.2850	15/4/43	21/4/43	Pontivy	Dorchester
41.BA.2913	5/5/44	11/5/44	France	Dorchester
41.BA.2969	5/6/44	13/8/44	France	Margate
41.BA.2975	14/6/43	17/6/43	Valenciennes	Folkestone
41.BA.2983	15/9/43	16/10/43	Mortagne	Folkestone
41.BA.2983	22/2/44	26/2/44	By Combined Ops.	Folkestone
41.BA.2995	17/11/42	18/11/42	Belgium	Folkestone
41.BA.3006	15/1/43	20/1/43	Belgium	Folkestone
41.BA.30114	20/11/42	24/11/42	Holland	Folkestone
41.BA.3014	16/4/43	23/4/43	Belgium	Folkestone
41.BA.3018	24/10/42	1/11/42	Montreuil	Folkestone
41.BA.3020	17/4/43	22/4/43	Pottes, Belgium	Folkestone
41.BA.3020	22/2/44	26/2/44	By Combined Ops	Folkestone
41.BA.3021	17/11/42	24/1/43	Belgium	Folkestone
41.BA.3034	24/10/42	26/10/42	Montreuil	Folkestone
41.BA.3036	16/4/43	18/4/43	Lubecour	Folkestone
41.BA.3039	15/1/43	24/1/43	Homoy, Somme	Folkestone

41.BA.3041	14/1/43	24/1/43	France	Paignton
41.BA.3046	17/11/42	20/11/42	Belgium	Folkestone
41.BA.3048	22/11/42	26/11/42	Belgium	Fuller Isaacson
41.BA.3049	16/4/43	18/4/43	Belgium	Folkestone
41.BA.3058	17/11/42	18/11/42	Belgium	Folkestone
41.BA.3059	18/9/42	28/11/42	Holland	Fuller Isaacson
41.BA.3062	16/4/43	3/5/43	Pas de Calais	Folkestone
41.BA.3079	14/1/43	17/1/43	Coutrail	Folkestone
41.BA.3104	23/10/42	24/10/42	N. France	Hursley
41.BA.3130	23/10/42	25/10/42	N. France	Hursley
41.BA.3264	13/4/43	26/4/43	France	Tackley
41.BA.3377	16/11/42	15/12/42	France	Gen. Sir H. Jackson
41.BA.3378	26/11/42	28/11/42	France	Gen. Sir H. Jackson
41.BA.3412	8/8/44	28/8/44	Lamouilly	Dorchester
41.BA.3436	29/4/44	1/6/44	France	Margate
41.BA.3447	28/4/43	23/4/43	France	Gen. Sir H. Jackson
41.BA.4016	14/9/43	28/9/43	France	Ipswich
41.BA.4055	20/5/43	24/5/43	Pas de Calais	Ipswich
41.BA.4058	12/6/43	14/6/43	France	Ipswich
41.BA.4686	16/12/43	22/12/43	Le Feilleul	Ipswich
41.BA.4911	9/4/44	13/4/44	Marne	Folkestone
41.BA.4916	30/3/44	6/4/44	Wetteren-Dedermonde	Folkestone
41.BA.4932	7/6/44	11/6/44	A. La Perthe	Folkestone
41.BA.4943	9/4/44	12/4/44	Donnemarie-en-Montois	Folkestone
41.BA.4992	9/4/44	11/4/44	Lens	Folkestone
41.BA.4999	6/8/44	8/8/44	France	Folkestone
41.BA.10243	9/8/44	29/8/44	Ancenis	Bognor Regis
42.BA.2607	27/8/43	6/9/43	Amiens	Hursley
42.BA.2979	6/8/44	9/8/44	Sens	Folkestone
42.BA.2979	6/8/44	9/8/44	Sens	Folkestone
42.BA.10250	28/5/44	25/6/44	France	Bognor Regis
43.BA.4908	10/7/44	14//44	Augan	Folkestone